KAMLA: Ascent Of A Woman

Rhona Simon Baptiste, a citizen of Trinidad and Tobago, has been teaching in Mainland China since 1998. Her background as a Science teacher and later as coordinator of CADEC (Christian Action for Development in the Eastern Caribbean) Women's Desk provided valuable insight into her Caribbean region. Later she teamed up with her husband and embarked on several adventures not least of which is living in China for the past twelve years. She returned to her native land in March 2010 in time for the historic 'gentle revolution' that saw the calling of an early election by Patrick Manning of the ruling People's National Movement and its replacement by the People's Partnership led by the first woman Prime Minister Kamla Persad-Bissessar.

Her published works include: *Trini Talk – Dictionary of Words and Proverbs of Trinidad and Tobago; Second Wife and Other Stories from China; Do you like Chinese Food?; Trees and Flowering Plants of South China;* and *Mandarin Ducks - and they lived happily ever after?*

Owen Baptiste is former Managing Director and Editor-in-Chief of the Trinidad Express Newspapers Ltd. He was Executive Chairman of the Caribbean News Agency (CANA) from 1990 to 1993. He was also Editor-in-Chief of the *Trinidad Guardian,* on the Board of Directors of the *Barbados Advocate* and was the founding CEO and Editor-in-Chief of the *Jamaica Observer* and founding editor of *Caribbean Contact.*

He launched *Caribbean Affairs* and started *Inprint Caribbean Ltd* and *Caribbean Information Systems & Services Ltd.* He has travelled widely through the Caribbean, North and South America and Europe and spent the last twelve years in the People's Republic of China teaching Oral English and Writing.

He has edited several books, journals, and magazines including *WePeople, Crisis, Trinidad and Tobago Under Siege, Caribbean Affairs* and *Duprey.* He has also written extensively of his years in Chinese colleges and universities and has a number of unpublished works in hand.

Anatomy of a People's Victory

Kamla:

Ascent Of A Woman

Rhona S. Baptiste

With an introduction by Owen Baptiste

DOUENS
PRESS
HONG KONG
LOS ANGELES

Kamla: Ascent Of A Woman

ISBN 978-962-86166-6-4
Published by Douens Press
Hong Kong
Los Angeles

Cover and book design by Marc Baptiste

Mandarin Ducks, a novel – available online

Dedication

To the Honourable Kamla Persad-Bissessar,
Prime Minister of the Republic of Trinidad and Tobago

Contents

The Honourable Kamla Persad-Bissessar
Prime Minister of the Republic of
Trinidad and Tobago

Acknowledgements

Alexander Selkirk was not as fortunate in his exile as I was and today I give my thanks to the JahajeeDesi2005@yahoogroups.com and to all the friends who interfaced with me each week between China and Trinidad and Tobago. They include: from Yahoo Groups: CongressofthePeople; CaribbeanHindus; CaribbeanTalk; OurGuyana; TheUnitedVoice; from Google Groups: TrinidadTobago; also: Government Information Services of T & T; JYOTI; Trinidad Express; Trinidad Guardian; Trinidad Newsday; Gregory Aboud; Karen Bart-Alexander; Steve Alvarez; Roy Augustus; Satnarine Balkaransingh; Raul Bermudez; Ronald Bhola; Cynthia Birch; Deosaran Bisnath; Eulah Borde; Hazel Brown; Stephen Cadiz; Madeline Coopsammy; Marlene Davis; Vernon de Lima; Winston Dookeran; Janet Gibson; Wesley Gibbings, Ashton Jimi Gonzales; Kenneth Gopaul; Monica Gopaul; Lennox Grant; Harold Charles-Harris; Michael Harris, Avonelle Hector-Joseph, Richard Hosein; Margaret Hunte; Laurel Ince; Inshan Ishmael; Fayaz Karim; Ian Lambie; Valerie Mahabir; Diana Mahabir-Wyatt; Sheila Maharaj; Mahendra Mathur; Anthony Milne; Peter Minshall; Roy Mitchell; Peggy Mohan; Rhea Mungal; Garvin Nicholas; Denis Noel, Clive Nunez; Peter O'Connor; Napier Pillai; Pooran Kanta, MF Rahman; Raymond Ramcharitar, Ronald Ramcharan; Deoraj Ramnarine; Lennox Raphael; Afra Raymond; Gregory Reece; Sonia Roach-Barker; David G. Roots; Ashaki Scott; Richard Seecharan; Raffique Shah; Parbatee Sirju; Sheilah Solomon; Eugenia Springer; Richard Wm. Thomas; Michael Thomas; and Debra Wanser.

My thanks go also to friends and family members who made the book and its launching possible; to Owen, Marc and She Xiuling who nurtured the mechanics of the publication; to Simon, Debbie and Victor who fed body and spirit; and to my sister Corinne, brother Ron and friends Eulah, Phyllis, Val, Leila, Barbara; Chester and Lynette Morong; and finally to those whose names although unmentioned have helped in making possible this memoir of my times in China, the United States and Trinidad and Tobago.

Rhona Baptiste

Introduction
by Owen Baptiste

Twelve years later: If the Patrick Augustus Mervyn Manning we saw on the political platforms for the May 24 general election is the same Patrick Manning that has been undisputed leader of the Government of the People's National Movement for most of this decade, then it was the will of God that stitched together the People's Partnership to seize power from this fool and his band of ne'er-do-wells who claimed to follow in the illustrious footsteps of Eric Eustace Williams. There is no doubt in my mind that generations of Trinidadians and Tobagonians, professionals and lay people who think themselves to be patriots, and the 9,736 voters in the Constituency of San Fernando East who showed unrepentant loyalty for the husband of Mrs. Hazel Manning and the disciple of the Reverend Juliana Pena, have a lot to answer for on Judgement Day for not acting more swiftly to rid the country of this smug and overbearing charlatan.

In China ten months before, as we debated the desire or the possibility to return to Trinidad, I could not gauge the enormity of the crimes being committed against the country under the guise of editorial freedom, environmental work, tertiary education and high-rise development. Early on in my self-imposed exile I found I had neither interest nor curiosity to go online to read the daily reports of murder, mayhem and malfeasance – just as I had no inclination to keep in touch with any of my former colleagues – and perhaps it was not surprising that I was unprepared when we finally returned home in March to watch the endless carnival of laissez faire, ineptitude and calumny. I recalled writing in August 2009 that I didn't think that I had any more blood to give to Trinidad and Tobago and the poisonous state of the country's politics, the incessant babble on radio and television that drowned genuine hope for comprehension, failed to rid me of pessimism and terror.

But the cacophony I noticed was what nearly everyone had grown accustomed with, having given blind and unquenchable support to Mr. Manning, to his protégé Mr. Calder Hart and to the Shanghai Construction Group that erected one monstrosity after another. The countryside was pockmarked with unfinished structures costing billions in taxpayers' dollars and bearing the footprints of workers from China and South Korea. At first it might have seemed a good idea – a lesson for Trinidadians and Tobagonians too greedy to be honest or too lazy to give a fair day's work – but it had turned out to be a kind of blight on the country with the Asians opening up a new form of indentureship to judge from the horrors in press reports about the life of Chinese workers on these government-to-government projects.

However, the alienation and exploitation did not seem to harm or bother Mr. Manning. The treasury of oil dollars was his personal Swiss bank and, having positioned Messrs. Hart and Company at the automatic teller machine he called Udecott, he had devised his own rules for tendering, procurement and life hereafter. As Louis XIV had said he seemed to believe, *L'état c'est moi*. And like Augustus Caesar he thought that he was rebuilding the nation and transforming the city of Port of Spain, which he had found of bricks and which he was leaving of marble. From time to time there were voices raised in protest of these violations, but he was impervious to advice or correction and those of his ministers with the temerity to condemn his arrogance came quickly to their ruin. He was a caricature of the emperor that opposition parties depicted him during the election campaign and he flaunted power and wealth and developed an environment in which only sycophants and cowards could find a comfortable existence, as party members or as patrons.

See no evil, hear no evil, speak no evil were the watchwords of his dispensation and with this a 20/20 vision and rhetoric that ostensibly held the key to a rich and proud life for Trinidadians and Tobagonians – scholarship, work, medical care and welfare – the over-confident geologist from San Fernando was allowed to rebuild and refurbish the Prime Minister's Residence at a cost of over $140 million and to staff it with foreign workers. Thrift was out, extravagance was in and the monthly bill for food and beverages was reported to be over $80,000. I believe he could have said that he was "rich beyond the dreams of avarice." Nothing in excess was written in the temple of Delphi, but Mr. Manning shunned all appeals for reason. As Matthew Arnold would have said, he bore the seed of destruction in himself.

It was clear however that other leaders had laid the groundwork for Mr. Manning's recklessness and cupidity. Over the years of political independence the abomination had jumped from political party to political party and was like a political swine flu. In the *Rights of Man*, Thomas Paine points out that it was not against Louis XVI but against the principles of the government that the nation revolted. The action of the Paris mobs was to clean the Augean Stables of parasites and plunderers. The story is analogous to what the government, led by Mr. Manning, was doing. His residence had become the country's Bastille and the actions of voters in Trinidad and Tobago were calculated to do the same: to rid the country of men and women whose interests were driven by greed and vanity.

It is clear that the promise and glow of the PNM were lost and it proves – does it not? – that political parties, like the men who establish them, become decrepit, die and decompose themselves when they lose all moral considerations for the public they were intended to defend and support.

Thus, after wrestling leadership from him, Ms. Kamla Persad-Bissessar opened the residence to handicapped children of the nation and to members of the media. She has made no secret that her purpose is to restore to us, as the prophet said, the years that the locust had eaten. And so she hoped it was a kind of cleansing and the right step to take to enter this house of ostentatious rapaciousness.

But there was more that was contemptible to the gullible population. The evidence showed that Mr. Manning's trust was neither in his Cabinet of Ministers nor in the Party's hierarchy. Instead it resided in a prophetess with a reputation for travelling to Africa and whose wisdom was about to be rewarded with a $30 million place of worship and abode. What force or faith had seized his judgement and had turned him towards this profligacy and style of living?

And who was the fairy godfather that was showering the prophetess with this benefaction? Could it be the same Udecott that worked wonders his prime-ministership to show?

There was no sworn proof of his involvement with the church until his Nemesis, the doctor's wife from Siparia who had cleansed her own party four months before, revealed correspondence about the construction of the church during the election campaign. Should the country believe the story of the mysterious PM? Or should it believe Mr. Manning that it was Mr. Hart who might have been the white knight in this rural adventure? In parliamentary debate after parliamentary debate and at press conference after press conference Mr. Manning had dodged the question and showed undeterred audacity in denying any knowledge of the construction of the Church of the Lighthouse of the Lord Jesus Christ on five acres of

Government lands at the Heights of Guanapo. If it were a political sleight-of-hand then, a subterfuge, it was disingenuousness that prevented him from coming to the Church's protection when villagers began to plunder the abandoned construction site in the aftermath of the election.

The Chinese have an idiom that you cannot wrap fire in paper. Whatever evil you do in the dark will come to light. Even for a Prime Minister who had put no limits to his ambitions this idiom had a warning; but he whom the gods wish to destroy they fill with unbearable pride. Now the time for reticence or avoidance had ended and he had fled Balisier House in disgrace, mourned only by those who worried where their next handout was coming from.

"The PNM is the party that loves you," the press and television advertisements had claimed with boring repetitiousness; but never in the History of the Peoples of Trinidad and Tobago had a political leader done so much to scorn the intelligence of his electorate and to destroy the confidence of men and women fired and freed by the emancipation laws of 1838 and by the revolutionary events of 1956 and 1970.

Why had the people of Trinidad and Tobago acted like sheep and allowed this barbarity and insolence to take place? Where were the sons and daughters of the men and women whose voices had opposed exclusivity, extremism and extravagance? Had they lost the anger Providence had given their parents when with Cipriani, Butler and Williams they had faced the tyranny of colonial powers?

Or, had these offspring squandered their inheritance for the profit they hoped to reap from a treasury filled with petro dollars and from a government that was oblivious of the crimes taking place – the robberies, rapes and murders that respected neither the old nor the young, neither pupil, policeman nor president? Was every outrage as benign as they chose to think?

And I? Had I left the safety of the Middle Kingdom to be a victim of predators in the land that had nourished my parents and siblings? And if by a miracle I should survive the villainy of politicians and felons, could I like Dr. Keith Rowley hope that when the government of Patrick Manning was shipwrecked in the voting shoals of Trinidad and Tobago that there would be a court-martial and that justice, and not the despicable culture of self-aggrandisement of the People's National Movement, would prevail?

On the night of Monday May 24 I sat before the television set and thirsted for revenge and an end to the criminal charade Mr. Manning had mounted during my absence from Trinidad. I wanted the party of Dr. Williams to suffer its worst defeat in decades. I saw a result of 35-6 as desirable to humiliate the party's leadership of Conrad Enill, Lenny Saith, John Rahael and Overand Padmore and to provide the beginning of a change in the politics of the nation – what Ms. Penelope Beckles who had been cast adrift by Mr. Manning would see as a chance to remould the party and to make it more relevant and more inclusive and less in the image of the fallen dictator.

The truth is I had had no inkling that my thoughts would be like that on the first day I had returned home and, indeed, mistaking the man I had known during his barren days in the House of Representatives, one of three PNM parliamentarians after the debacle of 1986, I had called him at the end of the first televised press conference I had watched. What genius had orchestrated it for the cream of the nation's reporters to look so poor, dishevelled and untrained? The questions and answers had provided no insight to the state of affairs in the nation and had revealed only the pathetic state of journalism and the perilous course of government. But in trying to get the

Prime Minister's attention was my purpose to provide him with a shield to deflect the arrows aimed at him from a corps of militant columnists? After all, he had a Minister of Information, an ex-journalist, who could have provided him with the judgement Prime Minister Persad-Bissessar now hopes that her own Press Secretary would do.

Or, was my intention to subvert the office of Prime Minister and to improve the skills of journalists who had demonstrated a wretched and humiliating inability in interviewing him and who had failed to get him to tell the public what was really taking place in government and what they should continue to expect in their lives and their work? But Parliament was prorogued, the snap election was announced, and his promise to call me the next week was abandoned in the paroxysms of the election campaign. And for the second time in my long career in journalism my brief amnesty with a Prime Minister failed to lead me in a new direction.

Today, when I recall the night of the election and the changing face of the map on the television monitor, from red to yellow to red to yellow and finally to a sea of yellow except in the northern and southern ends of the country, I know that Trinidadians and Tobagonians who have been given this respite must work untiringly to make sure that the PNM is not returned to government until the party has washed itself clean of the sins of its fathers. The 29-12 victory was a strong enough mandate for the coalition of parties that now form the Government and overwhelming proof that the country was fed up with the abuses of Mr. Manning. There will be always attempts to ridicule and to slander Ms. Persad-Bissessar and her People's Partnership Government, as Dr. Rowley showed with his scurrilous remarks about Wellington boots and dancing shoes. This sadly is the nature of our two-party system and the condition of Opposition politics. But for some years we must keep the PNM at bay and not allow them within miles of returning to the seat of power.

The results of the Local Government elections on July 26 in which the coalition of the United National Congress and the Congress of the People captured eleven of the corporations and in which the PNM held on to just three of the corporations were in keeping with the wishes of the people to put Mr. Manning and Dr. Rowley behind them. And already, it is clear that Dr. Rowley is not the kind of leader that the party needs to re-invent itself. His election style, characterized by pettiness and acrimony, seems not unlike that of the leader he has condemned and there is the danger that Mr. Manning, seeing this, would try to stage a comeback in Parliament to unseat him as Opposition Leader. This is a development the Party must not allow if it really wants to gain back the respect of Trinidadians and Tobagonians and party members like Ms. Beckles must understand that it is not silly rumour or mischievous newspaper speculation. In politics even a eunuch could still influence people he appointed to high places when he had the power to do so. For them it is a matter of misplaced gratitude as the burgesses of Port of Spain, San Juan-Laventille and Point Fortin showed.

II.

When we got back to Trinidad on March 9, I thought I would just watch, read and listen. I spoke to no one except family members, and it was not until the weekend that I phoned Sir Ellis Clarke to say I was back. I wasn't successful in reaching Mr. Isaac McLeod who at one time had declared himself to be a benefactor and friend and in China I never lost the feeling that I should be grateful to him for the courage and generosity he showed in standing by my dream to reverse the flow of information in the region.

Other people who had seen this opportunity never lifted a finger to make it happen.

"Are you back for good?" Sir Ellis asked.

"Yes," I said. "I am putting to test the idiom that you cannot go back home."

I forgot what he said to this. He probably said he was glad that I had come home. I remember Mr. Andrew Johnson – or was it Mr. Dennis Gurley? – of the Trinidad and Tobago Chamber of Industry and Commerce saying that to me when I paid my first visit to the Chamber's offices in Westmoorings in April and accepted its invitation to become a member of the Debates Commission. "I am glad you're back," he said as we shook hands and I wondered why he felt this way. I didn't remember having anything to do with him in the past. But I am aware that we come to know men by what they say, by what they do, and by what they write. When I left Trinidad in 1998 I had spent forty-six years as a practising journalist and had been Editor-in-Chief of both the Express and the Guardian. I had been also editor of the *Catholic News*.

My political commentaries had alienated many people and, as the late Frank Barsotti had said to me once, I had made a lot of powerful enemies. And maybe, I protested, a few friends who welcomed my frankness. But in Trinidad, he reminded me, friendship is a weak and unreliable reed.

I considered Sir Ellis one of the friends I had made. He had agreed to be Chairman of the Board of Directors of Caribbean Information Systems & Services Limited and I had hoped that his knowledge and counsel would be invaluable as we strove to establish an online information service. He had shown as much pride as we did in the Caribbean Basin Exhibit and, recalling the venture now, I remembered Mr. Basdeo Panday saying to me when as Prime Minister he visited the building on Frederick Street, "Why did you do it?" Why? Was it something the University of the West Indies should have attempted? Or, perhaps, Mr. Edwin Carrington, the Secretary-General at the Caricom Secretariat? He had seen what we were doing, had expressed his congratulations and praises and had gone away never to return.

We are accustomed in Trinidad and Tobago to look for quick returns on our investments and this was surely not what CISS would provide and it did not. Sir Ellis I recalled did not like the sound of the acronym, CISS. He shuddered every time I said it and he used to pronounce it *KISS*. When I was in China I would recall this idiosyncrasy of his every time someone explained that the number 4 is unlucky because the sound of it in Chinese is the same as the sound of the word for death. I wonder if this was Bhoendradatt Tewarie's problem as well.

For weeks I lived like a hermit crab, reading the three daily newspapers and watching the evening news on television. My world had shrunk and I recalled the Chinese idiom of a frog in a well. I had no interest in seeing Mr. Manning's tall buildings and the public servants at the Elections and Boundaries Commission and the Ministry of Legal Affairs, from whom I was trying to get a new ID card and birth certificate, seemed determined to frustrate me every time I went to them expecting that the documents were ready. In fact the bureaucracy won out and I never had the opportunity to vote in the May 24 election. The private sector seemed as inefficient or inconsiderate, once you had left it, and I had as much difficulty getting information from the Express for the National Insurance Board. Unlike as in China where I interfaced with hundreds of students every day, I was a complete stranger at home and suffered with the rest of the population seeking what was their right and what was promised them in 48 hours. There were some people – Roslyn Prescod was one of them – who met me on the street and who hugged and kissed me and said, "Are you coming back to the Express?"

Steve McPhie was another. But I never felt the same warmth and respect I had experienced from my college students and the teachers who taught with me in Guangzhou and in Beijing.

I remembered what I had told Sir Ellis: You cannot go back home. So would my fate be to return to China? And then one day, about five weeks after I had been living at the Sierra Leone Apartments in Diego Martin, Mr. Ken Gordon telephoned. A few days before, when I had gone for a medical examination from Dr. Winston Ince we had come within yards of meeting but he did not know this. On that same afternoon I had seen Professor Kenneth Julien but I hadn't recognized him when he had said on leaving Dr. Ince's office, "It's nice to see you people." Everyone had grown older and appeared embarrassed to see you, and I thought this was not a country for old men.

You needed youth to confront the frustrations and disappointments of daily life. And I was sure that I couldn't cope with the hypocrisy.

"How long have you been back?" Mr. Gordon asked.

"Five weeks," I said.

"And you never called."

"I didn't have your number."

"Nonsense!"

The truth is I had thought of calling him several times when I was furious over the news coverage in the Express, but I felt that to complain about the reporting was not something I should do. The credibility of the paper was not my responsibility and, as he was to say to me, it was no longer his responsibility also. I supposed it was Mr. Terrence Farrell's who two months later quit the One Caribbean Media Group as its Chief Executive Officer to go into family business. And yet it was clear to me that the weakness of the media was one of the major reasons for the tragedy of Mr. Manning and for the degradation of life in Trinidad and Tobago. Who was it, dear Father Clyde Harvey, that said all the faults of our age come from Christianity and journalism?

I think I would never escape the guilt and anger one feels as a journalist at a press one knows to be unreliable and untrustworthy. So was it true that it was not our business or was it only an excuse? As newspapermen our umbilical cords are attached to every newspaper and we have a responsibility to expect and to demand a high quality of accuracy and objectivity in the work of journalists. In fact I was to find out that he had a greater interest in their wellbeing as he had taken responsibility to raise funds for a journalism training course at the University of Trinidad and Tobago where he was a member of the Board and a few days later he copied me with a letter he wrote to Professor Funso Aiyejina recommending me to be a lecturer when the new university year began in September.

In the days and weeks that followed I began to read the newspapers more critically. I studied the columnists, the sections and the letters to the editors. I compared layouts, photographs, headlines and texts. The similarities were striking and though I bought all three dailies I knew it would not be a major calamity if I had purchased only one. Gone were the craftiness of Patrick Chookolingo and the classicism of George John. Imprudence had replaced intelligence and in all of the newspapers what was missing was an awareness that the press must be an example of excellence. It must hold up a candle in the darkness that surrounds us, as Mr. Thomas Gatcliffe used to say to me. But in the new secular world it appeared that this philosophy was missing and there was no example to emulate and, in a country where people were worshipping Principal and not Principle, the struggle to survive had challenged the editors of the three dailies, the Express, the Guardian, and Newsday, to pay slight attention to accuracy, integrity and competence. Getting the news out first seemed to be the only measure that News Editors insisted on and it did not matter if the information was incorrect or misleading. But this risk was not something that the reading public missed or ignored and for journalists the price of readers' skepticism is always a creeping demoralization in the newsroom. It is difficult to live and laugh with a weakness you know and despise.

Did the boards of the three newspapers really care about standards or truth? Or were they concerned only with circulation gains and advertising revenues? Was this the genesis of television coverage of political meetings that would say it was a "paid political announcement"? And was it why the Trinidad Chamber of Industry and Commerce and other institutions believed that it was safer to get their message out in advertisements rather than leave it to reporters to put the wrong emphasis on their news? On my way back to Trinidad I had stopped off in Los Angeles to pay a visit to the LA Times where Mr. Davan Maharaj who worked for me once at the Express is now Managing Editor. "I was in Trinidad recently," Davan told me as he showed me around his newspaper, "and I was shocked to see the low morale of the staff at both the Express and the Guardian. Perhaps when you get back you could do something to lift their spirits."

He was seriously concerned; I was non-committal. I had no such intention to interfere though after my conversation with Mr. Gordon I began to think of what I would do to correct the errors we had discussed. Trinidad and Tobago would develop in grace only in an environment of law, justice, peace and respect for all its citizens. But respect would come only when all its citizens believe that they have an equal opportunity to improve their lives through real work, fair income and social benefits. Newspapers are a way to provide this understanding but the news media had a problem: Readers, listeners and viewers did not trust them. Like the Government they pilloried they had lost the right to lead and like the Prime Minister they mocked they existed similarly in a quicksand of denial and distrust.

III.

The meetings of the Debates Commission at the Trinidad and Tobago Chamber of Industry and Commerce presented new opportunities to understand the frustration of independent groups of Trinidadians and Tobagonians with any plan to assist in building a new society. A bevy of young, intelligent and hard-working women, led by President Angella Persad and Chief Executive Officer Catherine Kumar, had given the Chamber a new face, but there was the need still to overcome its history of economic and political bias.

There was the lingering distrust of a population which was prepared to question every word and to investigate every act of the business community, whether it was in the city or in the country or in a house in Bayshore, to be involved in the governance of the country.

Indeed the new brigade of leaders at the Chamber was prepared to bend over backwards to prove their sincerity and patriotism and this, simply, was one of the reasons the Chamber had been working at the creation of the Debates Commission.

It was not an original idea nor was it strictly speaking an American idea. There were more than two dozens countries in the Americas, in Europe, in Asia and in Africa that had promoted the idea of Presidential and Prime Ministerial Debates, including Jamaica. The Trinidad Chamber had been working on a Trinidad and Tobago Debates Commission for more than a year when Mr. Manning called his snap election and precipitated action from the Chamber to initiate public debate on the issue.

Denied the opportunity to plan and prepare itself and the public of Trinidad and Tobago for another two years, the Chamber jumped into the election fray. When political leaders debate national issues, it argued, the public is informed. Its mission statement became "to strengthen the democratic process by staging debates on matters of national importance to assist the electorate in making informed political choices."

But to judge from Messrs. Manning and Enill's reaction, this wish of the Chamber was seen as an intervention in the political affairs of Trinidad and Tobago – which it was even if the Chamber's intention was honourable and it favoured no party.

I was invited to become a Commissioner as were Professor Rhoda Reddock and Father Clyde Harvey. Professor Bridget Brereton had been invited as well but she dropped out after our first meeting because of the Chamber's squeaky-clean policy to have no Commissioner who could be identified with the interests of any of the political parties by word, deed or association and Professor Brereton made it known after her first meeting that her sister-in-law, Lena Brereton-Wolfe, had been a candidate of the Congress of the People in 2007.

So am I wrong to publish this historical account *six months later*? Am I stigmatizing the Chamber and the Debates Commission by revealing my distrust of and contempt for Mr. Manning and the government of the People's National Movement?

The Commissioners, who included Ronald F. deC. Harford and Ian Collier, were never intended to be Moderators or Questioners; they were mainly responsible for the professional staging of the debates and for the topic and themes for the debates. Their goal was to have a more informed electorate that understands clearly political decisions taken by the government. But without the unreserved confidence of the contesting political parties in the Commission's constant impartiality, the Chamber had stated in its Code of Conduct for Commissioners, the Commissioners would fail in the pursuit of their objective to preserve the integrity of the Commission. This was an appeal for a virtual oath of silence and it was a condition that put a restraint on me as a practising journalist to comment on the absurdity of Mr. Manning's politics, and during the euphoria of the election campaign and afterwards I abided by the Chamber's rules and refrained from any public comment.

I had pointed out to Mr. Gordon that the Express lacked vision and enterprise and was failing to set the country's news agenda; television I thought was doing a better job. But what I found most disconcerting was the lack of interest from media houses in what the Chamber was doing. The planning had been going on for more than a year but there was no report of this activity anywhere in the media though journalists and shareholders from all the media had been involved in its discussions. I wasn't sure however that it was not what the Chamber considered as the best strategy because of its fear of an irresponsible media or a suspicious audience and its desire to avoid mischievous speculation. The suddenness of the news of the debates therefore might have precipitated the negative responses from Mr. Manning who said he had nothing to gain from a debate with Ms. Persad-Bissessar, and from Mr. Enill who complained that his party was not involved in the planning of the debates.

The debates as a result never came off and I wrote in my diary on May 18, which was to be the day of the first debate, that it was a loss of an opportunity for clarifying the issues of leadership, crime and corruption that worried the electorate. In an editorial I wrote on May 16, *The truth about the Chamber, the Debates Commission and the People's National Movement,* I said that the people of Trinidad and Tobago would not be hearing on the night of

May 20 a Leadership Debate between Prime Minister Patrick Manning and Opposition Leader Kamla Persad-Bissessar. But this lost opportunity I said was never the fault of the Trinidad and Tobago Chamber of Industry and Commerce and its brainchild, the Debates Commission, hastily brought to life when Mr. Manning called his snap election. I couldn't say these things openly however, just as my living-room views on the night of the election were personal and private. In order to preserve the confidence of contesting political parties, the Chamber had said, it was imperative that at all times appearances should project and reflect the reality of non-partisanship. Thus no Commissioner could make any public statement for or against any party or candidate.

I had accepted this interdiction so in writing this Introduction I am really abjuring rules the Chamber insisted on. I must therefore apologise to the Chamber and to my fellow Commissioners. To quote an Express columnist, who reminded me of my early days covering the magistrates' courts, "I am guilty, but with a cause." I believe I am writing a chapter of our History and to do this well, to write sincerely, I must remove the mask and muzzle that I wore during the general election period. But what I now make known should surprise no one. My views of politics and political parties in Trinidad and Tobago have been well documented in newspaper editorials and columns over the forty-six years that I worked as a journalist and I don't see my decision today as a revelation and a dishonorable act. I am aware however that the Chamber could be upset by its transparency and would rush to sever all connections with me. So be it. The end, as Shakespeare wrote, crowns all.

What does the record show? As early as April 27, the day that the Debates Commission had its media launch, Mr. Manning missed the point of the debates proposed by the Chamber when he said during a tour of

Tarodale Heights that he had "nothing to gain by a debate". And in doing so he misled the following of PNM devotees about the sincerity of the Chamber and the significance of a debate. And it was no surprise that Ms. Persad-Bissessar should pounce on this shockingly inept statement and repeat night after night on her campaign trail that Mr. Manning was thinking about himself and not about the population of Trinidad and Tobago. It was a pity because the debates were not about the gains of one political party over the other, in this case the PNM over the People's Partnership that included the United National Congress, the Congress of the People, the Movement for Social Justice, the Tobago Organisation of the People and the National Joint Action Committee. It was rather about the understanding of the Trinidad and Tobago population on matters of national importance.

I was certain that this intention of the Chamber and the Commission had been made clear to Mr. Manning. Indeed it was the subject of a letter of invitation that was sent to him and Ms. Persad-Bissessar on April 26 that informed them of proposed dates for the two debates and the rules governing the debates. "We believe," wrote Ms. Persad, "that these debates can play a vital role in enabling Trinidad and Tobago to join the growing community of nations that have made debates an integral part of their election process."

There is no gainsaying it: the Chamber had been scrupulous in its desire to be honourable and fair to both political parties and their leaders and even though the debates were suddenly in the public domain because of Mr. Manning's call to President George Maxwell Richards to prorogue Parliament on April 8, the Chamber believed that it had done the work that was required to stage successfully the debates. And public support for the events continued to grow day by day and justified the action and hope of the Chamber. On May 6 the Inter-Religious

Organisation, for example, joined the legions of people expressing support for the debates. "We are of the view," said its president, Pundit Bramdeo Maharaj, "that the debates would be in the best interest of the national community and that through such debates the nation as a whole would have everything to gain and nothing to lose." This was the opinion of the majority of Trinidadians and Tobagonians interviewed by members of the print and electronic media and finding its way on Facebook and Twitter.

At a meeting of the Debates Commission on April 16 I met Ms. Eleanor Henry, a consultant from the Jamaica Debates Commission, and in the weeks that followed Commissioners were introduced to Mr. Matt Dippell, of the Commission on US Presidential Debates, and Mr. Trevor Fearon, another of Ms. Henry's colleagues on the 2002 Jamaica Debates Commission. We learnt that Trinidad and Tobago was behind Liberia, Mexico, Peru, Cambodia and Nigeria – behind 27 countries to stage political debates.

But after the National Election was called on April 16, the Chamber was able to state in a whole-page advertisement that the Debates Commission was close to completing its debate framework and thereafter the Chamber moved quickly in the planning and organising of two national debates. But the early work of the Chamber had been unheralded and unknown as it sought to introduce criteria that would demonstrate its commitment for fairness in Trinidad and Tobago's unique, cultural diversity. Was this a mistake?

The Chamber's passion for secrecy had revealed the national distrust for the media and since returning home, after an absence of twelve years in the People's Republic of China, I was aware that this distrust was based on what is perceived by readers, listeners and viewers as distortions of the news. In other words, could the news we read, watch or hear be trusted? Would a simple statement be misrepresented because of spite, ignorance or laziness by practising journalists? The environment nowadays is one in which truth is compromised and the public knowledge, the celebrated right to know, is frequently manipulated and organisations and individuals retreat behind walls of advertorials, behind the security of "paid political broadcasts", behind "Sorry, no comment". Somebody once said that a journalist "owes nothing to those who govern his country. He owes everything to his country." Had the press now sworn an oath to this opinion and didn't concern itself with truth?

I am aware that outside of governments no other institution is so desirous of existing in a sane and safe environment as the private sector. It believes passionately that development, or, if you like, the opportunity for profit and luxurious living, could take place only in times of peace and with the bountiful support of contented individuals. And, if it could, business organisations would leave nothing to chance, to the whimsical understanding of untrained reporters. So, on the day of the Media Launch on April 27 the Chamber handed out press kits to the media that revealed the names of the Commissioners and the Moderators and the Code of Conduct for Commissioners chosen from various disciplines. They contained as well the criteria for participation by the political parties in the debates and guidelines for Moderators and Questioners. Transparency and openness and a spirit of fair play were obvious. It was never the Chamber's intention to stack the deck in the favour of any political party.

No commissioner attending the meetings in those weeks could fail to detect the surge of energy and commitment of the Commission's staff. They were a dedicated group of women that was consumed by the Mission Statement of the Commission and it is their trust, their bending over backwards to ensure that no charge of favouritism could be made against the Commission, that made Mr. Enill's remarks that the debates were rushed not just partisan but puerile, mischievous and dangerous to the public good. In a letter to the Chamber on May 10, Mr. Enill criticized the "approach" of the Chamber and said that the debate would have given the UNC "an unfair advantage." He said more and was devastating in his criticisms of the Chamber: "The People's National Movement," wrote Mr. Enill, "wishes to express concern to what seems to be a rushed approach to the staging of these debates contrary to the practice and procedure normally employed in staging these matters."

The week before he wrote this nonsense, Mr. Enill had said that Mr. Manning was "the victim of a sustained character assassination by opposition forces." (I am quoting an Express reporter at the presentation of the 41 PNM candidates at Woodford Square on May 2.) "Those who are opposed to us, and who are acting opposed to us are using the most extreme negative message campaign that we have ever experienced focussed [sic] on our political leader. They have united with one objective. The objective is to remove the People's National Movement by any untoward means and the means they have chosen to focus on is our political leader."

It was his job to defend the king.

Mr. Enill's was a brand of loyalty we could commend – up to a point. *Il ne faut pas etre plus royaliste que le roi.* This is undoubtedly what Mr. Enill had in mind. One must not be more royalist than the king. But Aristotle had said, "Plato is dear to me but dearer still is truth." The question is did he view the Commission's debates as simply a strategy of those in opposition to his party and his party leader? And why? Mr. Manning had said unequivocally that he had nothing to gain from a debate with Ms. Persad-Bissessar. Was Mr. Enill putting a different face on the PNM's refusal to engage the Opposition

UNC/COP Partnership in debating important social and economic issues and standards of leadership? Did he see pitting Ms. Persad-Bissessar against Mr. Manning in the same way he saw Mr. Percy Villafana's opposition to Mr. Manning when he was on his walkabout in San Juan? "I was appalled," the PNM Chairman said, "when a gentleman openly disrespected the Prime Minister of the Republic and the press made him a national hero."

What is the truth? Fifteen days before Mr. Enill's dyspeptic disagreement, on April 26, the Chairman of the Debates Commission, Ms. Persad, wrote to Mr. Manning and Ms. Persad-Bissessar, after meetings with both parties, that "(W)e would very much like to share the details of our plans with you and invite you once again to send your nominee to an information-sharing meeting at the offices of the Chamber this afternoon at a time to be mutually agreed. In addition we wish to invite this representative to attend a press conference scheduled for 10:00 a.m. tomorrow. This press conference will introduce the Commission and the framework for the debates."

The invitation to be present at the information-sharing meeting was not exactly slighted by the PNM whose representative explained his absence on the day that he was mistaken about the time or the venue and was available to take part only in a telephone conference. The representative from the UNC/COP Partnership attended and I would not be surprised if he thought that Ms. Persad ignored him while her attention seemed focused on the PNM Minister at the other end of the line. And the PNM representative failed to attend a second meeting to ask questions about the details for the debates. And yet I am not surprised. Mr. Enill had made it clear that debates are not the PNM way. "We see no reason for getting involved in the event," Mr. Enill told reporters at the launch of the Carbon Reduction Strategy Task Force on April 28, as the Guardian reported. "We go where it matters and addressing [sic] issues that the people are concerned with."

I am not surprised because we have made politics a road show of public ridicule and the temptation is to view any statement or gesture during an election campaign as favourable or hostile. So I am not surprised if the Prime Minister viewed the debate as another attempt to vilify him because he thought that the media, both print and electronic, were against him and he did not trust any contact with them. This has been the tradition of PNM leaders, the father of which once set ablaze the Guardian in Woodford Square. And this contempt was no doubt the basis for Mr. Manning's selection of Anthony Wilson, Juhel Browne and Hans Hanoomansingh for his pathetic radio and television interview on the eve of the election. I kept thinking of the nursery rhyme of the Three Blind Mice and the Farmer's wife who cut off their tails with a carving knife. The interview, it was clear to all of us watching and listening, undermined his campaign for re-election just as it added to the media's ignominy.

A political debate, as most Trinidadians and Tobagonians see it, is one of malice and slaughter and the suggestion of facing one's opponent in a neutral arena with gloves on could make even a man of Mr. Manning's combative energies uneasy. When we saw him flailing his arms on the campaign platforms and shouting imprecations at members of the People's Partnership, it was easy to understand that the sterilised environment of a television studio is not the arena he would relish. He must have thought wryly that what the Chamber proposed was like putting a 350-pound Sumo wrestler in a dance competition with Salome. I also believe that the people who followed the PNM campaign night after night would have preferred to see Ms. Marlene McDonald debating the Opposition Leader on her choice of clothes; or Mr. Colm Imbert debating Ms. Persad-Bissessar about her views on abortion. To them it would be, simply, a sideshow and not an opportunity to instruct the populace on the finer points of politics and leadership.

However, the debate that the Chamber planned was not a brawl; it was to be an occasion when the population would have been informed of intelligent steps the new government after May 24 would take to bring about solutions to the problems that plague our development and our daily lives. I think that the Debates Commission's advertisement that said, "*When issues are debated, people learn. When leaders debate, people win,*" faithfully illustrated the desire of the Chamber to raise the bar of political understanding in Trinidad and Tobago.

Thus on May 12 the Chamber felt that PNM dithering had gone on too long. "The Trinidad and Tobago Debates Commission," it said, "wishes to advise the public that the proposed debate scheduled for Thursday May 13th 2010 will not take place because of the decision of one of the political parties not to debate." But the Chamber wasn't giving up its hope to have a more informed and courageous population. The Debates Commission, it said, stands ready to accommodate a debate at short notice should both political parties agree on the need for such an event.

The message was clear: the Debates Commission was not folding its tent and silently stealing away. It hadn't been scared away by the might or malice of the PNM. Instead, the Debates Commission remained a permanent addition to the political landscape of Trinidad and Tobago.

IV.

This unchanging landscape of arrogance, demagoguery and conceit was the background against which the author of *Kamla, Ascent of a Woman* began writing her weekly Jahajee column from China and it had all begun with the murder of a little girl in Trinidad. Tecia

Henry was just ten years old and had been missing for four days when her body was found in a shallow grave under a house in Plaisance Terrace in Laventille on the outskirts of Port of Spain. She had been a student of St. Rose's Girls' Primary School and like other Trinidadians and Tobagonians she had become the victim of a barbarous crime that provoked protests by residents over what they saw as an inability of the police to find the killer.

But the protests were to show too that the government was not on top of the raging issue of crime in the nation. By the end of the year 2009 that Tecia died the number of murders in the twin-island republic had reached the frightening total of 509. The country came to be called the "Crime Capital of the Caribbean", overtaking the infamy of Jamaica, and foreign governments began to issue travel advisories against visiting Trinidad and Tobago.

The country's unstoppable crime rate had shocked and appalled the teacher and journalist in her classrooms in Guangzhou and every day she agonized that she could do little so many thousand of miles from Trinidad to console the family of Tecia and others mercilessly gunned down. How could she explain to her students that this was not the Trinidad she had grown up in and that she remembered? What evil had corroded the values that her generation had inherited from their parents, from their teachers, from their neighbours?

And then one day she received an email from Mr. Richard Seecharan in New York and his JahajeeDesi website presented her with an opportunity to identify with the hope of so many in the Diasporas and at home for a better life. It was thus the start of a series of weekly articles.

Her writings drew many varied responses but it did not seem to make any difference. The horrible crimes that the police said were drug and gang-related continued to stalk the nation like an inexorable evil scourge up to the time of the May 24 election. But incredibly it was not an issue that the People's National Movement was ready to confront on the platform or in a debate.

Still, this is not to say that Mr. Manning and his National Security Minister Mr. Martin Joseph felt all was well. Even though their attempts at solving crime appeared to focus on the purchase of sophisticated machinery like dirigibles and gunboats, their actions lacked credibility as they continued to fail to find a way to stop the bloodletting and the robberies at gun and knife-point. And even though they still looked for sympathy for what they were doing from a population that was wearied of the waste of taxpayers' dollars in everything that the government undertook they continued to show aloofness in their relations with the public and no one in the Party seemed to want to bell the cat.

Ignoring the row he had in the House of Representatives with Dr. Rowley over the excesses of Udecott, Mr. Manning had said that the PNM did not wash its dirty linen in public. It was clearly his prayer that we would believe this falsehood and that we would glorify him and enjoy him forever. And, not incuriously, there were many who did just this.

The results of two elections showed that many Trinidadians and Tobagonians closed their eyes and ears to his insanity and continued to revere Mr. Manning and to believe that the People's National Movement was the answer to the country's hope for a better life. This was the way that Elizabeth and Maurice Holder felt and they could point to benefits from the government's medical revolution of subsidized medicines that helped their family. This was the way Deborah and Victor Goden also felt. They hadn't received the HDC house they had applied for but they trusted Mr. Manning and the PNM more than they had trusted the government of Mr. Basdeo Panday and the old

United National Congress. And yet there was a growing number of wise men and women in the country who wrote for the daily newspapers, who provided the opinions on radio and television for better governance and justice, and who insisted it was time for Mr. Manning to go. Too many things had gone wrong and too many policies were flawed.

It was clear to the majority of the nation's 719,727 voters, for example, that lawlessness was the Number One issue of public concern in Trinidad and Tobago especially as Mr. Manning hadn't been able to find a suitable Commissioner of Police to take over from the retiring James Philbert. And even though he and his Minister of Community Development, Culture and Gender Affairs would have preferred to make Ms. Persad-Bissessar the issue of importance, turning the public's attention from crime, there was always the fear in May that violence would disrupt the campaign and the polls. And indeed there were minor spats, but nothing really dangerous to the public welfare as a Caricom team of observers led by Mr. Hugh Cholmondeley of Guyana and Dame Billie Miller of Barbados saw to their satisfaction.

Mr. Manning, brimming always with self-confidence, had felt it safe to believe that his record spoke for itself and there was no other issue in the campaign except the weakness of Ms. Persad-Bissessar's physical condition. Every night he made the point that she was just another female even when she showed she had the strength to tear his Party's Manifesto to pieces on her platform. "Same old, same old," she had said derisively of its plans for the nation as she shredded the expensive document. Nevertheless he conscientiously avoided the people's concerns about crime. It should not have surprised anyone therefore when after the night of May 24 the lawlessness in the country spilled over into the illegal seizure of state lands at Cashews Gardens and into the plundering of the abandoned church at Guanapo.

The truth is Mr. Manning failed the country but he hadn't been the only one to do so. Other Prime Ministers before him had failed us as well. They had left no legacy of benevolence and no example of a proper political life. They never grew into statesmen and never gave us values to enrich our lives. Instead we were bestowed contentions and churlishness. Now the question is would the People's Partnership be able to correct the wrongs of the past?

It is clear from the state of unrelenting crime that we do not have the luxury of Time but there is always Hope that springs eternal in the breast of man. And from May 25 the work of sustaining Trinidad and Tobago on the principles of law and order and justice had begun with a new person as Prime Minister – the 58-year-old Kamla Persad-Bissessar. Would a woman make the difference? Would the courage, stamina and intelligence of this woman put to shame the arrogance of the men who had occupied the office and position of Prime Minister?

I am banking on it. Her message to her Ministers and members of the Partnership on her first day was simple: Avoid arrogance and serve, serve, serve. "We have to be ever mindful," the new Prime Minister told her team after they had taken the oath of office at Knowsley Building in Port of Spain, "that the nation is looking at us expectantly. No one out there expects excuses; they want results. Lead by example. Follow and learn to listen. As of now each of us is on trial. We begin to be tested as of this moment. My caution is this: never be aloof, never lose sight of the true purpose of the position you hold. Stay grounded. Keep connected with the people. Earn their respect by the way you serve them. The people are the Government. Take these words and frame them on your desk."

Owen Baptiste
Guangzhou, China.

Rhona Baptiste in Guangzhou

1. LITTLE TECIA

GUANGZHOU: Thursday 18th June 2009

In the *Trinidad Guardian* online was the disturbing news of little Tecia Henry in Laventille. Actually it was there in *JahajeeDesi's* posting too. The ten-year old who went to the parlour for her Mom on Saturday morning at 7:30 was found dead days later under a house buried in a shallow grave. She was strangled, and stuffed into a hole pawed out by a dog.

How have we in our island Paradise of Trinidad and Tobago come to such a sorry pass? This started off as an email to my friend Eulah and then I thought I should share my concern with other Trinidadians and Tobagonians who must be as concerned as I have become over the incidence of crime in our country and the constant, almost daily, attacks on women.

You know, although Owen and I have been away from home for a very long time (since 1998) I don't think that a day has gone past when we have not spoken with concern for the islands we left behind.

In China we have carried our flag proudly and I know all this sounds like a lot of nostalgic ballyhoo but what it means is that we have never stopped caring and loving for the land that nurtured us. So what are the answers to the evil that now stalks our country?

I don't pretend to know what they are but I do feel that IF there is going to be an exorcism it has to start with ourselves. Yes, I know it is easier to bury our heads in the sand and lay blame at the feet of the Government, whoever has the power in Parliament, or at the fractured opposition or at the church steps.

No doubt we all think of ourselves as activists, ranting and raving in the safe confines of our oases. I might even seem to be one of them. But, fortunately, not all of us are like that. Some like Rhea Mungal in the south is rallying around the call for a public meeting to say no to Alutrint. We are asking those in authority for a Cost Benefit Analysis for Alutrint, she had written about the proposed Aluminum Smelter Complex.

All this may be good social activism, but is it enough? Have we really touched the heart of the matter affecting our new degraded quality of life? Have we reached into the wound and put our fingers into the throbbing nerves of hate and anger of our manhood? I say manhood as this is where the pain seems to be most. What has happened to our men?

Look at the future. According to a report issued by the United States State Department, gang-related homicides and other crimes will continue to increase in Trinidad and Tobago in 2009 and 2010.

As for we women, what have we DONE to our men? Why have we - literally speaking - let them get away with murder? We women must ask ourselves how are we to share the blame in this sorry state to which we have now degenerated.

To what extent have we examined the temptations of the oil money that have become more of a curse than a blessing? Have we taken a stand in the debate on any controversial matter; are we getting constructively involved in our family's or neighbours' affairs? or are we too busy 'minding our own business?'

But there is something more insidious than the money curse and gas smelters at the centre of the wound. It is an absence of love or something deep inside that frees one to really care about others. It's like we are unrelated. A little more than one million of us connected for better or for worst by Fate! Strange... such hate in our family... and Trinidad and Tobago is a land of abundant religions where each preaches forgiveness and love. So what happened to religion, to the doctrine that we are our brothers and sisters' keepers?

I've been thinking about us – women - single, married, housewives, mothers, teachers and other professionals and wondering to what extent by default we have allowed the 'chooking' and 'jamming' that fuelled the lewdness and which in turn imprinted a culture of violence and sex. By the same token have we not tolerated the breakdown in 'guardianship' so that President George Maxwell Richards finds difficulty in putting together an unblemished Integrity Commission?

There is I think a story like this in the Bible – the story of someone trying to save the cities of Sodom and Gomorrah, if only he could find five just men.

My heart joins in grief for our country and for the innocent victims like Tecia Henry who continue to be sacrificed at the altar of our insensitivities. What were her dreams? One of her sisters when interviewed a year later on television would say that she wants to be a doctor. Does she stand the ghost of a chance to realize her own dream for Tecia's sake? Or, will there be another family member to succumb to terror?

But all need not be lost. Wherever we find ourselves we must help to make this world a better place. In our quest for generosity, love really, and how we do so is up to each one of us.

2. THE ANATOMY OF VIOLENCE

GUANGZHOU: Thursday 25th June 2009

He said to me: Are the people in Trinidad and Tobago finally living in a world from which love has disappeared? Are we no longer our brothers' keepers? Do you remember how we once described the islands lovingly as: All ah we is one? Have the murders, rapes and kidnappings destroyed this belief and so we work, worry, sleep and die in what is an unfamiliar land today with no Williams nor Burroughs, Pantin nor Hassanali to protect us?

Why is it so hard for Trinidadians and Tobagonians to come together – forget the politics – and change the environment in which they live and enrich their lives? But isn't it true as well that crime, like war or an epidemic, abolishes all divisions though many might still keep their blinkered habit of ostentatious indifference?

I could feel his pain and anguish, but I don't think it is correct to assume that nobody cares and that nothing is happening to restore the goodwill we once had. In every crisis there are always people working to bring about a solution and as Stephen Cadiz reminded me this week Trinidadians did come together in 2007 to protest another brutal murder. No, there are people who care and who want to live in a country where it is safe to send a 10-year-old girl to the shop or to school. But I think crime is always with us and we have to learn to understand it and, understanding it, guard against it from swallowing the community.

"So what do you think we must we do?" he asked.

We could bring about change only if we understand the culture of violence that is fermenting in cosmopolitan Trinidad and Tobago, I said. I was aware that I was not the only one concerned enough to write. It is necessary, I said, to dissect the beast of violence so as to understand what is happening. The alarming statistics of June 8th 2009, from which Carmen Sanchez concludes that Trinidad and Tobago is now "the murder capital of the Caribbean," are a macabre milestone in our history. I am not surprised that she closes with this grim prediction by the United States Department of State: Gang-related homicides and other crimes will continue to increase in Trinidad and Tobago in 2009 and 2010.

It is not enough to gnash our teeth and cry about our situation, however. The problem is to find a way to dry our tears, even my own tears from China, as I understand *Newsday* had headlined my letter to the *JahajeeDesi* link last week. Tears bring some relief but tears alone will not heal our wounds.

He said, What we have to fight first is our history. I am not riding a hobby-horse here but colonialism and slavery have given us a bad start. We have a lot to overcome, as Dr. Williams showed in his *History of the People of Trinidad and Tobago,* which he published at the time of our Independence in 1962. "It was not the poor Governor's fault. Everybody in Trinidad was a lawbreaker. It was not a question of smuggling. It was an open trade conducted in broad daylight, in which all participated, men and women, young and old, adults and children." The year was 1611 and the period was Spanish colonialism. The French with their African slaves were not even there as yet, and that was to happen in 1783, almost two centuries later; while in 1845 the Fatel Rozack was to bring in the first boatload of East Indians as indentured labourers.

Fast forward another two centuries later and what do we have? Our people, as the inheritors and progeny of this concoction of humanity, seem not to have changed much. In spite of the British occupation in 1797 and eventual relinquishing the twin-island state to its self-rule in 1962, the more things change the more they remain the same. But we can squander our hopes in the recollections of this history. Once we recognize it, we have to move on. We don't want looking at our history to become the work we should be doing to understand and tackle the roots of crime and make Trinidad and Tobago a safer place for all of us.

So how do we deal today with people who break the law? Is our situation not unlike the Spanish Governor of that time? Williams quoted the frustrations of Sancho de Alquiza who in his capacity as one man Integrity Commissioner then wrote: "I was all alone in the Town and the people had done all that they could; to arrest all those guilty was not possible. I had neither the soldiers nor a prison large enough."

Even when we know this history, does it tell us how to escape the danger that surrounds our lives in our homes and on the streets? Consolation does not come as easy as it seems to those who must live with the violence, or for those whose distance provides a safe armchair of revolt. But I feel we should no longer take comfort in tired dogma and in self-flagellation. And I find that what's worse is the cowardice to put up with complaints about a wearied democratic system that leads to inertia and hopelessness.

All this, the lack of grace and graciousness, only serves to support Vidia Naipaul's loathing for the land of his birth and its people. In *A Way in the World* it does not take long to locate a familiar hostility in the words he puts into the mouth of Andrés Level de Goda. "Our hate, General, our hate. It isn't like the hate of other places." As he wrote before, nothing great has come out of Trinidad. I know it is a lie. And I know that a lot has changed since Spain and England ruled.

He says, Forget Williams, forget Naipaul. There's too much to do to restore pride and respect in our country. We have to combat crime and indifference with real love and respect for each other.

We must have understanding and a long patience, I say. I've just clicked onto Camini Marajh's *Express* investigative reports of the CLICO debacle. As she continues her forensic examination of the corpse that was once the robust stallion on St.Vincent Street, it makes one wonder again whether we can hope for justice in the world. I bristle with rage as I recall the arrogance of the CLICO group and its betrayal of loyal policy-holders. I know that its founder Cyril Lucius Duprey and faithful workers like Cyril Monsanto must be turning in their graves at the shameful events that are unfolding in Port of Spain.

With justice, he says, we will escape the scourge of lawlessness and corruption. With justice and with compassion. We need, as Camus said, to concern ourselves with the damned more than with those whom our world holds up as heroes. What this means is that we must leave our churches and our legislatures and go into areas of the poor and dispossessed. We must hold out hope to them.

3. THE 'P' WORD

GUANGZHOU: Thursday 2nd July 2009

Trinidad and Tobago is a sociologist's paradise, I tell my students.

It is a microcosm of 5,128 sq km (1,980 sq miles) as compared with your China's 9,596.960 sq km (3,696.100. sq miles). That means your country is 2,000 times our tiny land space! No where else in the world perhaps so many different roots have been transplanted in so small a land plot as ours over so short a time. There remain now two major root stocks from Africa and India grafting onto others and hybridizing into what used to be seen with pride as a delightful fun-loving breed of people. Each year festivals like Christmas, Carnival, Eid and Divali provided release valves for celebration and unbelievable joie de vivre.

My students understand. In China there is one dominant tribe – the Han - among the fifty-six ethnic divisions of their 1.3 billion people. The difference however with our Trinidad and Tobago is that 1.3 million people are concentrated on just those 5,128 sq km or 1,980 sq miles of island. There's water all around. Since Columbus opened up the flood gates in 1498 it is to the people's credit that they never previously succumbed to a 'pathological togetherness' - a syndrome as happens elsewhere when overcrowding breeds frustration, anger, hopelessness and the people turn on one another as in the ghettoes of Europe.

It is a term that describes the phenomenon in biology laboratories where rats that have lived together for long periods of overcrowding go crazy and cannibalize each other.

The students cannot understand why the online news that I share with them now is so alarming. They cannot understand why a country as rich in natural resources as we have should be making headlines with such horrible stories of hate and violence. They know I have started monitoring the crime stats on a daily basis even as I had them monitor media reports of China-bashing prior to the Olympic Games last year.

Like all good Chinese students they are aware that Trinidad and Tobago is more than the shallowness of Disney's *Pirates of the Caribbean*. They are aware of the richness of our oil and gas and the wealth of the people in terms of per capita income. They want to visit and enjoy the mountains and the seas and the warm hospitality that remind them of their own villages and towns. They see a paradise of opportunity even in the crisis I relate and they remember that their Hanzi characters are popularly translated into 'crisis' and 'opportunity' by Western platform speakers.

Lei Feng questions the numbers. If there are 640 acres to a square mile that makes it 1.2 million acres available to a population of about the same 1.2 or 3 million people! That gives each person a whole acre to himself! That doesn't seem like overcrowding?

It's going to take more than one class to explain Trinidad and Tobago's demographics and its descent from the euphoric Fete Capital of the World to the notorious title of Crime Capital of the Caribbean.

Lei Feng asks again: About your article from last week, what does Little Tecia and violence have in common with the news report of the Insurance Company that was bailed out by the Government? And isn't it just like what has happened in the United States and in Europe with its own banks and insurance companies?

Do you mean I am making a mountain out of a molehill?

No. I mean you could be disappointed but not surprised. It seems to me that what we are seeing today is the natural course of history, of evolution.

Is that the way you see crime, corruption and mismanagement of a country's resources? You think these things are natural in an emerging economy?

Stop. Tell me what you have in mind.

I say it all has to do with a particular 'P' word.

You mean words like Power, Politics, Pressure, and People?

Yes. All of those words are good, but the one with the strongest perceptible emotional charge is People because of the unreliability of human nature. Why, for example, does power corrupt, why are politicians insincere, and why does pressure cause men to abuse women?

There are other factors, Lei Feng says.

I am sure there are, but I recall the Spanish judge who told a group of parents, "I cannot tell you how to bring up your children. But I can tell you how to make criminals of them. Give them everything they ask for."

I think he is right, Lei Feng says.

Next week we will talk also about two other 'P' words that are important in the understanding of the anatomy of violence and the crimes that are shaking Trinidad and Tobago. They are Parenting and Planning.

4. PARENTING IS SERIOUS BUSINESS

GUANGZHOU: Thursday 9th July 2009

I look into the eyes of the 17-year-old. He stares blankly back at the world. The apparent lack of emotion could be a front for the passions that still churn wildly within him as well as an absence that betrays hopelessness. So why did he pull that trigger? Did the Devil really make him do it? Was it rage, desperation, greed, envy, jealousy, revenge? Was it all of these emotions or none of them?

The sum total of all this is a venomous hate that is fed by ignorance and bigotry. Those equate into hopelessness.

Where are his parents? I wonder.

These are questions that befuddle victims and lawmakers alike. To the Trinidad and Tobago public these chaps are 'Bad Johns', our colloquialism for criminals. In the past they were confined to their turf, which meant that they were born and bred in the country's shanties into a 'them' and 'us' society. So what monsters have these babies of the eighties and nineties morphed into?

Today as in some horror movie these aliens seem to incubate in their cocoons later to be transferred into a primary and secondary school system. Then they emerge armed with bravado and weapons to go on a rampage terrorizing young and old, rich and poor alike. So who are these creatures? And who are their mentors?

I'll tell you who they are. They are OUR children. We used to make light of it calling them the 'Children of Williams' as they swaggered past our store front on Frederick Street. The boys were 'dressed to kill'- baggies topped with colourful t-shirts that screamed Che, the Union Jack, or some pop icon like Michael Jackson or The Beatles. The girls too were equally aggressive, short shorts in peer competition with low cut tops, swinging tiny plaits braided in zig-zag patterns. Dress code and behaviour emulated role models who were often pop stars of street and stage. Freedom of speech meant freedom to spit out the m-f words.

They were on their way to the Savannah Panorama semi-finals – a rite of passage that saw thousands of youths go streaming past. They walked and talked with an attitude that was eerily foreboding. That was twelve years ago as I recall the words of a young woman on staff: "Their mothers worked hard to dress them up," Ann Marie Richardson said. "It must cost a fortune. Thank God I am childless."

Fast forward twelve years and these kids are now in their mid-twenties. Younger siblings have taken their place in the annual ritual of the national celebration with the blessings of the Ministry of Education. Figures pinpoint that these age groups are producing negative headlines. So too are news stories that reflect concern for the most unprecedented social implosion in the twin island-state. Its linkage to the country's good fortune in oil and gas riches provides more cause for reflection. It offers reason to study the wealth distribution and the effects of its trickle-down to the bottom of the barrel. Women especially are vulnerable. They are the ones who must hold home and hearth – that is, family - together.

Mothers are highlighted by psychologist Courtney Boxhill in a recommended article that details the importance of pre and postnatal understanding of child care. (*Express* 'Crime and Punishment' Nazma Muller, Sunday 28th June 2009).

Children come with a high price tag. The cost is not only emotional but a child sops up a lot of money. For a woman to DECIDE to bear a child is serious business. It requires making a pact with the unborn child for both their lifetimes. It is a biological and therefore even more sacred a decision than the social man-made institution of marriage I think. It makes a strong case for pro-choice where the woman must be free to CHOOSE to take this vow of responsibility for that new life for all of her own life. It's really all in her hands and she needs to understand this and decide accordingly whether to have a child OR not to have a child.

Life is too precious I say to risk an unborn child to chance or blame the pregnancy on 'an accident' or to hope that God will miraculously take over your responsibility. It makes a case for safe abortions.

Unfortunately, Nature does not bind the father to such obligations. Nature must be an optimist as she seems to take it for granted that *Homo sapiens* would fulfill his role as responsible provider alongside the nurturer. Unfortunately, it does not always work that way. Are women aware of this? Are we preparing our daughters for the 'what-if' possibility of single parenting? Would it have been different for Little Tecia's mother had she understood the real facts of life? Do her daughters even now?

Statistics from the *Household Budgetary Survey (1997-1998)* reveal that single mothers head about 12 % of the 14.4 % single-parent households in Trinidad and Tobago. What does it read now? I cannot find an update.

Andrea Duncan is somewhere in that figure. She is African but not unlike the Indian woman I remember who lived on the railway track by the Curepe Junction for many years with her several children. According to the *Express* (Yolandra John, Sat. 27th June '09) Andrea is the mother of 4 who considered giving them up for adoption. She and her kids were thrown out of their single room shack. The Housing Development Corporation has come to her rescue.

Andrea is good-looking and at a healthy 31 has another 20 child-bearing years ahead. Should it matter to us?

I often wonder about the woman who lived with her children on the railroad track. Are they still begging? What became of them? And what about their father?

Let me refer to Courtney Boxhill again: "So if we are really to deal with the breakdown of this society, we really need to go back, we need to start in the early childhood centres, we need to reach parents in poor communities. Although the sociologists say that poverty is not a direct cause of criminality.

"It's not, but you would concede that if I'm living in a shack with no running water, the frustrations that I have to deal with on a daily basis could impact on the quality of love, time and nutrition that I can give my child?"

Andrea Duncan need not be the only lucky woman... for the time being anyway. Somehow, as church-goers, teachers, or in whichever profession, we have to extend hands of hope to her and to the many more women, their men and children. Most importantly we must understand when all is said and done we are one family. WE must share the good words of pride and self-respect that bring true independence.

We all must get involved. Yes?

5. OF PATRIOTS AND THE DIASPORA

GUANZHOU: Thursday 16th July 2009

I say to him: "Anger can revert to joy, wrath can revert to delight, but a nation destroyed cannot be restored to existence, and the dead cannot be restored to life," It is a quote from Sun Tzu's *The Art of War*.

As veterans of many a skirmish if not full-fledged battles in our homeland, we are conscious that the wars are not yet over.

I tell him I want to understand the enemy better. I want to look into the eyes of The Beast that has been devouring the souls of our country's youths. Since Little Tecia went missing on Saturday 13th June only to be found strangled the following Wednesday, I have started monitoring the daily crime stats online to see how Trinidad and Tobago is faring.

I look again at the figures. Hardly a day passes that I do not record the criminality from the news of the three online papers. They are daunting. The fratricide ranges from the accidental deaths of Good Samaritans — teenagers recently — as both of these chaps were, through deadly altercations, to robbery with violence and revenge killings along with domestic assaults and kidnappings.

The gruesome investigation that I have undertaken reveals 4 murders 4 hours apart, and a total of 51 detected of the 242 murders at that point. It represents a 7% increase on last year's stats. That was on 12th June 2009.

Further analysis of the violence shows that 105 were gang-related, 26 drug-related, 17 due to altercations, 34 were robberies, 30 were revenge and 9 were from domestic violence. What were the missing 21?

The National Security Minister Martin Joseph reported that local law enforcement had succeeded in stopping drug inflows. This resulted in greater turf wars for the little that remained. And adding salt to the wound he said that as of June 17th there were 258 homicides to the 237 in the same period in 2008 and 130 in 2007. Not good news for our twin-island state.

I have trouble with the math. Between 12th June and 17th June - a matter of five days - the number of murders increased by 16 people? Have we gone crazy?

The graph continues to spiral with 284 murders recorded on the 9th July showing 9 more killings than at the same time last year. The National Security Minister reported on 23rd June that repeat offenders were clogging the prisons and 4,000 offenders were locked up. But equally worrisome were the 78 children he said who remained missing.

We are talking about being unable to find SEVENTY-EIGHT CHILDREN in our 'four by four' as we sometimes refer to our tiny islands.

At the root of all the internecine warfare is an anger which reminds me that *JahajeeDesi* reproduced an excellent piece last week on the subject by Robert T. Zackery. He explains that "anger is a natural response to perceived threats. Anger becomes a problem only when you don't manage it in a healthy way."

The crime stats show the high incidence of males from teens to thirties as both victims and offenders. I ask my Cyber Mate for answers. Responsibility is once more placed in the hands of the women.

She starts off with identifying the myth that women are programmed to believe that they cannot live without a man. She doesn't fall for that crap, but many women do.

She blames mothers who let their sons off the hook from doing household chores like preparing lunch kits or getting to the school bus on time. She sees it as allowing them to follow in their father's footsteps. (It may even attract teases from peers who will call them sissies)

Boys who don't father a child by sixteen fall into the 'mule' concept. He's not a man. (I find this one hard to comprehend. Haven't we gone past that bit of ignorance? I make a note to check with her on it.)

Women ALLOW no condoms because the men prefer it naked and no Tampax because nothing else is supposed to be there. (With all this new freedom of information - is sex education still not UNDERSTOOD?)

She is against women who do not have the courage to chase the 'No-Goods' who do not have their welfare at heart.

Women must set a good EXAMPLE of cleanliness, frugality, good manners, (and yes) church. (It remains the best spiritual and social support.)

Women must use the educational opportunities they have. These are INNUMERABLE now. She emphasizes this for self-improvement.

They must make use of health services that offer help. Contraceptives and pap smears are free and available. She cites an example of a woman in the environmental works programme, the mother of several children who is now a supervisor. She is proud of being independent for the first time in her life and does not take nonsense from her children.

There's enough information all around on STD especially AIDS and there are still outlets for the youths like Boy Scouts and Girl Guides to hold their interests. For the youths there are holiday jobs too.

Women must find out where the money is coming from and not accept blood money from drugs, robbing, and killings, etc.

They must punish not sanction irresponsible behaviour.

She ends by saying that women are strong but they must not collude with men for theirs and their children's destruction. (It takes enormous courage to fight the demons.)

My friend talks about the good, the bad and the ugly of the Community Environmental Programme now known as CEPEP. It used to be the infamous DEWD. Its notoriety continued when the ten-day programme to alleviate poverty changed its acronym to URP. But she makes the point that unemployment in the country is down to 5%.

From the positive feedback on *JahajeeDesi* and sparse coverage of Good News online there are innumerable opportunities for all to join in re-capturing our

T&T. But first we've got to deal with our own personal demons. Well, can we?

Yes We Can.

Yes We Must.

YES T&T! (I do love this one Stephen. It's upbeat and positive.)

When it becomes necessary to do a thing, he says the whole heart and soul should go into the measure, or we should not attempt it. Do you think there are Trinidadians and Tobagonians in sufficient numbers to bring about the change you hope to see?

I sigh deeply. If there is only one person who is determined to stand up against the horrors we are seeing, it is enough. It is not easy being a patriot in the Diaspora. I tell him that home is calling.

6. THE CULTURE OF VULGARITY

GUANZHOU: Thursday 23rd July 2009

Well, we reach! We are reaping what we have sown. Dr. Tim Gopeesingh's accusation of "ethnic cleansing" in the Port of Spain General Hospital continues to prove that Trinidad and Tobago, from top to bottom, is in dire need of a good old-fashioned bush-bath – a 'santiwah' of a gigantic order. But we'll get back to the holy water and other types of cleansings and leadership at a later date.

It all adds up, doesn't it? As of 16th July 2009 the murder toll hit 299, supporting Carmen Sanchez' report that identified Trinidad and Tobago as the murder capital of the Caribbean. According to the *Economist* Ms. Sanchez reported, the English-speaking Caribbean, which extends from the Bahamas in the north to Trinidad and Tobago in the south, averages 30 murders per 100,000 inhabitants per year, one of the highest rates in the world!

What is scary is that by comparison, the murder rate in both Canada and the United Kingdom is about 2 per 100,000. Her report continues: With 550 homicides in 2008, Trinidad and Tobago has a rate of about 55 murders per 100,000 making it the most dangerous country in the Caribbean and one of the most dangerous in the world! Sweet little T&T? What went wrong?

In looking at the latest casualty when I began this commentary on 16th July, businessman Henrick Lewis, 56, of Barataria was stabbed to death and his Mitsubishi Galant was stolen. Unnerving is the callousness with which life is being taken. Need there be murder during every robbery? What do we tell potential bandits: "Take what you want and go, but respect my life?" It is absurd even to think this.

Where really is that line between good and bad; right and wrong; moral and immoral? It's like there's a new breed of male animal out there that does not care or else does not think? They kill and then disappear. The drugs and the guns are one thing, the integrity of a people — that moral fibre of feeling good about oneself, about one's fellowmen, and about one's country — that spirit of national unity in a motherland — seems lost. It's no fun being Trini anymore. One member of the Diaspora on e-mailing me the bad news added, "Is a good ting we not dere!" Another woman on the infamous Block 8 in Laventille reported she wanted to get out of the country with her children.

We ask ourselves why? My Cyber Mate says the place is 'ungovernable.'

People say we saw it coming and they go over the past when morality in public affairs was lost — even before the public confession when one politician said on the platform that "all ah we tief". There was that time in Port of Spain, for example, when the good guys in the Junior Chamber, young men as guardians of the Nation, applied paint to cinema posters for *The Naked Maja*. Do you remember this clean-up campaign? It was a 1959 movie about Spanish artist Francisco Goya that starred Ava Gardner. With their paint brushes these young titans diligently painted brassieres on the bare breasts of Ms. Gardner. But not seeing into the future, many people scoffed at what they saw as moral pretence. Didn't these same young men play mas' on Carnival Monday dressed in their wives' bras, panties and housecoats and gyrated all over the city? Were they showing a double standard?

As the years passed, however, and as our Carnival degenerated into a street theatre of uncommon vulgarity, we could wonder when exactly standards of good taste began to slide into the gutters of the country and we chose to ignore the signs and ridiculed other people's attempts to stop the poisoning of our society.

Just think: every year Brazil's Carnival has been about sequins and thongs, but I cannot remember seeing a display of in-your-face vulgarity such as we witness in our Trinidad Carnival. It must explain why every year I fret whenever Carnival season comes around and the TV stations NEVER carry a thing about T&T's Carnival while the Carnival in Brazil and New Orleans is always in the news. And we boast that ours is the Greatest Show on Earth. What am I missing here?

I recall Carnival one year while I was waiting for Poison to inch onto the Big Stage. Next to me was a lovely-looking creature – a real 'winer girl from Princes town' – who was not satisfied with working out on her flag pole but directed her activities to a group of older men salivating at the edge of the stage. When she caught my eyes, she said, "I want to give those s.o.b.s a f--king heart attack."

There's something else. Recently someone sent me a video clip of the Trini export to the Labour Day Carnival in Brooklyn. I opened it up to my students to show off my culture and seconds later there are two of the hugest masqueraders – male and female obesities in G-string, one on top the other's backside like two fornicating sumo wrestlers, while close by are some women pumping away on their batons. I say in embarrassment that an exhibition like this makes a good case for governments that are paranoid about exposing their citizens to such western decadence. I am alluding to the Chinese 'interference' with the free flow of information through Google, Facebook and Twitter. But I am not sure that censoring the media and websites is the answer.

Now tell me, which mother would put her infant out there on the stage and encourage the child to simulate the sex act? We mothers in particular have a lot of questions to ask ourselves and a lot of about-turns to make IF self-esteem and public morality are to be restored to our people...to our nation. We've got to become accountable for our behaviour.

Our calypso too as a musical art form has hybridized from the original stock that was essentially a wit par excellence. As with the Chinese 'cross-talk' our 'ex tempo' originated to pit two contenders in satire and, naturally, intellect, in what we called a 'calypso war' of words. But what have we today? From Sparrow's subtle *Congo Man* and *Jean and Dinah* we now have sexual pictures that are as graphic and explicit as the acts of the performers on stage. Imagination is not challenged in its Soca or Chutney offspring and whatever good taste might have been salvaged by the innuendoes of *double entendre* is simply not there. What used to be adult fare behind the coconut branches of a calypso tent is now out on the street and available online for international consumption. Hard porn is how we sell ourselves as a nation of fun-loving people to the world.

It's gone past "we Trini jokey, oui!" to outright vexation at the ignominy to which we have exposed ourselves as we provide more fare for world-class literary exploitation. To tell you the truth I don't find us a funny people anymore and can be spared the sick e-mailed jokes of how best to know a Trini.

The media is last but by no means least in fomenting the culture of vulgarity in which we wallow and on which we have weaned our present generation. The daily and weekly press cannot be exonerated. They could be in the vanguard of our descent into depravity and the cause of the loss of our innocence. Add to that mess of potage the daily churn-out from low-class radio and television talk shows and what we have is close-to-the-ground garbage.

For a long time I have wondered what the weekly doses of centre spreads showing off gynecological photos of women would do to the status of our women, their men and their children. The guaranteed lies, half-truths and innuendoes dished up as a regular menu by dedicated 'journalists' could hardly have any efficacious value. Stories that stir up a weekly cauldron of venom only re-enforce bitterness and hatred between family members. Would this acrimonious brew not boil over one day to infect and poison the nation at large?

Isn't it blood-chilling to think that even as I write someone among us waits to fall Victim Number 300-and-something at the hands of one of our mentally and spiritually-impaired children? And still I wonder what could we do to stop the plague that is now afflicting us as a nation?

We all know that this answer bristles with controversy. And with anger.

7. THE MESSENGER NOT THE MESSAGE

GUANGZHOU: Thursday 30th July 2009

In my first article to *JahajeeDesi* on June 19th, I referred to a breakdown in Trinidad and Tobago's 'guardianship' that made it difficult for President George Maxwell Richards to put together an unblemished Integrity Commission. This 'voice out of the blue' attracted, surprisingly, an outburst of friendly fire warning me not to meddle in politics. My sister Corinne too was alarmed that I should "interfere with the President."

I was astonished by these fearful warnings about returning to a place that I have never really left, neither emotionally nor spiritually. But it has been an absence of eleven plus years and whatever 'objectivity' I must now bring to bear on home will be formed from hearsay and from the news and opinions I access online. And it is naïve, as he says to think that everything is the same in Trinidad as when we left in 1998.

Everything changes and I really should not be surprised by the fear that seems to be gripping Trinidadians and Tobagonians. Thus past week when thoughts of home strayed around the culture of vulgarity that contributed to the *comesse* in which our T&T society is now immersed, I suggested that this week I would explore the question of a new morality, or spirituality, that lost tribes go in search of.

It was purely coincidental (or should the word be ironic?) that last weekend the newspapers should headline the thousands that flocked to *Tribe's* Carnival band launch. I had been thinking in fact that we should stop the Carnival, re-organise our thoughts about it – the purpose it serves in art and fun – and start all over again. I am sure it won't be a popular suggestion but I think it is important for us to consider it if we want a change of heart in Trinidad and Tobago.

But let's us return to the need and power of spirituality. I guess it is no different from those times when people awaited the coming of Messiahs and re-settlement in their promised lands. Our history books tell such stories about Moses, Confucius, Gautama Buddha, Jesus Christ, and Muhammad.

But wait! He tells me. "Looking for a new messiah is not the answer. The next thing you will do is to call the names of Gandhi, Williams, Mandela, and Obama. But that's the problem. The country has lost trust in the messenger. Focus instead on the message. It's old and unchangeable like all the other verities of life. I mean things like honesty, love of thy neighbour, and accountability."

I remembered that he had said it was the messenger not the message that has been wrong. Nobody is hearing the message because they have turned away from the messengers, in whatever clothes they wear. See what is happening: Pastor and priest, professional and politician are making the time-worn pleas for good citizenship to combat the evil that stalks the land but no one is listening. It is the messenger not the message that they see and hear.

But what happens when we see only the messiah and ignore the message? It happened before with Williams. What happens when the messiah goes? Their man-God then disappears leaving a physical vacuum with disciples abandoned and left holding on to vague gospels.

There is, of course, the need for a leader he says but that person must come from anywhere in the society. That leader must be able to harness and articulate the message in order to bring about the necessary change in the people. The voice for change must come. In fact, it must come from the people. You remember the old Latin maxim, *Vox populi, vox dei?* The voice of the people is the voice of God.

But leaders and people cannot be in opposition with each other. Constant bickering and grabbing at each other's throats only drain away the opportunity for positive action and plays into the hands of a corrupt status quo. I talk of the familiar catechism and its messages on which we were weaned but he dismisses this old prop as well.

"If you are talking of a new spirituality you can't talk religion in the sense that we know it. There are heroes and heroines in the Church but change must come from within the masses that fill the streets at Carnival time not just at Easter."

Fill the streets? Are you talking of a revolution? I say, aghast at the idea but it has entered my head many times since I began writing again.

I am talking of a change of attitude in Trinidadians and Tobagonians regardless of race, colour, and creed. The people must WANT to live the set of values we knew as children and it must begin with the women, the mothers of the nation. Everything else is a sham and the people recognize this. It explains the need for thousands to go into denial by seeking release in tribes and in the fear of shadows.

8. THE WILD, WILD WEST

GUANZHOU: Thursday 6th August 2009

Come home. It is not perfect but close to paradise!

These words have absolutely touched my heart. It made my seven articles that *JahajeeDesi* has kindly exposed to the world worthwhile enough for me to keep on going. It comes from a fellow candidate who dared to contest the Trinidad and Tobago 1981 national elections under the banner of the ONR (Organization for National

Reconstruction). He wonders whether I remember him. He was a gentle, young professional who like so many of us at the time believed that change was possible by jumping onto the hustings rather than fence-sitting and griping about life after the Messiah. And change it did as from the ONR's marriage with the United Labour Front the National Alliance for Reconstruction was born. The rest is history.

Just when I was scrutinizing notes on my lethal roster of daily crimes that come via Cyber space his email arrived. But please bear with me. I have undertaken the grizzly task of recording crime from the online news by way of examining those that make headlines. The idea to monitor T&T's performance occurred after reading the stories of Little Tecia's demise and the one that banner-headlined us as "the crime capital of the Caribbean."

It is my way of confronting the demons. It also indicates the power of the media to showcase the criminal elements in the society. After all, the newsroom's maxim is, "if it bleeds it sells" and the advertising agencies buy that odious recipe.

Day after day of perusing the lead stories I note the types of crime, i.e. murder, robbery with violence or other. The names of victims and aggressors give some indication of their ethnicity, sex, age and location of home and place of crime.

There have been days when the number of murders soars and it leads one to wonder whether on those macabre occasions some alignment of the heavenly forces have called forth a diabolical streak of madness in our people. It's like we are creating our own version of Hollywood's Wild, Wild West or horror flicks. But there are those days when the numbers fall to just one murder victim enough to satisfy the notorious stats of one-and-a-bit averaged since my deadly recordings.

A good day is like today, Thursday 30th July, when all three on-line papers are free of gore. I write the letters FREE next to the date but there is still *Newsday's* Rhondor Dowlat's "Serial Rapist at large". It makes the point that we are not at all home free. But this monster is a well-documented specialist and is still free. He feasts on girls aged 13 to 17 and is still to be trapped.

My political colleague began his letter by referring to the *Culture of Vulgarity* article. "Your comments are not much different from many who have lived abroad for many years and keep in touch by reading the on-line newspapers and hearing the say of persons in the bracket that I suspect communicate with you."

That is true and I am aware that distance tends to exaggerate stories to the point, for example, that whenever bad news break in China, whether it is a flood or an epidemic, there is a real concern whether or not I'm affected. It works the other way around too as once on a visit to the Great Mosque in Xi'an, an Imam came forward to greet us with the words that he knew of our little country because we had a Muslim coup. That is the attempted coup in 1990. Bad news travel fast and wide.

"It is my view that T&T has moved on to be a most exciting and interesting place. I do not think that we live in fear, careful yes." For good measure my friend adds that he sleeps comfortably in a lovely suburb of Port of Spain. He continues to assure me that Trinidad and Tobago is "the laboratory for political, including race and class, development. The debates are clean and open. We take nothing for granted. To some it is *comesse*, to us it is dynamic development. The professional group that exists in T&T is second to none. There are some who do not appreciate it, particularly the non-professional educated."

He continues, "The country has moved on to a most exciting and interesting place." Of this I have no doubt and as some have indicated through photos of swanky buildings and new overpasses, it is what would be expected of a country that has been blessed with its own natural resources and the post 9/11 oil boom. No less. In fact, my expectations of a country that has come into such windfalls as ours I imagine should by now have erased the hell-holes of Sea Lots and Beetham Estate rather than hide it behind a wall, scraped away the misery of the Laventille Hills and shown off to the world a real model of urban and rural planning for its tiny population. Singapore and Hong Kong have proven that it can be done with limited space and much higher population densities than ours.

My fellow-candidate is worried about the company I keep. Be careful "of hearing the say of persons in the bracket that I suspect communicate with you." I am not too sure I understand this warning but before he extends that delightful invitation for me to return to our close-to-perfect paradise he warns me again... "Be careful who is your messenger. Their message is certainly not based on reality."

Perhaps he does not understand that I too am still in search of a messenger and that I am fully aware of the different kinds of messages that serve the different agendas of individuals and groups. I discriminate therefore I survive. Guess it is why some of us are so addicted to professions like teaching, journalism and law. It is like working on a thesis. With the painless facility of online information free for the plucking one can create his/her own bible to support whatever his/her premise may be.

Thoughts stray once more to back then in 1981 and later in 1986 when we innocents discovered the nooks and crannies of our constituencies - places with odd names like La Mango that defy syntax up in the Maracas hills at the back of Curepe. Apart from the hazard of ducking rotten eggs tossed at speakers, there are absolutely no thoughts of drive-by shootings to disturb the idyllic setting. Words like bandits, car-jacking, ransoms, kidnapping, and ethnic cleansing are not yet in our lexicon ...and Tobago is still a virgin.

Memories are filled with nostalgia. For those on stage who face the crowds, it is heady stuff. The night air is throbbing with expectancy as Baldy's loudspeakers blast popular calypsos and the red, black and white of flags, buntings and t-shirts initiate a classy trend of packaging the political product. Karl Hudson-Phillips as political leader is coming.The moment is a timeless adrenalin rush as we prepare to stand to attention for the national anthem of our country. And many of us can sing out the words too. The messenger at the microphone is about to deliver a message.

Yes, Ronnie Ramcharan, of course I remember you... and thanks for the invitation.

9. IS OPPOSITION POLITICS AN END IN ITSELF?

GUANGZHOU: Thursday 13th August 2009

Opposition politics creates a clear divide. It drives those in power to be constantly on the defensive while those in opposition must live up to the character of the dissenter. Democracy should always be a two-faced coin in order that men might govern with purpose and fairness, but we often see it as "we" against "they". As Eric Williams once said or implied, "Who is not with the People's National Movement is against us." But other wise men have insisted that one might be in opposition to one's government if one dissents but one is not necessarily against one's country.

In other words, we must see democracy as an arena in which people could disagree with one another without getting into a nasty fight. As Voltaire, who was not in government put it, "I disapprove of what you say but I will defend to the death your right to say it." That should be the spirit of democracy.

To be more explicit, the *Encyclopaedia Britannica* defines democracy as a "form of government in which supreme power is vested in the people and exercised by them directly or indirectly through a system of representation usually involving periodic free elections." And for the general public, "Democracy has come to imply universal suffrage, competition for office, freedom of speech and the press, and the rule of law. "

But democracy is also a paradoxical state - a seemingly contradictory statement that may nonetheless be true according to the *American Heritage Dictionary's* convenient online definition. Its two-faced-ness does not lessen the authenticity of the coin. To most of us democracy is the best of the ideals for good governance of a people by the people, for the people.... Are you asleep as yet? Yes. It's so much déjà vu.

We reaffirm our faith in it by casting a ballot every five years, thanking God that we have been blessed with adult suffrage and then pray for an honest tally of the numbers. The first past the post, individual and party, should win the respect of supporters and non-supporters over the ensuing years. That's the up side and it is great news for the winners. The downside however is that there will be losers and not only are losers an unhappy bunch, but the next four or five years lend themselves to the ready-made state of opposition politics.

This comes with more focus on an unproductive bullying of each other's side rather than any constructive problem-solving for the voters who live within the rules of a bi-cameral government. But the act of the two parties, working together at any time for the common good, is viewed as weakness or betrayal.

Let us consider Opposition Leader Basdeo Panday's call on Tuesday 11th August for a public investigation into the Drugs, Arms and Ammunition found last weekend at the St Joseph Police Station. According to Panday an investigation is necessary "after paying out approximately 80 million dollars to Professor Stephen Mastrofski and his team to transform the Police Service" The problem, said Panday, "lies solely with the PNM government and National Security Minister Martin Joseph, since there has been the poor implementation of change within the force and the failure on their part to establish a consistent standard of work ethic to prevent corruption in the police service."

Why do I think that Mr. Panday is now trying to close the stable's doors after the horses have bolted? Where was he when the contract was made with Professor Mastrofski? And didn't he and his party properly examine the terms of the contract and keep a watchful eye over implementation of the recommendations? Or, did he leave all of this to the Manning side of Government and to the Minister of National Security thinking that the job of security was theirs and not his? And if this is so, isn't Mr. Panday's attitude more evidence that the Opposition does not see itself as part and parcel of the Government's solutions for Trinidad and Tobago?

So who really are the winners and losers? In India, the much touted world's largest democracy, there remains a legacy of unrest - an inheritance from the British colonial divide-and-rule policy. If we are to heed the *JahajeeDesi* posting of Ronald Bhola on Tuesday 7th July, Arundhati Roy asks, "Is there life after democracy?" The link leads to her several points of view, one of them being remarkably familiar to ours – except of course for the numbers.

"Two decades of this kind of 'Progress' in India has created a vast middle class punch drunk on sudden wealth and the sudden respect that comes with it—and a much, much vaster, desperate underclass. Tens of millions of people have been dispossessed and displaced from their land by floods, droughts and desertification caused by indiscriminate environmental engineering and massive infrastructural projects, dams, mines and Special Economic Zones. All of them developed in the name of the poor, but really meant to service the rising demands of the new aristocracy."

In South Korea's multi-party democratic legislature the scene becomes hilarious if not pathetic when viewers witness angry members pummeling each other. Big men are seen fisticuffing each other because they cannot resolve their conflict in a civil manner.

In Hong Kong the British remnants of colonial democracy become ludicrous at times when TV cameras pan the legislative gathering and zoom in on the number of empty seats. One of the seemingly balanced reports on democracy in the Special Administrative Region (SAR) comes from the website of Henry C.K. Liu's *Independent Critical Analysis and Commentary:* "Democracy in the context of a world order of sovereign states needs a requisite socio-political milieu of national unity, loyalty to sovereign and social harmony. Democracy operates only under loyal opposition, not foreign-supported political insurgents. In colonial Hong Kong, national pride and loyalty to the motherland had been systemically erased by a century and a half of British imperialistic rule."

It could not have been better put but if there is a taste of bitterness in Mr. Liu's anti-imperialism stance it is no more sour grapes than what is happening in the mother of all democracies, the good ole US of A, and its present disagreements over confirmation of Sonia Sotomayor and the government's healthcare plan.

So what is the end-game of opposition politics? Is it an end in itself or a rational check and balance to the majority leadership? How self-serving is it compared with the original intent to serve the people?

One would surmise from the established bickering that it is to oppose, period. It is a clear divide. So much for "the common good" and leadership on both sides of the parliamentary process as so much time seems frittered away in pettiness, sabre-rattling and one-up-man-ship.

My Cyber Mate gives examples. When she responded to my query of why we had not as yet developed our Gulf of Paria coast with particular emphasis on the removal of the fetid swamp slums she replied:

"Re the Shanty town and Laventille bit that is exactly what Manning wants to do. The people Ron refers to object with arguments like:

- He wants prime hilltop property for his friends
- He's displacing people who have lived there for ages
- He's a dictator

"One union leader yesterday says he's going with his members to La Fantasie (PM's residence) for them to see how they don't and cannot live. They have the usual money dispute with the employer. Manning is responsible - again - according to them.

"And all sorts of reasons support why the residents must stay in holes and breed crime and a criminal population. They use these arguments to gain political mileage or because of shortsightedness. No vision. Little pride.

"The Hyatt is on the new, very attractive waterfront south of Sea Lots and the Port has been redone to international standards. Objections like peas when this was going on. The clean-up is slowly moving east.

"When the government responded to the traffic problem on the Uriah Butler/South junction and started the overpass which is working well now - objection! And so it goes. We need a Fidel!

"Some people in this country simply refuse to look ahead and uninformed spouting is their pastime. There is far too much confrontation everywhere. One good thing, domestic violence is exposed at every level at last and corrupt policemen and teachers are slowly being weeded out."

She ends by apologizing that she's beginning to sound like a PNM member.

"And I haven't given up hope despite it all. I'm glad to be here. These are tumultuous times. Change spawns eruptions. History has shown us this many times - repeats itself? Just look at Obama's predicament! He's not even American, according to the Republicans."

And talking about Americans as I write let's take a look at Sonia Sotomayor, the first Hispanic and third female justice as she awaits Senate confirmation to the Supreme Court.

Now that the ball is in the other court with the Republicans in opposition, according to Julie Hirschfeld Davis (*Associated Press* 8/4/2009) "the vast majority are lining up with their core supporters against Sotomayor despite her near certainty of being confirmed."

That is recognizably the nature of opposition politics. What is hard to digest however is that in the cradle of American democracy according to Ms. Hirschfeld Davis' report "the decision was further complicated for some senators in both parties after the National Rifle Association announced IT WOULD DOWNGRADE SENATORS WHO SUPPORTED SOTOMAYOR IN ITS ANNUAL CANDIDATE RATINGS." (My emphases)

Well, so much for democracy's "principles of social equality and respect for the individual within a community." North Korea's Kim Jong-Il must be holding on to his disappearing waistline and laughing out loud.

Postscript: Sonia Sotomayor was confirmed on Thursday 6th August 2009 as the first Hispanic Supreme Court Justice and third woman in court history of the USA.

10. CLUELESS IN AFGHANISTAN

GUANGZHOU: Thursday 20th August 2009

It was great to hear from two old classmates who fished me up on Facebook that is now inaccessible in China – thanks to what is suspected by the Chinese as western political interference in the Xinjiang riots. One wanted to share with me after half a century a re-written home page especially designed for our people. It is called Microsoft Windoes Trini Edition. It is of the usual cute and playful kind - a Trini jokey-ness that allows us to poke fun at each other with our infinitesimal penchant for laughter of self and language.

The thing is once I had smiled and forwarded it to a few chums it was time to return to worrying about the place that now preoccupies so much of my time. It was back to my monitoring of the daily online news that showed the murder stats in our beloved nation stood at 335 as of 19th August and climbing.

But the head was spinning out of control as there were so many other issues that needed attention if I was going to fix the world and from the other end of the globe what better place to begin than at home in Trinidad and Tobago. But then there was Afghanistan's apology for a democratic election that I was dying to get a hook on. And so it was a toss up between celebrating a relationship with *JahajeeDesi,* back to the blackboard of T&T's daily murder stats, to the international babble on a middle-eastern country's foray into democracy.

As it turns out, I am still clueless about Afghanistan's future.

The pantomime of free and fair democratic elections is currently taking place in a chunk of mountainous terrain somewhere in the Middle East. Afghanistan is a landlocked piece of somebody's real estate bounded by a multitudinous number of countries among them being Iran, China, Pakistan and a host of the other 'stans' with unpronounceable names. Try Turkmenistan, Uzbekistan and Tajikistan, for starters.

Now that the elections are in progress in the midst of a war between local militants and thousands of US and NATO forces alongside Afghan security forces, one is left to marvel at what manner of diplomatic spin is in place to suggest credibility at its outcome.

Jason Straziuso, an *Associated Press* writer presented on 14th August some bewildering facts and figures in his piece, "Observers see pattern of fraud before Afghan vote." It sent me to try to Google the lay of the land as I wanted to familiarize myself with what constituted 'the south' on the Afghanistan map.

His article stated that election officials predicted that militant violence in the south will prevent about 700 of the country's 7,000 polling centers from opening. If my math holds steady that works out to be a 10% error violation against the sacred business of ballot-casting. Now keep this number in mind.

Election fraud is taken by the international observers there as a given and monitors say they will tolerate a limited amount of fraud in the August 20th balloting. Jandad Spinghar, executive director of the Free and Fair Elections Foundation of Afghanistan, even admits that while the standard will not be the same as in the United States or Germany or France it compares just fine with any country in the Third World!

The reference to the difference in quality of standards between First (is there a Second and a Fourth World?) and Third World countries does not blow my mind as much as his statement of fact. Now hear this. "If the level of corruption or violation is under 10%, it will be acceptable for me," He says. Remember Mr. Spinghar represents the country's top independent election monitoring group.

But if this be the case well then incumbent President Hamid Karzai might as well don his emerald green chapan cape with nifty karakul hat, proclaim himself winner and continue on with his next five-year term. For if ten percent of the ballot is already compromised through non-functioning polling centres and, as the AP story continues to reveal other existing abnormalities, Jandad Spinghar might as well save himself and his country the trauma of attendant bloodshed and mayhem that stalk the big event.

Now what about the other abnormalities? They make a mockery of the democratic ideals along with those who strive so nobly to inculcate them.

If as the CIA says the population estimate is 33.6 million with half being under 18 that leaves us with a working total of let's say 16.8 million voters. Now bear in mind also that a census has not been taken since 1979. Also please note that the actual number of voters seem always to be tagged as "millions of voters" expected to turn out. Specifics are ill-afforded in this land of unspecifics.

Men (since women are not free to register in person) are registering up to 15 females from one family. Do these men have harems or what? This is happening in a conservative part of the country.

Karzai belongs to the Pashtun tribe. He is the leading candidate along with three dozen contenders. It is the dominant ethnic group of three conservative provinces. It is here that the women registered to vote by the men outnumber the men 3:1. There is no verifiable proof that these women exist. The AP story continues to make the point that in a more liberal province like Herat it is 2:1 in favour of a higher male count.

And as if the discrepancies were not glaring enough to boost a corruptible election, there are stories of voter registration cards on sale on the black market. One woman, an advisor to US military commander General Stanley McChrystal had personally bought 10 of them. The sky seemed the limit. It was possible to buy as many as 1,000 of them according to the report.

But even if we chalk these reports up to biased Western propaganda, bad things do happen in a free and fair electoral system. How else could one explain the year 2000 with George W. Bush and Al Gore in a battle for the White House and Volusia County in Florida with new words to describe suspicious 'nipple ballots with hanging chads and swinging doors'?

Today in collaboration with Robert Reid, Mr. Straziuso files an AP update on the elections in which Anthony Cordesman, former Pentagon analyst from the Centre for Strategic and International Studies, is quoted. The election he says "is not functional democracy by Western standards" but the important thing would be for Afghans to "feel the election was legitimate by their standards." I am wondering if the Palestinians felt so when they voted for Hamas and why didn't the West respect their choice?

But then so as not to feel too completely clueless in Afghanistan here is the analytical follow up. "If not," he wrote in a commentary, Afghans will "see the government as distant, corrupt, and ineffective, and empower the Taliban."

11. CELEBRATING A RELATIONSHIP

GUANGZHOU: Thursday 27th August 2009

Who knows how it gets started? You see an odd couple sauntering past and you chalk it up to there being no accounting for people's taste. One is tall, the other is short; one is thin, the other is fat; one is black, the other is white; one is Indian, the other is African. A relationship is like that – a strange and exhilarating love affair.

That's how it is for me as this becomes my tenth contribution (make that eleventh as Afghanistan got in the way last week) to Richard Seecharan's *JahajeeDesi2005* postings. It is a relationship that obviously was in place eleven weeks ago when a letter to a friend became the first article to appear on the group's email site.

What then was a mutt like me doing on an Indo-Caribbean membership listing and not in the multi-ethnic dailies where at one time I had naturally belonged at the *Express* and *Guardian* with circulation figures that were 20 or 30 times *JahajeeDesi's* modest membership of 3,323?

Prior to that, the unsolicited string of membership postings that appeared in my mailbox drove me to mood swings from renewing familiar scenes of what I had left behind in Trinidad and Tobago to exasperation at some of the hysteria that came through from a chain of Indo-Caribbean websites. Sometimes the reports revealed bigotry and xenophobia not to mention alarums of persecution and extermination of the descendants from Mother India. But old friends from all ethnic persuasions were responding happily to renewing contact with me and were at times apologetic for what they claimed was too racial a site and carefully tried to distance themselves from the extreme views of its writers.

I can't remember exactly when the courtship started and it may well have begun after a visit last summer to England where the daughter of a former Convent teaching colleague now resides. She subsequently appeared in my email and there is a faint recall that she introduced it to the membership list. It remained a one-sided affair with *JahajeeDesi's* weekly visits to my email address until one day in more recent times when I decided to succumb to the advances. That's how the first acceptance appeared when sharing the good news of my novel *Mandarin Ducks – and they lived happily together?* This piece of eccentricity about a western teacher in a Chinese classroom had just got itself published by an online publisher and was now available on websites online. The response was comforting and I remain grateful for the net-working.

Since this was the eleventh article and a return to columnist status with the self-imposed discipline of foraging T&T's online dailies for headline news, I decided to put aside the gore of criminal stats and political bickering to reminisce a bit about my place in the world of Trini Indian-ness.

In my English Writing classes the lesson always turned passionate with descriptions and distinctions between the "real Indians" from India, "native Indians" from the lands that Christopher Columbus drifted onto and "West Indians" who are a mélange of all the tribes in the Caribbean Basin. All these Indians now found themselves among those who were already there for better or for worse under circumstances following the Genoese sailor's accidental stop-over that day on the island Guanahani. The Italian in deference to Spain had promptly changed its native Arawak name to the Spanish San Salvador, or so the story used to be told. It lies in the Bahamas.

For good measure I showed on the screen the picture of a man whom I introduced as "my cousin... and theirs". He is the original native - a Carib tribesman who is short, stocky and with black hair banged out over an unmistakably Asian face. I asked them who he looked like and they were aghast to admit that he is so Chinese-looking. Indeed the chap looks like he's from around the corner on Yan Ling Main Road and is just clowning around in some J'ouvert loinscloth!

With finger tracing a connection on the wall map there is the clear possibility of Mongolian people trekking across the Bering Strait that links Asia to Alaska up there in the North East. Ex-governor of Alaska Sarah Palin would be thrilled to recognize her next-door neighbours as being from 'just over there'. A hop, skip and jump would have taken the foreign neighbours from the East across her territory and down the landmasses that were to become known later as the Americas and the West Indies.

Next comes a brief recording of a Navajo Indian Fire dance. The rhythmic thumping with its backup monotones are chants that replicate exactly what we saw on the Tibetan plateau in 1992. Even the circular feather head dress and chest garb on the dancers were surprisingly similar. What very interesting answers a reluctant history finally reveals!

The students are now on full alert and want to see some action from my country. I follow up with a one minute roll from a video called *Wild in T&T*. My son Simon helped the American producers with it and the clip shows a lot of beautiful people in Carnival revelry crossing the Big Stage in Port of Spain.

One of the girls being interviewed is an Indo-Trinidadian. No pasty imitation Barbie doll nonsense here that Chaguanas Mayor Natasha Navas seems to bask in being called – just a naturally sun-burnt Trinidad woman – the genuine article - bubbling with the sheer joy of celebration. In an inimitable sing-song Trini accent she replies that she's playing in Hart's and loving it. I explain to the class that she was born in Trinidad as were her parents and even her grandparents. The students emit an appreciative 'wa-a-ah' - certain sign of Chinese approval, and want to know if I had any Indian boyfriends. They love stories especially those with any scent of romance. I tell them well – er – kind of - as there was once a tall, handsome chap from Couva. He was round-faced with a gentility that reminded me of MP Alladin's who was my Art teacher at the extra mural evening classes at Tunapuna EC School and I had a serious teenaged crush on him. But Phil from Couva was really special and if studies had not got in the way, who knows? We could have produced a couple of the cutest little curly-haired red Indians running around the Caroni plains in Central. Once I asked him how he would introduce me to his family. He replied, "as the Spanish girl from Tunapuna." Sadly he would have made an early widow of the *cocoa 'pagnol* as he passed away some time after his own traditional marriage.

Was there any other? They press me for another story that they suspect I'm holding back on. Okay, so there was Pete T. We met at a prom for international students while we were both students. He attended the University of Detroit. He had an unusual family name so I thought he had anglicized it to match his obviously western first name. Over a real Indian dinner at probably one of the few Asian restaurants in the city at that time, he talked about his hometown. He was from Goa which is a small state on the western side of India with a history of Portuguese colonization. It was surprising how much culture we had in common. Today, thanks to the internet, search engines reveal that his name was indeed an authentic Brahmin family name in Goa. And to think that I threw up the opportunity to marry him, acquire genuine Brahmin status and live with his newly émigré brother in Toronto! Shucks! But c'est la vie! Fate was to hold in store for me other adventures nevertheless.

As with any relationship it's the little memorable things that count. For example in this present one with *JahajeeDesi* it was a simple discovery that grabbed my attention. It was the line in a story that said "he told Dooks to take his Jahaji bundle and go. "

Wait a minute! In the unending fascination with the Trini lexicon my own humble collection of colloquialisms in *Trini Talk* published by Inprint in 1994 had suggested that it may have come from the British "Georgie Bundle" meaning odds and ends tied together. I'd grown up with this incredible mix of languages fed by grandmother, relatives and neighbours from the Caribbean and with origins from far away places like Europe, China, India and Africa. Somehow I did not link the word to India. Now here it was in my face and a quick check on the net told me that *jahaji* means ship in Hindi. This was later corrected by Peggy Mohan, Trini scholar resident in India:

The word jahaji is Bhojpuri (not Hindi), and means (especially in places like Trinidad) someone who has travelled by ship to the diaspora lands: an original migrant. The Bhojpuri word for the ship itself is jahaaj. Bhojpuri is the language spoken directly east of the Hindi region.

In Hindi the word for ship is jahaaz. Since the story of the migration to the diaspora lands isn't part of Hindi folklore, a jahaazi would simply mean a sailor.

To further complicate the issue there is also a Bahamian claim to "Georgie Bundle" used to mean "possessions" like in Trinidad. How much of the Hindi rubbed off on the British colonials? I am still to find a direct connection to possible British origins however and the word directly linked with people arriving as indentures with their meager possessions from the boat certainly seems a more plausible explanation for the familiar "jah-gee" bundle.

And so the relationship continues as I check out for the first time other links to what is clearly Richard Seecharan's online baby and I've come to realize that there is an active community out there that connects Indo-Caribbean people around the world.

He has since straightened me out on the origins. "The *JahajeeDesi* group was started by my good friend, Mr. Deosaran Bisnath, when he returned to Trinidad in 2005 after living in the USA for several years. Since then he has also created several other groups - Caribbean Talk, Caribbean Hindus, Our Guyana, etc, and we help with moderating these groups. These are the leading online groups in the Caribbean. When he is not working and involved in his work as President of GOPIO Trinidad & Tobago, Mr. Bisnath creates and moderates similar groups in Facebook."

Lei Feng wants to know if I've got any Indian blood in my veins. I laugh heartily on remembering the black and white photo of a stately-looking woman on a mantelpiece in Washington. She could be a mix of any of the colourful ethnic combinations found in our parts now known as The Caribbean Basin. My cousin Myrna in DC says that she is a grandmother on our fathers' side and adds proudly "she was Buck Indian from Guyana".

That does it! "Buck" was the term associated with the offspring of an aboriginal from the former British Colony in South America and an African. It's like our own version of "dougla" where the blood lines of two great continents that are India and Africa come together. It's good enough reason for me to claim relationship with the Jahaji Diasporas.

After all, 'we Indian' by any other name still remains a West Indian.

12. THE TRINI WORK ETHIC

GUANZHOU: Thursday 3rd September 2009

Let's face facts. We don't like work. We hate it.

I know this is walking or rather talking - better yet - writing on the wild side, but as a national of the Republic of Trinidad and Tobago for all of six decades that makes me something of an expert on the Trini work ethic.

I KNOW our people.

But why should we want to work? The climate is more or less God-sent seeing that God himself is a Trini, with year-round tropical weather - no winters, lots of sun and water, rivers and beaches made for liming, lots of public holidays (a minimum of 15 days per year) excluding those unclassified like Easter Sunday, Carnival Monday and Tuesday, personal vacation. And when the going gets really tough there is always leftover pelau in Tantie's (or, dhal, in Bhowji's) iron pot which must by now have been replaced with a Zhongtian rice cooker. As for work shortages - don't give me that crap – work, like the poor is always with us. You just have to look for it. But then that takes time and energy - right? And a real Trini doesn't have either to waste in looking to FIND work.

What triggered these irreverent thoughts about my countrymen is the spate of recent news headlines calling for the Chinese to go home. Pooran Kanta wrote me last week questioning whether I was a recruiter of labour for Mr. Manning over here with accusation that they are taking away the people's jobs. Now as if that was not funny enough to think of myself as a broker in labour for the PNM government there was Emile Elias venting once more his anger against Chinese workers in Trinidad. This is what he said according to Ria Taitt in the *Express* on Wednesday August 27th:

"The Chinese were so smart, they were now using Western names for their companies, such as Times Construction, which is building the Chaguanas Administrative Complex.

"The only thing the Chinese could teach me is how they manage to go into a foreign country where they can't speak the language"

Why is this bit so funny? For starters I can't imagine anyone in competition, let alone teaching Mr. Elias anything new, and the idea of the hijacking so to speak of a country's economy without speaking the language is ridiculously praiseworthy. I mean - that gives real meaning to the word entrepreneurship. In this regard the Japanese were ahead of the game anyway ever since the Toyota and Datsun (later Nissan) made their first appearance at the Imported Motor Car Show in Los Angeles on January 9th 1958 according to *History.com*. They were previously in the USA under American brand names in joint ventures with Ford and GM.

Ria Taitt continues to report Mr. Elias as saying that these foreign workers invade the political network to the point where nationals are being denigrated and deprived of work.

Let's talk about that word denigrated first. Now the thing about Trinis is that I cannot imagine them feeling or appearing denigrated at any time. 'Denigrate who? What?' I can hear a brother asking. We do not KNOW the meaning of the word 'denigrate' and may well be tempted into reading something that looks more like the N-word somewhere in its middle. And so Eleanor Roosevelt's famous words that 'no one can make you feel inferior without your consent' is a maxim that is totally lost on our people.

Okay now let's tackle the words 'deprived of work'. To be deprived means to be denied something that is available. In this case it is to have available work taken away from a person. So the work is there but it is being given to someone else. The question is why deny the local people their livelihood and risk losing votes? And why once again the workers we are venting our spleen on are the Chinese?

Remember I said that work is always there. It was there when the earliest boatful of Chinese sailors landed in 1796. One story is told that they drifted by chance into Paradise, liked it, took up residence in Cocorite and introduced seine-fishing to the locals. In 1806 the first Chinese were imported to Trinidad.

Work was still there when between 1852 and 1884 some 2,645 came as indentures according to *The Chinese in Trinidad* by Trevor Millet (Inprint Caribbean Ltd 1993). The African slaves were now free, the East Indians were being freed up from indentureship and China with its own civil wars was ripe for a new kind of trade in human trafficking with the Colonies.

Then as now the answer as to why the Chinese came is more than just a case of supply and demand and the socio-economic implications with its euphemistic labels of 'contract labour' even then are better left for the academics to mull over.

But here is Taitt again on that report:

"And they could walk in with limitless workers, waive the work permit laws, break the health and safety laws, break the PAYE and tax laws... and be immune? Who is their Godfather?" Elias asked.

As for this remaining bit I am definitely not at liberty to respond to the good gentleman, being neither knowledgeable nor deep-pocketed to cross swords with him and venture comment or argumentation, as the Chinese students know it in Writing class.

To support my contention that 'we people' just don't like to work I will present two cases in point. But let me re-phrase that before tempting a blog of sophistry by *JahajeeDesi's* readers as to what I mean.

Work ethic according to the convenient *Wikipedia* is a set of values based on hard work and diligence. It is also a belief in the moral benefit of work and its ability to enhance character. To put it simply it is an attitude one brings to the job at hand. So what attitude do we - generally speaking - bring to our work?

I've learnt from my Cyber Mate that the Toco Bridge went up with speed thanks to the tenacity of Hazel Manning. She writes, "the Bailey Bridge up. Hazel Manning is Minister of Local Government. Never in the history of Local Government has a response been so quick. She would make a good P.M. All who know remark on her diligence, competence and ability to get people to work. Just look at her stubborn face!"

Methink my friend is fast becoming smitten with the PNM-ites but if I challenge her she will laugh it off as something akin to the Stockholm syndrome.

It is interesting to hear this report as it reminds one of the construction of a similar bridge over the Tacarigua River way back in the early days of DEWD as I think it was then called. It stood for Developmental and Environmental Works Department. This was during the reign of Prime Minister George Chambers when as the story goes he donned labourer's clothes and ventured forth incognito onto the Eastern Main Road site. There in the midst of the 'lahaying' he experienced for himself the source of the bridge without end.

My people all say that I will be surprised on my return as there are new roads and buildings everywhere. But I swear there are some things that will remain familiar. Let's recall a scene that my friend describes as it unfolds some weeks ago in front her place in Santa Cruz. She titles the subject Vision 20/20 SCENARIO:

WORKS Dept is cutting the grass on our road. It's 9.00 a.m.

A dumpling of a dougla woman, with a black handbag slung over her shoulder, is waddling along. I keep watch. She breaks several branches from off the poui tree, including one with flowers, and spends a long time wrapping a vine around the stems. Abra-ca-da-bra! A magic broom to sweep the cut grass!

She moves her arms overflowing with fat, in wide sweeps over the road and shifts from one leg onto the other.

An equally fat Indian whacker-man calls out to her: "Yuh wukkin'! De way yuh goin dere, doh forget dis part!"

He giggles and continues to do the rest efficiently. Further down, a young Indian woman has the real broom. She, too, has her bag over her shoulder. She's doing her wok systematically.

The workers' cars are parked about.

The orange rubbish truck comes noisily by. The garbage collector looks on contemptuously. The driver manoeuvers deftly through. They hail out to him.

Vision 20/20 in action. I think they're gone. Where? Maybe up the road. Maybe home.

Now this is no second-hand news reporting. Vision 20/20 is the Prime Minister's document for developing the country. This scenario is the real stuff and it is so loaded with socio-political detail that I am tempted to slap a copyright on its ownership, but she's keeping her own diary for posterity she says.

Now here's the deal. We are talking here of more than a quarter century into our evolution with the oil and gaseous blessings of some Divinity who is allegedly a native. Remember God is supposed to be a Trini! Our women folk are still dressed to kill with same handbag slung across shoulders 'sweeping' the road *soi-disant* with cut-bush. Is Time not of the essence for this lady and her magic broom? But - and here is where the socio-politicians and academics must go into overdrive in search of answers. There is a racial dichotomy of labour here - for why is it the dougla woman performs in one way while the Indian whacker-man and the young Indian woman perform differently? There is an order and direction on the part of the man, never mind he appears to be quite a 'mook' himself, while the young woman is serious about her work. She has a real broom and is doing her cleaning systematically.

The other players in the scenario are familiar too and one can only guess at the ethnicities here. The lumbering garbage truck with its contemptuous garbage collector, the blinkered truck driver, the final scene - as all disappear to where? Maybe home?

This little skit is but one in the repertoire of Trinis at work. Cyber space is flooded with ridiculously graphic examples. And it will do our people well to stop and make notes of these little scenes. List numbers, ages, ethnic orientation and comment on quality of work. You want to be on watch as my friend.

Arm yourselves with facts so that when you open your mouths at your village council meetings if they still exist, you will make your point. Take a stand. Hell! It's your country, and your money pays the workers and their leaders. You're the boss.

Perhaps we waste too much time whining about the predictable farces of the mundane as I've tried to console My Ron as he gripes over Manning's alleged snubbing of the only living of three Indian National awardees. According to Ron the Prime Minister did not shake his hand.

There is an entire thesis here for some diligent UWI undergrad. Has anything changed between George Chambers in the 1980s and Patrick Manning in the first decade of the 21st century?

What about the attitude to work among the swathe of ethnic groupings? It'll be interesting to take samplings from the different geographic locations just to compare the North, South, East, West and Central. Go ahead; prove me wrong when I say that we Trinis just hate to work.

Until then it makes a case for leaving the Chinese severely alone. As for their work ethic - well, that warrants another chapter.

13. THE CHINESE WORK ETHIC

GUANGZHOU: Thursday 10th September 2009

Bigotry like its sibling Jealousy is fed by hate, the monster of all passions. Love, in case you are interested, is its passionate twin. "I don't like you because you are the Colour Purple" is ridiculous because it is premised on a subjective irrationality about a random combination of blue and red pigments.

Or, how about this statement: "I hate you because you own a BlackBerry smart phone." It is another piece of ignorance that shows how irrational and ridiculous such passion is.

The thing is that these negative feelings are nurtured in the home and school, the latter being the place where I first learnt that the Chinese were a barbaric breed of yellow people who were atheists and believed in something called Communism. I didn't know then that all this happened after the Second World War, even though the Communist Party of China was formed in 1921. But the Communists came to power in 1949, at the end of the 8-

year War of Resistance against the Japanese in 1945 and at the end of a 3-year civil war.

A barbaric people? Nothing was farther from the truth as I was to discover when I came to China in 1998 to teach in Guangzhou that was still called Canton. The Chinese are no more the bunch of barbarians than those people on whom they bestowed the name *guailo*, meaning 'foreign ghosts or demons.' It was for a very good reason too, that name, as these were the people who came in, occupied the land, murdered, burnt and plundered. (Does all this sound familiar? Check out Dr. Shiva Bajpai's 6th grade social studies lesson in American schools in *JahajeeDesi's* Sept 5th posting – and then they turned around and penalized the natives with exorbitant fines for 'destroying foreign property'.)

Some years before, on the other side of Pembroke Street, my uncle Lennox was spouting such Red vocabulary that included words like Socialism and Marxism that were enough to have got him almost kicked out of St. Mary's College. He went on to indulge his contentious nature in studying International Law which somehow excluded him from mainstream practice and that is how he landed up as advisor in... yes...Mr. Panday's camp back in the eighties. But that's another story for another day.

Meanwhile across the street we stood in the hallowed portals of St. Joseph's Convent and devoutly joined hand in the Fellowship of Prayer that united Catholics around the world. We begged God at Assembly to deliver those pagans from the yoke of this monster that bound them to a godless state that took away people's homes and lands.

"Our own Chinese" were seemingly exempt. They were now praying with us, studying with us, living with us. They owned property and did business. They got jobs that were denied other Trinidadians. They were one of us and were even beginning to look like us. (The changes continued to this day. My Ron wrote last week that the newly-arrived Chinese he saw in the malls recently are even beginning to walk like Trinis!)

How different were the Chinese back then? The first time I visited a real Chinese home, at the back of Mt. Lambert, a classmate introduced me to her mother. She was as simple and as familiar as any country woman around Guangdong, and her hospitality extended to sharing a meal of rice and spinach with pork. I remember the frugality of the furnishings. Another time a student took me to her home in Park Street. The family lived in a crowded upstairs area above the shop. Amidst the darkness and the clutter an altar with a bronzed statue and glowing lights seemed to register on the subconscious.

A final memorable encounter was the christening of my neighbours' baby girl. They worked and therefore lived in the shop next door to us. It was the first time though that we youngsters were getting an opportunity to go behind the barrels of pigtails-in-brine and stacks of you-name-it to the cloistered scents of galvanized living quarters surrounding a courtyard. We kids could finally get to climb that blood-red plum tree that used to tempt across the ravine! The food was the real thing....different species of mushrooms, noodles, soups, meats, fish and greens and rice, of course. I remember too the salt-less-ness of it all and asking: 'Where's the pepper sauce?'

While husband and wife were busy running a mini-mart and rum shop which is where Mary learnt her first English words, their fellow-countrymen were diligently adjusting the blandness of the Chinese dishes to new heights of local cuisine so that pretty soon Mr. Chan's *Char Siu Kai Fan* and *Chow Har Look* were only vague imitations of back home. Restaurant dishes had now become spiced up into 'we Chinee food' that with the right combination of salt, sugar, vinegar and hot pepper still remain unsurpassed in this wide world.

But see... that's how nostalgia trifles with the fantasy of a Diasporean. Once after an exhausting two-week tour of mainland China as journalists we were being treated to a banquet in Shenzhen at which time one of the guides asked where we had eaten the best Chinese food. "In Trinidad." my partner blurted out before I could deliver a kick under the table.

All these reflections are leading to why the Chinese seem to possess this incredible propensity for work – a virtue or rather a quality that seems so elusive to the rest of us. It was a question that I put to him and his reply was to remind me that in Trinidad there was indeed a time when work was sacred.

One or two generations ago there were people black, brown, yellow, pink from the different tribes whose work ethic saw them laying down train lines, building magnificent houses, washing and ironing other people's clothes (as Eintou Springer used to remind her audience) and who are even now still planting the land so that the rest of us can eat... (and, yes, Pooran, we know who is planting!)

His own father he said held down four jobs so that the family could survive. We won't go into how many jobs his mother managed each day at home for their large brood in the backwoods of Caura! And so, like the Chinese, our people once KNEW the meaning of work.

The question remains, why is it then that China is still a powerhouse for labour and is still so attractive a work force to the world? At this point of re-editing China has just junped to No. 2 in overtaking Japan as the world's largest economy! (*CNNMoney*.com staff August 16, 2010). The story continutes soberly: It still trails the United States by a wide margin, but some economists believe China could even eventually unseat the United States as the world's largest economy. Although, it would probably take at least a decade before that happens.

One may be tempted to answer that it is the sheer magnitude of human resources available. Think: 1.3 billion is no joke number! It's four times the population of the United States! The population is as tempting to the missionary drooling for conversions as it is to the western capitalists thirsting for market share to provide profits from exploitation of its abundant labour supply. And while it might be as simple as that, the real truth of the Chinese work ethic could be what everyone shies away from facing: the Chinese attitude to life that is a religion and at its very heart is the sacrosanct family.

So while we were busy praying for the Chinese to get religion I had to come to China, cynicism bound with skepticism, to see for myself that these people already had and still continue to have religion. Once more it is the lot of social anthropologists, scientists like Desmond Morris (*Naked Ape*) and Richard Dawkins (*The God Delusion*) to compare the effects of "civilization" on established cultural patterns that have nourished the various religious beliefs, or vice versa. These are what make or break a people. But what China has taught me is that the Confucian principles for good citizenry that preceded Christianity by some 500 years are still alive and well among the Chinese population over the past two millennia.

As for religion, nowhere is it more alive than among the numerous beliefs and their believers that co-exist in 21st Century China. Such stories for the enquiring Westerner however, like the freedom to worship ancestors, Buddha and Confucius do not make as titillating a story for the seven o'clock Evening News as the quest for the underground practioners of Christianity or the persecution of suspect activists in the alleged guise of other denominations.

The precepts that fuel the spirit of work among the Chinese are best summarized in the words of Joseph Campbell (*Oriental Mythology*) as he says: The Chinese have maintained through thick and thin (they have had much of both) an extraordinarily buoyant confidence both in themselves and in the simple goods of progeny, prosperity and longevity.

And this is what Professor Joseph M. Kitagawa (*Religions of the East*) says, "The religious ethos of the Chinese must be found in the midst of their ordinary everyday life more than in their ceremonial activities, though the latter should not be ignored. The meaning of life was sought in the whole life, and not confined to any section of it called religious."

The enterprise or work ethic that our own forefathers held sacrosanct within the context of their religious beliefs is now no more. Our own present generation of children in Trinidad and Tobago (and indeed the west) for whom we have broken our backs in providing a security in a 'civilized world' free from pain now find themselves a hopelessly pampered lot. We have made their world a better place, to re-work a mantra of former American President George W. Bush.

Their expectations are high since they think that bread will continue to fall like manna from heaven – make that from parents. Our children lack incentive, creativity, maturity and immunity. They have had it so easy that they are now without that motivation for hard work born out of a belief to achieve. The national maxim, "Together we aspire, together we achieve," means nothing to them.

But new variables are taking place. It has not escaped my attention that the secondary schools in South and Central Trinidad outperformed in national scholarships along with its Primary school students of the Secondary Entrance Assessment examinations. Ronald Bhola's posting of *Time* magazine article and our Scholarship winners last Sunday tells it all and the pride shows.

Girls too are excelling, but it is cause for a critical analysis of what it says about our boy children, if not about performance levels between the tribes.

We must now take a long, hard and serious look at the ethnicities, religious beliefs and family cohesions that promote a healthy spirit of competition, achievement and pride in self and community one with the other. It is the only way there is going to be true national competitive performance between the predominant Indian and African families.

As for China and its enviable work ethic, how endangered is it? Next week we shall take another look.

14. THOSE NAUGHTY LITTLE EMPERORS

GUANGZHOU: Thursday 17th September 2009

Sorry, chaps. Nothing personal, but I have a problem with boy children.

What is this obsession with wanting or bragging about a son? It's like: "You know I've got a son..." and it is bellowed forth in that same grandiose tone as like: "You know I've got a $3 million Porsche." The need to say this, or the pride, is so out-moded and unnecessary. Or is it?

In ancient cultures there used to be a practical reason for wanting boy children to provide a hands-on in the survival business of hunting and slashing/gathering. Later as societies evolved with its acquired vanities, there was the need to want to ensure kinship through patrilineal family names. And then there was – always was - continuity...that compunction for the genes to perpetuate themselves into infinity which is what the original selfish biological purpose was all about.

Amazingly even in a more intelligent world, the 21st century still continues to witness the phenomenal adulation of the boy child. Some cultures take it to extremes to ensure that "You, woman, had better bring forth that XY chromo-combination or else..." Perhaps the 18-year old South African runner with the curious name of Caster Semenya knows something that some of us don't in opting to claim her gentler gender over the other testosterone-loaded one!

Well, okay, but how is this sociological observation leading us to the Chinese work ethic? I intended in fact that this column would focus on China's One Child policy that is producing a nation of spoilt brats, indulgently referred to as "The Little Emperors". But I got side-tracked again by an interesting event that the *Trinidad Guardian* reported on 11th September 2009 with the heading, "Damarie Hill feuders put down guns".

Apparently there are gangs in Sangre Grande whose intention is to recapture the original meaning of the Spanish name of "Big Blood" for the area. It is not with any known reference however to battles fought in this picturesque and verdant end of the East-West corridor between Native Indians and Colonizers. Rather the name is said to have come from the blood-red colour of the larger tributary of the Oropuche River. And it doesn't surprise us that the Spanish surveyors in the 1770s named its little sister river Sangre Chiquito.

These present-day gangs are unrelated to those who used to work collectively to till fields and reap harvests. Olga Mavrogordato in her *Voices in the Street* (Inprint Caribbean Ltd. 1977) speaks highly of the re-settled American Negro veterans who had a reputation for hard work and introduced the cultivation of rice. But that was the year 1815. Now a century later, these young descendants seem intent on fratricide and self-destruction. But what else do feuders do? If anything, the gangs today are more closely related to those we see on American prime time television.

The most important part of the news story however was that these youths were talked into going straight and all it cost was an initiative by Senior Superintendent Margaret Simpson-Brown. Mr. Manning, are you listening? There were no exorbitant fees paid by government to foreign experts, no excess rushes of adrenalin wasted by neither male police officers nor sanctimonious exhortations by the inter-religious organizations. All it took was a plain and simple plan that was organized and implemented by a couple of women in leadership positions.

So, are boy children troublesome? Could we really say this when we have had role models like Eric Williams, Rudranath Capildeo, Arthur Andrew Cipriani, Learie Constantine, CLR James, Sir Solomon Hochoy, and Lloyd Best?

In China the cultural pattern, lovingly promoted by grandmothers in particular, still holds. Newly-married couples are pressured into thinking that they must produce a darling little baby boy with that much-desired little spout like the one on the Chinese teapot.

Indeed they do and mindful of the One Child policy that was courageously put in place since the late seventies, the nation has been spared the trauma of having to feed 300 million additional mouths over a twenty-year period. Such practical people the Chinese! One downside of that policy however is the gender imbalance that overwhelms a society in which males predominate.

The overall male-female ratio was 119-100 in 2005. This was at a time when the UN suggested that 107-100 is normal for industrialized nations (Steven Ertelt, *LifeNews.com* August 24th 2007). How naturally we all accommodate this dominance thing!

Over the past twelve years, it has been a revelation to witness the passing parade of young teacher graduates and to hear their stories of 'entering the society'. There was a time when they returned with glowing reports of enjoying their teacher training classes in primary schools as the youngsters were 'lovely', 'pure' (meaning innocent) and a word they were fond of using, 'cute'. But you seldom heard, 'naughty'. This was reserved for the little brother in the family who could do no wrong.

Looking into the future, I would warn them that 'naughty' was a felicitous word in English meaning 'mischievous'. If anything it was a euphemism for what I suspected they really intended. And when it was applied to boys in class it meant that they were undisciplined and rude.

In recent years I think they are coming around to appreciating what I meant as they visit with toddlers of their own in tow. Some are fine enough but others are downright badly-behaved with screams and tantrums that betray a domestic indulgence and tolerance of their behaviour. Most of these children are the precious boy children who are dumped into the school system.

Enter my bright-eyed and bushy-tailed (mostly female) graduates who must apply the theory of pedagogy to a classroom of sixty unruly children, products of the single-child family. Unheard is the maxim of my father-in-law: To spare the rod is to spoil the child.

Teaching in China provides an incredible in-situ laboratory for the sociological transformation now in progress. For the new teachers entering their society, the generation of indulged children is going to be bearing fruit. The quality of the fruit remains as questionable as is the quality that we are reaping now in Trinidad from the children of the euphoric years of Williams in Damarie Hill in Sangre Grande.

Listen to what Senior Superintendent Simpson-Brown had to say: "I spoke to these young men, pleading with them to put down their weapons because they were either going to die by a police bullet or by one of an opposing gang..." (*Trinidad Guardian* 11th Sept 2009).

Those who live by the sword, our parents and teachers used to tell us, will die by the sword. We really don't need fortune tellers to read the tea leaves.

The story continues: Police brought in some 20 reputed gang members into the Sangre Grande Police Station late Wednesday afternoon....talks were also held with parents who expressed frustration regarding their sons' errant behaviour. "One parent said she was tired of speaking to her son and admitted he was in possession of a gun."

It sounded so familiar. Look at those words, their sons' 'errant' behaviour. Scary, huh! One parent said she was tired of speaking to her son! Does this boy not have a father? Or, is it more a case of like father like son?

I thought of my classrooms in China where girls outnumbered boys 7:1 in teacher training a decade ago but where the ratio nowadays is 14:1. What lies in wait for the Chinese population that places so much on its boy children? Will its fate be the same as what is happening in Trinidad and Tobago and for that matter in the United States and elsewhere?

Melissa Roderick, a University of Chicago professor and leading authority in school reform, reported some startling news in that Educators are slow to wise up to the gender problem. (*USA Today* 10/12/2006) One is led to wonder whether or not this 'slowness' to come to terms with the facts is due to a population being in denial. Men and sometimes women do not WANT to accept change, much more to question the underlying reasons for the change.

In China, as the classroom proves, change is dramatic and unprecedented. Is anyone prepared for the trauma it brings? My own fascination with China is its precociousness in catching up in thirty years with what it took the rest of us to do in three hundred!

The performance of the boys tended to be competitive with several of them succeeding in capturing scholarships to universities, but today the quality of the boy students seems in spiral descent. What is so different also is the attitude toward application and industry.

In other words what is changing before our very eyes is the spirit of applying oneself to the work at hand. So is the legendary scholarly diligence of the Chinese (male especially) in danger? How endangered then is the Chinese work ethic?

These are questions here, just as in Trinidad and Tobago and elsewhere that must be studied carefully. They are as complicated as the cultures and the shifting balance of 'enlightenment' between the genders and as the nature of the individuals that comprise the societies. I think that in *The Spirit of the Chinese People*, author Gu Hong Ming, helps us to find some answers. Trust me.

15. (MIS)UNDERSTANDING THE CHINESE

GUANGZHOU: Thursday 24th September 2009

Those who know do not speak; those who speak do not know. – Lao Tzu

"Hi, Auntie, we've arrived in Guangzhou."
It's a long time since we've had visitors from home. My son's classmate Jason is travelling with his teenaged son and we can't wait to exchange stories. They've been to cities in the north and now because of his interest in Zen the young man wants to take in the oldest Buddhist temple known as Guang Xiao Ci in old Canton. He is beside himself with the rampant capitalism that he is witnessing in a Communist country. I correct him: Socialist country, I

say, even as my students have corrected me stating with pride: "We have a Communist Party leadership but a Socialist system of government."

But the vibrant commerce is not all that attracts him. He's anxious to find fault with the dilapidated electrical poles that rushed past his train in the countryside and wants to know why they are not being maintained. He contrasts urban modernization with rural neglect.

Just like a newly-arrived westerner to have all the questions and answers, I think, recalling some of the foreign teachers at school who thought they could change the education system and make it more like the system they left in the United States.

Why does he feel he must interfere in the way the Chinese run their business? Is democracy, and the capitalism it breeds, the only way? Why did it fail the Greeks and the Romans? Why did Caesar and Pompey before him, think that they had to become emperors and alter the politics of Rome if it was doing so well and everyone was happy with it? Or, isn't it better in the world to let a hundred flowers bloom?

It is always the same. He risks sounding like the overnight experts sent to report on events in an exotic country and who turn out travelogues, books and blogs to sate the thirst of *Lonely Planet* adventurers. One can laugh at the industry of journalists who spend two weeks in a country and who are able to produce books on the people. The result of these 'authoritative' works is that the abundance of undigested information confuses rather than clarifies the messages. As a result China with its sheer size and population remains an enigma to foreigners. It explains the feeding frenzy when an 'abnormal' story occurs.

Who really understands the Chinese? I'm tempted to say, that I really don't know. But after so many years of living among the Chinese there are some analyses that I can make, particularly if the evaluation is derived with the help from a real Chinaman.

The help I'm referring to is from a Chinese scholar named Gu Hong Ming and what he says is as true today as when he first said it a hundred years ago. That's right; he has long crossed over into the ancestral world. But so relevant today are the words he wrote as World War 1 was being waged around him that the reader is still fascinated by his thoughts. In his book, *The Spirit of the Chinese People,* there is the provocative subtitle: A Paper that was to have been read before the Oriental Society of Peking. Thus the preface is signed and dated ' Peking, 20th April, 1915'

Now, as if what he has to say in his preface is not titillating enough, by page 11 of the unpretentious little book there is a footnote in which he refers to one Eugene Chen whom he describes as a 'clever Chinese Babu'. Now wait a minute. Isn't this our compatriot Eugene Chen? He's the Trinidadian whom we've been tracking whenever we visit a museum that exhibits the faces of Sun Yat-sen's short-lived government. In fact he was China's Foreign Minister after the 1911 revolution and the fall of the Qing Dynasty.

My God! How we Trinis get around!

Gu had accused Eugene Chen of being the instigator of 'piece of rowdyism' in orchestrating protests against Gu's criticism of the 'new Chinese woman'. Chen at the time was involved with a newspaper called the *Peking Gazette* and was stirring up trouble by publishing letters to the editor written by eager beaver newly-returned overseas Chinese students, he says. The alleged *comesse* involving Minister Chen is well worth digging into on another day. So also is a look at the beguiling Chinese woman.

But let's get back to the heart and mind of the ordinary Chinese person. What is it that makes this self-effacing, humble, most diligent, of God's creatures so much a Good Friday *bobolee?* Why is it that the rest of the world feels threatened by a group of people who have never occupied nor pretended to covet what is not seen to be their own?

Zheng He (1371-1433), the Chinese admiral, had reached the shores of East Africa. All he left behind, according to Siu-Leung Lee, PhD scholar, were 'some tribes near Kenya that are clearly Asian-looking. They also consider themselves as the descendants of Zheng He's crew.'

The Chinese ideology couldn't possibly be their political mission! Who wants to be ruled by dictators who monitor your media, sanitize your recreation, and interfere with your rights to plan your family? The western media never seem to get past these restrictions. As for the criminal law the Chinese do not wade though years of legality to prove a man's guilt while presuming his innocence only to free him or hang him on technicalities. Justice follows swiftly on the evidence to the corruption in government, in smuggling and in drug trafficking.

We westerners on the other hand with the Divine written into our constitutions believe that we must appear to be doing the right thing because capital punishment is barbaric. I think so too but the result as we are seeing in Trinidad and Tobago today is that criminals fear neither God nor the Law. And these are drastic times that call for drastic measures.

What is the real Chinaman like? Gu Hong Ming questions. He is worried about the disappearing original article and its replacement by the new progressive or modern Chinaman. He speaks with grace of the lowest class in which there is 'less animality' than found in the same class in Europe. He defends the gentility and docility of the Chinaman as being an absence of hardness and of a coarseness that is not jarring. He talks of the peasant as being ugly 'but there is no hideousness in his ugliness. He may be stupid but there is no absurdity in his stupidity. He may be cunning but there is no malignity in his cunning.'

I am captivated.

If all this is spoken like a true patriot, you should hear what he has to say about why the West does not understand the real Chainman and his civilization. The Americans he says are broad, simple but not deep; the English are deep, simple but not broad; the Germans (especially the educated) are deep, broad but not simple. The accolade for the character he thinks is more like the Chinese is bestowed on the French whom he confesses do not have the depth, broadness nor simplicity of mind as the others. But the French shares that nobleness of character with the Chinaman. The French have delicacy, he says, the quality of mind necessary to understand the real Chinese.

He attributes the quality to 'a pre-eminence among the ancient Greeks and their civilization' and it reminds me of the wish of Eric Williams to make Trinidad and Tobago the Athens of the Caribbean.

I have often kept the company of Gu on the coach ride out to the Nanhai Campus of South China Normal University. The bus-load of Chinese teachers chat animatedly and there is no jarring quality that makes one want to react negatively.

And hear this! There is always no vulgarity.

On the public transport there are times when the loudness of conversation in difficult Cantonese challenges sanity. And with their cell phones they can be as irritating as the pushing and shoving at bus-stops. Moreover, the haste to disembark from a plane when the seatbelt sign is still on looks like sheer stupidity. But you never think that they are vulgar.

So are we misunderstanding the Chinese today and losing the opportunity to adopt some of their finesse...their gentility or delicacy?

16. THE CHINESE WOMAN

GUANGZHOU: Thursday 1st October 2009

Today is China's National Day. It's a day of pride and pageantry not just in Beijing but all over China and wherever in the world the Chinese find themselves. It's a day that puts the spotlight on China's development and successes since the first National Day was held in Tian'anmen Square on 1st October 1949.

Sixty years ago Mao Zedong ignited the national spirit of the masses with the statement that "the Chinese people have stood up." After centuries of invasion, exploitation and civil wars, enough was enough. A new China was born. The unpredictable hand of history was to write off subsequent human foibles in Mao's leadership. And it was the responsibility of Deng Xiaoping to carry the Long March forward to the unprecedented burgeoning of towns and landscaped cities, each with its own intricate transit system.

As rat-infested *hutongs* and fetid ports gave way to incredible modernity and as families were relocated into the new excitement of home ownership with all its accoutrements, China is where the action is. Of course all this development comes with a price tag, same as it did for other developing countries. And at the heart of it all is the Chinese woman.

In China she is the feminine ideal identifying with the Motherland and behind the docility hides a feistiness that has provided stability to home and state. But this security is now being challenged as the sanctuary of the home and family where she has faithfully tended its traditions now comes under siege. The young Chinese woman faces a dilemma. As with her sisters elsewhere, just how far or how fast she should move in keeping with the times remains the paradox.

The Chinese woman - make that the Asian woman - holds an alluring appeal to the western man. It is a fascinating topic encouraged by the number of older men seen strolling the malls with lovely doe-eyed companions. We could give them the benefit of the doubt and assume that they are businessmen with their interpreters.

Or, we could gossip that the girls are really opportunists who want to escape to the West.

The men's devotion to these slim wonders of the world is enough to give the poor Western woman a massive inferiority complex. But luckily we have an overdose of self-confidence and we do not buckle under questions of appearance to ask what's wrong with our classy grooming? Our designer labels match or are casually designed to mis-match, while our hair must be coiffured so that we do not risk joining the ghastly exhibitions on Yahoo's OMG parade of bad taste.

But here too there's a certain charm about the Chinese woman. In trying to emulate the western cover-girl models, she dresses in quirky mis-matches – bolero over stringed tank tops; jeans or frilly billowing skirts with heels; flats or sneakers. These clothes are all made right here in any backyard factory. The night markets, especially in this world financial crisis, sell the non-exportable items, tank-tops and shoes, dirt cheap.

A second look at our willowy rivals will reveal that these creatures are truly simple-looking. So what's the big deal with these girls? Why are our men so captivated? None are remotely statuesque, bosomy, hyperactive starlets and models of western screens and catwalks. They don't even care for make-up: that's almost non-existent.

The Houses of Max Factor and Revlon depend on us westerners' cake-ing ourselves with mud, creams and slathers of lotions for their survival. For most young Chinese women mascara and eye-shadow are still just a fad. But to visit a Chinese shopping mall, the overload of cosmetics and glamour ads send strong messages of allure.

The Chinese woman's face is smooth, full, pale (not yellow), and youthful - youth as always promising a beauty even in its simplicity. Then there are those eyes, almond slits revealing varying shades of brown - not black as they are wont to claim that match their hair.

You've got to peer deep within to discover those whirlpools of emotion.

Behind the face is a well of tears that pour down on mention of Grandma's passing. Or else there is a handy paper packet of tissue to mop the overflow at the finale of the *Butterfly Lovers*, which is a Chinese classic that is as evocative to the Chinese audience as *Romeo and Juliet* and *Titanic* that they have watched many times.

In trying to complete for my *JahajeeDesi* readers what has turned itself into a series on China, my good friend Gu Hong Ming was about to accompany me on the ride out to Nanhai Campus once more. I was free to delve into his *Spirit of the Chinese People* for answers to the people-watching phenomena in the malls. Then pretty, young Dora rushed in to fill the empty seat that my deceased writer's work was occupying.

Since 'steups' is not yet into the Chinglish lexicon, she wrinkled her face on reading the book title and suggested that the more popular guru was Hu Shi, author of *The Chinese Renaissance*. Dora and her husband Sam were graduates of our Teachers' Training College and both are pursuing higher degrees while teaching out at the Nanhai Campus of South China Normal University. In fact Sam has already done his PhD study in Linguistics.

It was understandable why a modern young Chinese woman would pooh-pooh at the Confucian model of a Chinese woman as Gu has celebrated in his writings. At the turn of the twentieth century he frowned upon those young women who were leaving the gentility of the teahouse sing-song for the glamour of western style stage performance. Writes Gu: It is wrong for her to show herself in public; it is indecent, according to the Chinese idea to go on a platform and sing before a crowd in the hall even of the Confucian Association.

So in this Gu might be considered old-fashioned.

Dora's distaste for Gu's anger at the disappearing Chinese Madonna led me to empathize with the modern Chinese woman who is struggling to come to terms with her own enlightenment. Dora, for example, had struggled through a college romance with Sam. They eventually married; she teaching while seeing him though his doctoral programme that took him away to another city. Now she was still part-timing while producing a daughter and pursuing her own post-grad work. Welcome to the Brave New Gender-equal World, girl!

Dora is the new Chinese woman.

She finds herself bound by the traditions of 2.500 years ago that dictated the Four Virtues of the feminine ideal. First was the chastity bit. Of course! – it's what Everyman expects; she must have perfect manners - something that had nothing to do with intelligence; Second was her conversation whose dictate was like what we knew as children - they should be seen but not heard and when heard their words must be soft-spoken not eloquent nor brilliant (leave that for the men who were sent to competitive Imperial examinations in Beijing.) Third, looks must reflect personal cleanliness and good grooming - not necessarily physical beauty. Finally, she must be a workhorse and loving it in the home.

And as if that was not enough for this person without a personhood, there are the Three Obediences. An ideal woman must live for father or else husband; and she must live for children. In other words her sole purpose in life is to be a good daughter, wife and mother. She must be kept barefoot, pregnant and in the kitchen as our men still joke at home.

As recently as a generation ago this was the feminine ideal of the West sustained by religious dogma that was eventually to be challenged. In some countries they still hold. At the start of the 20th century, daring women like the Suffragettes struck terror into the hearts of fundamentalists like Gu. Meanwhile he continued to deify the Chinese woman's absolute surrender to her husband's family to whom he acknowledges she is really married.

The woman is at the very heart of the marriage ceremony as handed down through the ages and which glorifies family and naturally state.

Now before I diss the Confucian model as well as the Christian and other religious Madonnas as being irrelevant and obsolete, a couple of thoughts come to mind. One is the logic behind a Sri Lankan friend's thinking. She amazed me by announcing that she was going to New York to meet her fiancé whom she had never met. She was herself a post-grad student in London having worked and dated before in her country. This marriage, however, was family-arranged, she explained, "and who can better choose for my future happiness than my mother and father who love me?"

And then there is Dora who did her own choosing, albeit within the narrow confines of a boarding school where girls outnumbered boys 7:1

For this new Chinese woman she's asking herself whether she's eating her cake and having it, even as the cultures of East and West collide.

The coach speeds past fields attended by women and their men bent double against the landscape. They are all Chinese, but it is Grace Breedy's face that appears at the window. She looks down at her only son, 29 years old Travis, aka "Wet Money", gunned down in the George Street canal in Port of Spain. She holds a beer in her hand as she talks to an *Express* reporter. It is a bizarre image of a woman mourning her son, a woman alone.

Where is Travis's father?

With Grace Breedy is the mother of Travis's three children. He leaves them all behind - a son of eight, another of two, and a daughter who is just one. How is this family to forge a state on which social order from the family unit is founded?

"What are you thinking about?" Dora asks.

"I'm thinking about a woman at home in Trinidad who heard her son was gunned down even as he was talking to her on the cell phone."

"I am sorry to hear that. Is there something else?"

"Yes. She was free to choose her life as other women in the West are able to do but I am wondering if she had the chance whether she would trade places with the traditional Chinese woman."

17. OF BLACK ON BLACK, RED HERRINGS AND WHITEY COCKROACH

GUANGZHOU: Thursday 8th October 2009

Not everything that is faced can be changed; but nothing can be changed until it is faced. – James Baldwin

This is not going to be easy to write. It's about black people and talking colour is always a risky subject, as French President Sarkozy and Italian Prime Minister Berlusconi found out recently when they joked (I am giving them the benefit of the doubt) about American President Barack Obama's 'tan'.

The fact is ethnic jokes are nearly always in bad taste and only members of the race that is maligned are allowed to jest about their race. When someone else does it, the glove is off and the war begins.

So am I allowed to talk colour today and ask why young men of African descent in Trinidad and Tobago are killing off each other?

In our corner of the globe the question is a preoccupation with those of us who are concerned enough about the deteriorating state of the society. And the truth is Trinidadians and Tobagonians of ALL colours and creeds have good reason to be so. Trinidad and Tobago is the place we call home. We live next to each other and marry into each other's tribes. Against the black, red and white of our national flag, we sing our National Anthem in lusty voices that "here every creed and race find an equal place."

I have now a dossier of those gory stats that prove from daily news reports which include names and photos that those involved in murders as both victims and accused are predominantly black youths between the ages of 14 and 29. The starting point for me was the discovery of Little Tecia's body seventeen weeks ago. The ten-year old was strangled and buried in a shallow grave under a house in Laventille. Her story was the reason every week for me to want to plumb the depths if not the soul of what was happening.

A study of the cases shows that there are many common denominators linking these brutal acts. For example, apart from race, gender and age there are areas or locations where these crimes occur; there are the guns used as the most popular weapon of choice, and there is the unbelievable brazen-face in which one or more criminals are free to hunt in packs, posses or gangs and kill at any time, any place, anywhere.

An amazing 41,000 people WANT guns according to an *Express* story yesterday - 2,198 were granted licenses over the last eight years. In a population of 1.3 million that means 41 in every 1,000 people want to possess a gun! Is my math right?

Why are our young black men entrapped in this horror of violence at this time in our history? Have they just gone crazy? They decapitate their victim and then play football with his head! And then their hideous crime is transmitted by cell phone! (*Guardian* Tuesday, October 6th 2009). Is it just madness or are these guys competing with species of other races for sheer brutality and barbarity? Who has an answer to these atrocities and know how to prevent them? The Government? The Church? The Chambers of Industry and Commerce? The Media? Why are these youths self-destructing? Or, is the answer to be found in the Home and in the quality of Family Life?

We must ask ourselves what drives our youth to this barbaric state. There is the temptation to go the old sociological route of history with the starting point of the poor dispossessed slaves at the bottom of the community barrel while newly-arrived indentured Indians and Chinese were given a better deal. They had a head start with options for repatriation and land and even a pittance.

Y..a..w..n... Don't fall asleep on me. I know it is the same old boring stuff, but it is still being argued that these non-Africans had more or less a common language, religion, and a family. They had too that word that social scientists/psychologists love to use. They had self-esteem. Okay let's call it pride in a community. There was belonging and inclusion − very important positive attributes.

Then there is the temptation to blame the criminality on the black genes that allegedly encourage laziness and an attitude to lime, the proud word that we Trinis created. In our colourful lexicon "lime" means to idle away the time while talking, drinking and eating (free food) preferably.

Racists/bigots will take delight at this point to pull out references that prove the superiority of white over black. "Look at where 'success' is!" will be the gloat as they scan the latest *UNDP Index* and point to northern Europe where white people in Norway and Sweden earn lots of money and walk the streets freely. Some are even free to abort and to euthanize! Poor Equatorial Guinea brings up the rear at number 118 of the countries listed.

Or else there is always the temptation to blame it on the political leadership, from Dr Eric Williams through George Chambers to ANR Robinson to Basdeo Panday to Patrick Manning. What do we have here? Well the truth is the buck does seem to stop right there at the political top.

Or does it?

One cannot say Prime Minister Patrick Manning did not appear to speak for the entire Caribbean crime scene when he addressed the UN Assembly on Saturday 26th September. But 'Crime is our problem' can be mis-read as his words in the Juhel Browne *Express* story title appearing the next day. At any rate Mr. Manning did have to confess that where his country was concerned, despite the big energy sector earnings, T&T has seen record levels of crime, especially where homicides are concerned with the murder toll currently at 398. (It had not yet reached the unprecedented height of today's 415.)

But I have a colossal problem with Mr. Manning's red herrings. On which planet does this man exist? For instance he states according to the Browne story: The rising crime that is currently affecting Trinidad and Tobago and the Caribbean region has been caused by the loss of preferential markets for the export of bananas and sugar...

Although Trinidad and Tobago earns most of its revenue from oil and natural gas exports, it did also produce sugar for export until the closure of Caroni (1975) Ltd. in 2003. According to Stephen Kangal in *Trinidad and Tobago news Blog* 'Politics" 20th August 2007:

The principal reason given for the closure of Caroni Ltd by the Manning Government in 2003 was that it was a drain on the Treasury to the extent of $200m annually. After closing Caroni and giving their friends all the moving equipment they have now proceeded to the termination of the entire sugar industry by causing the private cane farming community to cease the planting of sugar cane. Sugar was always a problem with the culture of the PNM because they do not understand agriculture and food production.

As for the drug and guns according to Browne's story Mr. Manning had argued that "the security situation has been aggravated by the deteriorating economic situation in many of the countries", adding that the illegal drug trade has had a most corrosive effect on our small societies.

It was difficult to correlate the sugar industry closure which affected mostly East Indians in the central district with the massacre that was taking place among predominantly young Africans in the east west corridor and urban areas of Trinidad and Tobago. What was I missing here?

Two readers responded to the query that sought viewpoints on his address. Both dismissed the speech as being unworthy of response. Lenny Grant however admonished me to check with Mr. Manning's speech directly from the UN.

However, it was an *Express* Editorial (Thursday October 1st 2009) that satisfied my curiosity. For the interested few it will do well to take a look. But this is what I found interesting. It challenged the Prime Minister's words by stating that the region's growth economic rate was positive until last year and showed the humongous slide in cocaine trafficking between 2000 and 2005.

So Mr. Manning's correlation between Caribbean economic decline and deteriorating security does not quite hold - indeed, the opposite seems to be true. And nowhere is this truer than for Trinidad and Tobago, where the murder rate since 2000 has been rising in almost perfect synchronicity with oil and gas prices. Exactly where I think the buck passes before it stops!

To what extent is the entire society to be blamed? This has set me to do some further thinking about our sad young men and their death wishes. What exactly is the co-relation between the increased murder rate and the windfall from the increased national revenue? To what extent have we examined our ostentatious life style and the indifference it breeds?

Apart from Mr. Manning and a leadership that showcases an incredible ineptitude - where is the national responsibility lending support in this time of crisis? Have we self-examined to see how we contributed to the present disaster? It is so much easier to pass that damned buck by saying as my two respondents did: "I have not met anyone who listened to his address or was interested in what he said." And another replied: "For many it was a big joke!"

And hear this other one:

"To simply put it, this is a hollow and disconnected rant from a man that seems to be versed in hypocrisy and living in a mental fantasy world!"

There was once a time when a visitor to Trinidad could walk the streets of Port of Spain as freely as did the Englishman who came to train the *Express* staff in those early days of the seventies. On returning from a midday walk up to Rosary Church he announced that Port of Spain was a fine city but what did those chaps mean by hailing out to him with the words, 'Whitey Cockroach'?

Perhaps those were the days when we all lived in that fantasy world that the Prime Minister is accused of living in. It was a time when we tolerated each other to the point of joking about our races and happily called out to each other by racial epithets that drew blood elsewhere. Americans and Jamaicans could not believe we were for real the way we clinked each other's beer bottles while addressing each other by the "N" and "C" and "W" words.

The reality in present day Trinidad and Tobago is that we are all still confused about what is driving one young black man to blow out the brain of another young black man. More so is the clueless-ness on the part of our people as to how to fix the damage. And don't tell me that it is because the killer is jealous that the other guy is wearing a bigger gold chain around his neck. Don't give me that crap about turf...what turf... Block Eight vs. Block Ten? Surely by now the aerial blimp would have identified the blighted areas even better than the Google satellite images!

No, my friends. Something more insidious than jealousy and turf-protection is in question here. Something is radically wrong with the collective spirit of our nation. It lies in the apathy in which our attitude is reflected. As my friend in Hong Kong wrote: "is a good ting we eh dere!"

We are yet to become our brother's keeper and take responsibility for the crap that is now hitting the fan... or to put it more delicately we must now carefully examine the rotten fruit that we are reaping so as not to continue sowing such bad seed.

I will spend my eight days of China's National Holidays reflecting on what's going on back home. Even as I write the murder toll has crossed 415 and climbing to the predicted 500 plus deaths by the end of the year - black on black mostly. As for Mr. Manning and his red herrings, does the buck really stop with him? Or with those of us who dismiss the red herrings as a lot of baloney?

18. THE DREAM

GUANGZHOU: Thursday 15th October 2009

Too many stories of bullets, blood and rage. They follow me into my sleep.

Listen to my dream. It is crystal clear. I'm visiting family on Eastern Main Road in Tunapuna. Some pumpkin-vine relatives are living opposite Eldorado Road, sometimes called Dr. Murray Road after a not-quite-as-famous doctor of this time. It is in the vicinity of Turban Brand Curry factory, so I even smell the powerful aroma of geera and tumeric that the Harditsingh family is blending into those familiar brown packages we grew up with.

I'm standing behind a wooden door with jalousies that look onto a gallery. A gunshot rings out. Bang! It is followed by several others. Bang! Bang! Bang! A male voice screams then stops abruptly. I peep out.

There are two school girls in pink uniforms. Are dreams in hi-definition now and scented? They are under the corner shop opposite from where I am. Neither girl appears to have heard the gunshots. One girl continues reading her book. Four men seated around a table in the front yard of the old cottage continue playing cards. Not one of them turns around to look toward the sound of the shooting.

They are like the characters in an Alfred Codallo's black-and-white idrawing. But I could spy some people, some well-groomed office girls, looking down in horror from an upstairs building that once housed a bicycle repairs shop in the old days.

The dream ends with me still clutching the wooden door as a woman's voice - kind of like Miami CSI's Dr. Alexx Woods played by Khandi Alexander - calls out forensic evidence in a monotone. She is removing a glass shard from the body of a man lying on the road. Lieutenant Horatio Caine, the red-haired chief played by David Caruso, is nowhere around to bring closure with his signature sunglasses. The cast in my dream is all black although I do not get to see the victim nor the assailant.

I awoke from my troubled sleep and think about the dream. The scene is familiar and I could have read it in any one of the three dailies. Later, I decided to run it past my Cyber Mate. She's pretty good at this kind of thing. She is able to interpret from my "imachinations" the kind of answers to the nocturnal plotting that keeps the subconscious ticking.

Well?

The main theme, she says, is my plan to return home. I am fearful about this. The architecture is old-time, a longing for the innocence of childhood, also reflected by the young girls who refuse to take notice; the unconcerned blasé males choose to detach themselves from the violence around them. The girls are not diverted from their intellectual pursuits, even by gunshots. The smell of curry entices you back. Not everyone is touched by the violence but there are women who are horrified.

The bicycle shop again shows memories of your mother and the longing to return home. (Mummy worked at Fuller's Cycle Store on Henry Street for half her life.) The lack of colour shows despair. Finally, the removal of the glass shard indicates that women will take charge and provide the solutions. That's what I think! she says.

I told you! The girl is good. Who needs Freud?

Okay, so I'm into this highly emotive state of patriotism evoked by our present day descent into criminality much like what we see on American CSI crime clips. There is also the yearning for the good old days of growing up in pristine Tunapuna. "Bachac," our resident Bad John, was always around to 'protect decent people' (his words) when taking a las' lap on Carnival Tuesday night between Auzonville Road and Eldorado Road. As a teenager the only thing to break the euphoria was remembering to hustle the sign of the cross each time we chipped past St Charles Barromeo's RC Church.

It is amazing though how much blood of its own that Black on Black piece has drawn from readers last week! One is left to surmise whether or not it was the sensitive topic of race or the other tender nerve of a collective guilt that was touched. Perhaps it was a finger that pointed accusingly: "Hey! We are all in this mess TOGETHER and must take collective responsibility for cleaning it up!" What is the saying again... if we are not part of the solution, we are part of the problem.

A click on the mouse tells me that it was Eldridge Cleaver who declared this in a speech in 1968. "What we're saying today is that you're either part of the solution or you're part of the problem." And, ouch! That was the Leroy Eldridge Cleaver, African-American activist and member of the Black Panthers, with a checkered criminal history of his own.

The responses to "Black on Black" are worthy of note. Reactions are always so revealing as they tell where people are really coming from. It's a gut feeling, passionately sincere and usually well-intentioned. Among the fall out were those from old - albeit younger - media colleagues.

Chester Morong writes from Miami: "I could see you over the keyboard fuming...urging the computer to hurry up as you vent...as you keep saying to yourself: 'What a bundle of crock this man is spewing'... But what can we do, eh?"

Anthony Milne in Trinidad vented his own rage by sending me some sources of the problems he saw as being grounded in Caribbean neighbours who contribute unprecedented levels of illegitimacy, illiteracy and immigration. And he sent me to check out J.J. Thomas' *Froudacity: West Indian Fables by James Anthony Froude.* That was in response to J.A. Froude's *The English in the West Indies / The Bow of Ulysses.*

Then there was Lennox Grant who reacted with usual newsroom aplomb while pointing me to Vashty Maharaj (*Newsday's* Sunday editor and columnist), for her take on Prime Minister Patrick Manning's address to the United Nations, "to seek and find the text of his actual remarks, maybe on the *UN website.*"

Raymond Ramcharitar was enlightening as something he said added grist to my mill for stopping the Carnival and other bacchanalian celebrations. To make the point that we are collectively (yes, that word again) serious about fixing our country. This is what he said: The story (was) about an instantly forgotten *Express* front page of 22nd February 2003, when students attacked police. You read that right, students attacked police at a schools' Carnival affair...

I often wonder: My God! What is there to celebrate at this time of our misery? Isn't Carnival now a Celebration of the Macabre?

Richard Seecharan whom I am still to meet in person is the last among the respondents at this point and he quotes a Thought of the Day with characteristic fervour reflecting his own dream perhaps:

"If I allow bitterness and resentment to fester inside, it will make my relationships guarded and unsatisfying. The more I close down to others, the more I become a stranger to myself. By letting go of sorrow and negativity, I can keep my nature open and loving. Remaining open to life, with its constant adventures and opportunities to grow, is the only way to reach my full potential."

Curiosity about my Tunapuna dream however leads me to a website called *realmeaningofdreams.com*. Science is now providing us with the opportunity to understand the linkage between experiences and possibilities that you, the dreamer, can actually direct. Hmn-n-n-n!

According to researchers this phenomenon is called lucid dreaming and should we learn how to do this - it sounds kind of like the challenge of attaining Buddhahood - this means we are more able to think outside the box than in waking life. How interesting! This is the answer we Trinis are looking for!

We need to step outside our safety box of passing the buck and emerge from wallowing in irrelevant traditions (yes! including even Carnival where even a 'wee-wee' toilet truck has become a national debate!). We must CREATE or come up with some brand new answers to our problems. It's not going to be easy as we are talking revolution here. Gandhi did it, Mandela did it, and recently Obama has proven that change can happen without guns and in spite of guns. So, yes! We can do it.

The future of our country right now if we are to look at what DOMA (Downtown Merchants' Association) and some of our *JahajeeDesi* members predict is doomsday scary. Fifteen years ago we brushed away the possibility of 'coming like Jamaica' and Tobago was to be the forever virgin while exposing herself to temptation. Today we are running second to Jamaica as Silver Medallist for being the 'baddest boys' if we take heed of *Newsday's* 'Dead men tell no tales' (Thursday, Oct. 1 2009):

Tobago, our Little Sister Isle, has been ravaged.

Further deterioration of law and order in T&T will simply reflect that ominous warning of Dr. Williams' that what lies in store for us after the party he founded goes under, will be bacchanal at best or massacre at worst. The respite provided by the NAR and UNC governments and the re-entrenchment of the PNM clinches the bind in which we find ourselves. Credible leadership remains an issue. So how prepared are we for the 'massacre at worst'? Do we take up our *jahjee* bundle and run? To where?

Perhaps there are answers waiting someplace in that brain of ours for us to actually design solutions while in the Land of Morpheus. So much like the producer/director of a movie you can map or construct the future free from the Babel/babble of so many viewpoints. At any rate the accumulations of feedback have all contributed already to your collection stored up in your Dreamland computer.

In everyday terms we call it experience. You can call up one or the other at any time and decide how to use it to fix this ailing country of ours. It's what democracy should be about: Government of the people for the people by the people. Do we dare then to look for revolutionary solutions to save our precious country? By putting a woman in charge perhaps?

19. THE STATE OF ANARCHY

GUANGZHOU: Thursday 22nd October 2009

The worst thing in the world next to anarchy is government. – Henry Ward Beecher

This was going to be a column titled "Outside the Box." It was meant to stimulate interest in the urgency of doing things differently IF we are to save our country. And then the gunning down of Peter Garcia in the Rio Claro Court yard hit the cyber waves on Tuesday, October 20th. It seems to have been missed by the many whose heads were euphoric over the story by Andrew Miller (UK editor of *Cricinfo*): "Trinidad unity is a lesson for Caribbean" and with praise for Daren Ganga, Captain of the T&T Cricket team.

All the goodwill and answers and niceties of a one-nation unity that were projected into the column were bowled out as I read online reports of the mayhem in the dailies.

Two gunmen disguised as construction workers hung around the Rio Claro magistrate's court for two hours while the court was in process, and then using Uzi sub machine guns they finished off Garcia as he was led across the courtyard by policemen. Pandemonium seemed to have broken out: the police ran for cover, along with the magistrate and other legal authorities. The killers escaped but not before sending a grim message to the next-door police station with a barrage of firepower.

This is not *Tropic Thunder* and there is no Robert Downey Jr. here in fake jungle warfare. This is a war zone with real homegrown killers. Rio Claro, a sleepy country town in South Trinidad, is the setting for this episode. By now it must be a several grades ahead of a country town in the Middle East, even though one might be misguided into thinking that this deadly scene takes place somewhere outside Baghdad or Kabul.

The *Compact Oxford Dictionary* defines anarchy as a state of disorder due to lack of government or control. It is a society founded on the principles of anarchism. Trinidad and Tobago does not belong there surely. But *Answers.com* describes it as absence of any form of political authority; political disorder and confusion; an absence of any cohesive principle, such as a common standard or purpose.

Sorry folks, but we seem to be qualifiers here. Are we into a state of anarchy as Trinidad and Tobago continues its inexorable descent into chaos? So have we as a country reached where we are going? Should we describe our lot as a descent into the depths of Hell or the ascent to status of Gold Medallist for lawlessness? The new jargon would call it a "maxing out" into superlatives of a horror state.

From the writings on the wall, alas, the future speaks of a worst yet to come. At risk of sounding like a prophetess, it is the reality check that I hope these words impose as I do not see our plight as changing for the better. The situation will get worst before it gets better, if we read into some of the *JahajeeDesi* postings and the reactions from concerned bloggers. So how prepared are we for that coming day of reckoning? Do we remember that 1990 was real? Or, are we into denial of the unknown numbers who died in that Muslimeen uprising?

Vernon De Lima, prominent attorney writes: Please pray for us, as I assure you we are about to enter a very dangerous period of our history. Quite frankly I do not know who has caused it, and that really doesn't matter now. But to face this period we must. You know, Vernon, Madame Marie Curie once said that nothing in life is to be feared; it is only to be understood. As a defense attorney you are well-placed to know this. And, yes, it does matter who caused it so as to prevent a recurrence.

How close then are we to understanding T&T's predicament when we look at the definition of anarchy given above? Let's go over the first criterion. I will leave you to draw your own conclusions after reminding you of one day's news reporting. I am recalling Tuesday, October 20th and the killing of Peter Garcia. Let's call it a day in the life and death of T&T.

There was absence of political authority.

While there is undeniably a duly-elected political authority in the form of the PNM government with a corresponding opposition party in the form of the UNC one is left to wonder about the "political leadership" of both parties that has let the situation degenerate to its present state of terror.

Just look at this report. "Ambush" is the headline of the *Express* report by Richard Charan and Nikita Braxton of its South Bureau: "Murder accused gunned down in front court while escorted by cops" is the second headline. Peter Garcia was in handcuffs, police officers at his side, on the compound of a court, with dozens of officers nearby, when he was shot dead by men mocking the State's ability to protect. Garcia had no chance to defend himself and no one to defend him.

The police constables escorting him to the police station next door released their prisoner and ran after the first gunshot. The policemen who responded to the shooting came long after the suspects were gone.

When the gunshots sounded outside the door Magistrate Connor asked, "Is that gunshots?"

A police officer ran in to announce the shooting. People began screaming and ran towards the Magistrates' Chamber. Magistrate Connor fled first. Those standing outside the courtroom-witnesses to the killing ran into the courthouse.

No Court and Process officer was armed, the *Express* was told, because the Police Standing Orders do not allow for officers in contact with prisoners to carry firearms. Every word in the story is telling. Each word warrants questioning.

The same story reports the response by Acting Police Commissioner James Philbert: "Today we have lost some ground in the sense that criminals can be so bold face to do that. I want to promise the nation that we will find these men and bring them to justice in the quickest time".

The suspects were free last night.

The killing happened at 10.30 a.m. moments after Magistrate JoAnne Connor made a favourable ruling in Garcia's case.

Garcia, who five months ago was regarded as Trinidad's most wanted, was in court charged with wounding with intent to commit murder, and with the murder of Rio Claro businessman Simboonath Kumar. On the murder charge, the State was told it had one last chance to come prepared, November 4, to begin the preliminary enquiry. Garcia had already been discharged on two kidnapping charges.

This is what Jensen LaVende has to say on the same day. His report is: Magistrate: Too close for comfort: "President of the Magistrate's Association, Lucina Cardenas-Ragoonanan, said yesterday that the security system involved in the transporting of prisoners to and from court must be addressed."

Her comment came following the murder of Peter Garcia, a man accused of murder, outside the Rio Claro Magistrates' Court.

"This is too close to comfort," Cardenas-Ragoonanan highlighted as she sat in her Port of Spain Four A courtroom. In a release to the media yesterday, Jones P. Madeira, court protocol and information manager, said that the Judiciary is "deeply concerned" over the murder of an accused who was being led from the court to the nearby Police Station.

"That this could happen in the vicinity of a court and so very near to a police station give an indication of the boldness and the extent to which criminals are prepared to go to carry out their heinous acts," the release stated.

"The Judiciary would now redouble its efforts at reviewing its own security arrangements to ensure that no users of the court system would be put in to any risk" the release added.

Madeira stated that counselling would be arranged for the staff at the courthouse.

Political disorder and confusion.

On the same day the *Guardian* carries a report by Gail Alexander. Its headline is "Dookeran: T&T in state of emergency." It is a report on Political Leader of the Congress of the People Winston Dookeran addressing Sunday's NJAC forum.

T&T is in a state of emergency and the PNM Government is presiding over the forces of underdevelopment, political leader of the Congress of the People Winston Dookeran has said. Dookeran spoke at an NJAC forum to which he had been invited. Dookeran said he first met NJAC's Makandal Daaga at a 1969 meeting. He spoke about T&T's current status and how to proceed in order to take T&T "out of this state of emergency."

He said the issue of race in politics today remained "the most important cancer that we must get rid of if we want to build a new T&T." He added: "The issue of returning governance to the people of this land and having our institutions account to our people and our nation is our primary responsibility to protect our democracy and our freedom in our land.

"For almost 20 years those who have been in charge of the leadership of this country have either formed themselves into cabals or cartels in order to run against the people."

The front page of the *Guardian* of the day displays a banner headline: Murder accused killed outside courthouse. Below is a huge photograph of Diego Martin West MP Dr. Keith Rowley. It screams: PNM ON TRIAL "Udecott Affairs smelling". The Marcus Gonzales, Kimberly Mackhan report follows:

In a scathing attack on his political leader and Prime Minister Patrick Manning, Diego Martin West MP Dr. Keith Rowley yesterday said the affairs of controversial

State-owned Urban Development Corporation of Trinidad and Tobago (UDeCOTT) "smells to the high heavens." He said the PNM was being put on trial because of the support its political leader Manning was giving to the controversial State Board.

Newsday's front-page lead was UDECOTT WORSE THAN PIARCO by Sean Douglas on the same day, Tuesday, 20th October 2009. While one would like to read the interaction as vibrant, healthy democracy in action, they are reality checks that show within the ranks there is an in-fighting reflected in all other facets of the society. Watch the choice of words even in the reporting. It says that we are in a war zone.

"Pulling no punches as he fearlessly trained his guns on his political leader, Diego Martin West MP Dr Keith Rowley yesterday launched a scathing attack on Prime Minister Patrick Manning, declaring the Udecott scandal was ten times worse than the Piarco Airport affair and warning that come the next General Election, the issue would be about PNM corruption."

Absence of any cohesive principle, such as a common standard or purpose

Perhaps this qualification for anarchy is the most worrisome. In the absence of strong leadership at any level seemingly, who or what is to unify the people? Yes there are many patriots and each one is doing his or her own little thing, but where is THE messenger - not necessarily the messiah? Today's jargon will refer to "the critical mass" as that point at which the people say collectively enough is enough so that it will turn the tide of events for the better, as it couldn't get worse.... or could it?

Sometime back I spoke of the messages being there. We all know what should be done but it is the messenger who is needed. In my exploratory piece on the need for T&T as a nation to step outside the box to find the answers to our sorry state, I recognize that there are many still toiling in the vineyards.

Couldn't the messenger be the sum total of citizenry that must rise up TOGETHER to form a single resistance to the plagues? The French did it in 1789!

Irritating as it may sound as one blogger's ominous warning is not the ranting of a madwoman when she quotes from NJAC that it will take the assassination of people in high places to bring real action.

DOMA (Downtown Owners' and Merchants' Association) has reminded us in equally stark terms of the atrocities that took place in Jamaica and Guyana due to a breakdown in law and order. Will we wait then for real bacchanal to take place?

Raymond Ramcharitar in a recent *JahajeeDesi* posting speaks: "The Trinidad we're seeing emerge is merely a representation of Gunta life, which the black and brown middle & upper classes address by pretending it does not exist. That they know Gunta life exists, and wish to have nothing to do with it, is demonstrated by the banks' passing up the opportunity to disburse URP salaries. To get a better idea of the enormity of the upper and middle classes' denial: just think what it would take for the Banks to Refuse Money."

Nor is Sheilah Solomon's Civil Society Senate in place of a functioning government the delusions of another raving lunatic. It sounds like a brave new feasible option to me.

She says: "....Our society e.g. Lifelong Education. Food Security, Family and Child Care, Business, Finance and Economics, Health, Law, Professional Organizations, Sports, Culture, Heritage, Faith-based Organizations, Environmentalists, etc. etc. The reality of T&T is that all these groupings cut across the ethnic divides and represent the varied legitimate interests of citizens.

"The other reality is that such groups are already the ones holding the society together by providing a vast range of voluntary services in areas neglected or incompetently serviced by government arrangements - and that is why the Government tries to 'buy into them' as a means of control. So it's up to us to recognize the 'dependency syndrome' being developed within civil society itself and begin vigorous campaigning for citizen empowerment via a Civil Society Senate which will be just as qualified in the area of governance as the politically chosen 'representatives' in the House of Representatives.

"I am expressing these views on behalf of the Trinidad & Tobago Citizens Agenda Network, actively involved in Citizen Consultations since 1993."

Nor is Stephen Cadiz' voice crying out *Yes T&T* to be dismissed as it is an extremely noteworthy vehicle for mobilizing public sentiment against crime. He writes: "Your note on parenting and education says it all. I am reading a book entitled *The Bottom Billion* by Paul Collier which is about failed states and what can be done to correct the situation. T&T, not yet a failed state but on the way, may very well end up as one of them if we do not make an about-turn."

God alone knows the innumerable religious groupings and their leaders who are trying day and night to save bodies and souls from perdition.

There are so many other voices. I think of names too numerous to be mentioned crying out in that wilderness for a truly great little country to make that about-turn.

And then there are the Diasporeans like myself whose individual voices can still carry the message of salvation even in absentia. They too have never ever really left home.

20. SO WHO IS THE TRUE TRINI?

GUANGZHOU: Thursday 29th October 2009

I've been thinking: what is it that makes a REAL national spirit? But even before that who or what is meant by 'Trini to de bone.' These are the words immortalized in Michael Rudder's 2003 calypso to describe a true product of the twin island republic of Trinidad and Tobago. Listen to him once again:

Welcome, welcome one and all to de land of fete. When it come to bacchanal, well they can't beat we yet. Sweet women parade abundantly, De bredren dey full ah energy. Some people say God is a Trini. Sweet sweet TNT. (Jouvay.com)

I mean - which one of us would not succumb to images of the charismatic sweetness that Rudder inspires? It transports us into a magical homeland where the brightest reds of bougainvilleas tumble over walls, where food with its own unique aromas and flavours tickle taste buds like no where else in the world, and the people.. And the people? Well, that's what this piece is all about.

Who on earth are these creatures who number about one million and who populate a tropical isle or two with their ancestral burial grounds located in the four corners of the planet? And let's not forget the people who joined the colourful ceremony of blessing the ancestral burial ground on St.Vincent Street in San Fernando.

According to Yvonne Webb in the *Guardian* on 22nd October, indigenous peoples from our Arima, Guyana and Suriname in 'native garb' blessed the grounds before the $7million state-of-the-art community centre that had resumed construction. Unfortunately the ceremony was not without its own problems and Junia Regrello,

Permanent Secretary in the Ministry of Community Development, Culture and Gender Affairs, said that 'there was no evidence that it was an Amerindian burial ground, but in the face of concerns raised, the project was temporarily halted to undertake an investigation to see how authentic the claims were.'

Unobtrusive as this little story may appear, hidden behind the ebullience of the cricket news of the day, believe me it displays some of what goes into making the character that is called 'Trini to de bone,' and whose God, let's not forget, is also a naturalized citizen. The flamboyance of the performers concentrating on the blessing ceremonies, the costumery (never mind the native bits enhanced with Nike-type footwear), but most of all the audience and the commentator in particular are noteworthy.

The Permanent Secretary displays astuteness in having to try to please everyone. Note the diplomacy. "After consultation with the Amerindian community, they agreed to bless the site so work could proceed. We don't want to offend any community," Regrello said.

So the Trini character is of necessity a combination of many parts that must please its tiniest bit while remaining faithful as far as humanly possible to the sum total of all those parts. To be a cool, sharp-witted, bacchanal-fun-loving Trini therefore, isn't all that easy.

Okay let's take a closer look at this character. To see him at his best is during sport as beheld recently in the games of cricket when T&T experienced some days of exhilaration only to fall to New South Wales who won by 41 runs. The game has been able to successfully marry two of the major tribes and so the spirit of participation transcends barriers of ethnicity, age, politics and even sex. Most times anyway.

Sports-challenged as I am, it is with curiosity that I behold my Cyber Mate, a self-confessed feminist, and her total submission to the game of cricket. This is to the point where household chores are planned or abandoned in accordance with the telecast. She has explained away the macho-ness of the game by reminiscing about the days when she and her siblings used to bowl out each other in Arouca. Not with coconut bats and green oranges that I knew about but with the real cork ball and other genuine accoutrements she says huffily.

She is a little peeved at this writing advising me to get out of an area that I don't know, viz. the essence of cricket and sports in general. She is totally mad at my suggestion that she would want to re-fashion the Queen's Park Cricket Club out of its 'foolish antiquity' should she be given chance at a rebirth. She thinks my rambling about her in this column may be another of my 'crusading dreams' as she is still not a crusader.

Uh, oh! Lest this borders on a Rottweiler/Wajang debacle (names attributed to the present Leader of the Opposition) I'm tempted to take the easy way out and leave the essence of cricket to the connoisseurs.

So who really qualifies as a real Trini?

Let it not be said that this character - a national not necessarily a patriot - does not have passion for country. A look back at the brave front page of the *Express* October 24th announces: 'T&T falls in T20 final but wins respect from fans.' Curtis Chase captures the spirit of Cricket supporters Steve Khan and Gary Canejo reacting as another Trinidad and Tobago wicket falls during the Champions League Twenty/20 tournament final against New South Wales in India.

Faces of the two chaps in the photo recall memories of the Strike Squad's 1990 Word Cup loss to the Americans by one flipping goal! And big men cried. But God is a Trini so that more than the 30,000 of us packed into the over-crowded stadium on that fateful day did not get to meet our Maker after all. He alone knew what would have happened had T&T won that game.

Would the stadium really have collapsed?

Visions of red t-shirts, stalled steel orchestras, and a nation cheated of another fete were just too much and we had to look for scapegoats always conveniently placed to take de licks.

And then there was Germany 2006 when our Soca Warriors made it to the World Cup Finals but succumbed to the English. But we made it! It was like running second to Jamaica's Usain Bolt in Beijing Olympics last year - but we made it to The Bird's Nest! Like true Trinis we were there. We take consolation that we also ran. 'Tis better to have run than not to have run. There is a bothering memory of an American diplomat in Trinidad who liked to repeat the joke that "Trinis love to rush for second place."

But our collective soul was with Richard Thompson on that 9.89th second in the Beijing Olympics in 2008 after Usain Bolt. It was a margin of 0.2 seconds! How our bellies ached! So close to the Lightning Bolt! We bawled Oh, God! You're supposed to be one of us!

In the final he finished in second place; he was far behind winner Usain Bolt (9.69 s) but his time of 9.89 s was enough to win the silver medal and set a new personal best. His new best time made him the second fastest Trinidadian 100 m sprinter ever, after Ato Boldon. (Wikipedia)

We took it gallantly as always, consoled by memories of our Hasely Crawford having already won the first Caribbean 100-metre Gold in 1976 and joined the brethren celebrating with them in our own inimitable hedonistic fashion playing mas in Beijing Bird's Nest.

You see, we really are a nice people. Seldom do we get into brawls over matches like those rambunctious Britons although a story today did report the stabbing to death of 15-year-old Damien Duncan by a student from another school following a BGT&T Secondary Schools Football League match. The match was a Big Five semi-final between Presentation College (San Fernando) and Carapichaima High School, which was won by Pres 2-0.

Hopefully this is an aberration and we will continue to use sports as therapy for healing our nation and our fractured Caribbean.

The ball is now in the court of youngsters like Daren Ganga, Captain of the T&T Cricket Team, and manager Colin Borde as reported by Nagraj Gollapudi on 22 October 2009 who said: "It was a consensus on the part of everyone for us to approach our cricket in a certain way in terms of zero tolerance in discipline, the respect of people and cricket being the most important thing, and that all sacrifices should be made towards ensuring the quality of our cricket is improved."

Ganga, captain of the T&T Team, is reported as saying that before he was appointed captain, he was not happy with a lot of T&T players who were also in the West Indies side, because when they came back to the first-class set-up they took things for granted. "They never really placed the amount of value that should have been placed on playing for your country. That is one of the areas I recognized when I got into the captaincy role."

And here is Borde again: "You've got to find a happy medium if you want young people to learn. You've got to try and speak their language. It is not about them understanding you. You've got to try to understand them."

What else are people sayng?

For readers' information as to the real character of the Trini and our unique brand of democracy I have included a postscript by a blogger in response to Yvonne Webb's *Guardian* story about 'Amerindians bless burial ground' on October 22nd:

"I think that these Indigenous people should also bless the Prime Minister's residence, the Brian Lara Stadium and all other UDeCOTT projects.

"Mr. Junior Minister, if you pour concrete all over the site, of course there will be no evidence of any burial ground. You still need a lot of coaching from Colm and other seasoned cabinet colleagues before you start shooting from the hip. And your claim to not offend any community. What is that all about? You all offend the entire population daily. I guess we are not a community. (*Submitted by epsomsalts on 22 October 2009 - 7:01am.*)

And so who is the real Trini?

I guess he/she is a combination of all the characters mentioned above.

21. VOX POPULI

GUANGZHOU: Thursday 5th November 2009

These are the voices of two women, one white and conservative, the other black and militant, both Trinidadian by choice and by trial.

Diana Mahabir-Wyatt has laboured long in the vineyards of Trinidad and Tobago and has served her constituency of business and government employers with distinction. She has also never missed an opportunity, I think, to improve her understanding of the plight of the wretched of the earth. This is why she was able to admonish me last week for my own apparent lack of insider knowledge of the horrors in the world outside of Trinidad and Tobago.

To quote Mrs. Mahabir-Wyatt, the eminent labour consultant and former Senator: "I just got back from a Commonwealth Human Rights Conference in London attended by Human Rights Defenders from all over the Commonwealth, and having listened to their stories of trials and tribulations which were appalling, I could only thank God that I live in T&T where we can say anything we want to... and often do, criticizing the Government... never mind they ignore us... we are not arrested nor tortured for what we say."

But it so happened that on the same day I was sent Mrs. Mahabir-Wyatt's reprimand, I received the following rebuke from a blogger whom I believed I had quoted correctly in one of my earlier Letters from China: "Be careful how you interpret and rewrite these things in your writing because you can cause us to be arrested for sedition or for inciting people to commit a breach of the peace. Your interpretation and rewriting of what I said in my article could have the police at my door anytime. This is not the country that you left behind and the madness knows no reason."

Did I really err in thinking that Karen had seen the writing on the wall, as so many others outside of boardrooms have done? This is what I remember receiving from her in response to my article on BLACK ON BLACK, RED HERRINGS AND WHITEY COCKROACH:

"The young black boys are killing each other because they are simply not intelligent enough to know otherwise. The day they find out, everything will straighten out in T & T because there will be a mad rush to stop the flow of guns into the country. The untouchables will become touchables as the ratsasses rush to save their skins. The borders of our small country with four sides will become properly secured. Drugs will not come and go as it pleases and the education system will be thoroughly overhauled to produce productive, thinking people en masse.

"Suddenly we shall design an integrated, multi-sectoral approach to violence prevention after the public health model. Simultaneously we shall identify and use an appropriate model of community development that does not resemble the 'keep the ... wining and dancing' one that we now use. We shall also move expeditiously to salvage what is left of our culture and to preserve and pass it on to future generations. We shall finally be on the way to developed country status."

But mea culpa. Karen has corrected me. She referred me to Makandal Daaga, one of the leaders of the 1970 Black Power protests, whom I see is in the news warning of another debacle in our lives.

Was it Makandal Daaga then?

Oh, Karen, I am so very sorry. I do not want the police to come banging on your doors late at night. But you, me and Makandal could be wrong, misled by the mischievous media. Diana says that from what she has seen and heard that takes place in the rest of this evil world nothing like what you fear will happen in our Trinidad and Tobago, barred, and these are my words, the daily shedding of blood by our uneducated, uninformed and unemployed black youth.

"Have you forgotten what we really live like?" she asked me. "We are not arrested nor tortured for what we say. We have put our Chief Justice on trial and no one died as a result... we have put the head of the opposition on trial and he's still there talking all kinds of what anywhere else would be regarded as traitorous nonsense. We put the Chief Justice on trial and no one dies ... our Law Association comes out in public against the Attorney General and no one is arrested.

"The Commissioner of Police apologises to the public for the transgressions of his Police Force. And changes do happen ... mostly long after we protest ... there are tire burnings and marches and placarding fests.

"We do it in song and in writing, and the radio talk shows would be closed down any where else for the seditious things callers-in say, and they would be found and arrested for the things they fearlessly and often stupidly come out with ...

"Even the Prime Minister just tries to go in person to protest, but no one ends up anonymously in jail ... too many *macocious* people to know what is happening and criticize ... but then we go home alive to protest another day. We are fallible, wrong-headed and often, simply stupid, but we have more exercise of human rights than most of the Commonwealth Countries that I listened to with tears in my eyes."

This is among her reproaches to me, a tearful Diana returning to her paradise home after woeful days of listening in London to human rights abuses in other Commonwealth countries. "We need to improve and ensure that we do not end up like most of them, but for God's sake, Rhona, don't make us sound like we are what we are not. If you want to fight, come home and fight ... don' t challenge from a distance on the basis of what we all know are the sensational press reports that focus on the very real negatives and forget the even more very real positives which don't sell papers."

So it's not just crime, corruption and political mismanagement and ineffectiveness, we are fighting. We are also up against those nasties in the media who are only interested in circulation figures and who have Makandal Daaga warning about another conflagration. Shame on you, Ken Gordon. Shame on you, Tony Sabga.

Daaga has been reported by the *Express* to say that a revolution, the likes of the Black Power Movement, is coming, if the current Urban Development Corporation of Trinidad and Tobago (UDeCOTT) imbroglio is not corrected. Daaga, said the *Express,* made the statement when his National Joint Action Committee (NJAC) held a public consultation about UDeCOTT at the Curepe Scherzando Pan Yard in Curepe. "The problem here is your history," Daaga scolded his audience. "You have shown that you are capable of taking insult after insult, and outside of 1970 you would not revolt ... are you going to take that home and swallow it without pride, or are you going to stop this once and for all?"

Believe me, I'm in no way related to Daaga or to Nostradamus and it is possible that I could be, from this distance, a little paranoid. But the year 2010 marks the 20th anniversary of a cycle that has seen social upheavals in 1970 and 1990. Will another group of "imperfect and stupid" men rush to shake off the yoke of a government, an opposition and a middle class that have failed to understand their frustrations and their desperation?

The newspapers still do not understand, but should we ignore these voices, Diana, because they all sound like modern-day Jeremiahs? Should we assume that they do not really appreciate the benefits of living in one of the freest countries in the twentieth century? How prepared are we really for another meltdown of the social structures in our country? Is there a plan or a backup plan in the making? Or are we not reading the graffiti? Why do people wait for after-the-fact to wonder why, when the place was alight and blazing, like Nero they were busy fiddling?

If the truth be told, I would rather not be an irritant provoking such radical thoughts of gloom and doom. Far be it from me to wish another breakdown in a homeland that I love. It contradicts a sunny nature that would really prefer to ride out these Golden Years playing with grandchildren or introducing the fine art of Mahjong or Tai chi to my Trini neighbours.

The thing is the luxury of enjoying the good life (health, wealth, jobs, education, security) whether in China, Norway, or the Caribbean is directly dependant on the extent to which one understands the environment that makes such a life possible. The equation remains the same. It defies belief therefore that with the present environment at home, there is anyone in Port of Spain,

San Fernando, Arima, Chaguanas, or Scarborough and their environs who can truthfully speak of enjoying a good quality of life today. But guess what? There are some who do.

Let's take a trip down-memory-lane to 1970 and later make a stop over in 1990. In both instances, before the Black Power assertiveness and the two decades later invasion of Parliament and media houses by fanatical Muslimeen, was there ever an inkling that such upheavals would come to pass? How fickle is memory! We carried on in our usual clueless fashion.

But the writings were on the walls. We were simply not reading them.

According to TIME magazine on Monday, May 04 1970, this is what we failed to see: "Despite their deceptive tranquillity, the English-speaking islands of the Caribbean have been stirring uneasily for at least two years in the face of rising black militancy. On most of the islands, even the prosperous tourist Meccas, unemployment rates are distressingly high. The targets of black resentment are usually the well-off white minorities. Last week, on the two-island nation of Trinidad and Tobago (pop. 1,100,000), this resentment erupted into widespread violence."

Robert Walker in his BBC News on 03 June 2007 reminded us about that other episode in our history when he linked a current story of an alleged plot to blow up JFK airport in New York with Muslim extremists. He said: "Jamaat al Muslimeen first came to attention in 1990, when it tried to overthrow the government of Trinidad and Tobago. More than 100 armed men stormed the parliament building and took the prime minister and members of the cabinet hostage. There is little history of Islamic militancy in the Caribbean. But security analysts have suggested the region could be attractive as a base for terrorist groups because of its proximity to the United

States, its porous borders and because of the widespread poverty on the islands."

So unprepared were we that on that fateful afternoon of the attempted coup the Trinidad and Tobago Television broadcast with some strangely-garbed men with guns standing behind a head table of journalists made us think that we were viewing the cast of a Raoul Pantin revolutionary play. Crystal clear it is. I remember turning to my housekeeper and remarking about 'the play'. No joke! That was the first thought that came to mind. Little did we know it was the start of six days of terror that put Trinidad and Tobago under siege.

But we have forgotten. For better or worse, Time does that. What's more today we are oil and gas rich!

Those of us who survived the trauma of one or both social conflagrations emerged with varying degrees of burns so as to live to fight another day. The option is to go into denial that the fires really did not happen and even if they did, well, the third-degrees burns were not so bad after all! We have the best judiciary system in the world and the Trini God takes care of the rest. Right?

Distance lends either enchantment or distortion to the viewer. And therefore from as far away as China things do tend to take on a more exaggerated perspective and it is often with some bewilderment that one learns that maybe, after all, it wasn't so bad. It depends though on the viewers and the quality of their rose-tinted glasses at both ends of the distance. For example there was My Ron assuring me that home was all right to come back to and he had indeed not been touched by the misery of rampant crime... that is until he posted his own home-invasion by bandits.

I have been reading the daily news, editorials and columnists while keeping in constant touch with the *JahajeeDesi* postings. Every now and then I would get some direct feedback from a home-based member of the electorate at large. The blogging community is an important sector but dependant on which cyber feeder is opened one will get the predictable quality of feed-back. I speak here of those writers who use vowels in place of words; those who see the space as a platform for vomiting their biliousness or strutting their egos; or those whose intellect challenges comprehension.

The recent news reports of the police killings of three hijackers brought forth such a feeding frenzy of opinion on whether or not the police should be sanctified or vilified - democracy at work. With a collective sigh of relief, there were three fewer murderous crazies/psychopaths to deal with. Members of the Police Force involved were immediately elected to canonization status or as possible candidates for National Awards.

What is worrisome though is the middle rung of the social ladder which carries on as if they are in some reality-show immunity safety-net, secure and unaffected by the swirling cinders blowing around them. I spoke with one of these members of the electorate and can vouch that she is representative of those aforementioned safety-netters. She qualifies for the colour-coding of 'brown people' of which Raymond Ramcharitar speaks. 'High-brown' to be even more faithful to the pigment test.

She was convinced that things were on the upswing with business picking up. Yes, things were good. Prices were going back up. It was business as usual. Once again there was that pride in saying that I would not recognize the places that I had left behind twelve years ago. As for the people... these I would not recognize either. "They have changed. They are more selfish, not their usual friendly, generous selves and had become definitely more materialistic." But the violence is concentrated to the 'gang and drug group' she said, and they are killing off each other anyway. Did I read the good news of the police getting three of them yesterday?

I was curious about her political leanings. She is a Manning supporter liking Rowley at one time but not since he had got himself into the row with the Prime Minister. Most of the Middle Class feels the same way, she thinks and they believe that the people in opposition along with all the media had joined in unfairly lambasting Manning. *Newsday* that used to be partial to him had now gone totally the other way, she added. We hung up laughing away the notion that Trinis had indeed become too thin-skinned after indulging in some character-profiling of people we were both close to in the past.

I looked again at the two foreign reports on 1970 and 1990 for impartiality.

How will the 2010 report read?

22. WHO WILL BELL THE CAT?

GUANGZHOU: Thursday 12th November 2009

The more things change the more they remain the same. Every time I read the three daily newspapers online that is what I think. *Plus ça change, plus c'est la même chose.* It is attributed to Jean-Baptiste Alphonse Karr French critic, journalist and novelist (November 24, 1808 - September 29, 1890), but many politicians, including Eric Williams, have said it. People dpn't want change, Archbishop Anthony Pantin said during the 1970s. They just want quiet.

And I wonder who is going to bell the cat this time. Will it be the elected Opposition? Will it be an alert and intelligent media? Or, will it be disgruntled people of Trinidad and Tobago?

It is a feeling of déjà vu even as the excitement of re-entry increases. But the more I look forward to returning home the more I must brace myself for the jolt of landing on old stony ground and the disappointment of finding out that the surplus of oil dollars have not changed one iota the lessons of politics in Trinidad and Tobago. The politicians are still heaping curses on each other and the electorate is still mired in the ancient questions of "what we go do?" and "who we go put?"

Since 1981, with the death of the Father of the Nation – Dr Eric Eustace Williams, change hasn't worked out so well for us though the ship of state has rolled and yawed between the captaincy of the People's National Movement, the National Alliance for Reconstruction and the United National Congress.

And yet, I am aware that there are a lot of good people on board and a lot of good intentions and there is the hope that this combination will produce the formula we need to create a real nation of patriots. This hope might have been reinforced recently when Ken Gordon and Tony Sabga appeared at a function sponsored by the University of Trinidad and Tobago and at which Mr. Gordon spoke on the topic of "Nearly 50 years of Independence from a Publisher's Perspective - Now Nationhood".

It sounded like an old theme and one that Mr. Gordon should have had a close-up experience with as a publisher and politician. He was after all Prime Minister ANR Robinson's pick as a Cabinet Minister in 1986 in a marriage with Mr. Basdeo Panday that didn't last as long as the Red House fire. And so when he called on politicians to work together so as to address the problems affecting Trinidad and Tobago one sensed a certain futility or dejection in the slope of body-language, awareness that he is not really the anointed one to spark a fusion of national wills.

Forget body language. My question is why so late? Wasn't there this need in 1987, in 1988, in 1989 and in 1990 when the Publisher and Politician was in Cabinet with other ministers from the NAR Government? Or, did he know then, as he must know now, that many are called but few are chosen?

It seems churlish of me to point this out but those of us who expect to reap the benefits of a democracy and a life full of political promise must undergo, we were taught, the fatigue and the angst of supporting it. And that fatigue and angst indicts Mr. Gordon on two counts, one political and the other journalistic. I have no knowledge or idea of the role Mr. Sabga played at the lecture but in the *Express* Page One photograph with Mr. Gordon he seemed to have escaped the slings and arrows of both outrageous politics and media. I think Mr. Sabga has never really ever hankered for a power greater than his prowess in business and the wealth it has brought him.

I am writing this today because of Mr. Gordon's stated perspective for Trinidad and Tobago as a Publisher. It is no secret that in the *Express* he has great power at his fingertips moreso now that it has developed into One Caribbean Media.

When he was writing *War and Peace*, I learnt recently, Leo Tolstoy wrote that the most powerful weapon against political ineptitude, public ignorance and rampant crime was the diffusion of printed matter. The truth is the *Express* and the *Guardian* have often espoused this belief. But is it a stance that newspapers could have on one day and abdicate responsibility the rest of the week?

I don't think so and the more I am told the history of the media and the role of newspapers in society the more I am convinced that there is a quality of daring and responsibility that is missing in our newspapers today.

You are wondering no doubt whether China is a place where I could discuss the responsibilities of a free press. I am sure that not many Trinidadians and Tobagonians would think it is. But is it any better to do so in Trinidad or in the United States, my wily Chinese students – there are more of them on the Internet than in any other country, the United States included – counter, where even the press tsars of Main Street have allowed crooked financiers like Bernard Madoff to swindle billions of investment funds and pensions? They seem to have a point, but I am still reacting to my education and I recall that Henry Ward Beecher, an American clergyman, once said that "newspapers are the schoolmasters of the common people." I know that I have presented them with a two-pronged fork that they can and do turn on me. "Tell us," they say with undisguised triumph, "how organized religion and a free press have made if safer for you to return to your paradise home."

My eyes fill with tears of recrimination and remorse. I think they have been reading Diana Mahabir-Wyatt's messages to me.

The truth is I don't believe that anywhere in the world today is a safe place, thanks to Mr. George Walker Bush and his War Cabinet. But I take refuge in another American. Daniel Webster felt that newspapers instructed the public mind and animated the spirit of patriotism. Its loud voice, he said, would suppress everything that would raise itself against the public good and its rebuke would cause incipient despotism to perish in the land.

And then I caught myself. Did this happen when the absurd accounting for the $2 million flag was made known? Did it happen when the $10 million outdoor concert stage at the prime Minister's residence was announced?

As I read the farmers' threat to shut down the country against the Minister of Sports Gary Hunt's defence for his TT$2 million flag and Minister of Works, Colm Imbert's over (the more or less) TT$10 million for the stage at the Prime Minister's residence, I wondered how the *Express* and the *Guardian,* how Messrs. Gordon and Sabga, had enjoined these battles. And not hearing from them or from their editors I turned to another champion of the media. "An able, disinterested and public spirited press, with a trained intelligence to know right and courage to do it," said Joseph Pulitzer, "can preserve public virtue without which popular government is a sham and a mockery."

Only when it is not happening, when newspapers seem to be failing in their responsibility to be "the vigilant guardian of the rights of the ordinary citizen," will the government think of threatening the press, as Mr. Manning's Government is now doing, with a watchdog group of wannabe editors and moralists.

Well, as Mr. Gordon says, we don't want that because then we are sure to have no accounting for the mistakes and extremism of the Government. So go for it, Mr. Gordon. Go for it, Mr. Sabga. Make Mr. Manning's life a trial of nerves if he tries to assume a power that belongs to the people, if he and his ministers continue to pile error on error in total contempt for accountability. Go all the way. Call for their dismissal from office.

"I am always in favour of the free press," Winston Churchill said, "but sometimes they say quite nasty things." It's the only way to deal with self-righteous politicians in Government and in the Opposition. Be nasty. And save Trinidad and Tobago from the wrath of an authority higher than Parliament.

Politics and the public welfare are not mutually inseparable and they should have taught us by now that we cannot play mas' and fraid mas' powder. That is something that Karl Hudson-Phillips left with me.

On a much more relaxing note there were items of interest on the *JahajeeDesi* site. Not least among them was the heated response by members to a rather innocuous posting of Richard Wm. Thomas.

It suggested the coming together of the opposition parties to bury their hatchets and unite to challenge the incumbent People's National Movement in what is a familiar numbers game. It is not an original idea as in 1981 history records that the ONR's (Organization for National Reconstruction) loss to the PNM served to pave the way for the unprecedented easy win of the NAR in 1986 and it was all because of the numbers game. That NAR = ONR+ULF bunch, some of whom never knew what it was like to face an electorate on the hustings, had power handed to them by a stroke of luck played by the unity hand. But how easily we forget!

In a letter addressed to The Honourables Basdeo Panday, Austin Jack Warner, Kamla Bissessar and Winston Dookeran, Mr. Thomas' simple title was: Openly, now, asking you: "Why not?" But this question attracted an outpouring of passion that once more reminded me of getting caught up in distractions that make us not see the forest for the trees. It becomes more intense as the arguments become personal and serious answers are frittered away in petty squabbles.

By the time I got through the positions of Peter O'Connor, Richard Hosein, Steve Alvarez, Gregory Reece, Taran Rampersad, and MF Rahaman, I might as well have been quaffing beers at the corner pub and laughing out loud with them. Rhea Mungal was right when she replied early on: "Hi Richard, Solomon in all his wisdom would get a headache over this issue."

Mr. Thomas was on the familiar unity path I thought that Mr. Gordon had pointed out as the way to go. But it raised some old questions:

* How do we in this wonderful democracy of ours ALLOW guys at the top to get away with bleeding incompetence?

* Where are the checks and balances that our constitution provides?

There is no way I think that anyone could justify the expenditures from the public purse for the fantasies of Gary Hunt and Colm Imbert.

Which brings me to Ria Taitt's report in the *Express* on Monday, November 9th 2009 headlined: "Warner slams Ross crime proposals." The Chaguanas MP, wrote Ms. Taitt, also called on Senator Martin Joseph, Minister National Security, to inform the nation about the cost of retaining Canadian Cameron Ross and his team to produce a document that is pathetic. "The nation must know the burden on the Treasury of producing a crime proposal that reads like *deja vu;* one we have all heard of before," he said.

But why this late inquiry? Isn't the Government supposed to inform Parliament on the disbursement of public monies BEFORE the fact?

And then there is a ghastly-looking building, if I am to judge from the photographs, that is the National Academy for the Performing Arts, NAPA. It looks like a lopsided shuttlecock and is being built by the Chinese. But much like the Emperor's New Clothes it is seen "like a pearl" by Prime Minister Manning.

Ms. Omatie Lyder in the *Sunday Express* of November 8th reported that the cost was given by former Culture Minister Joan Yuille-Williams in response to a question by Opposition MP Dr. Tim Gopeesingh in Parliament in 2007, but the final figure was not yet revealed. The centre however was opened with great fanfare on Monday night by the Prime Minister at a cost of TT$480 million according to news reports.

What am I missing here?

Ms. Lyder who visited China from October 23 to November 4, on the invitation of the Chinese Government was able to interview the Director and president of Overseas Business of the Shanghai Construction Group (SCG), Tong Ji Sheng, at his Shanghai headquarters last Wednesday. His words are worth noting. And so too are those of the late Michael Manley, former Prime Minister of Jamaica who once jeered that T&T's oil money passed through the country like a dose of salts. I remember that Dr. Williams didn't like this sneer at all and the jokes people made of his statement that money was no problem.

These are Mr. Sheng's words from his interview with Ms. Lyder:

The SCG has observed that Trinidad and Tobago has two 20-year development plans and since this country has a big influence in the Caribbean area, "we hope to explore the neighbouring construction market" and to "turn our company into a local company based in Trinidad and Tobago."

All the big industrial countries had done it in the past; wasn't the American Halliburton an inconspicuous fixture in our Southland for eons? So why not the Chinese now?

The company also plans to include local labourers and overcome the big problem of how to better employ local resources, such as engineers, in their projects here as well as offer contracts to good construction companies.

In the last five years, SCG has also built the Prime Minister's residence and diplomatic centre, refurbished the old Piarco airport terminal in time for the Fifth Summit of the Americas last April, and is currently building the Ministry of Education Tower.

This is one Chinese businessman who knows clearly where to find lots of butter for his *mianbao*.

Do you not agree, Omatie?

23. S.O.S. (SAVE OUR SOULS)

GUANGZHOU: Thursday, 19th November 2009

Listen up, Mr. Manning. I am going to speak out loud and clear because I don't want you, or your ministers, or the raggle-taggle Opposition to misunderstand what I am about to say.

We, the people of Trinidad and Tobago are on a sinking ship and this is not the time for lies, half-truths and innuendoes. This is not the time for extravagant and wasteful projects that you think will raise the image of our country in the eyes of the world. This is not the time to ask members of the public to be nice and not to raise hell because you are going to host an international conference.

This is the time to raise hell.

You think I am a lone voice crying out in the wilderness? Well, I am not. The *Guardian* on 6th November wrote in an editorial: "Minister Hunt's handling of this matter (of the $2 million flag) seems to be less than adequate. But the expenditure on the flag and its erection does fall into a pattern of extravagance so prevalent in the operations of this Government. Within Mr. Hunt's own portfolio there is the waste being daily demonstrated on the Brian Lara Stadium, two years behind schedule and over by $100 million from the original cost (as revealed this week by the Housing Minister). Yet no one, not even the Sports Minister, is able to say when the stadium will be finished and what will be the final cost."

The editorial continued, "As part of a pattern of extravagance with public funds is the construction of a new building on the compound of the Prime Minister's Residence and Diplomatic Centre, to host 1,000 people in a concert hall setting."

It's time, Mr. Prime Minister, to wake up and see how far off-course the ship of state has gone and to realise that your confreres in the Commonwealth club are not unaware of our predicament. They know that mismanagement and corruption are not only a Trinidad and Tobago disease; they are twin evils that affect nearly every country in the world as this week's annual *Corruption Index from Transparency International* showed. Even Britain, the mother of the Commonwealth, has slipped to an 11-year low in the wake of its MPs' expenses scandal.

How the world sees us is, of course, cause for alarm. The vast majority of the 180 countries included in the 2009 index scored below five in a scale from 1 to 10. In the index, Barbados was in 20th place with a score of 7.4; Saint Lucia was in 22nd place with a score of 7.0; St. Vincent and the Grenadines in 31st place with a score of 6.4; and Dominica in 34th place with a score of 5.9.

But where was Trinidad and Tobago, Mr. Manning? In 79th place (tied with that incarnation of the Devil himself, China) with a score of 3.6.

By the way, Mr. Manning, did you see this week's TIME magazine cover story on the "Five Things the US can learn from China"? It repeated that China is the world's third-largest economy on the way to becoming the second and the largest foreign holder of US debt. I remember that when I came to Guangzhou in 1998, China was nowhere near the top of this economic chart and countries like the United Kingdom, France, Germany and Italy were way ahead of it.

So the cat is out of the bag, Mr. Manning. The world knows that we are in a mess. This is what our alarming crime rate shows. This is what the foolishness of your ministers' actions show. So there is really no reason why you should try to cover up our woes and appeal for a kind of false and fraudulent peace. Mr. Gordon Brown is chest-deep in manure as you are but he doesn't walk around breathing fire at people and the press who are pointing out the mistakes of his Government.

Listen up, Mr. Manning. The best thing you could hope for now is a press that is accurate. This is what I, too, rely on.

And on 13th November Yvonne Webb reported in the *Guardian* that you called on protesting prisons officers to be more responsible and you warned them against embarrassing the Government during the upcoming Commonwealth Heads of Government Meeting (CHOGM) in Port of Spain.

Speaking with reporters after a walkabout in your San Fernando East constituency, you said the officers had legitimate concerns and you assured the press that those concerns would be addressed. But you added: "Staying away from prison (work) does nobody any good. They (the officers) have a legitimate concern and it will be addressed, but people have to be more responsible in the way they conduct their legitimate business after all. What they trying to do...embarrass the Government? The Government will not allow that to happen. That won't happen."

Fine. If they break the law, fire them. Ronald Reagan did this to his air traffic controllers in 1981 when he fired 11,345 of them.

Do you remember?

But I want to add that the Government must be responsible as well and that the people will not allow the Government to embarrass them. Did the prisons officers have a case? They claimed, said the *Guardian*, they were under attack and have asked for guns to protect themselves after two of their colleagues were shot by criminals. Anthony Sinanan was shot and wounded on 4th November at the car park of the Golden Grove Remand Yard Prison, Arouca, while Ian Seegobin was shot dead three days later. These incidents fired prisons officers at the Port-of-Spain State Prison to stage a sickout in protest of the shooting of their colleagues.

The action of the officers delayed proceedings in the magistrates and high courts throughout the country, as prisoners were not brought to court on time. Minister in the Ministry of National Security Donna Cox said that the issue of giving prison officers guns was being considered.

It is clear that we are a nation in distress and we must do something to save Trinidad and Tobago. NOW!

I would like to think, Mr. Prime Minister that something is happening. I have read that your Government and Mr. Panday's Opposition are getting together to work on legislation re-the crime situation. Juhel Browne reported in the *Express* on 17th November that: "It was only on November 3rd that Prime Minister Patrick Manning met with Opposition Leader Basdeo Panday at the Diplomatic Centre, St Ann's, to discuss six pieces of legislation to deal with crime and also constitutional reform."

At times it could seem like I am over-reacting - I mean, being so far away from home and worrying about 1.3 million souls as if I have nothing else to do but crusade with what's left of my life. But hey! I watch the lavish receptions as people cocktail around Port of Spain, "the olds", as my students say, accumulating honours, women dressed to kill for charity, the young and the beautiful feverish over Carnival, or the politicians preening for the CHOGM Meeting that will bring together another round of cocktail parties and of talk shops.

I console myself, as Diana Mahabir-Wyatt reminded me, that maybe I've forgotten and things aren't so bad at home as they seem from this distance.

And then, BANG! BANG! Another young life is snuffed out right there in front of mothers and children in a Laventille clinic as the assailants continue their daily spate of senseless violence that is blighting Trinidad and Tobago.

It's interesting that Quintin Oliver that very week spoke in the same nautical metaphors of a ship in distress in his address at the two-day YesTT International Conference, themed "Strengthening Democratic Processes & Good Governance." Remember what he said? "Wake up, you have a crisis and you need all hands on deck to address it."

Here was an authority from Northern Ireland comparing his own country's experience of 4,000 political killings over a 40-year period with our own non-political killings put at 445 on that date 11th November only to jump to 451 by Saturday 14th. Will the end of the year total reach the 550 murders of last year?

Mr. Oliver identified two phenomena:
1. that the numbers were proportionally higher than that of his own country's, and
2. that unlike his Northern Ireland our violence was not politically motivated.

However, he remarked that it must be a cause of great concern and it should be the subject of the highest political and policy attention in order to try and diagnose the cause and find solutions very quickly. Mr. Oliver put it to the audience: "I understand you are in the top five murder rates in the world. Now isn't that extraordinary? Is that not the most important political issue?"

The most important political issue.

But apart from trying perhaps to shock his audience into awakening, it was what Mr. Oliver had still to say that sounded familiarly disturbing. "During the conflict in Northern Ireland those who lived through it found ways of shielding ourselves and the news bulletins that came on saying that another soldier was killed last night, another person was caught in gun fire, another assassination took place of a politician."

As I read the report, Mr. Oliver's words boom out like a fog horn to those who have ears to hear. But few are hearing as it is in an atmosphere thickly fogged up with distractions that allow people to continue *lahaying* on board, masquerading in eiderdown while feathering their nests. And so it's business as usual. Read carefully as he elaborates on the quality of the hands on deck.

"I wonder if some of the same factors take place in those societies that are afflicted by gang violence and gun violence and drug violence and whether people who in important positions who are opinion formers and decision makers have isolated themselves and do not see that this is a tragedy crying out for urgent policy attention..."

These are perhaps the most indicting words of his entire speech and one is left to wonder what will be the response to his SOS distress call. Will they be lost in the turbulent winds that buffet the Ship of State - a nation that continues afloat in a Carnival sea of Ship Ahoy euphoria? But even as I write these words I am aware that there are indeed people who are hearing the signals and who are prepared to join hands on deck in trying to steady the ship. The captaincy however is what remains at issue.

With the arrival of the upcoming Commonwealth Heads of Government Meeting (CHOGM), Mr. Manning, instead of worrying about an embarrassment from protesting prisons officers, must show himself to be in control at the rudder. This is not a time to worry about losing face. It's gone past the stage of cosmetics and face-lifts now. We have to understand that real leadership does not depend on appearances and photo-ops, or for that matter on convenient calls to a Higher Authority while relying upon a Prophetess.

What Mr. Manning and the City Fathers and Mothers should be waking up to is the reality of that scene in the Health Centre on Espinet Street last Thursday morning. The scene is graphic and it should torture them with nightmares.

A young man is sitting with his mother awaiting medical attention; it is vaccination day so babes are in arms and children are running around. A gunman apparently is alerted by a chap inside the waiting room that the man who is wanted is there. A gunman walks in and shoots him but as the revolver falls another picks it up and puts a bullet through the back of the victim's head. An eyewitness is reported as saying that one of the gunmen trots outside and along Old St Joseph Road gun brandishing. Just so! This is what our sweet little country has come to. I lapse into dialect, me alone at the keyboard talking to the silent screen. "Is better we did stay poor - oui!"

There are two aspects for consideration and understanding. Firstly, these youths have nothing to lose. They fear neither law nor god - man or deity. There is no one it seems that they respect. We must not forget that we have an Integrity Commission that is on hold while the Government searches for a few upright men as the prophet in the Bible story had searched for five just men to save the cities of Sodom and Gomorrah.

What else is spooky! Recently, in Barrackpore, five men jump out a car - one a 17-year old, stabs a man for having just five dollars for the taking. Police shoots him in the buttock, a second is held. The others escape into the forest. What is going on here?

These youths didn't just happen. WE CREATED THEM. We can run but we can't hide. They are "we own". It does not matter what colour section of the mas' band we belong to, whichever tribe, or religion, caste or class. We provided the ground and the fertiliser that nurtured the bad seed that produced the rotten fruit that we are now reaping.

Don't tell me, "it happening all about." I know that. I know that corruption and crime are worldwide. As an AP report from Washington stated on 17th November more than $98 billion in taxpayer dollars spent by government agencies was wasted, much of it on questionable claims for tax credits and Medicare benefits, representing an increase of $26 billion from 2008. The situation is so repugnant that US President Barack Obama is expected to sign an executive order by next week aimed at cracking down on government waste and fraud. Sure it's happening everywhere but my concern is Trinidad and Tobago.

I am aware too, as Huguette Labelle, the chairman of *Transparency International*, has said that "stemming corruption requires strong oversights by Parliaments, a well-performing judiciary, independent and properly resourced audit and anti-corruption agencies, vigorous law enforcement, transparency in public budgets, revenue and aid flows."

And, I may add, a vigilant and courageous press.

But talk to me about the brashness - or is it desperation - of our youths in T&T, who like some alien creatures out of a Hollywood apocalypse film seem to be multiplying and morphing into uglier and uglier demons.

Now this increasing bravado on the part of the young and violent calls for an action that is over and above the present legal measures that are in place. We are now in the big league and therefore big league solutions must be enacted.

Two news reports last week lead the way in what we must do IF there is to be immediate resolution of the criminality and we must do a *volte face* with respect to a national attitude. Patriotism cannot be bought with a flag.

The first was a *Reuters* report that spoke of 30,000 guns being seized from the streets of Venezuela next door during police raids this year. The country has one of the world's highest murder rates. Policemen said the report used blow-torches to chop up some of shotguns and pistols. They compacted weapons including home-made pistols into a 5-ton block, said Interior Minister Tarek Al Aissami. "Here we have weapons captured in operations during 2009," he said on state television. "This act forms part of the disarmament policies that we have been promoting."

It seems we have lots in common with our neighbours apart from sharing that lucky mother lode of oil and gas. Proportionately we are right next to them with their 13,000 murders in 2007 and 6 million firearms circulating among a population of 28 million. Crunch those numbers against our 550 murders last year in a population of 1.2 million in an area of some 1,980 as against Venezuela's 352,143 square miles.

According to the report, Crime has risen under President Hugo Chavez, who has focused on poverty reduction to tackle violence in poor city neighborhoods. So in looking for our own answers we must consider WHY there seems to be a direct relationship between poverty reduction and increased violence. The common denominator as always appears to be that filthy lucre breeding desperation at the bottom end and greed at the top.

And then there was a *Reuters* report from London that a "lawmaker who expensed fine wine, car, jailed." It makes interesting and pertinent reading for those crimes decked in white collars that the Trinidad and Tobago electorate MUST address. "A former far-right British member of the European Parliament who cheated on his expense money to buy fine wine and a car was jailed on Wednesday for two years."This fraud was so blatant," said Judge Geoffrey Rivlin to the 61-year-old Tom Wise, a former representative of the UK Independence Party, "I do not believe for one moment you were disadvantaged in understanding the system or that this fraud should be seen as falling into some grey area which you might not have fully comprehended."

Wise, who represented the UKIP before becoming an independent, spent a year channeling some 40,000 pounds (US$66,080) in taxpayers' cash into a bank account he secretly controlled. He maintained a 3,000-pound "secretarial assistance allowance" he received every month was for his researcher, but paid her just 500 pounds while keeping the rest for himself, buying a car, expensive wines and paying off debts.

Is the story familiar to us? Is it something that we suspect is a practice in Trinidad and Tobago? Should it be a warning to those bright-eyed and bushy-tailed political aspirants breathless as they wait in the wings to get inside the halls of Parliament and who like Tom Wise can't wait to get their feet beneath the desk in a government position?

They should realize that Tom Wise wasn't so wise after all!

24. MOTHERS OF THE NATION

GUANGZHOU: Thursday 26th November 2009

Dear Ms. Esther Le Gendre,
It is clear that our schools and colleges have not turned out to be the halls of learning our forefathers envisaged. Free secondary education was supposed to give all the children of the nation an opportunity to make them better men and women. That, I think, was Dr. Williams's aim. But today our schools are more like war zones where teenagers kill each other as was cruelly illustrated last week when two students were knifed to death.

They were not isolated cases. The *Express* in an editorial on Tuesday 25th November that was headlined, "Bloodletting among our young" wrote, "Whenever a schoolchild is killed by another schoolchild the national reaction is shock bordering on despair. And in Trinidad and Tobago it seems to be a recurring tragedy with two schoolboys recently being knifed to death within days of each other, one 18 and the other 13. Moreover there have been others before with the most damning, perhaps, being the killing of Shaquille Roberts who, last year, was stabbed to death in his own school yard, even as his schoolmates, seeing his blood pouring out, begged him not to die."

It is clear that the present education system is not working for our children. It could be obsolete and we need, not to put up fences, but to build parallel structures of understanding, compassion and competitiveness. We need to reshape our world. Some years ago the Brazilian educator Paulo Freire said, "The ability of humans to plan and shape the world for their future needs is what separates man from animals. The oppressed majority must be taught to imagine a better way so that they can shape their future and thereby become more human."

I'm thinking metaphors these days. School is the cradle for the youngster just weaned away from the security blanket of parents. Home and school provide the four corners of the cultural box. The creature emerging from this cocoon is imprinted for better or for worse some eighteen years later as a citizen to make his or her contribution - positive or negative - to the society or to the world at large.

Let me go back 28 years. It is one of those heady tropical evenings in Trinidad and Tobago. The ONR (Organization for National Reconstruction) bandwagon is doing the unthinkable. I say unthinkable as no one had dared in 25 years to seriously challenge the incumbent PNM (People's National Movement) during which time the venerable Dr. Eric Williams had been at its helm. But it is 1981 and he is dead. George Chambers has been the anointed one to replace him by the party faithful. Baldy's boom boxes are blaring forth the warm-up to a constituency meeting in the Morvant/Laventille area. It is under somebody's rum shop on the Eastern Main Road. He dared to let it happen on his sidewalk in PNM territory!

Among the young hopefuls with Karl Hudson-Phillips on the platform is Dr. Hugh Spicer whose passionate rhetoric promises an overhaul of the medical system that is responsible for the high child mortality rate in the area. But out from the thick of the restive crowd comes a woman's belligerent voice: "It ha plenty more where dem come from!" She is responding to his statement that babies need not die because of poor health care and she is cheered by her neighbours.

I often wonder about that woman. Is she the mother who laments today that the devil has taken over the country? Or, is she the one who is afraid to identify her son's killers because she KNOWS who they are? Or, maybe she is leaving it in the hands of an overburdened God? It seems as though we have on our own hands a group of women who simply did not get it back then and who even now holds the choice - no longer is it an accident - to bring a child into the world. We're talking child-raising as being a serious business. And you, Ms. Le Gendre, as Minister of Education, have your hands full to educate not just all those mothers who have failed to bring up their children in the right way, but also the country's 14,000 teachers for whom TTUTA speaks.

We are aware, aren't we, that our teachers today are not of the same kind as our teachers of yesterday. They are not the dedicated headmasters whom we knew and under whose teaching we trembled at times. They were strict and they understood that they were role models. This reminds me of the Chinese idiom, *Ming shi chu gao tu* – it is the strict teacher that produces superior students. But the dedication was disappearing years ago. When I visited my sister-in-law in England last year, for example, she was reminiscing about her own career in teaching at St. George's College in the late sixties and she said, "I remember one of my colleagues saying, *They expect us to come to classes and teach too!* I know that we shouldn't lose our sense of humour, but it was a joke that illustrated the coming demise of sacrifice and nobility in our schools.

In her 2008 address to students, teachers and parents of the nation Ms. Le Gendre called on them "to make this an exciting year as together we face the challenges and (will) reap the rewards of our efforts. Let us take responsibility for more efficient service delivery, improve our telecommunication – including our information and communication technology – share our achievements and enhance our reputation."

Since then, that reputation becomes increasingly questionable as she struggles to find answers in an education system gone haywire. Not only is there an alarming increase in male teenaged crimes in the country but the age bar seems to be falling as the earliest teens get in on acts of criminality.

By Friday, November 20th 2009 Minister Le Gendre faced the media with answers that ranged from suspending pupils in the brawl between East and West El Dorado Secondary schools. A divider fence was to be repaired with urgency. Security guard services were increased along with more police patrols in the area.

So, okay, the good minister may console herself that things are now well in hand BUT since that date we have had TWO more school boys murdered by their peers. According to the Gyasi Gonzales report in the *Express* on 24th November, another schoolboy was knifed to death as school violence has once again reared its ugly head along the East/West corridor.

Yesterday's incident occurred in St Joseph, near Curepe, where the victim, Dillon Griffith, 18, a pupil of St Augustine Senior Comprehensive School was killed by a single stab to the chest. Only last Friday, 13-year-old Malik Hillaire, of Barataria Senior Comprehensive, was stabbed mere metres away from his Barataria home. With the knife still lodged in his chest Hillaire was taken to the Eric Williams Medical Sciences Complex where he was pronounced dead on arrival.

The *Express* was told that during the melee one of the boys handed the other a 12-inch long dagger and it was plunged it into the chest of Griffith. Two suspects - aged 17 and 18 - were taken to the St. Joseph Police Station. They were being questioned by Homicide Bureau detectives up to press time last night.

In Hillaire's case, a 15-year-old boy remains in police custody.

Scare after scare continues and so Ms. Le Gendre must understand it is NOT ALL RIGHT and things are NOT IN HAND.

I'll tell you what is blood-curdling about that gang inter-school warfare. In the Akile Simon report in the *Guardian* on 18th November, this is what we read:

Head of the Northern Division Snr. Supt. Joseph Edwards says police are doing all in their power to curb gang violence which has escalated between some students of the El Dorado West and East Secondary schools.

During a telephone interview yesterday, Edwards confirmed the fracas, saying there were incidents among students of both schools, on a daily basis. He described the latest incident as an ongoing feud among troublemakers at both schools. "We have been working with the PTA, principals, parents and all other stakeholders in order to identify the troublemakers," he said. "Students are not willing to come forward and give information on the troublemakers."

Both schools accommodate some 3,000 students. Shortly after 10 am, some of the pupils of both schools squared off in reprisal for the stabbing.

Sources said the incident stemmed from a fight between two female students from separate schools, over a PH taxi driver, who operated between the school and Caura Junction.

Speaking with the *Guardian* after their classes were dismissed, some students from the Gaza declared they did not want peace, but war, to the end. Attempts to contact the principals at both schools on the incident proved futile as several calls to the school's phones went unanswered. Several calls to the cell phones of Education Minister Esther Le Gendre and Communications Manager at the Education Ministry, Rory Subiah, also went unanswered.

Read again and again Madame Minister for each of the words above is telling. And why is there not a hot line from your office in the Ministry of Education to re-assure the nation that you people are at the nation's service?

So what is going on here? I notice that an attempt to bring together the nation to lock down the country for two days failed depending on whom on which side of the fence was speaking. But the teachers staying away from school which TTUTA (Trinidad and Tobago Unified Teachers' Association) hailed as a success makes one question the thinking behind the action. In what way does staying away from a system in crisis warrant a mark of excellence?

The TTMA's suggestion to come up with a better plan begs the question about unity and purpose? So are we Trinis serious about the state of the country? Or is it that (as I keep harping upon) the message simply does not have credible messengers?

According to TTUTA's president Rouston Job thousands of teachers across the country heeded the call to "stop and reflect" on issues affecting them as they stayed away from classes on the planned nationwide two-day shutdown by the People's Democracy yesterday. In a release, TTUTA general secretary Peter Wilson said preliminary surveys revealed 60 to 65 percent of the 14,000 teachers stayed away from classes to send a clear message that, "now is the time for citizens to intervene and demand resolution to the many vexing issues that distress our lives."

But National Parent Teachers Association (NPTA) head Zena Ramatali was not happy with the action of teachers. She said she found the teachers' decision to stay away from classes as being "very unproductive and unfair to children at this stage of the school term." She said she would like to know what teachers had to benefit since the students are the only ones who will be losing out on an education. Ramatali said while teachers stay away from classes "to reflect", she hoped those who stay away from classes regularly would reflect on living up to the expectation of becoming a better teacher. She said she was also hopeful that the two days would really bring some introspection in terms of delivering quality education.

Here we see conflict – disunity and inability to even get the story straight. Is this a healthy democracy at work or what? But let us return to the critical state of our youths' brain waves. Are we looking here at a lost generation? There was a time when errant fathers or working mothers were replaced by extended families and always...always, a solid grandmother who made ends meet to nurture one or more children deposited on her doorsteps. There was religion that proffered social and spiritual support; and there was the village. Outstanding amidst the support group was the school. The head master or head mistress and teachers were the role models and many are the memorable tales to be told.

So where do we go from here with this generation of 'lost children.'? Is there any hope for salvation? And what about their parents? Are we to write them off too as a lost cause?

They are questions that I must put to the women of the nation. I am talking about women like Mrs. Hazel Manning, Minister of Local Government, Dr Jean Ramjohn-Richards, wife of President Maxwell Richards, Education Minister Esther Le Gendre and all those women who now head government departments like Marlene Mc Donald.

vocal minister in Community Development and Gender Affairs, women in business, religious and social services, retirees, professionals especially now where they proliferate in the legal and medical institutions. I am addressing this to women like Diana Mahabir-Wyatt, Sheilah Solomon, Dr Eugenia Springer, Hazel Brown, KB and to others like Rhea Mungal and Monica Gopaul who subscribe to *JahajeeDesi* and Caribbean postings. And of course to women in the media.

Yes, I know each and everyone of you are toiling in the vineyards, but it seems to be the labours of Sisyphus. What do I in China know? But distance provides the beyond vision 20/20 to see that whatever we are doing at the moment in T&T is NOT working and while the band aids may have kept down the rates of murder and violence to 1.2 per day, the truth is that IF we are to become a better place to live like Norway and Denmark, we must find and institute new ideas....new directions. The old ones are just NOT WORKING ANYMORE and we are a nation adrift.

When are we going to understand that the old ways are irrelevant and obsolete much like in Paola Totaro's *Herald* Correspondent report? Hear this. "A damning British report has warned that the Commonwealth is out of touch and must undergo radical reform to regain relevance and clout." Well, so much for TT$235 million dollars of our taxpayers' money for the razzmatazz party about to take place to facilitate the wake of a dying if not quite dead institution that is CHOGM (Commonwealth Heads of Government Meeting) in Port of Spain.

Women have now come into their own as numerically we now hold more key or leadership positions than before. At this time in our history when we face failed systems that obviously continue to churn out desperation at the bottom and greed at the top we must look for a revolutionary turn about in leadership. It must NOT be a replacement of what we are casting out, but a genuine new direction in responsibility and a new spirituality for the nation.

For us women, it is a lesson that applies to most places in the world where we women are turning out sissified men or else those who would kill to prove an illusion of manhood. It is a lesson that I keep in focus here in male-centric China. We women are responsible for the quality of our men - sons and daughters. *JahajeeDesi*'s has just posted Andre Bagoo's "Carnival" published in *Boston Review* that reflects our phenomena.

It is difficult to talk meaningful change to Minister Le Gendre as she may be entrapped in a system that is obsolete and vision-less. But it is a message that is necessary to repeat and to remind ourselves that from the moment (and even before) a new life lands onto a shared hospital bed it is imprinted with stamps of hardship and want. A catch-arse environment speaks to the young brain of rejection and nihilism that is even more so when the mother takes him 'home' from the hospital ward. Is there someone to advise that names like 'Hell's Yard' or even the implication of 'Sea Lots" are negative stimuli? Can a child feel good about himself with such an address to write down in class? And what about the nicknames allowed on that child – names like "Lucifer" and "Rape Man" can only do more harm than good in school yards recognized as "The Gaza" and "The Gully".

There are two areas that can be dealt with at a later date as we look back on Paulo Freire. One is the concept of teacher-student / parent-child teaching each other; the second is the concept that 'authoritarianism' may have to accommodate 'humility' in the learning exchange. This is difficult for us in T&T where familiarity breeds contempt and tribes persist comfortably in meaningless *vieux causer*. Old talk and one-upmanship.

And so the task is Herculean for Ms. Le Gendre and the rest of us who care about our nation. We have no choice but to put heads together WITH HER and work for the goal of making the only box that we have a better place for all the tribal members.

Well, can we? There is nothing wrong about this ambition but public servants must understand that serving the public calls for humility, self-sacrifice, passion and an appreciation of the real meaning of the word patriotism.

There is no room for arrogance.

25. OF BLACK GOLD AND BEAUTIFUL WOMEN

GUANGZHOU: Thursday 3rd December 2009

I had been warned. "You don't know enough about Esther Le Gendre," he said to me last week. "You are not familiar with her work as you are with the work of Mr. Manning and Mr. Panday. She is a newcomer in our national politics and she could be a hindrance and not a help in bringing about changes in our education system. You are going to be easy on her and draw the wrath of people who work with her and are familiar with her timidity or her arrogance." And it does appear that he was right.

My call on Mothers of the Nation to put heads together with Minister of Education Esther Le Gendre last week stoked the fires of fury in a number of Trinidadians who have been frustrated by the lady minister's lack of support for indigenous works. Ms. KB, for example, criticized my naïve generosity. She blazed against Ms. Le Gendre's insensitivity to projects directed to alleviate the mess at the bottom of the society. Her rage was aimed in particular at the minister's attitude toward the "black and ugly" wretched of the land while "blue-eyed white men" were courted, wined and dined and paid large sums of money for reports that were neither original nor perceptive of the special problems we face in Trinidad and Tobago.

This is not a racial thing. It is calling a spade a spade and not a garden implement. But the intensity of their anger made me think once more of our uniqueness. It is heartening to know that we must be the only place in the world that is so comfortable with racial epithets. We know too how to laugh at ourselves and at others so easily! Mind you, Ms. B and the others were not laughing.

By the way, this reminds me of another email, one I received from Shivana Dipnarine in response to my comments on the current behaviour in our schools, the shocking murderous attacks on students. "These things," wrote Ms. Dipnarine, "do not happen in the Denominational Schools!!!! The Denominational schools do have their challenges and they are certainly not squeaky clean but they do not have this killing madness!! Why? Most of those denominational Schools are Indian and they win the vast majority of scholarships every year!!!"

When we look at the statistics and the results of national examinations, it is easy to think that Ms. Dipnarine's protest is justified. And I am sure that the teachers in other denominational schools have the same kind of pride and satisfaction that their students are doing fine. The problem is they live in the same world as the students in government schools, which appear to be the incubators of teenage crime. My point is, they cannot be smug and unconcerned and the adage my grandmother used to say, "If your neighbour's house is on fire, throw water on your own," comes to mind.

I remember something else. Sir Hugh Wooding once said it was the black man's ability to laugh at himself that saved him from the humiliations he suffered in slavery. And in our calypsos and picong, we show year after year that we can make a joke of race most of the time. I am sure that it is this Trinidadian sense of humour that has saved us from racial conflict in the past. This ease in talking about race, I am sure, must have impressed our Commonwealth visitors last week.

And then I read Vashty Maharaj's report in Sunday's *Newsday* (29th November 2009) on what she says is a marginalization of the Indian community. This came two days after a *Newsday* interview with Manikant Thakur, a radio journalist with *All India Radio News* Service Division in New Delhi, which validated our little country's success with racial harmony. Said Mr. Thakur, "This is my first time and experience here in Trinidad and I found the country to be great with all the different races... Everyone here of all different races lives in such harmony and peace which is really great."

The wonder is that there are so many people in Trinidad and Tobago who believe that discrimination could be not only happening TODAY and they think that tribal divisions seem to be intensifying as yet another cause for alarm in sweet T&T. But the truth is that I do feel irritated when the face of T&T is promoted to the world as a "one-dimensional" reflection of Africa. I guess there are Trinidadians who could be touchy about this. But where do we put the blame? On the Government or on the Opposition?

Suzanne Mills on Friday 27th November 2009 had already published her article, "Manning, the most disliked person in town," and proceeded to ask the Prime Minister if he likes what he feels? – a question aimed at his luxurious, I think, lifestyle. There is the feeling that Mr. Manning, as Captain of this drifting ship, SS Trinidad and Tobago, along with Ms. Le Gendre, as one of his first mates, have been ignoring the crew and have a lot to answer for. Daily more and more, there are accusations of neglect and discrimination.

So while all the bowing and curtseying to the visiting Queen Elizabeth II and her princely consort was going on back home in T&T last week, I was taking questions from wide-eyed students in a Chinese classroom about my paradise islands and the lavish spending on yet another international meeting. I also wondered if the good Queen remembered during the speeches and the dinners, the calypso that the Mighty Sparrow had sung years ago about the strange Briton who had climbed into her Buckingham Palace bedroom.

My students were curious about what was taking place in a hitherto unknown corner of the globe, known to them only because of Walt Disney's fantasy with Johnny Depp in *Pirates of the Caribbean*. They were curious too about an education system and a democracy that have allowed a miniscule population to let things get so out of hand.

After all, we are not talking about the classrooms of sixty-plus kids that they are about to face! Neither are we talking here about an old-fashioned education system that is based on Confucian principles set in a socialist system. But they are not living in the past and China is not today the backward country that American and European media tend to portray with their stereotyping of peasants and factory workers and the prevailing myth that the majority of Chinese work for US$1 a day, or a month. I cannot remember which now. I am so tired with this slander.

And oh! Spare me the did-you-eat-dog idiocy.

These students are from rural towns and villages but many of them have won scholarships to the city. They attend a Provincial College for teacher training during which time they receive a 5-year tutoring in Education as English majors. They know why they are in college and they make every good use of modern-day technology. Their sights are on making the 21st Century the century of China. They are aware of the problems but they are not afraid.

Last week in preparation for a weekend visit to Wuhan on the Yangtze River, I asked the students in my Oral English class to work in groups to come up with information about China they would provide a visitor. After ten minutes they were able to present information about the weather, clothes, food, places of interest and such details as arrival/departure, internal travel and accommodation costs. They had cell phones and electronic dictionaries in hand with ready call numbers and credit card facilities. There was no need for textbooks or the library or even the classroom Internet.

Yahoo by chance carried on that day the report that American students are resorting to more mobile phone use in the classroom! But China has the largest number of cell-phone users and the largest number of people on the Internet. We are almost in Isaac Asimov's classroom in the year 2155. In his essay on the classroom of the future, the 11-year-old Margie writes in her diary on the page headed May 17, "Today Tommy found a real book!" Sometimes in my classrooms I could feel it is happening already.

Later that day there was the chance to talk to my writing class about the women vs. men relationship that is a favourite topic of mine as I see it at the heart of the present problems afflicting the planet. And just as I was about to defend the system of "freedoms" with a personal little encouraging adage that it means discipline and respect - lo and behold - up popped on the overhead screen the on-line *Newsday* report on 27th November 2009 by Sean Douglas.

We read that Prime Minister Patrick Manning was at the first dinner for Commonwealth dignitaries attending the Caribbean Heads of Government Meeting and once more he says something that left me with a queasy feeling in my chest. I guess after you have spent millions of dollars to host the CHOGM there isn't anything interesting to tell your guests. This was Mr. Douglas' report:

Highlighting the attractions of Trinidad and Tobago to his guests, Manning said the country produces 700,000 barrels of oil, assists its Caricom neighbours with a Petroleum Fund, and has some of the world's most beautiful women within its mix of ethnic groups.

It's great to know that our Prime Minister thinks that Trini women are among the most beautiful ethnic mix in the world, but, geeze! was it the forum to say this and to show off our women with commodities like oil and gas and the technology of the recently built National Academy of Performing Arts! The Prime Minister actually announced then that it cost more than the Sydney Opera House, the Shanghai Concert Hall and the Beijing National Theatre!

So much pride!

Mr. Manning's surprising tribute to our women, mothers and daughters, came with the announcement that the country faces a $7.8 billion dollar budget deficit. There was a $7.5 billion deficit in last year's $45 billion budget but said Mr. Manning, the Government was not unduly worried about the deficit. Do you remember that ditty we used to sing? The king is in his parlour counting all his money, the queen is in her chamber eating bread and honey? Is that what is going on nowadays in St. Ann's?

There is more and I am quoting still the Douglas report. Mr. Manning said, wrote Mr. Douglas that the US credit ratings agency, Standard and Poor's, recently upgraded the status of Trinidad and Tobago, even amid the global financial crisis. He boasted that this country had three weeks ago taken possession of "one of the most advanced opera houses in the world" as he referred to the National Academy for the Performing Arts (NAPA), where the CHOGM opening ceremony was held.

Opera Houses! Ay, Mama Mia!

That piece of our news was meant to provoke the students into considering their own positions as they get ready to step out into their own society. They've got to ask question and must be unafraid to seek answers.

I say to them that the responsibility for turning out the large numbers of problem or no-problem children is our business. It is evidenced from the reports of those graduate teachers who return to visit and who imply that we must examine carefully the source of the problems as they relate to home, school and society. They say that they no longer like teaching. The students are becoming more 'naughty', which in Trinidad and Tobago translates into 'unmanageable'.

The truth is I love teaching and it probably explains why one year added up to twelve in such a happy environment where learning so easily becomes a two-way exchange. The discussion today is to consider whether we are turning out boy children who are too softened by the attention that we bestow upon them or else they become so arrogant that they go to extremes to prove their manhood. What do they think?

They turn to the text where a student has written a model paper about "Three types of Parents". They fall into categories of being the monarch, the servant or the friend types. I do a quick self-examination on where I/we may have helped or failed our own children. Were we intolerant, autocratic, and self-centred? Or, were we soft, good-natured and easy-going? Or were we the writer's ideal among parents – those who treat their children as good friends discussing their interests and listening attentively to their thinking?

One thing leads to another and pretty soon there is a question that stumps me as Lei Feng asks: "So who do you think is a real man?" I put the question on hold.

It is distracting me from what I really want to talk about and that is the two-way exchange as Paulo Freire so marvelously puts it in his treatise on education. Listen to what he has to say on the goals of education: Our relationship with the learners demands that we respect them and demands equally that we be aware of the concrete conditions of their world, the conditions that shape them. To try to know the reality that our students live is a task that the educational practice imposes on us. Without this, we have no access to the way they think, so only with great difficulty can we perceive what and how they know. There are no themes or values of which one cannot speak, no areas in which one must be silent. We can talk about everything, and we can give testimony about everything.

Let me say this in another way, as John Lyons of *2001 New Foundations* interpreted for us: Education should raise the awareness of the students so that they become subjects, rather than objects, of the world. This is done by teaching students to think democratically and to continually question and make meaning from (critically view) everything they learn.

What Freire said and what Lyons said can be condensed into one word – RESPECT. It is applicable in and out of the classroom, in the home or in the halls of government. Everywhere. But sometimes it is not possible for Prime Ministers and Ministers of Education to know this.

"Wait," I said, as he was about to leave.

"What is it now?"

"Did you know Esther Le Gendre?"

"I have a vague memory of her. I think she was somewhere in media but I don't recall it clearly."

"Could you have helped me more?"

"No. I think that Ms. B has done a good job of telling you what kind of person our Education Minister is."

26. OH GAWD! DE CHILDREN...

GUANGZHOU: Thursday 10th December 2009

It was a heart-wrenching cry from the gut of Beryl McBurnie. She used to sit in her living room that doubled as an auditorium in her Panka Street home and watch the children go by. They were multicolored – little Black ones; little Indian Ones; little Mixed ones; and, to satisfy Anthony Milne's appeal for inclusion of the European presence, there were little White ones.

These kids you see were from the St James Secondary School in the historic area of St James/Mucurapo, a catchment area for all the tribes that is the setting for our VS Naipaul's *Miguel Street*. They were about 14 - early teens - and their speech and attitude already in the mid-nineties were similar to those mid-teens we watched with amazement as they swaggered up Frederick Street on Panorama weekends from the four corners of the island. Our high tech *Caribbean Basin Exhibit* with first-ever touch screen computers was farthest from their minds.

For those who had the privilege of knowing Ms. McBurnie, she was a True Trini whose life was dedicated to a concern for the betterment of her world and that was Trinidad and Tobago. The afternoon I visited her she was watching the children through her wrought-ironed windows as they moved against the grey-washed background of the Mucurapo Cemetery walls. She groaned, "Oh Gawd! De Children!" Her face scrunched up (in sadness or was it fear?) and she gestured with typical Belle Dame drama turning to fix her eyes on mine speaking silent words. An unfinished sentence dangled in mid-air. I've often wondered - were those words of pity or horror... or both?

In hindsight one is saddened at the lost opportunity in pursuing what is clearly now a prophetic call - a warning that something horrific was about to possess the souls of our children. In life one thinks there is always time, so the rest of her sentence is lost. I never returned to question her further. In China I read that in 2000 she had to leave her beloved children behind.

But the children of Ms. McBurnie and Dr. Eric Williams persist and continue to present the huge problems that she foresaw. Wherever those two compatriots are they must be aware that we do not hold the monopoly on problem children. In tandem with our turning point which could easily be put at that July 27th 1990 when an independent Trinidad and Tobago really lost its innocence, its freedom - a topic to which we will return - there was an even more ominous pandemic that would reach our backwaters. It took the form of an open season on a new information technology. Communicating as we knew it was becoming obsolete.

Today not only is there a whole lot of demons possessing and destroying the souls of so many of our youth in T&T but just take a look at youth elsewhere on our planet.

Last week gave new meaning to a new word that is "Schoolies." They are the 'lost children' of the nineties who according to brand new Yahoo7 links from Down Under report that it is not only an "innocent" sun, sea and sand bash for school leavers in Australia. It is big business that attracts teenagers to party like crazy ultimately leading to the extremes of drugs, booze and gang rape as reported this year. Queensland's Schoolies 2009 seem to have out performed the American Spring Break with its own unparalleled brand of hedonism for the young.

As if that was not enough to make me want to start a website advocating the banning of human conception indefinitely, there was yet another word to join the futuristic world of lexicon. It was "sext' like in "text". The relationship of course is intrinsic or implicit as it means... well... let me allow Nick McCallum to explain it in his November 25th article titled "Sext up" He says it more originally:

> Call me old fashioned, call me an old fart, but this is a 'new age digi-drama' I simply don't get. I don't understand it. I can't comprehend it.
> It's 'sexting'.

It's the apparently common practice among teenagers of taking an explicitly private photo of yourself on your mobile phone and sending it to your boyfriend or girlfriend. No prizes for figuring out what happens when the relationship goes sour. Out of spite or revenge, the photo hits cyberspace and is everywhere, seen by everyone... at the very least severely embarrassing the person involved, at the worst tearing apart his or her life, destroying reputations and relationships forever.

I'd heard of this happening back home among school kids with cell phones but I'd dismissed it as a "Nah man! Somebody wants to *mauvaise langue* my sweet T&T again." And then...guess what? One of our own beautiful female icons exposes not only her feet of clay but...

And then there was that marvellous paragon of virtuous American manhood THE Tiger Woods in whose mouth the proverbial butter seems unable to melt and who even has had a church named in his honour. All that is now dishonoured with one little touch of the hi-tech. button that recorded his shenanigans, not to mention the spoofs that keep a-twittering.

Now tell me this - I put it to my class last week - "Why would anyone want to show off in video their intimate love-making and private body parts to anyone else...period?" I elaborate a bit more..."in one case there are three people tumbling around in search of orgasms ...so who else should care?" It's an opportunity to introduce them to the French *ménage à trois*. I direct it to one of the few boys in the class. Chen Yue replies: "Maybe they sell it for money?" But this is the beyond-comprehension part. "No!" I tell him "there's no money here."

But Chen ought to know, for according to a Canadian researcher all men watch porn videos. Professor Simon Louis Lajeunesse, reported this week (*AFP* December 4) that All men watch pornographic videos but it does not impact on their sexual habits or their relationships with women.

Really? I want to ask him? But this follows and I wonder how many of us teachers are aware that boys may seem to mature AFTER the girls cross into puberty at around 11-13 but Lajeunesse's study shows that men search out pornography that relates to their earliest sexual fantasies, generally conceived at age 12 at the onset of puberty. They are not looking for new tricks to show off. All men watch porn, and it is not bad for them.

Some students suggest that it is a peer group thing but as I re-read Nick McCallum on *Yahoo7 News*, there is the harking back to that other pandemic of Information Technology that crept into the early nineties. And here he quotes a film writer Jamie Roberts who has made a film directed to youths to counteract what has become a full-blown madness:

"Unfortunately we have this, I guess, mentality that anything goes with technology and that our morals and values have gone out the window."

I agree whole heartedly and join McCallum in saying that he's right and that's a very ominous sign for the future. It means it's a major problem our entire community must stomp on. Now.

This reminds me that last week brought a valuable response from Valerie Mahabir. It linked with McCallum's 7 News report in that here was another concerned citizen looking for answers to the disturbing question of what to do with our youth. Each comes from opposite points of the globe.

As a retired government secondary school teacher Ms. Mahabir quoted one of the cases in which a suspended student was re-admitted after his parents obtained a letter from Ministry of Education. He had deliberately damaged a door at school and warned by the principal not to return to school until the door was replaced at his family's expense. The principal had no choice but to comply. The door was replaced at the school's expense.

This bit of news is therefore timely to Akile Simon's *Guardian* 7th December report that more than 1,000 students have been suspended in the last five years from schools in St Patrick County. The first response submitted by: Ah Trini Too on 7 December 2009 - 2:51 a.m. is right on target with: *Here's an idea.....also make parents accountable for their children's inappropriate actions.*

We will address Ah Trini Too's response along with new interesting feedback that is coming out from inside the belly of the school system itself. And just in case readers may think that the "privileged schools" are exempt from this kind of waywardness, there are several reports that I will refer to at a future date.

Ms. Mahabir was able to share several other interesting points as her contribution to this series. But, I wonder, is her concern being tapped into as valuable material in planning for the future?

She makes the point that the Abu Bakr attempted coup in 1990 was the Pandora's Box that we botched in fixing and put in denial and which up to today is plaguing us as we have not got to the root of that cancer that struck on that afternoon of 27th July. She puts it eloquently: *The children observed authority humiliated and set about their own re-enactment in the classroom.*

I repeat. Is her concern along with others being teleconferenced with the nation and is there open discussion to distill the valuable bits so as to begin correcting the errors of the past? One thing more. It is a good example of government's insensitivity to details of the people's needs.

Ms. Mahabir continues: As early as the 1970s when the existing system was in the planning stages the physical layout of the schools with the staff rooms isolated from the students was predicted that it could "ultimately lead to gang violence." Dr. Selwyn Ryan made mention of it in a recent lecture she said. The report was shelved in the interest of political expediency and a scapegoat was made of the teachers. On the other hand, in one "prestige" school, the staff room is so located that teachers are still able to keep an eye on the children even when classes are in recess.

How much longer can we continue with this don't care attitude on the part of a blinkered government, an opposition splintered and adverse to tribal sharing and which could provide viable option?... And then there's the citizenry, groups in the country that feel powerless? And afraid.

My sister and friends continue to warn me. "You coming back, but don't interfere with de government." I wonder what Ms. Diana Mahabir-Wyatt would say about their warning.

But Ms. McBurnie's incomplete sentence still hangs in mid-air to haunt and taunt that there is a lot of unfinished work still to be done.

27. WHAT PEACE ON EARTH?

GUANGZHOU: Thursday 17th December 2009

Sorry folks, but this year I really can't enjoy the black cake I have tried to make once more with imported Bacardi White rum. It approaches RMB 200 (about the same in TT$) per bottle at times. Cherry Brandy? No problem. There are a zillion varieties available lined up with Great Wall wine labels on shelves.

Let's scratch pastelles. Although you may have heard those shrieks of delight when I discovered my first banana clump on campus in 1998, I've never been able to make a good pastelle outside of home base though. And even then no following of Mama's *cocoa 'paignol* rituals in preparing the Christmas delight came close to the freshly ground corn somehow called 'mas' at that time. This was to be the delicate envelope for the seasoned minced meat within, which tied up like a culinary gift wrap in banana leaves, was then steam-boiled in salt-kine brine.

I track down that word which must have Spanish origin and guess what? According to *GourmetSleuth.com* "Masa" is the Mexican word for "dough". It refers to the corn dough used to make tortillas, tamales, as well as other traditional Mexican dishes.

What incredible linkages! Probably it is the same in Venezuela from whence came the peon ancestry!

Our mother collected the moist fist-sized balls somewhere in a barrack yard on George Street. That began the round of shopping for the right cuts of fatty pork, lean pork and beef all to be hand ground into a mouth-watering minced-meat filling seasoned with lots of hot pepper, chives, thyme and other backyard grown herbs like *shadon beni*. It is a kind of cilantro known by the Indian name of *bhandhania*. The Central Market was then located on Charlotte Street.

My efforts (despite help from the *Naparima Girls' High School Cook Book*) consistently produce a tough outer casing that never failed to attract the question from my family members: "Oh! Is that paime?" This is in reference to a heavy corn savoury that we grew up with. It was encased in banana leaves and was steamed likewise.

The *poncha crema* this year is missing its generous squirts of Angostura Bitters, no thanks to the accounting shenanigans at that once proud Siegert institution and keeper of its family secrets on the Eastern Main Road in Laventille. The absence of *poncha crema* this year is compensated for only by the ginger beer that is overdosed with a thick cinnamon bark that has to be a distant cousin of the Haitian mauby bark.

That and the cloves and Xinjiang raisins with dried Chinese dates are the additives and, believe me, the week-old brew turns out really quite good. Its golden colour looks like ginger beer, the slightly syrupy flavour with definite sting tastes like ginger beer and a good fizz builds up with time. It even smells like ginger beer. It's Trini ginger beer all right!

This reminds me that the first time I ever tried out ginger beer as a young bride in Trincity. The bottled stuff exploded with a series of staccato pops in the middle of the night. If that were to happen now, to some young bride in any of the suburbs of Port of Spain, it would surely be cause for several heart attacks!

This year the annual pilgrimage to the neighbourhood wet market however, was bittersweet with thoughts of home. Diasporean nostalgia is at work.

It gets in the way of the usual picking around the plump, green ginger piled high on the concrete counter. It's not called wet market for joke as everything here is freshly green and constantly showered unlike the delicate misting from overhead displays at the modern supermarkets. Chinese people believe that the fresher the healthier. The marketplace is an enjoyable experience and reflects the soul of a country. It is the reason why I often took guests with me to the POS Central Market or to Tunapuna or to Chaguanas on a weekend.

Still curious about how a Trini manages to survive Christmas in China? Well... there was that one time that is worthy of sharing with my one or two *JahajeeDesi* readers. In order to impress on the students that the Christmas table back home is a serious challenge to their Spring Festival overload, we undertook to invite whomsoever we met to one of the five parties that were evolving annually. As in Trinidad word gets around and pretty soon the fetes were becoming an institution. A true Trini REGARDLESS OF COST must carry the flag of celebration all the way, right?

It is We Trini, not the French, who invented true bacchanal. Agreed?

Why five parties? Well there was the college leadership to satiate, and there were members of the foreign teachers' fraternity, then there were the English major classes that had to be split into three evenings that took us into the western style Old Year/New Year's bash.

On the very first celebration I managed to communicate with Fei, the Canteen head cook, to include my order on his wet market daily shopping list. The arrival of his motor bike and his loaded side carts assured me that all was in place for the big West Indian Christmas Feast.

I will not bore you with details except to say that because the Chinese are not into western-type ovens, (the cavernous ones more designed for hops bread -- which incidentally they introduced to T&T) all the black cake was reduced to German bundt cake size. It reminded me of *My Big Fat Greek Wedding* when Toula Portokalos' family saw her mother-in-law-to-be proffering her little German home-made cake at their first inter-family gathering.

It still beats me how those legs of pork I ordered could translate into a multitude of baby pigs' knuckles that defied the original intention of being sliced into ham. It was meant to accompany the hops bread! But Chinese is not easy. Nor is English as they remind me. Much gets lost in translation.

This week is a time for me to reflect too on the traditional greetings that were delightful family trips with old friends Mikey and Mary Mendez and their brood to photograph quaint scenes in the Trinidad countryside, or else capture the reddest reds of the hibiscus or poinsettia to print and send off as Christmas cards. Time was too when I had sketched a family seated around a table with the message: A family that prays together stays together. The electronic greeting cards were fun later on and absorbed some of my time in diligently selecting and sending off the appropriate ones to family and friends.

This year the cheery scenes of animation and fun are no longer funny and fall flat on an old brain that registers reality of what is taking place on an earth that is far removed from that stable in Bethlehem. The understanding of its original celebration that was the birth of a child - symbol of peace, innocence and goodwill is dwindling. It's like trying to find a four-year old who believes in Santa Claus.

My Cyber Mate thinks that I'm becoming too melancholy and a party-pooper burdened with the woes of an unfixable world. She sends some "solid words from Colin Powell" as she thinks I'm in need of the power of positive thinking. The advice - words that amount to 'soaring with the eagles, rather than gobbling with the turkeys' - is jaded.

I'm restless. I want something new to excite me. I tell him.

"Thinking of home again?" he asks.

"It's difficult not to." I reply, as waves of nostalgia flood me with the jingle bells and red-capped waitresses moving around the tables at the neighbourhood Pizza Hut. "Oh Little Town of Bethlehem" is being piped over the mall speakers. It competes with 'Silent Night" "Jingle Bells" and "Mamacita" from in-house audios. The mall itself is a-glitter with 'Christmas Father' and fir trees with baubles.

Who would think that you would hear "Oh come let us adore Him... Christ the King" in this "godless" society? But the Chinese are curious people. The first time I heard the carol was when I was aboard a domestic flight somewhere over China. I swore there must have been a *guailo* pilot in the cockpit but no - this was a CAAC flight! The next time we were to hear it was at campus noon break when on a sunny day in May the airwaves were broadcasting the sweet crooning of Perry Como's "Oh come let us adore Him..... Christ the King."

Christmas in China is not a novelty. The missionaries in their enthusiasm to convert heathens and garner heavenly merit with the number of souls saved had long brought the good word to the East. After the demise of the Three Wise Men, countless numbers were to head toward the lands of the rising sun in a bid to save the world.

If the Chinese are even now still suspicious of foreigners they have every reason to be. This religious crusade from the West wanting to save the world (and in particular the Chinese) has been going on for a long time. Historians say that as early as the 4th century evangelization took the form of one Assyrian Christian missionary named Nestorius. His zealous disciples resulted in Tang Emperor Wu Zong persecuting the converts with the adoption of ant-religious measures in AD 845. (*Christian Missionaries in China on line*)

One Christmas I decided to accompany my Hong Kong *laoxiang* home mates to the French gothic-styled

Sacred Heart Cathedral known as Stone House or *Sec Saat* by the natives. Its story is worth telling. It is a magnificent structure in old Canton, the district that the European occupiers seized on the Pearl River as a convenient trading site. Congregations at Mass now are heavily represented by such resident communities as the Filipinos and Africans along with the Europeans. Yes. I'm talking about INSIDE mainland.

As the story goes during the British occupation in 1846 Emperor Daoguang promised compensation for churches and property destroyed during the Second Opium War. The site was originally the residence of Ye Mingchen Viceroy of Guangdong and Guangxi. The residence was completely destroyed and the Viceroy captured by the British.

Are you reading?

By 1861 the agreement signed by the Qing government gave the Société des Missions Etrangères de Paris the rights to the land. Watch the weakness of the Qing leadership at work here. There is so much more to tell and we have not even got to the part about the lucrative Opium business.

History can be so enlightening!

Information reveals that three years later the foundation stone was laid on June 18th 1863, the Feast of the Sacred Heart. Money came from Catholics in France and Bishop Philippe François Zéphirin Guillemin first vicar apostolic of Guangdong was in charge. French architect Nancéen Léon Vautrin designed the cathedral with its neo-Gothic design.

Wikipedia has been helpful here as it took a while to unearth who indeed was the architect.

While traveling around China what has been most fascinating for me is the degree to which foreign occupiers arrived, plunked down their flags in the name of that innocent child born in a cold, mangy stable and proceeded to build monuments to themselves. Incredible how some things just don't change!

"What are you thinking about now?" he asks. "Peace on earth?"

"I am thinking of the sham of it all. The Nobel 'Peace' Prizes; the 'Pommecythere' National Awards; Opera Houses; Walls that provide an illusion of safety and the solution to students' loss of hope."

Do you know, I say, that the Qing puppet Emperor Xianfeng in his decree of approval for the Gothic Cathedral, wrote: "From now on, war should be stopped and peace be sincerely kept forever". He spoke of war and peace even as he was signing over the people's birthright into foreign hands.

Rhona Baptiste in Beijing

28. AND GOODWILL TO ALL MEN!

BEIJING: Thursday 24th December 2009

The Christmas message from that Child in Bethlehem is not an easy one. You must love your neighbour as yourself; find peace upon this tormented planet and you are expected to bestow your own goodwill upon fellow men. At least so goes the story. It was about 'the army of angels' who appeared in the heavens to help the Angel of the Lord deliver his message of Jesus' birth to shepherds tending their flock on that wintry night somewhere in the Middle East.

During this past week of Advent when most of the Christian world was preparing to celebrate the birth of Christ it has been most interesting to watch the *JahajeeDesi* message board light up with another promise of things to come.

The online news reports were a bit livelier with coverage of the Trinidad and Tobago electoral battle within the UNC (United National Congress) opposition ranks where it is time for party members to elect a new leader. There are comments too on Dr. Selwyn Ryan's polls that if we are to be guided by stats reveal some intriguing feedback from the population.

I've always thought that polls are like legal defense having one thing in common. You can always find what you want to support your argument. Whatever the means the end can always be justified. But for those for whom the bells were tolling the good Professor has come back nicely with a defense of his own titled: "Politics and parties...and politics" in the *Sunday Express* on 20th December.

These are his opening words: "The polls that I have done over the years in my own name or as *St Augustine Research Associates* (SARA) have always been the bane of controversy, much of it unjustified.

"Perhaps one reason for this is that they have never been particularly preoccupied with the question of who will win the elections or with the number of seats which the parties would get. What we also saw were many dissatisfied, angry, depressed and confused PNM and UNC supporters adrift and looking for a political resting place. Many want to switch, but they cannot readily cross over to the third way party, COP, since the act of voting is for many a tribal event which involves extended families and members of bonded communities.

"The poll has been attacked by both PNM and UNC spokesmen, though more loudly by the PNM. As indicated above, the SARA polls and its successors have been bitterly attacked by political leaders and party supporters on all sides of the political fence for the past 33 years."

Vying for attention was another piece on the same date titled: "Backing Bas ...or Ramesh" by Mr. Raffique Shah, on Sunday, 20th December. These are his words: "I am backing Basdeo Panday for leadership of the UNC in the upcoming party elections. I have taken this decision, not after long and hard examination of the issues at stake, or any analysis of the future of UNC, but purely because Bas is a man. And this country of warped minds where people are whimsical in their outlooks, man must back man."

"Uh huh!" I thought, here we go again. The male/female battle is now engaged. It has now become the parasitic twin to ride the back of the black/indian one.

After excusing himself as did Professor Ryan from any perceived political alliances, he exposes the real reason for his stance. This is what he says: "I am backing him because I am blasted vex. Vex because suddenly all kinds of women - those who hate the UNC, most of them diehard PNMites or 'nowhereians' like me, are crawling out of their holes to support Kamla Persad-Bissessar."

He continues: "What's their reasoning? She is a woman. Nothing more. 'Her time has come,' several of them are quoted as saying of their decision to support Kamla. 'What we need are more women in leadership positions,' another chimes. And this gem from yet another female leader: 'It's time a woman leads us into the next century!'"

T&T's seasonal Politics of Race and now Gender has begun. It is open season to show our real colours and watch bigotry and sophistry at work, but let's get into that another time.

Anyway what the Ryan polls say BEFORE Ms. Persad-Bissessar's announcement is especially fascinating. According to the Selwyn Ryan poll in the *Express* on Monday 14th December on the coalition of the COP and the UNC, there was scarcely a unity of choice:

"When asked to indicate whom they would wish to see prevail in the leadership contest for the UNC, Panday or one or other of the dissident so-called 'RamJack' faction, which includes, inter alia, Messrs. Jack Warner, Ramesh Maharaj, or Winston Peters, Warner was the choice of 30 per cent, Panday 14 per cent, Maharaj 11 per cent and Peters 2 per cent. Close to half the sample, (44 per cent) did not express a preference.

"It is, however, interesting to note that Panday only received 19 per cent of the votes of those who were Indian, as compared with Warner's 32 per cent. He, however, did better than Maharaj, who got 14 per cent.

"In an experiment intended to pit potential candidates against one another in 'playoff' groups, we asked respondents to indicate their choices if they were limited to the given groupings. The responses for the respective groups were as follows:

"Patrick Manning does very poorly against Keith Rowley who leads him by about 24 percentage points in the 'playoffs'... and by 6 per cent when all candidates are included ...Manning also does poorly among Indo-Trinidadians. Only 6 per cent endorse him compared to 22 per cent of the Afro-Trinis.

"The second observation is that Winston Dookeran is favoured over Panday... When this particular finding is disaggregated by race, Dookeran remains favoured over Panday. He also trumps Persad-Bissessar... Maharaj is an 'also ran'... Persad-Bissessar is also leading Panday in the national stakes.

"Another observation is that Manning would be in trouble if he were to come up against a united opposition that excludes Panday...

"The final observation is that when all the 'wannabes' fly the gate, Rowley is the odds on favourite with Dookeran in second place, and Manning in third place, just barely ahead of Persad-Bissessar.

"We must, however, bear in mind that these hypothetical popularity stakes do not tell us anything about who will win an election since elections in Trinidad and Tobago are not conducted on the basis of proportional representation or run offs. We should also bear in mind that the various performances vary depending on who is in or out of the hypothetical 'play off' group."

It was no surprise therefore that hottest on the cyber links was the declaration of Ms. Kamla Persad-Bissessar to contest the January 2010 UNC elections for the position of Party Leader. It turns on end the stakes and subsequent 'play off groups' alignments of the Ryan findings above. It is with interest therefore that one examines the contributions of individuals on this wonderfully open and accessible technology and to follow their lines of arguments that support one or the other position.

What the debate comes down to is, should all go well for her? Can she, a woman, competently fix the Republic of Trinidad and Tobago?

First in consideration is that she must first win her party leadership which means a hot battle with the incumbent Basdeo Panday, iconic leader of the party, and Ramesh Lawrence Maharaj, a contender for the coveted position.

Will either be satisfied to play second fiddle in the position of Queen Consort? Human nature says maybe not and will test the political maturity of unsuccessful men in both contending parties such as we see in places where women have succeeded as their country's top leader. I am thinking here of Indira Gandhi, Eugenia Charles, Janet Jagan, Margaret Thatcher, Gloria Macapagal-Arroyo and Aung San Suu Kyi, just to mention a few. How did they interact with their men who surrounded them?

Secondly, should she make it past the first post in leading the Opposition UNC, can she provide whatever it will take to win over the marginal opposition numbers from COP (Congress of the People) and NJAC (National Joint Action Committee); (NAR) National Alliance for Reconstruction, Tobago Organization of the People, and other fledgling parties and fence-sitters to support a party that makes no bones about its ethnicity?

There will be some supporters of the PNM mature enough to give her a vote of confidence in place of Dr. Keith Rowley the hottest contender for the PNM leadership. Those are the ones who understand the freedom of the democratic process to vote for the best person to speak for them. These people are the ones who are confident enough and FREE enough to chose whether or not it is all right to 'dead ah PNM' and still remain a loyal 'Trini to de bone'.

Thirdly, what IS the 'whatever-it-will-take'?

Let's examine this whatever-ness.

What is necessary is an understanding of the fact of T&T's racial politics. We must understand as well the absolute necessity for a change of spirit toward Nationhood; that is WE ARE ONE PEOPLE. If we understand this everything else will follow.

But Kamla Persad-Bissessar should know. She is a veteran politician and has hung in there with loyalty to her maximum leader Basdeo Panday thus far. For example, she must know that it does not make sense replacing a black PNM with 'an Indian PNM' anymore than it makes sense putting in a woman because she's a woman. Some of us were rooting for Hillary Clinton as after George W. Bush she seemed the best qualified person for the US presidency and it so happens she was female.

Then along came Barack Hussein Obama who seemed a God-send for an America that needed a breath of fresh air – a new karma - in its re-thinking and direction. Who would have believed that a black man with an Islamic Muslim name would be chosen to lead the people (whose constitution is founded on a WASP-ish Judaeo-Christian ethic) out of the land of bondage?

The USA suddenly seemed resurrected and hope sprung once more in the American breast. But of such strangeness is politics made.

For Trinidad and Tobago now is the time for radical change. It has to happen NOW. We do not have the luxury of time so that the challenge is to win the hearts and minds of all the people. This includes the fractured Indians, Africans and the rest of the tribes in a genuine coming together of unity that is more than just ole talk.

So what does it take to restore peace and love to a country paralyzed in a FEAR OF LAWLESSNESS that must be understood before it can be checked? THAT IS THE PRIORITY. The question then is: Can a gentlewoman do it? Or should that vanguard position be held by a snarling Rottweiler?

Such leadership calls for a bigness and generosity of spirit that overrides the pettiness that can be so distracting and damaging in the machinations of a democratic process. She can take a leaf out of Barack Obama's book and dare to hope at her own audacity. This calls for a lot of self-will, self-confidence and focus.

The woman bogey will naturally be pushed and played against her so that every fibre of her feminine nature will be challenged. Mr. Shah for instance has declared his hand. She has to be reminded that women can cry and it is as much a strength as is the masculine inhibition of passion not to do so. Women give birth too. And that's a labour of both love AND physical strength. How convenient it is to forget! But these are little reminders that will come from the ground swell of support when the time comes to remind her that it is all right for a woman to be on top.

Even if Kamla Persad-Bissessar survives the inevitable bags of dirty tricks that she will find herself even unwittingly embroiled in at times, whatever ideals are pledged to an adoring electorate before the seat is won will be overturned by the realities of office. Let her check on Barack Obama once more.

It is the reason that despite the attempt on the part of Dr Eric Williams to institute a People's National Movement as a truly representative cross-section of the country, it did not take long for the realities of office to confront him. The ambition of holding on to power and the pragmatism of much-needed ballot numbers pushed the PNM into becoming institutionalized into a Party with an African bias (or base).

Some other realities include bigotry perceived or otherwise. Many are the stories for the falling apart of a really good-looking representative slate of that first PNM roster that included such luminaries as Winston Mahabir, Gerald Montano, Patrick Solomon, Learie Constantine,

Kamaluddin Mohammed, Isabel Teshea, John Donaldson, A.A. Thompson, John O'Halloran and Muriel Donawa-McDavidson. Let's not forget also that it was a time when we had Sir Solomon Hochoy as First Governor General in the post-Colonial period.

But Kamla Persad-Bissessar has a number of firsts too. Her biography states that she was the first woman to act as Prime Minister of Trinidad and Tobago; first woman to be appointed Attorney General and Minister of Legal Affairs; first woman deputy political leader of the UNC and the first woman Leader of the Opposition. She certainly sounds all right to me to lead Trinidad and Tobago into its second decade of the 21st century.

"During her two-year occupation of the office of the Minister of Education," it has been said, "Persad-Bissessar was successful in establishing Universal Secondary Education, removing the dreaded Common Entrance Examination, replacing it with the more modern Secondary Entrance Assessment SEA, and establishing some 32 new secondary schools in the country, among other major achievements." But to me that is de damn thing self! She has a foot into the education system which is at the heart of the present breakdown in the social fabric of the country.

"Her life goal and mission today still remains working towards building a more just and equitable society for all persons in Trinidad and Tobago."

Well herein lies the real challenge as pleasing the various components in our T&T just eh that easy!

Hear me again. The future of the country depends on a truly national representative leadership so that ALL members of the different tribes feel that they have a stake in THEIR country.

Genuine nationals and supporters who helped to put her there will easily become side-lined in the rush of those train-bearers who want to share the spotlight and the largesse that such office brings. The dirty game that politics is must be well understood in order to win gold, not silver or bronze.

In order to understand what Ms. Persad-Bissessar is up against one must understand a bit of the country's electoral history and of this she must be acutely aware of what lies ahead of Bas.

She's a bright and mature young woman at 57. What better could we wish? What better do we deserve?

But why am I trying to pontificate to the good lady and you readers at this special season of the year? It's time to go pray at that Roman Catholic Cathedral here in Beijing whose foundation dates from 1605. I've promised My Ron to continue the historical reporting of China.

So to him and to all you *JahajeeDesi* readers, may the angelic words of that celestial army on that first Christmas bring Peace and Goodwill to you, yours and our beloved Trinidad and Tobago.

HAPPY CHRISTMAS!

29. FAREWELL TO CHAIRMAN MAO

BEIJING: Thursday 31st December 2009

We've come to bid farewell to Chairman Mao. His cherubic face, stoic as always, looks down from on high, picture-framed as he is on the red embankment entrance to the Forbidden City. We drive past him on the way to our hotel which is in the centre of the old foreign legation where I am about to re-discover that old church called St. Michael's.

I've promised My Ron to stay closer to history as I detect a warning from his last email to steer clear of politics. (Is there a difference?) He is beginning to sound like my sister Corinne... or is there a hint of chauvinism somewhere that I should leave the messy game of politics to the 'brighter' sex? At any rate, it is going to be a week away from my work station so I'm clueless about that favourite corner of the world and the dynamics of the vibrant democracy on holiday down there in my hometown.

Christmas Eve in China finds us looking for a Peking Duck restaurant on a quiet, grey-walled side street. There are three chattering men behind us heading home from work, plastic dinner bags in hand. Although it is half-five-ish in the afternoon, night is settling in and the wind is edgy. The temperature is minus ten degrees Celsius and I can't wait to spot the neon signs and lanterns that should welcome us into its warmth.

Our guide is a Mongol-looking chap (yes, Chinese like other races don't all look alike!) who is on the way to his car. He is very helpful and soon we see the drawing of a duck on the wall and a tall cook in apron and chef's hat beckons us into an alleyway. It used to be one of the poor people's *hutongs* just outside the Forbidden City and next to the legation quarters where the majority of Europeans lived in the old days. It was a time of segregation from the Imperial dynasties of China and Europe.

The restaurant is local with a calculated dingy hole-in-the-wall-ness a deliberate ploy to attract tourists in search of authenticity. We go past the heating coal brazier into one of two rooms with walls that display pictures of celebrities like movie star Jet Li who dined there many moons ago.

A huge golden-braised duck is brought for our inspection and then carved into thin slices to be dunked in a thick molasses-like sauce. They will be joining rectangles of cucumber and slivers of spring onions in a wafer-thin relative of the roti skin. This is folded envelope-wise with chopsticks or fingers and eaten along with other dishes ordered. The cozy dinner ends on a high as a result of the number of refills of chrysanthemum tea and our party heads back onto the main road while wishing everyone Merry Christmas.

An old chap tries to lure us into his tri-ped transport but settles into riding alongside as he responds to our *Shengdan jie kuaile.* He is thrilled to reply in English "Happy Christmas" and is curious about two little islands in the Caribbean Sea next to South America.

The atmosphere is festive enough as we arrive at St Michael's Roman Catholic Church. It was built in 1902 as the French Embassy church. It had its first Chinese parish priest in 1952, and reports say that it was closed in 1958, to re-open on December 23rd 1989. It is located in the old Legation Quarter, Dongcheng District.

Now this period of China's history is particularly interesting as this Dongcheng District on the north-east of the Forbidden City was the place that saw real combat action at the start of the twentieth century. (Do I hear someone saying no politics?) The Boxer Rebellion saw bands of the peasantry take up the crudest of weapons and imbuing themselves with a supernatural fervour gave the Eight-Nation Alliance quite a scare. To ridicule their fierce martial arts stance the nickname of "boxers" was bestowed upon them.

One may ask so who were these members of this 'coalition of necessity'? Who were these fools to face an enemy armed with guns?

Seven of the eleven foreign ministries in Beijing comprised Austria-Hungary, France, Germany, Italy, Japan, Russia, and the United Kingdom. They all were occupiers who contributed the 20,000 troops to the face-off. Their stakes were as usual very high - exclusive trading rights to certain parts of China and it was seen as dividing it into "spheres of influence." As reported on The Boxer Rebellion website (*Small Planet Communications*) some even claimed to OWN the territory within their spheres! The Germans, for example, were powerful in

Shandong, the home province of the Chinese sage, Confucius.

The eighth member of the coalition, er, alliance was the military forces of the United States who responded to the siege on the diplomatic legations. They were in the area anyway!

But geeze! This is what makes the whole political game of Grab-It so fascinating as the sub plot involved the Americans who had their own axe to grind. By acquiring the Philippines, they too had become an Asian power. In 1898 the territory was ceded to the United States under the terms of the Treaty of Paris. "Now, with a strong base of operations just 400 miles from China, American businesses hoped to take advantage of China's vast resources. The foreign spheres of influence, however, threatened their ambitions."

To add further interest to the *comesse*, Herbert Hoover who was to become the 31st president of the United States of America was honeymooning with his bride on Chinese soil while scoping out the countryside for minerals. Like our Mr. Manning and Dr Rowley, he too was a geologist. As a young mining engineer he found himself in the thick of things patrolling the barricades of the seaport of Tianjin where the forces were going to land.

But history is so remarkably predictable. It seems that we are condemned to repeating our mistakes!

I have previously scoured the websites and reference books to identify the source of the rebellion of people power that caused unknown numbers on both sides to die. However, being this far away from my work station I must fall back on the convenient *Wikipedia*.

One of the first signs of unrest appeared in a small village in Shandong province, where there had been a long dispute over the property rights of a temple between locals and the Roman Catholic authorities. The Catholics claimed that the temple was originally a church abandoned after the Kangxi Emperor banned Christianity in China in 1715. The local court ruled in favor of the church, and angered villagers who claimed the temple for rituals.

As if that was not enough cause for the villagers to go mad and attack the church building there were other reasons driving these passions of hatred.

The exemption of missionaries from many laws further alienated local Chinese. In 1899, with the help of the French Minister in Peking, the missionaries obtained an edict....

So you see in any age "do so eh like so" for when the tables turned and the people took up arms against the injustice there was no 'turning of the other cheek' on the part of the occupiers.

This brings us to Christmas Day and the promised visit to that other cathedral whose foundation dates to 1605. It was built by the French in 1904 and named in honour of the Immaculate Conception.

Ironically it came after a visit to the bookstore on Beijing's *Wangfujing* in search of Richard Dawkins' *The Selfish Gene*. Remember - he is the evolutionary biologist who like Charles Darwin said many things that people did not want to hear at the time. I'd already become hooked on his *The God Delusion,* so it was not without some pangs of guilt that I found myself participating in a French High Mass on Christmas Day.

It is also known as *Nantang,* or the South Cathedral to the locals. Amidst the beauty of the Gothic arches, stained glass windows and nativity crèche, the service despite the glorious French language was uninspiring. What was missing as I reported to my *laoxiang* homemates in Hong Kong was the spirit. Perhaps it was the all-European procession of priests and acolytes with a token African youth; perhaps it was the lack-lustre sermon that reflected nothing to remind us that we were now into the second challenging decade of the 21st century; perhaps I just missed the drums, and guitars and vibrant *Gloria in Excelsis Deo* of the Filipinos and Africans in the churches of Guangzhou and Hong Kong. Music and dance too conspire so much to invoke the spirits!

To tell you the truth I never cease to marvel at Man's creativity of beauty surpassed only by whatever Supreme Being he calls his God. But what holds the curiosity even more is the manner in which Man uses God for his own self-embellishments and promotion. Why do I say this?

As I gazed upon the imposing structure that was rebuilt for the fourth time in 1904, the congregation of mainly French and other foreign embassy staff could have been a scene from somewhere in time. The handsome couple in the pew with their two blonde children was the same faces in museum daguerreotypes. The altar with lavish embankment of flowers and figurines in crèche were the same. The familiar smokiness of incense was as ever present as the Latin and Greek incantations. But most striking of all was the apartness even when time came for an exchange of neighbourly blessings.

I wondered how the new converts felt, for they were not admitted into the same services as the foreigners from what I have read in similar research done on Hong Kong's evangelization about that time. Further perusal of *Wikipedia* reveals that "the exemption of missionaries from many laws further alienated local Chinese."

For history buffs or those fascinated by the intrigues of politics which equals religion plus state, just listen to this. It is an ongoing human story that counteracts the 'peace on earth goodwill to men' message of the Jesus birth:

"In 1899, with the help of the French Minister in Peking, the missionaries obtained an edict granting official rank to each order in the Roman Catholic hierarchy. Local priests, by means of this official status, were able to support their people in legal disputes or family feuds and go over the heads of local officials."

Now, not only did this ploy manipulate the laws of the land but it was an effective means to divide and over rule a weakening Qing dynasty, not to mention the wedge driven between converts and their 'heathen' kinsfolk. But there is much more to this familiar story.

After the German government took over territory in Shandong, many Chinese feared that the missionaries, and by extension all Christians, were part of an imperialist attempt to "carve the melon," that is, to divide China and colonize the pieces separately.

Therein lies the heart of the xenophobia, that is, the fear or suspicion of the Chinese for foreigners whom they still refer to as *guailos* or 'foreign devils'. History with its patriots and heroes - yes even like Mao Zedong - whom the west would prefer not to acknowledge even as they canonize the Dalai Lama, was to save them from a fate worse than the carvings of two other melons, namely, the great land masses that are Africa and India.

But there are still two other churches to visit despite the mercury falling to minus 14. One is the Roman Catholic Cathedral - *Dongtang*, the East Cathedral, known as St. Joseph's. A small church was first established in 1653, but later rebuilt into an imposing Romanesque structure in 1904. Here I was to witness a Chinese priest hearing confessions and Chinese people worshipping at the altar and crèche.

The other visit was to retrace the footsteps of former US President Bill Clinton to a protestant church. *Chongwenmen* Church or Ashbury Methodist was built originally in 1870. It was the first American Methodist church and the largest existing Protestant church in Beijing. We traced it to 2 *Hougou Hutong, 4*

Chongwenmen Neidajie (near *Chongwenmen* subway station) in the *Dongcheng* District.

It is less pretentious in structure than the flamboyance of the Roman Catholics' steeples and Baroque carvings. The spirit here is sombre enough and very Anglo-protestant looking. Its dark wood panels and furnishings with stained glass windows while displaying the family of Jesus, Mary and Joseph are devoid of crèche scenes.

The rounds of visits to sacred sites that day ended with a stop at the *Lama* Temple. But that is even earlier political history for another day. The religious belief then entangling with state would have been Buddhism arriving all the way from the Indian subcontinent via the Himalayas and the Silk Road.

My interest in China's history got a boost after reading *The Boxer Rebellion* by Diana Preston. Suspicious as I am about western writers on China, her extensive reliance on diaries and letters, plus extensive research from both Chinese and western perspectives, won me over, but only somewhat. It was enough however to whet my curiosity for further investigation. The human story of a people protecting their birthright from foreign predators (sometimes in league with the locals) seemed to be a familiar and on-going crusade.

It is recommended reading for those interested in why China and the West still view each other with hooded eyes even as we approach the year 2010.

And now to you, Richard Seecharan, and to *JahajeeDesi* readers, may the New Year bring you even more understanding and an appreciation of the SO MUCH that there is still to be celebrated around us.

Peace and Respect.

Rhona Baptiste in Guangzhou

30. 2010 - DARING TO HOPE?

GUANGZHOU: Thursday 7th January 2010

We are one week into the New Year already! Time is moving on. It is not static but filled with dynamic energies. Web surf into 'What is Time?' speaks to me. It is remarkable that the most real feeling in perception of time "the present" cannot be measured in any units of time. Present is duration-less, it is an infinitesimal. On the timeline both the past and the future which are seen as durations in time encroach on the present.

So what does that really say? Time, like Love and God, remains a mysterious something around which we poor creatures feel humbled simply because we just can't understand any of them.

I have still not gone into the dailies on line but have caught a glimpse of the year's closing homicide figures for Trinidad and Tobago as standing at 508 bodies found and 904 missing. It was taken off Richard Wm. Thomas' diligent 'guarding of the guards' in his customary circulars to Editor/Head of news desks.

It is for this reason that I felt that I could not respond to Richard Seecharan's 2010 survey of readers to participate in a questionnaire. As My Ron reminded me, if you do not live here, you will depend on third parties for your information. You will depend on the press and on 'educated' persons with their particular perspectives for your information and the difference between that and reality is like chalk and cheese. You must be on the spot and have lots of ole talk with all types and sides.

So my observations I thought could be very out of place. The Chinese put it more colourfully: It's like hen talking to duck. Or, it's like our own saying that "cockroach eh have no right in fowl party".

Nevertheless I tread where angels fear to walk. And so as to who will be elected Leader of the UNC I can only wish that Ms. Kamla Persad-Bissessar will be given that opportunity. Who will be elected Chairman of the UNC? I am unable to choose the nominees not being familiar with Messrs. Jack, Vasant, or Other. Missing is the question in the event that UNC wins the National elections - then who will be President? To this one we will all have to call on God to put a hand in our affairs. For some time now He has appeared most unwilling to do so.

Will there be Local Elections or General Elections in 2010? I can only guess that based on the uneasiness with Mr. Manning and the queasiness of the electorate it will be called as early as possible. It is the norm of political uncertainty rather than the combat strategy from the book of Sun Tzu's *Art of War.*

Will there be more murders in Trinidad in 2010 (more than 500)? To this I can only hope that good sense will prevail so that we surprise ourselves into sanity and respect for each other's lives. So the answer is No.

Will PNM expel Rowley from the party? I will vouch that Rowley being a born and bred PNMite, he will not be expelled. But then one must remember that Political Survival is unscrupulously indifferent to the sensitive feelings of friends and comrades.

Will unemployment in 2010 be higher than the 2009 rate of 5.8%? I am unable to answer this, along with this one: Will the PNM government have to borrow more money to finance their spending?

It is the same for: Will Calder Hart be hauled before the courts in 2010 and Will the PNM government call in the IMF in 2010?

I reluctantly go along with a Yes for this one though: Will there be massive civil disobedience and refusal to pay the Property Tax in 2010? Isn't it written in the Chronicles of Fate that this will happen? After the frenzy / hypnosis / intoxication / hallucination of Carnival, it is inevitable that the realities of daily life will bring about the proverbial straw that will break the camel's back. Whether the straw will be another senseless murder; or retaliation against a show of police force, or simply just the THOUGHT after watching someone's ostentatious indifference as he drives by in his car or SUV – only Time will tell.

As with some of the other questions I cannot answer the following: Will there be economic growth in T&T in 2010? Will the PNM government increase taxes in 2010?

For this one: Will there be increased foreign investment in T&T in 2010? Again I can only speculate that human nature being what it is, commerce or trade will attract the most unlikely bedfellows – sellers and buyers alike. So depending on the attractiveness of the return on investment, yes, direct foreign investment will increase.

Will CLICO bailout require more than $10 billion? I cannot answer this one either. Ms. Camini Maharaj is much more competent I think to deal with this suggestion. Will anyone from the previous CLICO management be charged for the CLICO debacle?

Will the PNM government bailout HCU (Hindu Credit Union)? Unfortunately, I am not familiar with this at all.

Will the PNM government continue to give money to Caricom countries, e.g. OECS, Air Jamaica?   For window dressing I think this is a possibility. Our face abroad is boo what with the bad press and I understand now why there seems to be an exclusion of both tourism and 'we Carnival' from mainstream foreign news. It is because our National Festival's on-going deterioration into gross vulgarity - it makes viewers and audiences want to puke. Ugh!

I've just opened up the *Express* and discovered Andy Johnson's "Muddled would-be meddlers" on 31st December. It talks about the radio airing of risqué tunes that are at the heart of the mayhem-in-denial taking place in what used to be Sweet T&T. And the "wining" season is only just getting started, he says.

Now tell me you holders of the fort: Is there any Moral Authority down there to guide the nation between Right and Wrong? Have we forgotten the difference between Good taste and Bad taste? But more on this later.

Will the PNM government survive 2010? This is hazarding an answer I know, but I do not think so.

B-U-T so much depends on the UNC members' ability to THINK and ACT and UNITE rather than messing around with political has-beens who see party and self before country.

And finally: Will Winston Dookeran still be the leader of COP at the end of 2010? My memory of this good gentleman remains just that - a gentle man who is fortunate enough to have survived the vagaries of politics in health and spirit thus far. I do think so.

But I have strayed far from the original intent of this piece. The idea was to continue the Christmas sight-seeing with a visit to the Beijing Center for the Performing Arts. I wanted to see how it compares with our own National Academy for the Performing Arts (NAPA). The truth is I can't wait to get down there to see what Mr. Manning and his government has done with my and your money in my absence.

With reference to the half a billion TT dollars worth of building that he exults is "like a pearl" I want it to thrill me in the same way or even more so than did the one I've just visited. After all, in Omatie Lyder's story in the *Express* of Sunday, 8th November what we are told however, is that

Prime Minister Patrick Manning thinks it is more beautiful than the Sydney opera house in Australia!

Therefore I look forward to the 429,093 square-foot Academy that features the following:
- 1,500-seat performance hall;
- Two practice halls;
- Teaching rooms;
- State-of-the-art lighting and sound features;
- Stages designed to showcase pannists and other artistes;
- Hotel;
- Landscaped surroundings, including seating areas, water features and greenery;
- Parking facilities.

And yet the first question I want to ask Mr. Manning is how will it sustain itself?

Now bear with my own exultations over the massive upside down rice bowl that floats on a frozen lake in Beijing. The people call it "The Egg." As we walk around its perimeter it is no illusion. There is no access to the igloo shape across the ice floes on the water. The design on the face of the glass dome holds the attention as it reveals itself to be of contrasting shades that suggest the swirl of the Yin Yang Taoist symbol for harmony.

Suddenly you come upon the entrance in a garden. The fee is RMB 30 each (same as our TT dollars) and visitors then enter an underground corridor that is a green-house garden, above which is the moat-like lake! Sunlight penetrates the crystal ice and rippling water to reveal hanging posters of concerts and sculpture amidst the reds and yellows of anthuriums, poinsettias, azaleas and heliconias with the ubiquitous balisiers to remind us of home.

What is particularly nostalgic is a visit to the Exhibition Hall on the right where the costumes of famous performing operas and stage shows are exhibited. They are tastefully displayed with accompanying information.

Other paraphernalia like props along with Minshall-ish sketches of stage and design further enhance the miniature presentations.

I think of past visits to the Victoria Museum opposite the Deluxe Cinema (are these still there?) where wonderful costumes of retro Carnivals gathered dust even as their creators like Saldehena and Bailey and Lee Heung were disappearing from the annual pageantry. Have we done something about show-casing our own creativity in an educational and classy manner too? Have we built money-earning features into it? I speak here of on-going (local) maintenance like cleaning and landscaping, coffee shop, souvenir shop, CD/Video shop, among other possibilities? Classy ones. No tackiness, please!

But of course we must have put a lot of thought into an expensive structure that has to be more than a landmark! We must have sat down in consultation with those concerned and thought as did the Chinese that this is not for the here and now. Such opulence is not for 'the gimme-gimmes' but for the future and the children. The mission statement that greets visitors to the Beijing Centre says it clearly:

Our philosophy, which governs our approach to everything we do, is grounded in three guiding principles: to be national; to be creative; to be international. To be national is to be rooted in service to the general public.

As a public funded cultural facility, the National Centre for the Performing Arts strives to serve the cultural needs of the Chinese populace. The Centre has been tasked by the central government to help raise the cultural awareness and enrichment of all sectors of Chinese society. To help achieve this objective the Centre operates a wide-range of education programs that includes arts appreciation classes, lectures and special cultural exhibitions.

I have no doubt that the PNM government has taken all the above into account in providing us with our own Academy for the Performing Arts. Our creation of the steel pan music said to be the only musical innovation in the 20th century; and the calypso hybrids that are soca and chutney soca; our classical musicianship and our Carnival creativity deserve no less. Can you imagine how Jamaica would have bolted with such luck! Remember Bob Marley was to greet me in a Cantonese taxi back in '98! His messages are international and forever.

Clear through the glass from any view inside that beautiful edifice is The Great Hall of the People to its East and Tian'anmen's Chang'an Avenue on its West. As we join the old and the young, the rich and the poor, the infirmed and the able-bodied in wonderment of the NCPA (originally named National Grand Theater), designed by French architect Paul Andreu, pride shows especially on the faces of the old-timers.

Time - that old immeasurable entity curtails a further sharing of experiences of the proud structure the Chinese refer to as "The Egg." Time too would tell how the people feel about "Our Pearl."

31. THIS IS MADNESS!

GUANGZHOU: Thursday 14th January 2010

It's eleven o'clock at night in a city high rise. Imagine the quiet of an urban community of 30,000 in suburban Guangzhou. There is the occasional honking of a car horn, an impatient driver negotiating the never-ending road construction, but it's like the night before Christmas in any civilized country. No creature seems stirring not even a mouse.

I've had enough of marking end-of-term papers so what a relief to escape into Cyberspace! There're always *JahajeeDesi's* offerings among others, a choice of old timers' jokes from one classmate in particular who seems addicted to surfing risqué stuff and just as I'm wondering why, up pops something from another old friend, William Greene. He wants to share with me a cute video reminiscent of Tiger Woods' up-to-the-recent bedroom dilemma. It is an old spoofy sitcom with Carol Burnett as the suspicious wife who takes a turn in husband Harvey Korman's tail as he muffs his answers about a caller in the middle of the night. He swears it's a wrong number until she surprises him sneaking out. It's a hell worse than Elin and Tiger Woods'!

But anyway I decide it's time to open up Len Raphael's recent email attachment. Suddenly the night air is filled with the sweet, sweet familiar voice of Sparrow's 1995 tune, "This is Madness." It is social commentary at its best and datelines the existence of the murderous quandary in which our T&T is now entrapped. Like The Bird, we keep asking ourselves how did this happen to such nice people? When did it get started? Total madness, he croons. So what is going on?

Calypso now morphed into a hybrid strain called soca is rooted in social commentary and provides a musicological (yes, I've checked. It is a word.) calendar on the country's post-Columbus 'carbon' footprint. And so I up the volume like any good Trini and simply cannot resist getting up and chipping around to the bitter sweet lyrics that The Birdie is delivering. If there is a single moment that I bleed for my country it is now. We living in a state of undeclared war... his words are loud and clear.

You see I've already scanned the major postings and thoughts are running wild over a number of stories that have appeared this past week.

First of all, there is the return of Mr. Basdeo Panday who as leader of the Opposition UNC is greeted at the airport from his Christmas vacation in the United Kingdom. He announces that his doctor having given him a clean bill of health, he is now ready to take on a lion and is in warrior mode. Great showmanship all right BUT isn't it a little pathetic that the good gentleman should be engaging in robber talk at risk of burdening his aging heart? He anticipates an impending battle for leadership within his UNC camp.

Following on this was the declaration by Sunil Ramjitsingh, UNC Member (Reg # 04 2008546) in a public letter re: Harassment and intimidation by Political Leader and others at UNC Headquarters today.

It does not speak nicely about attitudes inside the camp.

There is the on-going feeding frenzy of the UNC bandwagon supporters with voices from all sides creating the biblical Babel that overrides the plague of killings that continue. By January 11th the *Express* reports nine murders for the year which makes it just about one a day.

Consolation from all the war-mongering and barring of fangs via the on-line news comes in the form of two postings. Both are from the gentler of the two sexes.

Ms. Anjanie Ramharrack writes: I was disappointed and disheartened that our Political Leader, Mr. Basdeo Panday, can voice with such passion his intention for "war" upon his return. Why "war" amongst our own. Why can't this election be calm and completed without the said intention? Why can't we as a people (UNC) show the Nation that we CAN accomplish so much more through TEAM – Together Each Accomplishes More work?

Why indeed, Anjanie?

You ask why does politics have to include insulting and degrading remarks about each other. The question may appear as simplistic and naïve as LA's Rodney King asking the LAPD: "Why can't we all just get along?" Dear Child, it has to do with a chemical called testosterone that in turn triggers the male nervous system to respond to challenge. But look up the term "gorilla dust" and you will catch the drift.

On second thought let me help you. It comes from the 1998 *Hindu Today*, "Is India Nuclear Threat Mere Gorilla Dust?" When two male gorillas confront each other, says the paper, they're too canny most of the time to actually fight, so they resort to the tried-and-true political tactic of intimidation. Both scurry about in frenzy, grimacing menacingly, beating their chests and tossing clouds of dirt into the air. It's a serious encounter, full of powerful and primitive energies, a test of testosterone. Soon one becomes convinced that the other could win the threatened physical engagement, and retreats. It's called gorilla dust, and nations stir it up all the time.

And we have not even got to the Big Gorillas as yet when PNM begins squaring off with UNC!

I am sure you represent many of our Trini youths who are appalled at the behaviour of our old timers both in and out of opposition politics (make that Leadership period) who pursue their own personal gains without considering the real issues of the people. No wonder young people are turned off! It's a fact we old people have messed up, even with good intention at times, mind you!

As Sparrow's words waft over the stillness of the night, 'we had no money but we used to live right', I think of the other lady writer. She is Ms. Dzifa Job whose tag line is Colin Powell's "Giving back involves a certain amount of giving up." I like that. The woman in me reads 'sacrifice' into the message. I understand fully the meaning of 'giving up something in return for having to give back something'.

In her musings on the same day as Anjanie's she posts an excellent commentary in response to the recently published 'Small Arms Survey on gang violence in Trinidad & Tobago' titled 'No Other Life: Gangs, Guns, and Governance in Trinidad and Tobago' She writes with the same passion for a beloved country. "As a nation we are riding the back of a Tiger with no idea on how to get off. While I hope that it doesn't take us another seventy-four years to get rid of the ruling cabal; I can't shake the sinking feeling in my bones that we haven't hit bottom yet - and if we wait too late, 'crapaud might as well smoke we pipe!'"

She continues: "If gang affiliation and running afoul of the law has become a way of life for some as the report suggests, then we must all shoulder some responsibility for creating a culture where the rule of law is not respected." Let me repeat that: We must all shoulder some responsibility for creating a culture where the rule of law is not respected. These words are particularly strong in her message.

Now Ms Job's comments follow upon the international Robert Muggah and Dorn Townsend's report on TRINIDAD - A GANGSTER'S PARADISE. The reading is chilling and cause for another reaction - this time from an anonymous writer titled "A Trinidad Reflection".

"We are being forced to live out a real hell in our land of birth and our children's cries of terror are not being heard ... Ignored by the Foreign Press. We all have close friends and neighbours who have been affected ... We are talking about abhorrent merciless crimes being committed against Babies, Little Children, Wives, Husbands, Dads, Mums, Boyfriends, Girlfriends, Grannies and Grandpas.

"Stabbings, rapes, choppings, eye-gougings, scalpings, shootings, disembowelments, kidnappings, murders, are now the order of the day for far too many of us ordinary people and our closely tied ones. Many are so traumatised that they are emotionally numb now. No more laughter, no more tears ... just numb ... no more cuddling for the young ones ... just this paralytic numbness going on ... and on ...

"Can anybody hear our silent cries for help ... It's getting worse now. Getting closer by the day. Will it be like Rwanda, a mini-Bangladesh, or Auschwitz, perhaps, Darfur?

"Every skin colour now ... But only one liquid colour flowing. Blood Red."

It is a cri du coeur made all the more painful as the author is afraid to sign his/her name. For the writer and for the two lady writers above it is some consolation that perhaps salvation will come when the money runs out. Mr. or Ms. 'annonymous' asks: "Is the luxury of balancing billions in overseas bank accounts more important to them than life itself? ... And when the oil and gas run out or the "credit crunch" comes ... We know ... Just jump on their planes and again desert the sinking ship ... like so many did in 1970 and 1990."

As I pick up on the hysteria of my country how I wish it could be otherwise! In fact there is often the doubt that maybe – just maybe – as Diana Mahabir-Wyatt once rebuked me (and My Ron did too until he was confronted by home-grown terrorists), perhaps – just perhaps, T&T is going through a bad phase and we will soon come out of the nightmare. After all, democracy is alive and well. "Have you forgotten what we really live like?" She had asked. "We are fallible, wrong-headed and often, simply stupid, but we have more exercise of human rights than most of the Commonwealth Countries that I listened to with tears in my eyes".

It is perhaps because of this we're-not-so-bad-after-all attitude why my peers and kinsfolk do not make mention of the terror that only some seem to see stalking the land? I have been advised to steer clear of politics by those who do not understand that Politics IS Religion. It is THE GOD that holds each of us in its hands. So Politics IS to be understood. Politics should be compulsory on the curriculum along with Money and Integrity/Values/Respect from kindergarten. It used to be called Civics in the old days.

Two old friends on discovering that 'I once was lost but now was found' on Facebook stopped communicating after I forwarded to them one of these *JahajeeDesi* columns.

There are those who are so into denial that there is absolutely nothing wrong at home! And then there are those who advise that survival (I take this to mean 'quality' (white picket fence) survival is possible if only I can live AROUND the badness! The last person who suggested this is a sister-in-law who has lived abroad for umpteen years and whose own sanitized life connects to home through the occasional telephone call. Then she is told the good news of nieces and nephews who have made it successfully through to UWI and now have cushy jobs back home. So she asks me: "Maybe you are reading too much bad news from the media?" Well, am I?

Okay, 'nuff said for this week. I'm back to correcting exam papers. I'll leave you to share my nostalgia with Sparrow's "This is Madness."

Let me rewind to Sparrow and you too listen carefully as he sings of 'sorrow and pain' revealed in his song...'ah wish ah was wrong...'

The man Francisco Slinger - like so many of us - is hurting.

And now there is Haiti.

32. HAITI'S DAY OF JUDGEMENT

GUANGZHOU: Thursday 21st January 2010

HAITI, Monday 11th January 2010 ... How hateful to see a country relegated to permanency among the poorest of the poor nations in the world! How despicable to see pot-bellied children eating mud cakes! Shame on Caricom and you pompous heads of Banana Republics! Shame on you Ban Ki-moon and the rest of your impotent UN members! Shame on you fat cat businessmen! Shame on the rest of us! As for you developed countries beginning with France... Judgement Day is at hand!

HAITI, Tuesday 12th January 2010 ... On the screen is a picture of a black woman caked in white mud, eyes bulging frighteningly as they reflect the devastation of a nation's latest calamity that assails thousands of her countrymen.

There are pictures from the recent earthquake measuring 7 points on the Richter scale that has just struck Port-au-Prince, the capital on Tuesday afternoon. It has brought more misery for the people of Haiti. It is as if they haven't had enough of Hell. Where is God? Does God hate so... or is this about love? Is He testing them... AGAIN?

Amidst the misery some find Him as they hold hands singing and chanting in consolation to a Being that has let this befall them - no doubt for a purpose. But of such is belief programmed...and maybe it is just as well...for without their gods what else is left? Anarchy?

HAITI, Thursday 14th January 2010 ... ABC reports one source of the tragedy: Haiti disaster blamed on pact with the devil announces the Yahoo headline. American televangelist Pat Robertson has blamed the devastating earthquake in Haiti on a pact between the impoverished nation's founders and the devil!

It is as idiotic and insensitive as actress Sharon Stone's pronouncement at the Cannes Festival on the Wenchuan Earthquake in China in 2008. She said that the Sichuan earthquake was bad karma for China's treatment of the Tibetans, a statement which she was quick to retract after Christian Dior began pulling her out of their store ads in China.

"My erroneous words and deeds angered and saddened the Chinese people, and I sincerely apologize for this. I'm willing to participate in any earthquake relief activity and to do my utmost to help Chinese people affected by the disaster." But her pockets were pinching.

Amazing how money talks! Dior too made haste with damage control by putting distance between them: "We don't agree with her hasty, unreflecting remarks and we deeply regret them. Dior was one of the first international brands to enter China and has won the affection and respect of the consuming public. We absolutely do not support any remark that hurts the Chinese people's feelings. We express our sorrow over the compatriots who lost their lives in the earthquake in Wenchuan, Sichuan, and we extend our sympathy and condolences to the people in the disaster area."

Aha! So you see! Even the language is damage controlled. Note well "compatriots".

Now maybe Richard Dawkins who continues to remove the mote from my eyes with his latest book, *The Greatest Show on Earth – The Evidence for Evolution,* (and no - it has nothing to do with Trinidad's Carnival) will view this latest disaster to remove thousands of people at one fell stroke from the face of this earth a bit more pragmatically.

You may say callously.

I can hear him saying at an Oxford lecture podium "No - it is NOT God's will. There is no God until scientifically proven... in fact..." he will continue..."it has nothing to do with the unnatural or the supernatural but with the natural." Since he's an atheist, unlike the linkages to a supernatural as the two people above will want to attribute blame, Dawkins will more likely question the whys of such catastrophic happenings from a cause-effect starting point.

As an evolutionary biologist he will point out those huge fragile populations that are vulnerable to risk, be they as end source in the food chain or as casualties of natural disaster. Man, poor, and usually black, brown or yellow and heavily concentrated in population densities is just another statistic of Nature's seeming happenstance of its physics.

More infuriating than scientifically fascinating is the man-made story of Haiti, the bi-fingered western edge of the historic Caribbean island of Hispaniola on which Christopher Columbus was to put his pox on that fateful day of his arrival in 1492. Never mind the local people, the Arawaks, called it Ayti, meaning the 'land of mountains'. Nah man! El Capitan Colon promptly christened it *La Isla Espanola* meaning The Spanish Island.

Things, I tell my students, were never ever the same. All hell broke loose as he returned to Europe with his exotic specimens. The floodgates were opened as more Spaniards and their neighbours arrived in a search of El Dorado, so that by 1697 they were ceding the buccaneer-infested third on the west to France. One thing led to another so that by the end of the 1700s Saint-Domingue (Haiti) was the world's richest colony.

To make this wealth possible the 30,000 white French planters by this time were riding the backs of 450,000 black people bound in chains and forced from their West African coast homelands. Nature being nature, played her own mating games too as the next thing you know there were 25,000 free mulattoes (or mutts) forming a new racial caste with their own subsets to complicate matters.

Now let's return to Pastor Robertson's words that I find so abominably intriguing. He said the curse was evident when Haiti contrasted with its neighbour the

Dominican two-thirds which if you remember were retained by the Spaniards. "Dominican Republic is prosperous, healthy, full of resorts, etc. Haiti is in desperate poverty. Same island..." he preaches.

Speaking on his television program *The 700 Club,* Pastor Robertson said the pact happened "a long time ago in Haiti". And the spin that follows will surely have CLR James along with the players in his *Black Jacobins,* turning in their graves. "They (meaning the Blacks)," the pastor continued, "were under the heel of the French; you know Napoleon III [sic] and whatever. And they got together and swore a pact to the devil...They said 'We will serve you if you will get us free from the prince.' And so the devil said, 'OK it's a deal'. And they kicked the French out."

Now shouldn't there be some kind protection of the innocent from such hogwash? And please let's not start debating by pulling out the American First Amendment as I will be tempted to reply with - so why isn't there a universal law to protect the innocent from irresponsible public speech, or proselytizing which is calculated mis-information to win converts?

Mr. Robertson said after the pact, the Haitians "revolted and got something – themselves - free...But ever since they have been cursed by one thing after another."

Well, so much for the Yahoo ABC story - a gospel according to a modern day cleric of the only successful black slave rebellion in history. Bear with me, dear readers, but it's a chance to share a bit of CLR James' *Black Jacobins* with you. I don't know why I'm doing this as it is much like preaching to the converted. But it assuages my grief over the damage that a bigot like Pat Robertson is wielding over a captive international audience.

Now consider this: How are the likes of Robertson and Rush Limbaugh (who is not backing down from his claim that President Barack Obama is trying to score points off the Haitian earthquake), how are they to understand the Haiti that was created by the curse of a political situation of white dominance and black enslavement? Do even West Indians, although in an 'educated Caribbean,' have any idea of the meaning of being kidnapped for slave labour? And what about feudalism? How many of us have truly experienced the Haitian - or the Tibetan - situation? We do seem to know a helluva lot about the Holocaust though. Why? Is it a case of the golden rule...he who has the gold makes the rules?

HAITI Sunday 17ʰ January 2010 ... Sunday Express Raffique Shah's "Reparations, not handouts, for Haiti" is an excellent reminder of what must be done for Haiti NOW.

I tell him it is the first honestly intelligent response to Haiti's latest tragedy. Reparation is long overdue and is the least of the right things that 'developed civilized' countries like France, Britain and the USA should do in righting the wrongs of so much human misery they have wreaked in conquests around the globe.

He replies with an attachment by Sir Hilary Beckles, Pro Vice-chancellor and Principal of the Cave Hill Campus, UWI. The University of the West Indies is in the process of conceiving how best to deliver a major conference on the theme rethinking and rebuilding Haiti. It also summarizes the "popular perception that somehow the Haitian nation-building project, launched on January 1, 1804, has failed on account of mismanagement, ineptitude, corruption." Or, I might add, "negritude".

HAITI Monday 18ᵗʰ January 2010 ... Bad news continues even as poor Guyana pledges US$1million on par with rich T&T's million. Prime Minister Manning out of consideration for putting stress on the ravaged country with one extra pair of hands does not consider sending helpers and he himself joins other leaders in Dominican

Republic for another talk shop rounds of promises. He is to be supported later by former president Sir Ellis Clarke who thinks our soldiers should not be sent to Haiti.

Newsday's Darcel Choy on 16th January reported him as saying: "Necessary factors should be considered before a decision like that is made.

"One would have to consider surely not only sending people but what do you send with them, can you at this stage guarantee relative safety when there are still a number of aftershocks. How do you cooperate with others, it is not a matter of Trinidad and Tobago simply, it is a worldwide matter and Trinidad through its part will play its own role."

Meanwhile John Travolta was preparing to fly his own Boeing 707 jet to Haiti with medical supplies and doctors as well as a crew of his Scientologists to perform 'healing'.

At home the homicides continue as newspapers report the murders up to 24 for the year! At any rate Mr. Manning and his government seem impotent to deal with the situation.

By quirks of Fate, many of the West Indian islands escaped Haiti's experience for better or worse because we did not have men of the ilk of L'Overture and Dessalines to fight to the finish.

Now look at Caricom, seemingly as sterile as the recent CHOGM (Commonwealth Heads of Government Meeting). Shouldn't the Caribbean Community be working and planning ALONGSIDE if not AHEAD of the Americans to help Haiti stand confidently and permanently on its feet? But that takes PLANNING and dedicated selflessness. We should have been INSIDE Haiti already helping out with that same spirit of family as do the Chinese after each of their catastrophes.

HAITI Tuesday 19ᵗʰ January 2010 ... "Anarchy" screams *Newsday* as Haiti descends into mob rule. A looter is beaten to death, his body dragged through the street to be set alight. The death toll is put at 200,000 but who really knows?

Just when I'm thinking that could have been us, *The United Voice* posts online something called 'A little Haitian history' It comes from Garvin Nicholas and is a must read to our children. For what John Maxwell the author has to say in the *Jamaica Observer* of Jan 17th should be compulsory in all history books of the world as the lions continue to tell their side of the story of the hunt. "No, Mister! You Cannot Share my Pain!" And against that picture of the white-caked woman in rubble he articulates her grief.

It is addressed to the Americans: "If you shared my pain you would not continue to make me suffer, to torture me, to deny me my dignity and my rights, especially my rights to self-determination and self-expression. Six years ago you sent your Ambassador Extraordinary and Minister Plenipotentiary to perform an action illegal under the laws of your country, my country and of the international community of nations...."

He writes here of the US interference with the kidnapping of President Jean-Bertrand Aristide and his wife. Mr. Maxwell then erases the propaganda that it is the Haitian people who are responsible for denuding the Arawaks' Ayti – "land of mountains." He says:

As Marguerite Laurent (EziliDanto) writes: Don't expect to learn how a people with a Vodun culture that reveres nature and especially the Mapou (oak-like or *Ceiba pendantra/bombax*) trees, and other such big trees as the abode of living entities and therefore as sacred things, were forced to watch the Catholic Church, during Rejete - the violent anti-Vodun crusade - gather whole communities at gunpoint into public squares, and forced them to watch their agents burn Haitian trees in order to teach Haitians their Vodun Gods were not in nature, that the trees were the "houses of Satan".

In partnership with the US, the mulatto President Elie Lescot (1941-45) summarily expelled peasants from more than 100,000 hectares of land, razing their homes and destroying more than a million fruit trees in the vain effort to cultivate rubber on a large plantation scale. Also, under the pretext of the Rejete campaign, thousands of acres of peasant lands were cleared of sacred trees so that the US could take their lands for agribusiness.

Are we bright extensively-traveled Caribbean people aware of this? Does CARICOM know of this? Why then aren't they preaching it from the pulpits?

Well, if this isn't a precursor to the Agent Orange story, the defoliation caused by chemicals used by the 3 million Americans armed forces in Vietnam in the 1960s and early 70s! And the destruction of North Korea's rice plantations in the 1950s.

We never did have a L'Overture, nor a Dessalines. We never had to fight for self-determination. The dying Empires made it easy for us 'lucky ones' as it was in their interest to let go of what had now become their dependents. But then what a price we would have had to pay, eh, in a fight to the finish? Ask Fidel Castro. He is still around to tell you about hegemony, recent occupations, and the ostracizing of an entire population that comes when a people attempt to pursue their own self-determination. One lethal form it takes in the punishment of daring to go a 'different' route is denying them the life-blood of commercial trade by what is known as embargoes and trade tariffs.

Yup! Patriotism/Nationalism IS about blood, sweat and endless tears. Well, so much for the meaning of sovereignty.

As Haiti now relies on its survivors to continue its destiny as a uniquely independent black nation there is the marvellous spirit of humanity alive in those who help to pick up the pieces.

Such a one is Pierre Chauvet (Bobby) as posted in one of Richard Wm. Thomas' communiqués on January 16th. It is an eyewitness' report on the situation in Haiti in which he thanks helpers, and details the destruction but he ends as only a true hero will speak.

Port-au-Prince has been destroyed twice already, in 1750 and 1770 by previous earthquakes. So has been Cap Haitien in 1842. Both cities were on stand by for this repeat cycle of every 150 to 200 years. Port-au-Prince got hit 2 days ago and will be on the list for many more years. Recent generations have forgotten to build accordingly, because, surprisingly, many very old Gingerbread houses are standing up, including the former residence of President Petion built around 1810 which currently serves as the Ministry of Social Affairs.

Both cities were rebuilt by survivors at that time. The spirit of those who want to stay in the country nowadays is to rebuild and to build better with para-seismic and other standards and norms.

I will be part of that spirit.

Until next...

Pierre Chauvet (Bobby)

HAITI Wednesday 20th January 2010 ... It is difficult to resist a comment on Bobby's "recent generations have forgotten to build accordingly, surprisingly; many very old Gingerbread houses are standing up..."

Surprisingly? Did recent generations really FORGET? Hm-n-n-n... Recent generations NEVER did have an option to trade and build houses on foundations of rock as did the architects of Gingerbread or Plantation houses built around 1810. The plantocracy had FREE labour to build their ornate European-styled replicas. No surprise here, Bobby.

But to end on a positive note, here is a latest response from Raffique Shah. He writes: "Bottom line: Haiti must be rebuilt from the ground up, very literally, and the effects of the earthquake give us that starting point. You should see how Trinis are pouring out their all to give to Haiti. We are really a nice people when one gets past the scab of the few villains who give us a bad name."

33. HEAVY METAL IN CHINA

GUANGZHOU: Thursday 28th January 2010

No - it has nothing to do with the joys nor anguish coming out of Haiti in the Caribbean today. Instead I SCREAM is the title on the advertisement for an open air rock concert Chinese style. It is the coming of age of young people and their music in the East and while it might have taken Mötley Crüe some time to arrive in Guangzhou, nevertheless, western musical acculturalization is at work. No wonder Beijing is nervous!

Who says it's never too late for anything? Well that's how I found myself last Saturday afternoon at a Chinese version of the 1969 American Woodstock. The site unfolds at the far end of a peaceful stretch of what I call My Secret Garden. It is approached on the west alongside a restaurant that is as mysterious as Jamaica's Spanish Town. In the daytime you never can see any action around the couple of parked cars in its front lot.

We go past some friendly guards into an old garden with workmen renovating dilapidated buildings into up-scale studio offices. There are art galleries among others yet-to-be- converted and historic plaques say that they had once been active in serving the Communist Party during past decades. Dominating the structures however are tall paper barks, walking rubber trees, and Java apples interspersed with shady walk paths and goldfish ponds.

Apart from some cooks cooling it outside the big restaurant on the south side of the garden, the walk becomes more interesting as we head east and we run into busy cameras held by what must be Chinese paparazzi. They are chasing a pair of ultra slim beauties clad in mostly black clinggies. Through the greenery we can see others posed for photos that will soon adorn the transit advertisements or flash across video screens in taxis, subways, malls or television.

The main drag is an open campus that welcomes visitors to a free concert in both Chinese and English. The words spell out I SCREAM and for good reason. The noise is deafening. Just a couple more extra decibels on the amplifiers will do the trick in modern warfare. They stun the enemies' ear drums and have already turned up in Iraq and Afghanistan. Adding to the excitement are rows of youthful entrepreneurs on either side of the driveway where they are displaying hand-made bric-a-brac, t-shirts, and you-name-its.

At this point the garden becomes a wide swathe of lawn with shapely Cuban palms and there against the Titanic-looking side of the Guangzhou newspaper building is a monstrous stage with all the gadgetry and electronic paraphernalia that a modern concert demands.

We make our way past groups seated on the grass and closer to the three young men who are responsible for the cacophony from the speakers. On the high stage the lead singer is in mad imitation of a blend of the two Michaels – the King of Pop and the King of the Basketball court.

Since conversation is impossible with the amplifiers on high decibel, it is time to check out the audience. The average age is say nineteen and it reminds me that it is the age group of my students who surprise me with their musical versatility. Their familiarity with hip hop, Indys, rock and heavy metal is far removed from the high-pitched tones of Chinese classical operas like *Legend of the White Snake* or *The Butterfly Lovers* of their parents.

After an eternity of noise another frantic lad appears with another group. His antics remind me this time of an argument with a friend who, like Barack Obama, is the black/white genetic combination - except her father is English and her mother is Ugandan. She is vehement that dance rhythm is largely environmental and not genetic so she does not buy into my 'wild' statement that black people are born with a specially selected gene for natural rhythm.

Before us is a good example to prove my point as Chinese boys like White boys just don't have it. Somehow the gene for dance rhythm is absent or turned off altogether and so the resulting movements despite weeks if not years no doubt of practicing the moonwalk is anything but smooth. We are not talking here of the perfection of trained disciplined steps like those in that choreographed dance routine of the Philippines' jailbirds.

In fact, it is a pleasure to witness older couples on the dance floor doing their one-two-three-dip thing. And the Chinese do love music and dance. So we are not talking of the precision of the Olympiad gymnasts or of those street performers paraded by Guy Laliberte for his *Cirque du Soleil* Spider Man antics. I'm talking about natural, fluid, inimitable movements that black people display whenever there's a beat.

But this crazy little chap on stage has a following! Apart from the man asleep under one of the Cuban palms (he looks like a worker who came with his buddies to check out the scene/screams), the Cantonese heavy metal singer has a solid support side up against the stage front. They are grooving to his sounds, hands in the air.

Now remember I spoke about the African possessing a rhythm that seems to be an inborn thing. Someone from our group now hails out "Hey! Look! The Brothers!" New excitement fills the air as the crowd stage side thickens.

On stage now is a meticulously garbed emcee in white linen suit and tie. With him is a Chinese Barbie in white satin outfit – the micro-mini flare skirt allowing a peep at peek-a-boo undies as she bobs up and down to the rap rhythm. The chap introduces themselves in Cantonese as a Hong Kong Hip Hop side with guest performers from America. The Brothers – African Americans both tall and handsome enough hail from New York and Atlanta. They are casually dressed with sweat rags dangling from side pockets. It's like one grabbed the other while rapping: "Hey Bro – grab the 'fro, just remember we've a gig to blow so let's go go go!"

Like many of the other foreign entertainers in mainland China however, one gets the feeling be they guitarist from Boston or pub side from Sao Paolo, that they are on stage for pocket money. The impression left to the one or two discerning foreigners in the audience is that they are nothing but a 'pick-up' side and window-dressing for some young Chinese entrepreneur.

In an educational exercise straight from the boom trucks of Machel Montano's Carnival crowd teasers come the lessons to the Chinese youngsters below. The couple explains the lines in dialect and the students are to respond eagerly as The Brothers slip effortlessly into action. They move in sync with the street rap that the four of them are now belting out.

Never mind the words, the steady drum beat is infectious and soon hands are waving with or without those neon-lit plastic cylinders that have been strategically placed around the lawn.

One of my young friends curl up two of my fingers and now with thumb and pinky out I am soon jabbing the air with the index in making a point of defiance (or is it in agreement?) with the rest of them. It is in imitation of the brothers and the Cantonese couple. I am told that the finger sign stands for 'heavy metal'. It goes with attitude, Chen Wei advises laughingly. The stage side is re-sounding to the 'yeahs' and 'nays' in a pretty close follow-fashion of Trini 'put yuh hands in de air'. And yes...the crotch-holding – (or is it protecting?) - hand movement is part of the act.

Back at my work station I do a little self-educating as to what exactly is heavy metal. The free convenient encyclopedia *Wikipedia* says it originates with rock music of the blues and psychedelic type. That figures, I muse...Originating in the late 60's in the UK and the US it employs electric guitar, bass, drums, vocals and keyboards.

The information becomes weirder as I read on.

The bands that created heavy metal developed a thick, massive sound, characterized by highly amplified distortion, extended guitar solos, emphatic beats, and overall loudness. Heavy metal lyrics and performance styles are generally associated with masculinity and machismo.

O-ka-a-ay! …. You don't need to go figure...

After all, it did take me a little time to hook into jazz. Now I'm addicted to a CD acquired by chance at the South African Embassy in Beijing. It was recorded at the 8th Cape Town Jazz Festival with *Caribbean Jazz Project* and for kindred spirits it is worth every effort to lay hands on it. Trust me! Accompanying pan music sweet too bad!

Now just when an old-timer should buzz off and go find a rocking chair and a pair of knitting needles or a can of Tsingtao, or better yet, the Bible, the term 'distortion' beckons me to go look it up. The frantic little young man who was tossing himself around the stage comes to mind. The music he was making certainly qualified for this musical genre of discordance.

After wading though tons of genretic terms like 'turbo distortion', 'electronic compressions' and 'fuzz tone pedal' not to mention 'warping and woofing' I've come to the conclusion that anyone who can deliberately doctor an instrument with punching holes or joining wires to achieve an accidental sound of extreme distortion would have to be bloody out of their mind. Such resulting noises range from a desirable 'warm fuzz' to screaming 'bites', 'grits' and 'crunches'.

My mind wanders back to that educational Saturday afternoon at the Chinese Woodstock.

I SCREAM was certainly a far cry from the energies of those young people who gathered for "An Aquarian Exposition: 3 Days of Peace & Music", held at Max Yasgur's 600-acre dairy farm near the hamlet of White Lake in the town of Bethel, New York. That was from August 15 to August 18, 1969.

I think that there is no message or purpose in the Chinese version on this lovely January afternoon in 2010. What do these comfortable, well-heeled youngsters have to protest about? There is no making of a point as did the Woodstock hippies of the Sixties. Remember that was about peace and love in a troubled world in the age that was the dawning of Aquarius.

Or...is there?

So let's take a look at the Age of Aquarius once more. Just when I thought it was an astrological period that had gone past, and not having former *Express* colleague Gail Massy to guide me accordingly, I learn that we are still within the 2,150 years of its zodiacal cycle! A website called *The Sixties* throws further light on the 1969 assemblage of young people.

The term, Age of Aquarius, long used in Astrology, assumed its new significance for young and uninhibited devotees when the musical show Hair linked its popular rock lyrics to an unforgettable melody and provided a new zany explanation for the way rock audiences faced the vicissitudes of life. It denoted boundary violation, carefree abandonment, humor, and a venue for imbibing in booze, dope, nudity, sex, and upbeat music, mostly but not exclusively rock.

As I read on, their message of protest becomes evident.

People, mostly young, tired of the pompous clichés and worn out admonitions of their parents, decided that with the dawning of the Age of Aquarius they would no longer need the sanctions of the hegemony to survive in life. Instead they put their faith in an open set of values that were at the same time naively honest, revolutionary, and kind, but those which, above all, celebrated life. For most celebrants their revels represented more than appeasing appetites, as the "roaring 20's" parties did; the new generation had a cultic concern for making and living in a better world, and backing away from repressive cold war behavioral codes and the military mentality that characterized American political rhetoric.

Aha! Therein lays the protest. It was a rebellion against the status quo that preached mealy-mouthing by parents and a government that acted in contradiction to the realities of life. So what does this have to do with our well-behaved teenagers on this harmonious Chinese landscape in Guangzhou?

As the golden orb begins to dip over there in the west, we leave the campus scene tranquil except for the throbbing of the boom boxes. A young man in red sweater with white design saunters past. The letters are huge and spell out words clearly visible in English - white on red hood across his shoulders. F*CK YOU, it says.

Well so much for freedoms, cultural penetration and peace and love as West penetrates East... again....

The message is there all right.

No wonder Beijing worries about the effects of the degenerate west on their 5,000 years of culture.

Rhona Baptiste in Hong Kong

34. IS IT GOODBYE TO THE OLD?

HONG KONG: Thursday 4th February 2010

I love Hong Kong! It is happy, it is exciting and it is an international city.

Now I did not say I 'prefer' Hong Kong because there are several mainland cities that would give the Hong Kong Special Administrative Region, and in particular the significantly rich Central, a run for its money. Beijing and Guangzhou are much more affordable places to live in and they offer a quality lifestyle that is as superior even as the battle with pollution continues.

But Hong Kong is really expensive. For instance, a three-bedroom apartment of 146 sq metres (about 1,600 square feet) in Guangzhou with all amenities from security to hot water and gas could be had for a monthly rental of 4,000 renminbi (US$ 570). However, the same-sized apartment in Hong Kong will cost approximately US$9,734 a month! This is according to a report from the 2008 EBA communications website. It is 13 per cent higher than it was a year ago when the equivalent apartment would have cost approximately US$ 8,592! The report states in fact that on average a three-bedroom apartment in a popular expatriate area in Hong Kong is 15 per cent more expensive than in Moscow, which is the survey's second most expensive location for rental accommodation.

If you are smart you don't brag that you are a foreigner in Hong Kong! If you do so, this will automatically convert the local currency into immediate US$ notwithstanding the present state of degeneracy of that currency. But what else do you expect when Hong Kong's per capita is put at US$31,849!

The entire area known as the Hong Kong Special Administrative Region (HKSAR) measures 426 sq. miles with a population of seven million people. That is about one-sixth the size of Trinidad with five times the population. What is little known is that outside of the hustle of the world's most densely populated city is a sprawl of countryside known as the New Territories and outlying islands rich in history and culture with its hidden nooks and crannies provided by an amoeba-like coastline.

Hong Kong is a Shangri-la for writers, poets, movie makers, artists and artistes, history buffs, gourmets, shoppers, buyers, sellers, traders, the works. It is one of the most cosmopolitan cities in the world and there are mosaic faces and garbs representing those who visit or live together cheek by jowl in one vast bazaar. But, oh! I've forgotten the princely preoccupation of them all – it's gambling. As a leading world international finance centre, Hong Kongese are traders in stocks, bonds and other forms of chance, like lotteries and horse-racing. Mahjong is a favourite pastime too.

But perhaps I just love Hong Kong because it is easy to identify with a history in which the British took control of the island in 1842 and planted their flag in the name of Queen Victoria. More than three hundred and fifty years before, Christopher Columbus had done the same in the Caribbean, that time in the name of King Ferdinand and Queen Isabella of Spain.

And so these imperialists, like Napoleon's armies in Haiti, imprinted their culture that has left us with an awareness of a hybrid life that evolved into something pretty much as familiar as back home in the Caribbean. Amidst the towering high-rises there is delightful European–styled architecture, lovely old gardens and shady streets with trees wearing identification bracelets for nature lovers.

Where Hong Kong becomes really intriguing to this visitor from the Caribbean is in its politics. With the return to mainland China on July 1st 1997, the Special Administrative Region (SAR) brought about the accommodation of two diametrically opposed political ideologies: communism and capitalism. It was Deng Xiaoping's idea to retain on the one hand the capitalist economic and political system of the colonizer, while a return to the mainland meant that it would be beholden to Beijing as the seat of the socialist system.

The angst of the British handover after 150 years to Beijing is well reflected in the writings of the last governor Christopher Patten. It must have been emotion-packed therefore when in his farewell speech he said grudgingly: "The story of this great city is about the years before this night and the years of success that will surely follow it."

For the territory's first Chief Executive Tung Chee-hwa, to whom Governor Patten had symbolically handed over the lowered British flag, the onerous duties of leadership had begun. For Mr. Tung and his successor Donald Tsang, Hong Kong's Basic Law that serves as the constitutional document provides no end of challenges. Although it was drafted in accordance with the Sino-British joint declaration and signed by both Chinese and British governments in 1984, it triggers heated debate in Hong Kong's Parliamentary sittings. In 1997 it replaced the Letters Patent and the Royal Instructions when the former colony of United Kingdom was handed over to the People's Republic of China.

Now the absolute fascination of Hong Kong is the familiar evolution of a people within an environment created along similar lines wherever the British have occupied. As it happens in all other British colonies, the success of this transfer of power is in the interaction (or lack thereof) between the leadership and the masses in the socio-political system.

It is seen each time the television cameras display empty seats of the Hong Kong parliament in session. It is seen each time there is a protest led by well-known opponents of the Beijing leadership, and often by a character called "Long Hair". Leung Kwok-hung is a self-proclaimed Trotsky-ist and a member of April Fifth Action, a radical socialist group. The amazing thing about democracy is that it provided him with the opportunity to win a seat in the 2004 LegCo District Council election!

And yet, democracy seems to be the privilege of those in position of power to be or not to be present at sittings, or to the privileged 'elite' in the Hong Kong society, many of whom are expatriates and local professionals. The politicized masses always seem to protest in a remarkably orderly manner behind horizontal banners. The banners display Chinese characters, and the marchers are usually dressed with kung fu headbands or kitchen pots on head - depending on the nature of their protest - advance stoically to present their letters to the government department in question.

So how then does this schizophrenic policy of "one country two systems" function? Why are there questions about the Chief Executive's accountability seemingly more toward Beijing than toward the democratically elected LegCo? Who are these people anyway and how are they elected? What about this adult suffrage question and why was this not instituted when the British were in control? What about the apparent hero-worship of the last British Governor Christopher Patten?

As happens in the so-called British West Indies, these are questions that do not elicit easy answers. But it is not that there are no answers. For example, that brilliantly explicit piece by Michael Harris in the *Express* on Monday, 14th December 2009 provides chilling insights to the problem of leadership. In his article, "Our leadership paradox in the Caribbean," Mr. Harris gives clear indications of why democracy western-style appears to be so confusing and self-serving to the few.

After a recent visit to Jamaica what this UWI lecturer found striking was the response to editorials in the *Gleaner* that called on the nation for answers to problems facing their country. Not only was Mr. Harris struck by the almost unanimous view of participants that a key component of the problem was the failure of leadership in the years since Independence (and this despite a number of charismatic leaders since then). The key political legacy in all these countries he found was a model of governance in which all power and authority resided in the person of the governor, the representative of the imperial power.

This explains why Christopher Patten continues to be lionized whenever he sets foot in Hong Kong to sign copies of the books he writes while paying a ritual photo-op visit to his favourite custard tart shop - Tai Cheong's Bakery in Central.

Mr. Harris' article would do well in *South China Morning Post* as this is what he says about adult suffrage that so many in Hong Kong are hankering after missing out on the opportunity while the British was there: The only real change in the model had come a few years before political independence with the general introduction of full adult suffrage which meant that the masses of people could no longer be completely ignored but had to be wooed periodically for their support.

But the disengagement that follows after a visit to the polling booth is of paramount importance and Mr. Harris' investigation into why despite political allegiance to leaders and parties, they (leaders and parties) have failed to engage or to politicize the people in an on-going making or forging or creating of their own destinies should not fail to jolt us from complacency. Leaders, who in taking over the colonial model of governance, he says, are, in fact, our modern-day governors. The problem is that they are incapable of transforming such overwhelming authority into genuine political power, if we understand political power to be the ability to persuade and commit.

Permit me to add, "to a self-determination of their country." That should be what true empowerment of the people in a true democracy should be all about.

At a time when Trinidad and Tobago has embarked on a pathway of change with the stunning victory of Ms. Kamla Persad-Bissessar to her party's leadership, it is a time to think of new directions, new meaningfulness and the obsolescence of charismatic governors at all levels whom we have inherited.

From the deck of the cross-harbour ferry, I watched the receding shoreline of Central with its latest prized building – a phallic-like structure thrusting upward to a clear blue sky. It is the 88-storey Two International Finance Centre.

I thought of how difficult it was to find a local author who could give me a picture shot from his side of the hunt. The bookstores are cluttered with expats like Mr. Patten – all authorities or 'foreign experts' who see the political game from their side as the hunters.

Back on the Kowloon side, my thoughts drifted back to Michael Harris and the hope that he engenders as I looked toward a return to a Caribbean homeland. Beyond the wake of ripples that the ferry dispatches while docking is the South China Sea. Farther away it reaches the wide Pacific Ocean that comes ashore on western side of the United States. Then a hop, skip and a jump from the state of California I will be on the more familiar shoreline of the Atlantic Ocean.

I think of Mr. Harris as another of the lions writing his side of the hunt where on the chain of islands in the blue Caribbean Sea is what many of us in the Caribbean Diasporas call home.

But wait.

Mr. Harris ends with what is surely a most exciting starting point for further discussion. And action. And hope. He says, as we look at Ms. Persad-Bissessar's recent victory:

Here in Trinidad however all the signs point to a total collapse of the old politics and with it the old political parties. That eventuality surely must present us with a golden opportunity to fashion new institutions of leadership.

How earnestly we hope that this is so, Michael.

Rhona Baptiste in Guangzhou

35. A CLEAR AND PRESENT DANGER

GUANGZHOU: Thursday 11th February 2010

Today is our mother's birthday. She loved Carnival so I'm dedicating this piece to her and hope that wherever she is it will reach her gift-wrapped with a forever love from us three children, four grandchildren and two great-grand daughters.

She was born Ivy Colastique Fairley in the year 1906. Had she lived this long she would have been 104 and Trinidad and Tobago in the year 2010 would have become to her - as to so many of her generation - the strange place that it is today.

Her name speaks of a gracious time when girl babies were given a first name from some favourite aunt as happened in her case, so that several cousins bore the same English name of Ivy after a beloved aunt on the Fairley side.

According to the Roman Catholic tradition of her mother she was baptized with the saint name of the day of her birth and that happened to be the Italian St. Scholastica's whose life span is put at (c. 480 - February 10, 547). Because her Spanish mother was brought up by a French patois-speaking grandmother, the saint name became the Colastique she grew up with.

The Fairley family in Tunapuna is a story for another day because according to deceased Teacher Tiny (Ann W. Murray) who was a repository of local history, (*Memoirs of the Good Shepherd Church 1886-1936*, by Ann W. Murray and Hyacinth E. Clarke, Inprint), the Scotsman and his 'dark-skinned' wife and their brood were pillars of the Anglican Church of the Good Shepherd on upper Morton and Freeling Streets. I don't remember this great-grandmother being referred to as African in those days which she clearly must have been.

The reason for this peek into family memoirs is because it is the reflection of many of our people in Trinidad and now Tobago where miscegenation continues apace. It is a fact of our Caribbean heritage. It is difficult therefore to find a family that does not have its gene pool swirling into and mixing with other colours of the palette from around the world.

Where this is leading is to the clear and ever present dangers – let's call them bogeys of race - from which we in T&T simply cannot extricate ourselves. But race, regardless of its wavelengths emanating from the broader spectrum of 'racism', like bigotry or discrimination, continues to be the great divider that crops up in the most sophisticated of social groupings.

One would think, for example, that after the acceptance speech of President Barack Obama as the first black president of the United States of America in 2009, the country with the world's highest ranking as a developed country would have been marching forward after resolving its black/white racial conflict that co-existed with the birth of their nation!

Check out the American history from the inauguration of George Washington as its first president in New York City in 1789 to Deosaran Bisnath's recent posting on 'Genealogy for a Nation of Immigrants' by Alessandra Stanley.

Instead 221 years later what we have is the on-going distractions of race that interfere with the urgent political issues at hand. For example, the latest US congressional budget estimates predicted a $1.35 trillion deficit for this year as the economy continues to slowly recover from the recession. However, much ado is made by a media just waiting to pounce on gaffes the like of

Senate Majority Leader Harry Reid after remarks he made about President Obama's race and dialect.

In Trinidad and Tobago, after centuries of living together on a piece of earth that measures just about 1,980 square miles, it seems as if we are more than ever divided by race despite the securing of our Independence from Britain in 1962 and a democratic system that promises free and fair elections with adult suffrage among its multi-ethnic people.

And yet, phobias persist in some quarters as to whether one's child is marrying 'dark skin' or 'light skin', 'African' or 'Indian', 'straight' or 'curly hair' if we are to judge from some of the postings that appear on this *JahajeeDesi* messaging board not to mention local and international articles that appear online. Race or racism (shucks... there goes sophistry again!) is alive and well at home it seems.

Such unproductive postings are self-serving and solicit the biliousness of some members of the blogging fraternity. One is apt to think of it as a self-flogging fraternity. Amazing how time and education affect this irritant that is race! Can we hope that race and tribalism is more the pre-occupation of the 'over-the hillers' rather than one that consumes our present-day more liberated youngsters?

In a society such as ours born and forged of so many ethno-religious beliefs shouldn't the litmus test for approval of an in-law by now – should it not be such better – meaning more wholesome - survival traits as selfishness vs. unselfishness; tolerance vs. intolerance; charitableness vs. greed, honesty vs. corruption; and so on? I guess this is what Confucius had in mind when he crafted the principles of his Good Citizenship.

But hold on! Aren't these the virtues that religions irrespective of whether they are Christian, Hindu, Islam, Spiritual Baptists or other 'good beliefs' have taught us born as we were on top of each other's religions and bred in the shadows of so many symbolic places of worship? Don't they each and every one spell out "Good Citizenship" – as our "brother's keeper" kind of thing? I have always marveled that democracy, the world's most-touted political ideology, could be corrupted into policies of hate, greed, exploitation and destruction that are quite the opposite of what its original creators had in mind.

Our gallery on the Eastern Main Road looked out onto parades and street theatre of all kinds. My favourites, apart from Carnival, were the funeral processions which represented the uniqueness of the tribes as they proceeded into Cemetery Street opposite our house to bid farewell to their dearly beloveds. For us neighborhood children it provided our first lessons into an amazing cultural diversity and religious tolerance.

The Roman Catholic procession led by Irish priest chanting rosary and acolytes swinging censers of incense in front of the flower-decked hearse was as magnificently baroque as were the Protestant Anglican and Presbyterian funerals where the ministers and choir dressed in somber clothes sang hymns like Rock of Ages straight out of 17th century England. These people were more or less 'light-skinned' people with more 'dark-skinned' ones among the Anglicans, Moravians, Adventists and others. The Presbyterians were mostly 'brown-skinned' East Indian people.

I liked to see the decorum of the Friendly Societies' protestant funerals with men and women wearing sashes of purple or those who carried banners with such titles like the Rose of Sharon to signify membership to a particular fellowship. It was the first time I'd heard the word "Rosicrucian" and the alleged bizarre rites that accompanied the passing of a member to the other side. These funerals were mostly of 'black-skinned' people.

And then there were the East Indian funerals. It is where we kids developed an appreciation for tassa drumming as the Hindu funerals bore its own special characteristics with the pundit leading the procession as the coffin was borne aloft. These were brown people.

A Madras funeral was particularly engaging as bare-backed men wearing dhotis danced in front of the coffin. This we understood to signify death as a happy occasion and one for celebration. The Indians in these funerals tended to be black-skinned rather than brown since they originated from the hot tropical south of India we were told.

We could recognize the Islamic type of funeral as the corpse was shrouded in white cotton and exposed on a bamboo pallet borne aloft with wailing women wearing orhnis following behind. The Muslim men wore crocheted skull caps or else like others elsewhere, cute little boat-shaped Nehru hats with white tunics over pants. Here again we saw brown people.

I know I tread on dangerous ground here, but it is what I remember. For example, the hijab was an unknown word to us as was the burqa. This womanly 'shroud of the living' was to appear in Trinidad with the advent of Abu Bakr's introduction of the Muslimeen after their attempted coup in 1990. The outfits were exotica that we students would gaze at on the pages of *National Geographic*. In the fifties as conservative Convent girls of Cambridge Higher Certificate, we could not reconcile the modesty of these women in the photos with others shown with their sultans in harems. That was the real exotica of the Islamic Middle-east as it displayed the fabulously erotic belly-dancers with an erstwhile hidden sensuality.

The elegant yet provocative sari was to be seen at weddings and certainly was not common place in everyday wear or even at funerals.

The Shouters or Spiritual Baptists were a curiosity too as the mourners wailed themselves into a frenzy behind the coffin while attendants waited to see if the spirit possessing the dancer would cause the person to collapse in a faint. We always hoped that the spirit would take complete possession of (usually) the woman's body before the cortege turned into Cemetery Street. Men were dressed like shepherds with staff in hand while women were bedecked as nuns, or nurses with scarves and aprons with head ties. These were all black people - African people.

But there were other lessons for us youngsters to learn from these street theatre performances too. I remember once as we watched the passing parade of cars and lorries with their electoral candidates way back in the fifties from our front gallery, my mother sighed deeply and commented on the tribal followings of each candidate. It was probably her first glimpse into the racial shades of politics.

For what she saw developing was the birth of party politics Trinidad style. With adult suffrage coming into play and people grouping themselves into cheerleaders to root for their particular political representatives, it was neither the organized social/class/caste divisions of the funerals nor even the socio-ethnic bandings of the carnival masquerade. This was a raw, animal passion of tribes pitting themselves one against the other, fangs barred in confrontation, gorilla dust being whipped up.

It led my Mum to comment naively perhaps, that she wished all Indian and Africans would intermarry and the resulting Douglas could then intermarry with the Others – they being the minority Whites, Chinese and Mixed in the population. How neat! I thought at the time. Later at university, on meeting with Gregor Mendel and Crick and Watson's teachings on the possibilities of genes and while unraveling the mysteries of the DNA workings of the chromosomes, I thought that she was probably onto something after all.

The difference remained however that what one could hope would materialize in the experimental lab just did not hold for what happens in the real lab of complex humankind.

Trinidad and Tobago remains a sociologist's paradise and an evolutionary scientist's wonder lab. Unlike most of the other Caribbean islands, history has bequeathed to it two major tribes, namely the Africans and the East Indians, who were deposited for the most part north and south of the Caroni River.

Let's not forget that there was NO CHOICE in the matter of homesteading. We got plunked in either the flooding muddy basin of the Rio Orinoco as it poured out from the belly of Venezuela or left to fend for ourselves on the foothills with the dying cocoa and coffee plantations.

Long after the demise of the British Colony, the muddy brown waters continue to rush down from the Northern Range above Arima, flow south to San Rafael and turn west collecting tributaries from Talparo farther south, and Tumpuna and Cumuto in the north and east. It effectively separates the East-West Corridor on the northern foothills from the Central Plains on the south. It is a recipe for perennial flooding now that it is open season for squatters and marijuana planters.

That was the Mason-Dixon line that became deeply etched with the birth of Independence in 1962 and the entrenchment of Dr. Eric Williams' People's National Movement with an African face on the one side while the East Indian face was registered on the Democratic Labour Party of Dr. Rudranath Capildeo on the other. The geographic location of both major tribes as was already mentioned was the happenchance of a colonial history.

The die was cast and to this day, African versus Indian remains the tug-of-war for political power over the twin-island state made all the more tempting because of the coffers that its accidental oil and gas windfalls generate.

Over the years as my mother's 'douglarization' of the African and Indian families was taking place along with the follow up 'browning' of the lightened mixtures in the pot-pourri, nevertheless the unfortunate consequence of race continues to rear its ugly head especially at election time.

It is the time to show one's true colours by aligning with the candidate on one or the other side of the Great Racial Divide. It is a time when the past five years of 'harmonious' living is rent asunder and one migrates to one's tribe in much the same way as one finds oneself called in a Carnival band to get-in-yuh-section. The oddities meaning Syrians, Indians, Mixed or French Creoles are the profiteering opportunists who would align with whichever racial side their bread was being buttered.

Rarely would an African jump the tribal line in obvious allegiance with the other side.

But politics is a time for so much 'chupidness' that it brings to mind once more that relevant piece from Michael Harris's 'Our leadership paradox in the Caribbean ' in the *Express* on Monday, December 14th 2009.

It is a time for electoral rather than for political mobilization since after the celebration of the victors and laments from the vanquished, it is back to business as usual. We must continue to eat and drink, fete, ole talk and mate with each other. For over the next five years the frantically possessed voters having cast their vote for their tribal leader possess no powers of constraint on the exercise of governmental power by their leaders.

The further result was (still is) a critical disconnect between the political leaders in government and the mass of their supporters.

It is this critical disconnect that we, the masses of supporters on BOTH sides of the Great Divide, must now address. Whoever wins or loses - and there has to be one of each, namely a government that must lead and an opposition whose duty is to provide the checks and balances - we all must understand that we have work to do. IF this democracy of ours is going to work and become a model for others, we've got to do it TOGETHER.

So are we REALLY committed to pulling off this ideal? Shouldn't this be the proud hallmark of a True Trini? Wouldn't it be really neat to travel the world and stick out your chest and say: "Yes man! I'm from Trinidad and Tobago. Neither Afro nor Indo Trini. I'm a real Caribbean person."

I would like to assure our mother on this her 104th birthday that for the next five years we are going to put our house in order. We the people of Trinidad and Tobago will not only pledge ourselves to a unity in which we can move forward for the greater benefit of ALL our people BUT we will accept our accident of race with equanimity without having it run our lives to ruin with pettiness.

What's more, Mum, we pledge to be our brothers' keeper so that our poor black Little Brother Haiti would be helped out of its misery from circumstances that must not be allowed to happen again...NOT ANYWHERE ...NOT EVER.

Is the Caribbean Community listening? The G7 meeting seems to have heard the cries of concerned people in our islands!

36. DRINK AND BE DAMNED!

GUANGZHOU: Thursday 18th February 2010

As Trinidad and Tobago staggers awake from its annual bacchanalian revelry of indulging its flesh and its fantasy, it is time to take a look at the essence of a society that reflects the purpose of its existence. Let's call it a country's Mission Statement. I know... I know... it was a wonderful Carnival (according to all the online press reports) and sweet pan reigned, but let's return to reality.

A T&T Mission Statement? Reality? What exactly is that? Well, it is when someone invites you to share with them the purpose or rationale or raison d'etre of their lives. It is an enticement or a wooing of your interest to want your participation. Someone wants you to be a part of their world. It is much like inviting you to be a part of their Company. Caught my meaning?

So what is the first thing a Trinidadian or a Tobagonian might tell someone about his country? A ready sales pitch could be: "Man, you must come for Carnival! It's the greatest show on earth ...T&T is plenty street theatre... plenty food and drink". Should you be an old-timer you will do a 'dry wine' and sing for your listener: "Rum... glorious rum... when ah call you - you bong to come." Is this what our Mission Statement should be?

Let's look at it another way. Go find one of those newly-arrived bona fide Chinese labourers and ask him about his country. Soon enough you will be invited to come to China for the Spring Festival. It is their country's big fete and it coincides with our own Carnival dates. But there is in place in China, as in other countries in the so-called western world, an ideology that holds people together to aspire and to achieve a higher quality of life than gluttony and fun.

We didn't invent the Carnival and for those curious enough about festivals it is interesting to note that the celebration of the Chinese Spring Festival is a reunion of family about the same time as the ancient pagan spring festivals that celebrated the end of winter and the start of Spring and new life. As the Chinese idiom says, *Yi nian zhi ji zai yu chun.* Or, a year's plan starts in spring. Christianity, we see, positioned the dates of Christmas and Carnival at times in the year already celebrated as festivals by people in the known world.

The former marked the birth of Christ in December when village, town and city wore the somberness of winter. The latter, Carnival's pre-Lenten celebration, was a hedonistic time for indulging the flesh before putting it into denial for the forty days of prayer, fasting and abstinence from meat. Hence carne vale, Latin for 'farewell to meat'. This was placed at the end of winter and forty days before the death and resurrection of Jesus Christ whose own birth is the internationally accepted dating point before and after that first century of his fabled arrival.

Now let's take a look at what happens in India and in T&T too. On reading of UNC Political Leader Kamla Persad-Bissessar's observance of the festival Maha Shiv Ratri last Thursday, a background check delivered the answer that I expected, namely, that it was a Hindu Spring festival. The website reveals very interesting stuff about Lord Shiva as being a dissolving force in order to create anew - death and rebirth here being a familiar theme as with the Christian celebration of death and resurrection.

And then there is Holi, definitely a fun festival that begins on Sunday, February 28th and ends on 1st March this year. This Hindu festival speaks of full moon and Spring harvest and spraying each other with coloured water we know as abir. Now all this comes from a website titled 'Holi - Hindu Festival of Colours' with an introduction by Subhamoy Das. The paragraph that is familiar though is titled "Don't mind, it is Holi" and proceeds to tell:

"During Holi or Phagwa, practices, which at other times could be offensive, are allowed. Squirting colored water on passers-by, dunking friends in mud pool amidst teasing and laughter, getting intoxicated on bhaang and reveling with companions is perfectly acceptable. In fact, on the days of Holi, you can get away with almost anything by saying, "Don't mind, it's Holi!" (Hindi = Bura na mano, Holi hai.)"

It sounds as familiar as, Doh mind nutten, is we 'mas. And now look at what follows! Just watch how it connects with those pictures of women-in-liberation last weekend! Can this really have been our last Carnival? Certainly not after that colourful assembly of my Mum's 'red people' at Adam Smith Square on Carnival Tuesday? Once more My Ron encourages me to come see for myself. But Subhamoy Das continues:

"Women, especially, enjoy the freedom of relaxed rules and sometimes join in the merriment rather aggressively. There is also much vulgar behavior connected with phallic themes. It is a time when pollution is not important, a time for license and obscenity in place of the usual societal and caste restrictions. In a way, Holi is a means for the people to ventilate their 'latent heat' and experience strange physical relaxations."

Ah! So it's a letting off of steam too, eh!

Now the joy of instant research that this wonderful world of IT has provided titillates one into further discovery and can easily distract from the purpose at hand. For today's column was really triggered by Krishna S. Narinedath who posted his vexation on *JahajeeDesi2005* on Sunday 7th February. And it had to do with Carnival. So angry was he that he titled it, 'Shameless Coolie Rum Singers' and went on to berate Chutney Soca Monarch

Ravi B (Bissambhar) for a "Rum Song" that is denigrating and in bad taste.

I understand Mr. Narinedath's anger especially since 35,000 bmobile text votes, the first ever used, earned the singer the cash prize of TT$200,000. It does seem a lordly sum to promote the idea that it is okay to become inebriated and have your woman join in the "Ah Drinka" - the title of his rendition.

When I look at the disintegrating fabric of our society where law and order is challenged with a murder rate that stands at 64 up to Carnival Tuesday (that is 64 murders in 47 days!) and a judiciary that is back-logged in solving an on-going rate of homicides there is justifiable cause for alarm. This becomes even more dangerous when treated as did the *Express* Thursday 4th February that announced too optimistically perhaps in its Editorial 'Welcome moves to boost judiciary'.

I am not being over-sensitive, I hope. The editorial went on to declare without giving specifics that the judiciary, however, has made significant improvement over the past decade in reducing the backlog of court cases. And it spoke of over 10,000 matters outstanding in the High and the Appeal Courts, and perhaps another 400,000 in the Magistrates' Courts!

Geezanages! This is madness!

Who is fooling whom that this unspeakably dangerous situation can be regularized even by waving a wand for an additional 1,000 members to boost the judiciary?

One reads frequently of stories like the one I've just pulled up by chance from the *Guardian* on Thursday 17th January 2008. It really is heart-breaking. Shaliza Hassanali reports on a twelve-year-old pupil found with condoms in her school bag. She is one of three pupils who have run away from school. They come from broken homes. And *Newsday* on 9th February 2010 relates a

Form Three student as fatally stabbed in the chest by a 15-year-old.

So what continues to be going on here? We are not talking isolated cases; we are talking REGULAR occurrences that threaten to become an acceptable way of life! But we feted as usual over the past weeks, will continue to do so and it's business as usual now with mountains being made of molehills on Mr. Manning's front lawn. Was precious water being used for the Prime Minister's gardens out of season? What will WASA do about this? Well, if we can't get a license to fete on de beach we go do it in de bus.

Know something? Were I standing in the wobbly shoes of the Prime Minister I would have stopped the Carnival and used the two days in a national consciousness raising, get serious convocation. It could become a week's retreat. Let the people write their own Mission Statement - perhaps one that would ban alcohol with fines imposed as with breaking the water curfew. People would have been employed as guardians and the whole twin-island family would have undergone a renewal experience.

Now don't tell me I'm bringing my conservative diatribe or any religious evangelism to a country now recovering from Carnival and gearing up for the Holi days of freeing-up.

Truth is I want to get back to Ravi B's rendition which 'celebrates' the heart of many a broken home. I have no idea what the rhythm is like but this I know from the often unintelligible but infectious rap beat. It could easily offset the negatives of the song's message. But people like Mr. Narinedath and Dr. Suruj Rambachan, my fellow candidate on the old ONR hustings in 1981, have a right to take offense at the singer's lines that invite the woman to 'Just break ah seal gyul and take some liquor with me'. The message is negative and once extracted from the euphoria of the fete or lime, it registers as not funny at all but as terribly pathetic long after the fete is over.

When are we going to grow up? When are we going to take ourselves seriously and define where we are going? Where are we really taking that delicious pan that has outdone itself at this year's Panorama? Where are we really taking Carnival? I heard that Trinidad and Tobago was in the Hong Kong New Year's street parade this year. So we did get on to Hong Kong's TVB Pearl Channel. But guess what? It was introduced as "Pan from British Notting Hill's Carnival" and my friend became excited only when she recognized four little T&T flags on the four corners of the truck! Where was Minister Gary Hunt when we needed him?

But again I'm being distracted from Ravi B's Chutney Soca. My own angst comes from the futility of the man telling his woman 'Gyul when U kya beat them, Gyul when U kya beat them, You have to join them. You know U kya do no better...' To begin with I have a problem with the written dialect that seems to swing between 'text-speak' and the 'traditional vernacular.' Most scary of all though is the idea that an intelligent human is unable to DO BETTER! "So gyul doh fight it! Succumb...give in...drink de rum...keep me company in mih dotishness!"

Does Ravi B have any idea of the potential for catastrophe that his 'jokey' lyrics could cause among his friends and family and thousands of other Trinidadians and Tobagonians? Has he ever experienced the return of a deadbeat father to a home where wife and kids are terrified at the monster that they must call husband and father as he stomps around the place that is home? In the case of a mother who drinks it is just a step away from hard drugs and the road to insanity.

Now this calypso-in-bad-taste comes at a time when the Manning Government has just to its credit instituted a breathalyzer programme for the country's drinking drivers. It comes at a time when the country's social performance is in such bad shape as to rate it as one of the world's most dangerous places in which to live. Isn't that cause for all our alarm?

Does it take an Irishman to tell us we have a crisis on hand? Remember Quintin Oliver's words at the YesTT conference when he remarked that it must be a cause of great concern and it should be the subject of the highest political and policy attention in order to try and diagnose the cause and find solutions very quickly. He then put it to the audience: "I understand you are in the top five murder rates in the world. Now isn't that extraordinary? Is that not the most important political issue?"

If this isn't a wake-up call for messages to be serious yet entertaining, I don't know what it will take to make us become a society of responsible individuals. It should begin perhaps with calypsonians who wield such great influence with a captive audience on its radio and video waves. They remain the voice of the people.

This is a time to remind ourselves that the Mission Statement of our Trinidad and Tobago must be as positively uplifting as we can make it. The messages can no longer be a celebration of drunken and disorderly behaviour. The price of those 'rum songs' is just too damning.

Rhona Baptiste in Los Angeles

37. WELCOME, IDIOCRACY

LOS ANGELES: Thursday 25th February 2010

I have been in this City of the Angels since Sunday evening, the same day that I left Guangzhou, and I have heard that *Idiocracy* is the name of a Hollywood movie that bombed. The storyline is the number of intelligent people having babies has declined, while the number of stupid people having babies has increased, so soon enough we are in a world that is overrun with idiots.

Ouch! I think we are there already.

We are experiencing life in the raw in downtown Los Angeles. At the bus stop there is an African-American young woman occupying the waiting bench. She is bouncing around a cute two-year-old, hair heavily braided with beads. An older daughter and a son are fidgeting alongside while a skinny guy - the father perhaps - hovers around.

A paunchy man of questionable ethnicity appears. He's pleasant enough and uses the arrival of a Hispanic woman, who is pressing her three-dollar belts on us, as the moment to engage. Time was he says, while shaking his head sadly, when life was better. Now jobs are hard to come by. He remembers when he could afford a seven-dollar pizza. Now he has to settle for a three-dollar one that costs him a long ride over. He's curious about our origins. I tell him and he asks, "Is it as bad there as it is here?"

I remember the warning from Marc: "Do not engage." But we are Trinis and it's hard to be indifferent to people who seem to be just curious about our looks and accents? We are, aren't we, proud about our good luck to be born in Trinidad? It is obvious that we don't fit into the background poster, which reads in huge type that 'We help people grow and thrive in Los Angeles'. The 'we' being Kaiser Permanente, a health insurance business that owns the comfortable acreage of real estate around us.

Los Angeles has to be one of the craziest places on this planet. Why else would a city with such a mind grasp on the world attract the Church of Scientology? Our bus goes past a site that promises another man-made monument to its beliefs. There is an expansion of membership if we are to judge from the colossus about to be erected for and by believers. What is it with these people who believe that they must lay down treasures on earth?

The creator of this Church was Ron Hubbard whose legacy attracts some of Hollywood's finest. So what is the basic tenet of his church's beliefs? Well, for one thing, it offers the connection with extra-terrestrial beings, which nevertheless could only be acquired with lots of non-believers' support at the box offices of the world. It is itself the stuff of which fantasy is made even if it is nothing like ET. The movie, I mean. But when one sees names like John Travolta, Tom Cruise and Will Smith in its galaxy, there is cause for wonder.

So, yes, arriving in the USA in the year 2010 must indeed be a culture shock for the innumerable immigrants like that chap in the film, *The Legend of 1900,* who was the first to spot the Statue of Liberty and shouted, "A-mer-ee-ka!" Could it have been the same for our middle-eastern housekeeper? I had asked her help about the apartment's microwave, having always had a suspicion of laser beams that could zap a cup of coffee into an IED (according to Margareth Chen in Hong Kong) and turn bread into dough.

Well, anyway, the house-keeper's English vocabulary comprises two phrases: "Okay!" and "Yeah-yeah!"

Could she have been subjected to passing a grueling Immigration interview before she was allowed to put hand over left breast and pledge allegiance to *The Star Spangled Banner*? And was I being cynical when I thought that, thanks to Mr. Bush, Washington owes many Iraqis, burqas and all, a lot for the plunder of their country?

Well, anyway, by the time our little outing takes us past innumerable freaks, downwind of the gigantic letters that spell out HOLLYWOOD, we make a stopover at Archlight. This is an entertainment plaza where I recalled another visit to Los Angeles in the summer of 2008. I remembered that I had written at the end of it my impressions in *Imprint*, the Hong Kong Women In Publishing Society (HKWiPS) anthology. It was a kind of farewell letter to my friends in Hong Kong and it was inspired then by what I had seen of the American MTV Awards 2009 on TVB Pearl.

The video introduction of the Emcee began with the young man parodying the movie *Slumdog Millionaire* by a self-immersion in faeces only to emerge and expose himself 'in the nude' (thanks to computer wizardry) while showing off his backside to viewers. Onstage in his opening jokes to a live audience of millions worldwide, he punctuated his welcome with assuring the audience that it was okay to fart at will. What was I missing I thought? Or was it that the line between good taste and bad had blurred or rather disappeared into non-existence?

Again while risking the accusation of apologist for the Chinese it is understandable why the fathers in Beijing view with queasiness the degree of Western decadence to which their 1.3 billion population is exposed. Where one draws the line in censorship and morality vs. amorality continues to be the preserve of religious and political doctrine in each sovereign state. It is what should be respected.

Up to the time that the first awardee took centre stage to receive a tacky-looking pop-corn trophy, both garish presentation and dress code epitomized an absence of class. And by this I mean an absence of good taste or style. The much touted Low Cost Budget on which the evening's show was made possible could have become the challenge for an incredibly remarkable presentation.

Now don't get me wrong. I'm neither prude nor Victorian. I enjoy good adult risqué stuff as much as any other liberated member of my peer group. And my sons and their friends seem to think me so cool as to have included me to attend the premiere showing of *Tropic Thunder*. Arm-seat loaded with real buttery popcorn and mile-long hot dog lathered with yellow and red goo I sat back in one of Hollywood's Archlight cinemas to enjoy some quality time relaxation with the young people. I remembered it all today as I looked around the lobby advertising such films as *Avatar*, the current movie-goer's choice.

Seconds into *Tropic Thunder*, the audience is awash in mud with a battalion of make-believe US combat soldiers competing with each other in vulgarities. The Mother f-ing word has become a Part of Speech and mayhem reigns amidst a Babel that my youthful companions find hilarious. There is no embarrassment registered on my sons' faces or on their companions'. After all, we are now all adults!

As the movie thundered on, one calamitous event followed another in even more ridiculous succession. I could not help but bemoaned the enormous sums spent on Ivy League education that should have elevated my sons' taste to a more cerebral fare. The explosions of land mines and in-your-face gore reminded me of how careful we were as parents to protect them from violence. "Please, no gun gifts" was the gentle reminder to friends and relatives.

Nowadays, as I prepare to return to my Caribbean home for the first time after 12 years in Mainland China the reality of crime statistics that I now monitor on a daily basis is daunting. My homeland once recalled with nostalgia as a Paradise, where church and state with its multi-racial population co-existed more or less happily together, now is no more.

China has provided me with a security blanket over the past twelve years. Like the Buddhist monk Vicki Mackenzie in her Himalayan *Cave in the Snow* there has been much time for reflection and search for that difficult to grasp chimera-like/willow-the- wispy male-linked Nirvana. The daughter of a fishmonger from London's East End, Vicki (Tenzin Palmo) emerged from her cave after twelve years to champion the rights of women to attain a gender equal spiritual enlightenment.

The daunting task of fixing the world so as to leave it a better place remains a continual challenge for us all. Albert Camus was preoccupied with it and bitterly so at times. His notes on the meaning of his work are scathing: *So many men lack grace. How can one live without grace? We must really get down to it and do what Christianity has never done: concern ourselves with the damned.*

Yet at times he is sympathetic to those intellectual non-activists who were looked down upon by fellows in the French resistance and many of whom died for the cause. He acknowledges in his notes that it was inertia or ignorance which accounted for people's failure to act. I take consolation in the words he puts into Tarrou's mouth. In *The Plague* Tarrou says of people, you just need to give them the opportunity.

I am going home after this Los Angeles visit. It's not long now. There's a lot of work still waiting to be done. The world is still waiting to be fixed into a better place.

38. WALKING ON STARS

LOS ANGELES: Thursday 4th March 2010

On hearing news of the latest earthquake in Chile measuring 8.8 on the Richter scale, my friend's daughter Nikki back home swears the end is near. Her mother suggests she joins Prime Minister Patrick Manning's Church. Be careful though, she adds, as a member of his flock you will be open to persecution.

It is this irreverent and cynical attitude to life that keeps a lot of us going. It explains why for eons Man has consoled himself, if not with a believable religion, certainly with the lighter unbelievable side of laughter. This comes as a counterweight to the manic-depressive bouts that tempt him into retreating from the trials of daily life.

Look at Marie Osmond's son. *Celebrity News* reported that he was suffering from depression and loneliness so for the 18-year old Michael Blosil, his leap from a 15-storey building on Friday night was the solution to his problems. Depression and loneliness in this land of Walt Disney and the American Dream!

But of this kind of tragedy is life and death in the tragi-comedy of the city of Los Angeles.

It has been described as a collection of cities without a centre and you understand why as you roam from Thai Town through Korea Town to all the other ethnic groupings of Towns that manage to survive from day to day. One wonders how it succeeds with its polyglot populations where whites are now in the minority.

One reason is the release that comes with looking and laughing at the ridiculous. It is for this reason why from the cross-talks (*xiang cheng*) of China's stand-up comedians to the calypso and extempo of our own Carnival's double-talk (*double-entendre*) and picong, we discover kindred American spirits in the likes of individuals speaking out for us on provocative issues of the day. In the USA, release from daily pressure takes the form of self-immersion in soap operas, street songs and theatre. And thank God for the stand-up comedians.

Thanks to these voices important lessons in social education are shared with a populace unfamiliar with the complexities of academics and their polemics. When will we awake to the fact that ordinary people just do not get some of these messages? The irony is that the common people are the ones who most need to understand what is being dished up to them in a daily dose of government talk-shops, lies and false promises otherwise known as politics. It is the same politics that enable some to live on Beverly Hills while others must scrounge on the streets.

Educating the people is an area where newspapers can become a forceful medium for the messages that can play so much more of a dynamic leadership as can movies like *The Soloist*. In this drama a news reporter (actually from the *LA Times*) investigates the life of a vagrant on the streets and discovers the incredible story of a genius violinist who just could not compete. He dropped out of the competition, preferring insanity to suicide. The reporter's interest on a person-to-person basis results in the rehab of the homeless chap he has befriended.

The streets of LA provide innumerable stories for the visitor to interface with and are of much more human interest than the Guinness Museum that seems to be in a state of dereliction as are so many other iconic institutions. It is the human drama in which the real characters you meet are as if from a book - the living history of life that is now the American West.

So this is why HBO was welcome the other night as it churned out more than an hour of straight comedy from Bill Maher. Just look at this quote:

What's so great about the internet is that it enables pompous blowhards to connect with pompous blowhards in a vast circle jerk of pomposity. Guess one can substitute the word 'internet' with 'politics'!

His mouthing on individuals from the Pope through Osama bin Laden to God the Divine to Tiger Woods are nothing short of irreverent in its topical and thought-provoking snippets he calls "Religulous". No wonder Maher is so hot with ratings that continue to spiral upwards.

It is another exhausting day out in this arid, sunny native land of the Cherokee people where tall, thin tufts of California palm trees like feather dusters air-brush the landscape. Cherokee is the long-forgotten presence of a native tribe of people on a street sign. It is dominated by the other familiar mountain sign with huge letters that spell out HOLLYWOOD. Tacky shops along Hollywood Boulevard display T-shirts with messages from the sublime of Che Guevara's and Bob Marley's revolutionary spirits to the ridiculous prints of obscenity on how to keep your mate.

We are in the Mecca for locals and foreign visitors who must gawk and tread the footsteps of their idols - movie stars of yesteryear like Grace Kelly and Lawrence Olivier. It is with awe that tourists point their cameras at the bleachers that line the sidewalk at Highland and Hollywood. It is where hopefuls of the hallowed and the profane will walk in anticipation of the Oscars on Sunday next.

Doting fans will pose or talk with an imitation Batman or Marilyn Monroe who appear for a photo-op for which US$1 must be doled out. After all, these people are working, and like the pimps and prostitutes manage to escape the radar of the IRS.

But let me walk you through the blocks whose sidewalks are the shrines at which so many come to worship. These are the tiles inlaid with the gold gilded star shapes with names inscribed of past and present pantheon of celluloid deities.

On this cool morning in LA when a drizzle actually threatens, a good breakfast is hard to find within walking distance between Western and Highland. There are innumerable dingy places and stepping over the galaxy of stars provide only passing interest to the actual circus that is coming awake.

There is the Museum of Death advertised with a large skull and Old Glory in front of which sits a picture-perfect vagrant. He lights up when a partner alights from his bicycle. There is a positive side to the groups of misfits however. Along the way with the exclusive Hollywood Hills on the right is graffiti that advises, 'Violence solves nothing'.

True enough on this strip one group of homeless assembles passively at the corner at Whitley and Hollywood. They are the colourfully bedraggled collection of humanity who looks like *j'ouvert* morning revelers walking past the star clusters that belong to James Dean and The Supremes.

By ten-thirty a whiff of marijuana signals the awakening of the city. And why not? The State of California has legalized the sale of marijuana so medical marijuana pharmacies are ubiquitous. The City of the Angels is coming alive with a couple of store fronts now pushing open their shutters.

It is a time to wonder what will become of this famous American West Coast city, if we are to judge from news reports that California's budget shortfall is now estimated to be $26.3 billion.

How to fix this is reflected in Meg Whitman's TV commercials as she makes the case to save the state by voting her in as a replacement to Governor Arnold Schwarzenegger. Her platform plank is "building a grassroots organization second to none".

I think of Kamla Persad-Bissessar at the home that I am fast approaching. Her star is certainly in its ascent from all reports and so too are the hopeful asteroids that are clumping ever closer into her Milky Way. With her recent appointment of four new senators and the adrenalin rushes of an impending election, it will be an ongoing curiosity to see how she will devclop her team.

I am concerned that the change in a future that some of us envisage for Trinidad and Tobago can well threaten to become a replay of the past where questionable messengers will assemble with empty messages and the fiasco of leadership will be the same as when the 'Rainbow NAR' got their chance and blew it. We should examine WHY it was blown.

Where is an exciting new blood? Where are the people who will create a new energy for meaningful change? Are we going to put back in the old tired blowhards like Bill Maher's internet people? *What's so great about old politics is that it enables pompous blowhards to connect with pompous blowhards in a vast circle jerk of pomposity.*

So where are the young people? Where are the women?

As for women and where their representation is concerned, listen to what is happening at this very liberated feminist end of the globe in the USA.

State News Shot November 2009 an American website reports that it is harder to recruit women to run for office.

Are the women of Trinidad and Tobago willing to join with Ms. Persad-Bissessar for prominent positions? Or, will we see men who are unabashedly crawling out of the woodwork? Many are those already excited at the prospects of shining in that star-studded galaxy that is political office and the lure of privilege and power.

Rhona Baptiste in Miami

39. DAY OF THE IGUANAS

MIAMI: Thursday 11th March 2010

It is getting as close as possible now to stepping on home soil. American Airlines flight 280 has touched down at Miami International Airport and although the sun is as hot as ever, the temperature is a cool 58 degrees F. The Chinese winter jackets are as welcome here as they were in Los Angeles.

We are to stay with the Chester and Lynette Morong family in Miramar and familiarity with Le Jeune Road and Palmetto Expressway rushes back as though twelve years never happened. Miami is as always post-card perfect. Coral buildings against a clear blue sky with fluffs of clouds above; blue fringe of a beloved Caribbean Sea below and beyond; coconut trees...

The Florida landscape is pleasantly monotonous. The large chunk of expropriated Everglades is neatly cut into living and shopping communities. Somehow a comparison with that other coastal city that is Tinsel Town speaks of an energy – a characteristic that seems absent in this people-less town. It is not like downtown LA and certainly not like Guangzhou with its teeming millions. Miami is a city that is dead.

The charm of coming closer to home is being with friends who speak the same language, make the same jokes, re-live the same experiences. Excitement increases as photos are shared over bake and buljol. West Indian fare that has been traveling to North America over the years is now permanently available, from doubles to patties and jerk this to jerk that. It is good to be coming back home.

Our Trini hosts remind us with that irrepressible humour that there's always dinner from the lake as we watch the ducks and their ducklings waddling across the lawn. The strong glare outside encourages a stroll alongside the water. On the little deck is a large brown-skinned iguana, immobile and contemptuous. A younger green-skin, suspicious of our intentions, splashes into the water. Was it just a joke? Or, did the iguana know the fate of some of the ducks?

A neighbour comes up to say her husband has tamed the larger, older creature with breadcrumbs. The result is a longer basking in the sun. However, this reptile knows too that humans are not to be trusted and there's a point for man as for animals at which indiscretion becomes folly. As I stalk nearer, with camera instead of crumbs, it eludes my camera finger and flings itself into the water.

Later, we are shown pictures of the Port of Spain waterfront. There's the harbour − impressive buildings against a background of lights twinkling from the hills of Laventille. The foreground is lit up with bursts of fireworks from the Gulf of Paria. By day the video reveals that the Caroni Swamp is still there and against the intensive development with ritzy apartments, the mountains still appear green. I'm anxious for the reality check.

There is that shuttlecock building of the controversial Performing Arts Centre that I anticipate in the real. Yes! Trinidad has done well for itself. But then nothing less should be expected with a budget that was boosted by former US President Bush's invasion of Iraq in March 2003. The aftermath saw the price of oil skyrocketing to over US$100 a barrel.

By 2006 we could read a report on *www.news.co.tt*. Breaking News that Prime Minister Patrick Manning in his capacity as Minister of Finance stated:

• The size of the Trinidad and Tobago Economy has doubled over the past five years.

- GDP has grown by 8% in 2006 so far and the total growth for 2006 is expected to be 12%.
- Inflation stands at 9%. Government aims to bring it down to 7%.

They are impressive achievements but in Miami my queasiness increases with my first look at T&T's news in print. The daily and Sunday newspapers that I was given at the Trinidad and Tobago Consulate at Brickell Avenue all look identical! The layout is garish and news stories are confusingly difficult to read. There is no difference between the newspapers and, from what I remember as the Patrick Chookolingo legacy, they all seemed to be daily siblings of those weekly tabloids.

In both Los Angeles and Miami I found readers who cited their preferences as the *Express*, the *Guardian* and *Newsday*. Readers it was said chose all three because if something was missed in one paper they might get it in the other. So much for the news; what about intelligent opinion? The feeling was: "Dey eh have no newspapers no more. If somebody want to write someting it go get in."

The Trinidad and Tobago Consulate in Miami at No. 1000 Brickell Avenue brings back memories of the time when it was a stomping ground for my door-to-door sales of *Caribbean Affairs* – the quarterly journal that survived a period of nine years. The décor of the Consulate is certainly timeless with its colourful touristy panels and framed photos of government leaders.

There was a moment of pride as we drove past to enjoy a temporary luxury of what the Miami Intercontinental Hotel and the Marriott offer. It was where the annual Latin America/Caribbean Conferences took place. That was time to showcase the publications that we were involved with from our little corner of the Caribbean.

Which reminds me - there is a full page advertisement in Sunday March 5th *Miami Herald*. There is a conference scheduled for 17-19th March at the Miami

Beach Convention Center. It is to be held over a period of three days with 45 panels/workshops and it is billed as the largest economic and development conference ever held on Haiti.

It is a bit confusing. Which one is this? Is it the same one that Rickey Singh questions in his 'Investing or capitalizing on Haiti?' (Wednesday, 17th February 2010). He raises concerns about Caricom's involvement (or lack of) scheduled for March 9-10 and bearing in mind its own involvement in next month's special conference that will consider the orderly integrated social and economic development of Haiti.

Mr. Singh continues about his concern and mine: engaging in traditional humanitarian rhetoric, the organisers, many of whom are linked to private security corporations and not all with flattering credentials, state on their website *(www.investmentsummits.com)*

Good so far. Linking the Montreal Conference with the Investment Summit in Miami may be tactical. But are the objectives the same - in the best interest of Haiti's reconstruction?

Now to tell you the truth what is of great concern in the future of Haiti's re-development at a time when US$ billions must be administered is trustworthiness. Once again the question is who to trust. The integrity of those who have already positioned themselves as caretakers of the coffers and designers of Haiti's future are the suspect security firms and providers of business summits. This is especially so as more information surfaces about the possibility of oil and gas on which Cuba, Haiti and Dominican Republic float.

In Miramar, I watch the iguanas basking in the Florida sunshine. What do they understand about suspicion and the nature of the creature called Man alongside whom they must co-exist? Can they trust the one who feeds them with crumbs? And could they trust the newcomers who point strange weapons at them?

As Trinidad and Tobago draws closer, it is with the same suspicion as the iguanas that I view my fellowmen. It is a country where I think crime remains the major issue; where the President is unable to identify members for an Integrity Commission; where the Police Service is headed indefinitely it seems by an acting Commissioner of Police; where both Government and Opposition are tainted with charges of corruption, inefficiency and mismanagement; and where the Judiciary is in a state of nervous solicitude.

I sit in the sun and question the country to which I am returning and trying to discover the answer for such a need. Was it nostalgia, but nostalgia about what?

It used to be so easy to hum Valentino's 'Trinidad nice Trinidad is a paradise.' And to believe it.

Rhona Baptiste in Port of Spain

40. RETURN TO PARADISE

PORT OF SPAIN: Thursday 18th March 2010

I didn't feel this apprehension when we were leaving for China 12 years ago. When the truth was out that we were going, everyone had asked me, "How could you think of living in a Communist country?" I guessed it was because of our outspokenness, the frankness with which we expressed our opinions. But I never felt any apprehension in 1998 of leaving democratic Trinidad and Tobago to live and work in the socialist People's Republic of China. And for 12 years nothing happened to embarrass or to terrify us.

But as soon as I was back on Trinidad soil on 9th March, there was another kind of feeling: consternation. Had we expected too much from our visits to Harbin, to Tianjin, to Jinan, to Qingdao, to Chengdu, and to Wuhan? Did we expect that our oil billions would provide a landscape that was rich in new buildings and with an environment of tree-lined streets? I had been warned that returning home would be a shock. Trinidad and Tobago, my friends wrote, had changed and I would not see any of the old highways and streets, the old buildings. Even the Beetham Estate had been walled in. But was it all an illusion of development?

It is 2:30 pm as American Airlines Flight 1647 prepares to touch down at Piarco International Airport. Beyond the tropical haze that swathes the parched city and clusters of buildings are the mountains. They still stand sturdy but beleaguered as Man and Nature continue their unrelenting assault upwards. Match box buildings straggle ever further up its ramparts while landmark St.

Benedict's Monastery seems to hang against a torched escarpment.

Eyes scan for the new airport terminal building that is promised to surprise the newcomer. I am surprised. It is not where the old one used to be so the disembarking now takes the arrivals along long narrow corridors with iron rails and escalator. It leads to a bank of Immigration booths. I don't see anything especially remarkable and that is worth the millions of dollars poured into the building. The difference is the glass-domed ceiling.

When we leave the airport and drive past an adjoining structure that looks like the tent of a bazaar - *lagniappe* to the main airport building – my brother Ronnie jokes that it is probably part of the cost over-runs. Now all joking aside, is that tacky, low-ceilinged structure, where one of the features is described as a 100 ft-high cathedral ceiling, is that our eighth wonder of the world airport? The cost listed online is $123 million but people are still being tried for ripping off ten times this amount.

You know, we should be ashamed of ourselves for letting this travesty of expenditure happen in a place that prides itself on being a democracy. Wasn't there an opposition in place when this thing got started? What about the electorate? Were they asleep or feting?

I often wonder how a population well acquainted with world-class travel facilities could ever feel good about the structure. It is not only poor in quality and appearance but a continuing embarrassment to the nation cloaked with an on-going pall of corruption. I am thinking that this thing should be torn down immediately and a proper one built with lessons from the Chinese. Now, I did not say *built by the Chinese*. I think that it is ridiculous to have foreigners build our icons. Where is our pride?

One of the memories I hold dear of my stay in China is a classic portrait of two men. We were visiting the newly-built state-of-the-art Library in Shanghai with its rotary escalator for search and delivery of books; lofty ceilings and gardens with shops intended to encourage family visits. There were two old men still dressed in their signature blue clothes and Mao caps. Hand behind back they were looking upward at the architecture with undisguised pride. Memories like this hurt when we see what we have allowed in our own cities.

It is not long before we are on the Churchill Roosevelt Highway to Port of Spain with the promised traffic jams. Overpass highway leading south and junction at Nestle's bring us in contact with young men pressing imported plastic kites and bottled cold water on to commuters awaiting the traffic lights change to green. It is a scene that I remember and I am uneasy with it as I used to be 12 years ago, but I realize that people work sometimes on what they are comfortable with. And it is better than stealing.

It is good to see the Caroni Swamp still on the left albeit the eternal fires of the *labasse* that continue to smoke from some hellish underground and the fetid green of the swamp mud is evident. It has been a victim of urban blight for a long time now and is said that it too is earmarked for development.

Sad to say the Coconut Growers' Association that provided memorable whiffs of coconut oil that we remember as school kids still discharge its white murky waste in open defiance of health and environmental laws. Is there no intention to enforce the law? Or, is this too what freedom is?

We come upon the open Gulf of Paria waters that must be a challenge to the law with its invitation to illegal smuggling of drugs and guns. How accurate I wonder is Mr. Dorn Townsend's *Trouble in Paradise* which on March 11th 2010 said:

Of late, Patrick Manning, the prime minister of the tiny island nation of Trinidad and Tobago, has been publicly contemplating deploying the country's navy to patrol the Antilles for drug smugglers. His statements might come as a surprise. For one, Trinidad and Tobago barely has a navy: just three 140-foot offshore patrol vessels and some patrol crafts. Additionally, the country, renowned as a Caribbean vacation spot, generally has no need to defend itself.

But not everyone in Trinidad was caught off guard. The drug trade has made the island paradise a very violent place. At the same time, oil wealth has given the Manning government the means to assert Trinidad and Tobago as a regional power.

Over the past decade, Trinidad's murder rate has risen nearly 400 percent; last year, the rate in the capital city of Port of Spain rivaled those in Johannesburg and Baghdad.

As we drive through Port of Spain, my companions defend the Manning Government. They say that the media and the Opposition have joined forces to discredit the PNM's good works. They are very pleased with the success of the overhead blimp, helicopters and the offshore security vessels. They say we must remember that Trinidad and Tobago is just 48 years old in its independence and must be given a chance to grow up. We cannot compare it with First World countries like the USA and the UK with centuries to their credit.

It is almost refreshing to hear the other side of the T&T politics seeing that ever since I started writing these weekly pieces for *JahajeeDesi* some 40 weeks ago, it has been with an ongoing onslaught on the ruling PNM and its seeming failure to govern. This I have absorbed from the three dailies on-line along with the lively contributions from the *Jahajee* members and other Diasporeans. So now I will be my own judge.

The unabated criminality is what continues to disturb and it is of this that I have been evangelical. It called forth from my readers the need to come home and see for myself. And this I have now done.

Actually it was the murder of a ten-year old girl named Tecia Henry in Laventille that catapulted me into this series of writings. Now even as I return to Paradise, it is with trepidation that the saying, One can never go back home returns to me. Fixing things become more difficult in an environment that has become unrecognizable.

At any rate, it is wonderful to enjoy the mountains, the trade winds and the tweeting birds. It is wonderful to be home.

41. PORT OF SPIN

PORT OF SPAIN: Thursday 25th March 2010

It is said that one cannot go back home, the idea being that return holds too much nostalgia of times that were good and meaningful. And things change. It is true. A stroll on upper Frederick Street is rife with bitter-sweet memories of a dream now dead. The blue building that once promised hope to the futuristic wave of electronic information for the Caribbean is unfamiliar in its decay.

The Scott Building opposite is now a tacky government complex that houses the Elections and Boundaries Commission registration office for procuring a much needed ID card. It reminds the public that this is where you register to become a bona fide member of the electorate. It is the democratic privilege that some people die for.

I am re-introduced to how government works. Mr. or Mrs. Joe Public is sent through a screening device by a man who seems to be holding the fort for someone who went to the bathroom. He is casually dressed and wears a bemused look on his face as he sends the hand bags through. A back room is filled with people packed into its air-conditioning comfort. There is an atmosphere of impatience as those seated wait to be called, and those called await more information often time frustrating.

There is an absence of welcome in the shoddiness and any pride that should be associated with registration for citizenship goes through the door as one gingerly avoids the greasy prints that form a circle around the door handle. The neatly-dressed receptionist is patient and accommodating however.

The situation was repeated on a subsequent visit to the Ministry of Legal Affairs offices on South Quay where the public is accommodated in a darkened cavern that is an embarrassment to electoral promises. A tent has been thrown up somewhere in the back for the overflow of those on the waiting list. Nature blesses them with a comforting breeze.

Credit must be given though to some staff managers, supervisors and especially to the clerical staff who must interface with the daily members of a frustrated public. Sometimes one wonders whether staff has been trained in a courtesy that would assuage the agony of long waits especially for those from distant parts. Confrontation and disgust are inevitable. My question is how can serious national pride be engendered here? How can one feel good about oneself and one's country?

The hot mid-morning glare limits gawking but rather encourages curiosity on the immediate sidewalk with its hole-in-the-wall businesses, street vendors and passersby and always... always those wretched of the earth we call vagrants. There is no tourist poster rainbow-ethnicity here. One may as well be in sub-Saharan country.

The strangely crowded narrow East/West thoroughfare with actual trees sprouting from the pavement is Park Street! The air smells of pelau and curry as if in reminder of the two major tribes each contesting a perpetual stake in the nation's bubbling cauldron of *comesse*. We are in Spin City and everyone has a good twist to the yarn they weave.

Park Street is as unfamiliar as is Cyril Duprey's Colonial Life Building that once was so proudly a homegrown financial institution. The founder of a successful insurance company must be turning in his grave at what greed has brought into disrepute. Today the company is in Government's hands – a rescue operation designed to stave off a collapse of the financial house of cards. Its tentacles are far-reaching from business inside the country, to the Caribbean and beyond.

The lobby, once free to policyholders, is inaccessible until you reveal your innards to tight-faced security guards and even then access to the inner chambers requires staff escort into the large darkened foyer that seems to be shrouded in disillusion.

Opposite on St. Vincent Street the Red House is being renovated, so it's a trek past legal people cloaked in self-importance to the diagonal walk across historic Woodford Square. Nothing has changed here and even the bald spots reserved for resident vagrants seem as allotted as they were in 1998.

What then did I expect of Port of Spain twelve years later in the year 2010? They say that God either in presence or absence is reflected in the details. He is certainly not in that dingy sign at the south-eastern gate. It speaks of a colonial proclamation of bye-laws for the Borough of Port of Spain. It hangs rusty and forlorn against the queue of taxis with drivers hustling their fares.

Let's face it: Port of Spain is a disgrace. The blight may well have begun that ominous day after the Black Power protests in 1970 when Dr Eric Williams entrenched the People's Mall on Pereira's corner at Queen and Frederick while closing his eyes on the Drag Brothers' leather works on what was once called Marine Square.

In order to satisfy the immediacy of political patronage, quality urban planning was sacrificed. Its name had changed to Independence Square and now what might yet become an incredibly beautiful garden east from Tamarind Square to the Cathedral of the Immaculate Conception and westward to the waterfront is now known as the Brian Lara Promenade.

Are there any remarkable features you may ask? Captain A.A. Cipriani still stands at the cross roads near where Salvatori Building is now no more – a black wall demarking its northern boundary; across is a KFC franchise touted to sell more chicken than in Beijing; and somewhere I've seen a clump of wild flowers that is symbolic of survival in the harshest of conditions. It is the *Lantana camara* or Wild Sage called by a derogatory name in China for its putrid scent.

On Frederick Street I am relieved to see the original French balustrade wrought iron work on the old Stephen's/Miller's buildings. Like the other historic places such as the Railway Station, the Cathedrals and the Magnificent Seven these are all lost amidst the hodge-podge of edifices that crowd each other. History and culture are once more in ignominy.

Where have all our architects and city planners gone? In any other country, such historic landmarks define the character and pride of the people! Just think New Orleans and you see that iconic wrought iron balcony in the French Quarter. I guess if there was anything to be saved during Hurricane Katrina it would have been that one piece of curlicue iron!

Was it then the urgency of fixing the city that precipitated Prime Minister Manning into a construction frenzy that now haunts him in the form of current investigations into UDeCOTT, the Urban Development Corporation of Trinidad and Tobago? Whatever the inspirations divined or otherwise that have led him to the present hysteria of unpopularity, it is difficult to exempt the country as a nation from being collectively guilty about the present state of the nation.

Whether by compliance, by ignorance, or by omission, Trinidad and Tobago finds itself wallowing in a sea of confusion that leaves its Prime Minister dead and buried if we are to listen to the words of media commentators. Each one spins constant stories that court lies, half-truths and innuendoes with the truth being somewhere in between.

And so along with individual opinion that can be gleaned when waiting in line at a public services counter or in a taxi, let it not be said that the twin-island state is not highly 'politicized.'

The thing is while all this is commendable for a free society as we pride ourselves and as Diana Mahabir-Wyatt once reminded me, there is seldom an opportunity for constructive opinion that will lead us out of this land that is now in a bondage of criminality and white collar wheeling and dealing.

This past week after wading through the attacks and defenses on and by Mr. Manning that ranged from the hysterical to evangelical and having witnessed the diss-ing and subsequent canonization of Mr. Percy Villafana for blocking the PM's entry into his yard during a walkabout, it was a time of tragi-comedy.

This week began with the super-sensitive letter of Michael Harris to Kamla Persad-Bissessar popular heir-apparent to the waiting throne. It warns her to keep on track with her coming mandate to governance. The columnist's message was a heartfelt plea for her to lead the people out of bondage and to climb El Tucuche with them in order to seize their lost self-hood and sovereignty.

Mr. Harris's sincerity has touched us all – souls wandering in a desert of daily survival – some with deeper pockets much better able to do so than others. The shadow that is cast over all - super rich and super poor alike however - is the uncertainty that threatens each time we hear what sounds like gunshots followed by sirens regardless of whichever gated community we may reside. Each time I hear of another community protest with burning tyres accompanied by unbridled anger, it is a reminder of how perilously close to hate, mayhem and anarchy people are to political instability. Just think 1990 and what IF a man by the name of Abu Bakr had taken control of a hostaged Parliament and media? Can it not happen again?

The most powerful statement for me since my return two weeks ago has taken the form of these particular words in Mr. Harris' letter in Monday's Express to Ms. Persad Bissessar:

The danger to our nation arises because the old regime of government and politics, of maximum leadership, of racial polarisation, of corruption and bobol, of squandermania and malfeasance, of insufferable arrogance and dictatorship, is collapsing before our eyes. Nothing can halt that collapse.

But that old regime, as perfidious as it is, constitutes the order that we know. Should it collapse before a new political order can be pulled together, the consequences will be either anarchy and chaos or a resurgence of authoritarianism so draconian as to obliterate any possibility of democracy and freedom for our people for decades to come.

If you understand this, if you truly believe this, then you must be absolutely clear as to what your critical role in this drama must be.

These lines should be read and re-read by every one of our citizens and understood, but there are other words too that are ominous for Ms Persad-Bissessar and I see it reflected in several responses on the *JahajeeDesi* message site. Mr. Harris speaks for the nation when he reminds her that opportunism will find a way to the top and alongside her. And so he warns:

Finally it is not your role to rush to put together any accommodation of parties or persons. It may be that in the fullness of time the need for such an accommodation shall become indispensable to the transition.

The most prophetic task for the lady therefore will be in identifying a cadre of True Trinis who understand that country is first in a pact of serving the people. Such patriots are there and waiting to be called upon as they are not going to be pushing themselves forward. It is not their style. They are to be found among the young and the old, the rich and the poor in this group that is the Silent Majority. They have no axe to grind; no baggage to carry and their greatest asset is generosity combined with humility in the love of country. Trinidad and Tobago comes first before the arrogance and greed of self.

But am I being naïve?

And, as Mr. Manning is still discovering after eight years as Prime Minister, the lady must watch her promises to an electorate that can easily become disenchanted when things do not go their way. She must understand that "It eh have no real jobs for all the boys and girls after you win an election." A reality check will bring an honesty that is really what the people want.

If I may add a humble postscript to the thoughts penned by Mr. Harris, it is to tell Ms. Persad-Bissessar to remember to walk always with a crap-detector, as a certain Nobel Laureate once warned me about living in Trinidad and Tobago. The crap in the media and the spin. The crap that is everywhere.

42. IN SEARCH OF SUPER STARS AND BOBOLEES

PORT OF SPAIN: Thursday 1st April 2010

There's a real temptation to trivialize the crises of today and to wish us all on April 1st a Happy All Fools' Day. But we've been there already and now it's time to move on. It's been three weeks since my return to a Paradise that was and it's difficult to reconcile the wonderful little pictures that I've been painting to my Chinese students with the reality that now presents itself on the home-spun canvas.

Trinidad and Tobago is no more the innocent, harmonious society where we laughed loudly and cussed each other only to hug and make up again. I am finding it a clutter of disgruntled people intolerant of each other's point of view and bent on self-destruction. Laughter still comes easily but there seems to be no good sense behind the jests. Of course, I could be too wary or too suspicious and could be accused of scanning the laughter for genuine empathy. Put the blame on my grandmother; she used to warn me that "not every skin teeth is a smile."

But our people are truly strange. We are yet to be engaged by media colleagues who should want to share an interest in the excitement that is now China. What comes over instead by those barely interested in our Chinese connection is a perverse curiosity in whether we have ever eaten dog!

Nevertheless it is heart-warming to meet and greet family and old friends who welcome you with the same ease as if it was yesterday since we'd seen each other. The behaviour is the same. Loud guffaws follow a piece of nonsensical memory that recaps funny incidents and ridiculous circumstances. Walking into a mini-mart to pick up the dailies, for example, becomes an adventure to interact with everyone talking politics. T&T epitomizes democracy at the grassroots level, but it is a democracy in which almost every politician in turn is corrupt, inefficient and untrustworthy. And therein lies the Achilles' heel of our democracy, the seed of indifference, revolt or anarchy.

I am anxious that before sinking my teeth into the political culture of the country, I must first examine the social fabric of the place I left behind twelve years ago. So what then is the people's culture of Trinidad and Tobago? What is the heart of our nation? There was a time when I took foreign visitors to the market places in Port of Spain and Chaguanas. "This is where you find the soul of a country," I would say to them. It was the reason that led me to explore the marketplaces of Guangzhou and other Chinese towns and villages so as to understand better the real people who comprise the masses.

The soul of a country is to be found in its people's sights, sounds, smells, touch, taste and, perhaps most of all, in that intangible sixth sense of an insight or intuition defined as a power of perception. It is definitely independent of the five senses.

This is my focus today on what seems to be a continuing search for heroes or superstars, as veteran political commentator Ferdie Ferreira refers to them, as he recalled the ascendancy of Ms. Jearlean John. And there are bobolees. It is the performance of superstar, bobolee and ordinary woman and man, the comradeship or competition of each member of the group that constitutes the culture of our people.

Last week I watched a TV programme hosted by Mr. Fitzgerald Hinds, a former PNM Member of Parliament. It took viewers into the heart of Chaguanas where Mayor Natasha Navas and Deputy Mayor Orlando Nagessar along with *Crime Watch* Ian Allen and a representative of the Congress of the People (COP) were panelists.

The topic of the Borough's development introduced such words as 'aliens' with reference to other citizens who come in to find employment or perpetrate crime. The minutes were uninspiring segments held together by a host who struggled with involving his scanty audience. Chaguanas which is historically home to a large segment of the East Indian population did not appear to be represented in the audience.

All could not be well in the bustling heartland known as Central, judging from the anguished tirade of two members of the audience who came to the microphone and from the defensive mode of the panelists. Listen to this bit of nonsense. In response to Mr. Hinds, Deputy Mayor Nagessar explained away the apparent snub that was the exclusion of Chaguanas councillors from a visiting delegation from the City. The deed (or misdeed) for which the mayor took responsibility according to Mr. Nagessar, was now past and all was one love in the Borough of Chaguanas. The lady meanwhile sat in sullen silence.

But there's more. There's so much more *chupidness* in this land of the calypso...soca....chutney soca...or shall we just say in this land of bacchanal? Scandal, *mauvaise-langue* and rumours are what feed the nation's obesity.

The *JahajeeDesi* message board continues to light up this past week with what only a newly-returned Diasporean would consider a storm in a teacup. I am treading here without the fear of angels, but the source of the anger - "Errol Fabien is a national disgrace" – has attracted a vituperousness centred on an artist who seemed to have switched allegiance from one political camp to the other. It does make one wonder about the meaning of freedom of choice. Apparently Mr. Fabien committed the crime of making an advertisement in support of Vision 20/20, the PNM's brainchild.

Tolerance, the handmaid of respect, is certainly not present.

Is there some instrument to measure the degree of wastage of passion and energy and thought that might well be placed into some positive means of fixing this blighted country of ours? Look at our countryside! We are letting it compete with Haiti's deserts!

Okay. I must understand that people are vexed...damned vexed at a government whose good works are obliterated by those that they have screwed up. The present sagas of corruption in high places and wastage of money overshadow any attempts at clarity and explanation by members as demonstrated by replays of debates in Parliament. There is now a special television channel for our parliamentarians, and what the Government is doing appears in the myriad of media companies, both print and electronic. Talk about Information overload! It explains why the nation is so *bazodee*. In local parlance that means stupidly confused.

In one such programme I was able to hear the presentation of Opposition Senator Suruj Rambachan and the respondent PNM Senator Tina Grunland-Nunez. It was followed by a post-Cabinet press conference with MP and Minister of Finance Karen Nunez-Texeira. All conducted themselves properly in addressing the people's issues. It was good to see that the people's business was being attended to by an articulate colonial-type government and opposition with such professional competence. Never mind the empty seats that were reminiscent of Hong Kong's government meetings.

There is however a certain bite-up-ness in the atmosphere. For the new reader, this is a colloquialism that means a state of dissatisfaction that results in a kind of permanent negativism. But it is more than just depression that causes one to find fault and exist in a state of dejection. It is a lot more than that. For the clinical psychologist there must be a term to describe the state of deriving satisfaction from lamenting one's woes, passing them on to another thereby exonerating oneself while flogging the *bobolee* in word or deed. Is it a persecution complex?

(Again, for the new reader *bobolee* is the colloquial term for the Judas effigy stuffed like a scarecrow that is dragged thought the streets on Good Friday and given a thorough beating.)

While this state of misery is certainly not a monopoly of small island states, nor larger ones whose sheer magnitude of size and population numbers tend to dilute the pressure of the 'bite-up-ness', there is a sinister aspect to this national character that I'm trying to come to terms with. The reason is that it is consuming our people with its nihilistic culture that could lead ultimately to... to what? Self-destruction?

This thought, frighteningly enough, obliterates good sense and throws one into hysteria, rage and hate. The line between sanity and madness becomes blurred. This is when one becomes branded 'PNM till ah dead' or 'UNC to de bone'. It is like a religious fanaticism that is a fundamentalism. It nurtures martyrdom and provides a *cause celebre* for suicide bombers.

I know... I know...we have not reached there. Pray God we never will if we are to have the confidence of Mr. Gregory Aboud, president of the Downtown Owners and Merchants Association (DOMA), in a recent morning interview about his 'beautiful Trinidad and Tobago'.

For the non-Africans and non-Indians, whether French Creole (the category of the lightest skinned) or Other – that is racial mixtures or Chinese, the association with African PNM or Indian UNC will sooner or later SEE you as branded into one or the other of the two major tribes. The Syrian-Lebanese community is a swing vote whose supreme power was demonstrated this past week when they invited the Prime Minister and his lieutenants including the new-ly appointed UDeCOTT's Jearlean John to a private meeting at the home of Mario Sabga-Aboud in Goodwood Park.

Of particular interest was the celebration of Spiritual Baptists' Day on Tuesday with UNC Leader of the Opposition Kamla Persad-Bissessar sporting an incredibly huge African head-dress. Cute, but, oh, was it necessary? Couldn't sincerity refrain from anything so burlesque? And at the other end of the political parade PNM's Dr Keith Rowley was ecstatically embraced and fired the devotees into a tribal "Welcome Home Brother."

Interesting place this homeland of ours! It remains a veritable sociologists' paradise where the masquerade never stops.

Another spotlight this past week centred over the sum of TT$80 million dollars in additional expenditure that will have to be spent in correcting errors in the National Academy for the Performing Arts (NAPA). This was the gospel according to Mr. Rubadiri Victor, interim President of the Artists' Coalition of T&T who has claimed there had not been adequate stakeholder consultation. He did so at a news conference at The Professionals' Centre, Mucurapo, on Thursday according to a *Guardian* Saturday, March 27th report. He said the state-of-the-art edifice had conceptual, technical and programming flaws.

The ongoing trouble with life in these parts is that it is difficult to extract truth from spin. You see – on the other hand Junia Regrello, Parliamentary Secretary in the Ministry of Community Development, Culture and Gender Affairs says it will cost about $20 million to attend to the niggling issues like lighting and flooring at the National Academy (NAPA). He exulted over the magnificence of the place adding: "I admit there are grey areas that need to be worked out. I know for a fact we have to change the flooring. It is laminate."

Did I hear correctly? The floors of a public place designed for major training and performances are LAMINATE????? Like somebody really tief we chupidees! According to the news report Regrello appealed to the population to be "patient and give us time to work it out." Is this gentleman seen seated while testing out the 3-star-to-be-upgraded-to-5-star hotel bed for real?

Listen to him further on the 'ABOUT $20 million' which is the sum for all the things that need fixing, to get the facility properly functioning and going. He said, "It is the first time I have toured the facility. It is fantastic. I am saying that as someone who has performed in the Royal Albert Hall, (London). I am sold." Does all this money come from an infinite oil well in the Gulf?

And did we hear him say THE FIRST TIME! Please refer to his title. He is Parliamentary Secretary in the Ministry of Community Development, Culture and Gender Affairs! Know something? Were I in that position I would have been camping outside with those Chinese workers, sharing their instant noodles and connecting with people like the venerable Dr. Pat Bishop and Mr. Victor instead of risking the inevitable fallout by side-lining them.

Mr. Hayden Paul, chief construction engineer, admitted to such ill designs as an overly deep orchestra pit and undersized stage entrances. But he says the cost of such flaws was not yet worked out. The media tour was organized by the Ministry of Community Development, Culture and Gender Affairs, MP Marlene Mc Donald. However according to one report just two questions were allowed the media.

Like many in the electorate I am yet to be convinced that the UNC PLUS is ready for replacing the present government. If one is to judge from the accusations of impropriety on both sides of the room after listening to replays of Parliament, there remains the taunting 'who-we-go-put?' Besides, we are still to understand their vision - not manifesto - which does not necessarily have to be alien to the present PNM's Vision 20/20. To throw that out would be like tossing out the baby with the bath water. It is an error of judgement that newcomers to any situation make in desiring to wipe the old slate clean.

In last week's quotation from *Express* columnist Mr. Michael Harris, the most pertinent statement for me remains the one in which he reminded that "perfidious as the old regime may be (namely the PNM) it constitutes an order that can collapse into anarchy, chaos so draconian as to obliterate any possibility of democracy and freedom for our people for decades to come."

After listening to replays of parliament in session I am yet to see the "PULLING TOGETHER OF A NEW POLITICAL ORDER" or an amended vision. More pertinently though I am still to see a community of people standing together who will put Trinidad and Tobago before anything else in cleaning up its mess. It must be a community of new caretakers the people can trust. Unfortunately, the country is still to SEE them.

I now put it to Ms. Kamla Persad-Bissessar: Are such people so hard to find? Do you think you would find any among the rubble of past governments? Or are you like Mr. Manning hoping that power is all you need to mend this nation?

43. FRIGHT OF THE HONEY BEES

PORT OF SPAIN: Thursday 8th April 2010

That's right! The bees are running scared and they are in flight. Nature is under siege. It's a topic very troubling to my green heart. It comes at a time when there is a temptation to write Richard Seecharan thanking him for allowing me the opportunity to share his

JahadeeDesi messaging space over the past 43 weeks. It's time to stop penning troubling thoughts about home that started on the other side of the globe.

Who really cares anyway? It seems so depressing!

Now into the fourth week since my return from China, I continue to feel like an outsider looking on at the passing parade as Trinidad and Tobago pursues its date with Destiny. It is difficult to re-connect.

The distractions of the daily media and talk shows that my Cyber Mate and My Ron promised are indeed spell-binding as heads swing from the sparring apologists of one political camp to the other. To tell you the truth were the T&T General Elections to be called tomorrow I would not know whether Mr. Manning's PNM or Ms. Persad-Bissessar's UNC PLUS political party will merit my vote.

You see I am yet to be convinced that either one is sensitized to the awesome responsibility of global care-taking.

Leadership today is so much more serious than pandering to the annual celebrations of the Spiritual Baptists, Christian Easter or to the Divali and Eid religious festivals. It cannot be only about 'playing mas' which equates with playing political games.

Leadership today requires so much more than superstars and bobolees. It has to get past the navel-watching of defensive partisan politics and temporary highs that oil prices promise to the bigger picture beyond that.

In 1968 Marshall McLuhan invented the concept of the global village. Today the effects of colonialism have affected every corner of the planet leaving a world where cultures mix, overlap and collide, literally causing shifts in both its cultural and geological platforms. Trinidad and Tobago is a microcosm of it all and more.

In driving through the countryside, of interest are the housing developments that show off a nouveau-richness in the newness of structures and newly-painted facades. There must be an undoubted pride in the increased number of new home owners and the cheek-by-jowl business places speak of active trading, and all that is good.

But not only is there a madness in the name of development but there are the devastating consequences of an unplanned exploitation of the land and its waters. It is amazing how we think that land, forests and sea are limitless. Here at home we equate quantity with 'bush' or 'water'. For example: *Hear nuh man! It have grog flowing like water...*

In another instant we run *to cut down de bush*. It is as if we hate plants and must therefore get rid of them. This is the thinking that makes me fear bulldozer and electric saw as they threaten to remove yet another chunk of land or still another tree.

To hear Mr. Gary Aboud on the C Channel on Tuesday morning was to relive the *deja vu* of people trying to save the Savannah. Tired but persistent he was making the plea for government legislation and people awareness for protecting the nation's aquifers from the deadly land compression of construction.

The interdependence of man on water and of rivers and seas is a difficult lesson to teach and not even the cost of converting salt water at the cost of billions of dollars to taxpayers seem to strike a chord. And so we continue to self-destruct.

Radio Talk City with Fazeer Mohammed and Jessie May Ventour was highlighting the rough-handed treatment of side-walk vendors along with the proposed development of the Queen's Park Savannah. The Peschier family land of 232 acres was 'donated to the people' of Trinidad and Tobago. But even this is questioned in the book *Voices in the Street* by Olga Mavrogordato who credits the public space to the foresight of Governor Sir Ralph Woodford who purchased it from them in 1817.

In the eighties while flying over Florida, it was with awe that I watched each time a newer chunk of coral limestone was being carved out for yet another housing estate. The Everglades was shrinking as inexorably as the green lungs that are the Amazon forests.

Other flights north to New York revealed down below brown patches one after the other that linked town with states. Where was the greenery to balance this madness named progress or development?

Travels throughout China were no different and the 40-minute coach ride from Guangzhou to Nanhai was to convert green farmlands to dusty manufacturing and residential complexes with the omnipresent mechanical cranes replacing those of the avian kind. What was the cost? My students were hardly impressed by my words that one morning they will awake to find that the pollution has trapped them indoors.

It was the same casualness that greeted my alarm at the ashen mountain-scapes of the valleys of Diego Martin, Petit Valley and Maracas. One youngster, bright lad with the curious Hebrew name of Gideon and whose IQ the family promises will crown him the next Dr Eric Eustace Williams, quickly reassured me that the hills will soon come alive again with the first rainfall. It is the same up the islands. His brilliance was reserved for defending the rights of Mr. Calder Hart, past chairman of the scandal-ridden Urban Development Corporation of Trinidad and Tobago (UDeCOTT), who has not been charged with any offence, he reminded and who therefore is innocent until proven guilty.

It is Mr. Calder Hart's embedding with a government in so large and intricate a construction business that leads me back to Nature and the Caura

Valley. It is said - and I do remember - that bush fires are a recent phenomenon dating from perhaps the seventies. There is a correlation here with the oil boom when Trinidad and Tobago got its first real taste of money. What else then can one expects after the tsunami of oil revenues from George Bush's 2003 invasion of Iraq was to trigger in his own quest for oil?

Caura Royal Road, north from the Eastern Main Road at Tacarigua, is resplendent in its housing developments that carry such exotic names like Pigeon Peas Gardens. In fact from the old Orange Grove estate houses, past the Anglican Church with the Orphanage opposite; across the memorable bridge on the Eastern Main Rd., where Prime Minister George Chambers was said to catch the workers off guard when he dropped by incognito, all things are spanking new.

We ascend to the Caura Sanitarium health facility where the burning is evident. The precipice lips are blackened so the familiar dumping of garbage is about to begin its new cycle – sight and stench evident to the nature lovers who travel upward to where the river still trickles as streams. Road and shoulders are maintained, but two miles up the damage from the bush fires continue to blacken the hills.

On family lands on the left there is the unexpected presence of a cell tower. It is another man-made threat to the environment and on Man himself in this unceasing search for gold – or gold mining as the buzz word appears to be. Amazing how Trinis see money in everything! It has become THE GOD and we disciples have earned for ourselves the undisputed title as Arabs of the Caribbean.

Cell towers in the desire to satisfy our egos, or in our need to communicate, are a fact of life. Cell phones are like cars. They are no longer a luxury but a necessity in view especially of the prevalence of crime. So the cell tower cancels out the risks of cancer and other radiation mutations by dint of its sheer must-have-ness. Cells now, mutant children later. Of such is the urgency of money with a very fine line between it and greed.

On the familiar grounds two sentinel mango rose and mango vert trees are gone. Adjoining the questionable cell tower is an unusual tree. Small green leathery leaves and aerial roots merged into bark with strapping foot roots binding the stony ground tell me it is a *Ficus*. Yikes! This is an invasive sub-tropical species! How did it get here? Like the few alien pine trees that the Forestry people have managed to sustain, these plants have replaced the natural ecosystems' varieties with the vanishing of the original forest covers that controlled water in its sustaining of life.

My eyes wander around for the golden cassias and buttercup that provided nectar for the Old Man's apiary. There is a scrawny cassia, mangoes and cashews surviving the drought with a pair of coconut trees on the curb. The fruit is so emaciated that not even its yellow promise of being Chinese dwarf coconut seems to attract the curry river limers who drive past in their motorcades. The sugar cane estates of Orange Grove are now no more. They have been taken over by Government's Housing Development Corporation.

Suffer the little honey bees.

A lonely honey bee buzzes past me under the *Ficus*. It is said to be the Africanized type that has expropriated the industry. They are hardy but dangerous so I do not move as advised. What does it matter? The handsome little fellow seems lost without food. Its nectar comes from plants that need water and water needs plants, if it is going to be retained in the soil. The interdependence of Nature - one on the other is a reality that we have either forgotten or simply never learnt. It is what I say to Mr. Joefield who is selling fruit and provisions at a junction in the village.

We have finally arrived three miles further up the hairpin curves to what was the old village of Caura. It is where many of our *cocoa paignol* grand parents came from. La Veronica RC church replaces the original that succumbed to the infamous Caura Dam and the scandal that activist Jean Miles exposed in the sixties.

Cocoa and coffee cultivation has given place to an ambitious–looking project of dwarf pawpaw. Sustenance for these depends on the trickle of river water now in drought mode so it qualifies as stream. Nevertheless groups of people take advantage of the ankle-high water to frolic. Government has provided park-like facilities and there are even signs that speak of trails the most important among them being the road to a burnt out El Tucuche.

Mr. Joefield's stall displays pawpaws, pumpkins, plastic-bagged oranges that cry out for vengeance and some dried provisions all testifying to the brutal dry weather. The solitary shade tree provides point-of-sale advertisement as he has bedecked it with plastic bags of colourful hot peppers and tomatoes - a maxi variety of the cherry type size. The entire scene is not an enticement to go back to the land. When he announced the price of a flask of honey was TT$40 he reminded me that at the supermarkets the cost of a rum-bottle size was TT$140! The last price the Old Man was asking was TT$36 for a 26-oz rum bottle. But then that was over twelve years ago and certainly before the financial tsunami that turned us all into rabid capitalists, gold-diggers and extortionists.

The ridiculousness of the situation of our burnt lands, lack of water and high food prices is reflected in the news stories like that of Peter Balroop's in the *Trinidad Guardian* 4th April 2010. Smokers who have been seen as one of the offenders for starting bush fires may not only have contributed to the vicious cycle of nature's degradation but to the financial profits such as West

Indian Tobacco Limited (Witco) recording of a 23.6 per cent increase in operating profit over 2008, with a profit after tax of $258.4 million!

You know, God has to be either a dunce or a very funny being with a sense of humour.

But just in case you think I'm sounding like sour grapes, this little story on catching up with life in T&T should bring a smile at just how incredibly funny we are as a people.

My good and faithful housekeeper Adelcia is now into retirement at her family plot in Chin Chin, Cunupia. She often returned from weekends with bundles of dasheen bush, baghi, ochroes, oranges and plums from the fertile plains of Central. In response to my query of how the gardening was going at a time when fruits are all imported this is what she had to say.

The chickens were picking around and destroying everything she planted.

Well then perhaps she was gathering a lot of eggs?

Oh no! She groaned. Her nephew's blind sheep was finding them before she did! Her family still had to face the supermarket for everything.

At that point I suggested that I drop a couple of Chinese farmers fresh from Guangdong onto the land...

44. THOSE RAGA RAGA BOOM BOXES

PORT OF SPAIN: Thursday 15th April 2010

Writing is lonely business. One takes consolation that as with the rest of the universe you put your thoughts out there and Nature – let's just say, God -- does the rest. Mostly though, one ends up talking to oneself. This is how it was with me this past week when a couple of the responses filtered in on my 43rd contribution to *JahajeeDesi*.

"Fright of the Honey Bees" was an ongoing concern about Man's unrelenting self-destruction of the place we call home. Its messages were naturally out-staged by Prime Minister Patrick Manning's call to President Max Richards to dissolve Parliament. There will be a National General Election on Monday May 24th.

The frenzy as to why he dropped this bombshell becomes as obvious as the mounting pressures that surround his office. The piece reflected my ambivalence of "who we go put' and enamored as I am with the idea of newness and change from the Hon. Kamla Persad-Bissessar heading the next government of Trinidad and Tobago, there are urgent questions to be answered.

One of them was my indecision about voting for whom, if at all. My cousin Margaret chided me as follows: All true. But re politics, remember a no-vote amounts to a vote for whoever the rest of us choose, though I agree the choice is not enticing at all.

My Cyber Mate in very succinct language responded: I think Manning used a master political stroke. That's all I'm doing with the contenders - analysing the strategies used to wield the sword through each other.

She continued in response to my observation that: Westminster is for the civilized white people. We never got the thing right for our islands. We don't seem to recognize our size and how fortunate we were with all that money which could have taken our descendents through many an eon. She concludes by saying: I eh votin. I've done my bit.

That's what I love about us.... at times. Our freedom of speech.

And, finally, thank God for My Ron who in his usual prompt response to my postings had this to say: Would you believe that yesterday evening I was sitting at the Tranquillity tennis club having a drink after the game and macoing the Balisier House screening when a honey bee gave me the most painful but natural sting on my leg!

I leave you to guess how cute a reply I was able to click back to him!

In distilling the tons of information and opinion that are blitzed on continuous media waves my own opinion centres around the cool and dispassionate 'state of play' of Mr. Robin Montano in his guest column, *The Election Game* on Thursday 8th April. The Congress of the People, (COP) he states has management capability as its greatest asset but is unable to sell itself. Beside it is broke, and many are those who defected to the other side.

This other side being the United National Congress (UNC) that has Ms. Kamla Persad-Bissessar as its most visible asset. "In addition, the UNC has a solid base of fifteen seats and an organisation that can perform in the six marginals.

Money may not be a problem for Kamla, he says, but the biggest danger for the UNC comes from within. 'The Panday factor,' as he terms it, is described as follows:

Kamla has several dissident sitting MPs that she must deal with: There is the old Bas' himself, his daughter Mikela, his brother Subash, Kelvin Ramnath and Ramesh Lawrence Maharaj.

He described Mr. Jack Warner as a formidable asset of the Party. He seems to have unlimited funds and has proven himself to be a shrewd and capable politician who does not lose a battle... or at least not easily. (Mr. Panday's threat to oppose Mr. Warner anywhere as an independent candidate shows perhaps a shrewd wit.) He (Warner) clearly has great organisational skills and is not somebody to be taken lightly at all.

In other words, Kamla has to have a plan in place to deal with these very possible exigencies. Failure to do so could present an image to the country of weak leadership.

I cannot agree more with Mr. Montano. As for the People's National Movement Mr. Montano continues:

"The PNM's greatest strength is its formidable organization. No other Party in Trinidad & Tobago is as organized as is the PNM. This organization extends down to a fundamental understanding of its supporters and how best to ensure that they turn out to vote. Do not discount this ability!"

So why is it then that like Mr. Montano I am inclined to bet a dollar to a doughnut on Ms. Persad-Bissessar? Okay, I'll tell you why.

The Republic of Trinidad and Tobago under the watch of the PNM government with Mr. Patrick Manning at the helm has thrown the country into jeopardy. The well-being of a nation first of all - and I hope the comfortable Fathers and Mothers of the Nation are listening – is its ability to provide a safe and comfortable environment for its citizens.

But how do I escape the feeling that Trinidad and Tobago is now a lawless society?

Even as I pen these thoughts, there is a consciousness of being gated into a community with neighbours whom I have never met. The building itself is a jail with wrought iron and triple locks; the traffic on the main road is alive with heavy machinery on its way to further carve out the mountainsides of Petit Valley.

And then there are the gut-shaking decibels of passing vehicles.

The booming amplifiers shout to me of an unbelievable disrespect for others as the noise is as horrible as it is unnerving. The thing is the music is not even enjoyable, but abrasive. It is a music that speaks of defiance and anger rather than of pleasure and gentility.

Macho car-owners seem to compete with each other in noise polluting as the raga-raga 'musical' cacophony vies with the raw strength of other car or motor bike engine's horsepower in speed while accelerating or in the hauling of increasingly large loads. Therefore from as simple a case as deliberately provocative noise which constitutes a public nuisance there is the larger and more immediate concern of a criminal bravado.

Over-riding it all there is lawlessness in the land which people seem to have accepted. Indiscipline has become a way of life.

Now let me return to my Cyber Mate's cynical comment about 'white people'. I understand fully what she means. We both were born and bred in the same colonial era that was ruled by Britishers who imposed their system of governance upon a raggle-taggle group of heterogeneous peoples they collected mainly from Africa and India. Therefore we have adopted certain 'couths' which have us frown upon civil service supervisors who chew gum at their desks or electoral candidates who yawn with wide open mouths while seated on a televised political platform.

Over the years this post-colonialism when viewed from the bottom up is replete with realities that we must now come to terms with. The view from the top cons us into thinking that with ridiculous wig and black robes we are secure within a judicial system of Westminster with legislation – law and order that speak of a near-to-ideal democracy. Every four years or so we dip our finger into red ink and vote freely in what is called our right to adult suffrage. Democracy is what people die for.

The real 'white people' of whom Cyber Mate speaks have returned to their homelands where they continue to rank first among the world's nations with development bound to successful places in which to live and enjoy a good quality of life and law and order.

In the United Kingdom, for example, the final score according to an "International Living 2010 Quality of Life index" website rates them with a numerical 73 taking into consideration the cost of living; leisure and culture;

economy; environment; freedom; health; infrastructure; risk and safety; and climate.

Now think Denmark where old NAR stomper Lennox Raphael resides. Copenhagen its capital is celebrated as the city with the best quality of life. It is rated 76 on the International Living index. And who ranks first? France tops us all with a score of 82 followed by Australia with 81. Our T&T comes in at 57. On comparing Australia with ourselves one is left to munch on the cynicism of my friend who says - and let me repeat again:

Westminster is for the civilized white people. We never got the thing right for our island. We don't seem to recognize our size and how fortunate we were with all that money which could have taken our descendents through many an eon.

So why is it that we 'indigenes' never got it right?

As I look at the latest figure of our criminality it stands at 142 on 9th April with an ongoing spate of young black youths as assailants and victims. I listen to the accelerations outside on top of the raga raga decibels...as I smell the fires burning off the once-forested hills...as I safeguard water with the same diligence as I must watch guard property... there is a feeling of anxiety for what lies in store for us as a nation and those descendents our inheritors my friend speaks about.

Do we CARE about them?

The People's National Movement with Mr. Patrick Manning at the helm has had TWO successive terms of office in which there was ample time to put right basic strongholds of our democracy, first among them being a respect for law and order. Legislation implementation and punishment are the rightful pillars on which trustworthiness in a society's leadership is forged.

Where the People's National Movement is concerned, despite my free access to the waterfront adjacent to the 5-Star Hyatt on Wrightson Road; beside the free access to medicine and my grandchildren's education; beside my increased pensions and free boat rides down south; besides all these entitlements that would be expected of any government anywhere with a windfall of US$85 for a barrel of oil, SHOULD I TRUST THE PNM with my country for another five years? It is as simple as that.

Sorry, Mr. Manning, but I've been testing your government's trustworthiness over the years, and it just does not seem to measure up.

People in and out of your camp are concerned. So this is neither personal nor otherwise. It is a concern about COUNTRY! It is about those people – YOUR PEOPLE whom I sit next to while waiting five weeks for a birth certificate down at the Ministry of Legal Affairs on South Quay!

We are a miserable looking lot!

Now the next question I must ponder upon is this: Should I risk putting in a new equation in the form of Ms. Kamla Persad-Bissessar and the UNC PLUS whose leadership skills have not yet been tested and whose vision for T&T in this global village of ours is not yet crafted? This plan as with the PNM's Vision 20/20 which really is their manifesto is the pledge that each contesting party must provide the electorate. We are not yet seeing plan nor representatives in whose hands we can safely entrust our country.

Sorry, Ms. Persad-Bissessar, but you and your crew are still to inspire me. I am not surprised to hear the radio show host telling his audience, "I don't like Mr. Manning but I am voting PNM." The inevitable decision would be to put that X next to the devil that one knows rather than to the other who is also known! For let's not fool ourselves. The performance of the UNC under Mr. Panday's leadership is not one that leaves a trail that smells of roses!

We must not allow ourselves to be confused with promises made in the heat of the election frenzy. Last Monday's launches of both political platforms and candidate screenings testify that the feeding bacchanal has begun. Watching the presentations of both parties was just so much déjà vu. As for listening to the daily verbiage tossed out on the airwaves one is left aghast at its vulgarity.

Will we ever mature?

Beside Mr. Robin Montano's words about the UNC's own concern for a fundamental understanding of its supporters and how best to ensure that they turn out to vote is the overriding concern: CAN MS. PERSAD-BISSESSAR SHOW US A SLATE OF CREDIBLE OFFICE-SEEKERS IN WHOM THE PEOPLE OF TRINIDAD AND TOBAGO CAN PLACE THEIR TRUST?

The 2010 Trinidad and Tobago election should be won on the merit of those men and women within the political party who can best convince the voters that they are for putting Trinidad and Tobago first. But will it happen?

45. LOST – A VILLAGE AND ITS PEOPLE

PORT OF SPAIN: Thursday 22nd April 2010

Brasso Seco is behind God's back. Presumably God remained in Arima somewhere by The Dial where Pennelope Beckles was being favoured by supporters as a PNM candidate rather than the diplomatic post she rejected. It is the sleepy Blanchisseuse area back of Arima with a handful of houses in the village about fifteen miles inside the northern range. In Spanish the name means 'dried woods' and the name was perhaps someone's attempt at Trini humour as the area was originally very wet and covered with thick rain forests.

About eight miles north of Brasso Seco is Paria Bay and the last of the Crown lands that we inherited as a people.

Time was when we drove up the Arima/Blanchisseuse Old Road to collect a dried branch to be used as our Christmas tree. It was an annual ritual which began with throwing the kids in the car and four miles up the twisty road we would stop and begin scouting around for the perfect branch that would be subjected to the spraying of white 'snow' and decorated with light bulbs and other Christmas baubles.

The intention was to discourage tacky plastic imports at the time. It took some years afterward to realize that not only was a Christmas tree not an integral part of the birth of Jesus, but that the Christ child was born in a miserable stable in a desert town somewhere in the Middle East. Not only could there not have been snow in Bethlehem (Snow is very unusual, as you'd expect at a latitude of about 31 degrees north; on a level with Algiers in North Africa – *Yahoo answers*). Altitude is put at 2,350 feet. But in all wishful thinking the child was a bouncing brown-skinned baby boy who looked more like an Arab. To be honest, if we are to go by the disputed Shroud of Turin on which his adult face is imprinted, he does look more like Osama bin Laden!

Okay...okay...I'm just speculating here and risking the wrath of Roman Catholic ex-communication... again. But back to that old road to Brasso Seco. It used to be a delight to follow the hairpin curves, as they wound their way upward from the foothills where the Arima city limits ended. Twelve years later the road remains broken by an old landslide and so we must return to the circuitous hill of Calvary skirting the Holy Cross College to re-connect with the hairpins.

Downhill from the newly painted Temple Village is the first quarry that was once small business. Today it is humongous with great hills of aggregate that is needed in the name of our national development. Heavy duty equipment as we drive further up testify to on-going activity even as the blight of bush fires blanket the lower reaches of the Northern Range. Every landowner now wants to get into the act either as gentleman farmer or quarrying magnate.

Asa Wright Nature Preserve is synonymous with old friend Ian Lambie. How can I forget him labouring for the past forty years plus in the vineyards to keep that place going! In China I'd surfed for his name on the Asa Wright website. Every other name is there but his. But then I remember the idiom about prophets being devoid of honour in their own country.

By Saturday morning I connect with him. From Tobago he assures me that he has been duly honoured. How great! I shrug when he tells me that it was expats who nominated him. We relive old times on the phone. He updates me on Asa Wright. It was a sanctuary even before the term ecotourism was buzzed. From the original 193 acres it has now increased to 1,300. Of that Government 'gave' them 250 acres in exchange for the quarrying lands that were 'hopsed' from them.

In T&T nothing is without a story of government arrogance and 'bold-faced-ness' - period - so he tells me about the time when people with familiar names were in power and the attendant attitude that accompanies the holding of power.

It is difficult not to bemoan the loss of a strong sturdy green backbone and watershed. But even more heart-wrenching is the rate at which we humans CONTINUE to rape the lands with speculation on how much each parcel is now worth. For much like Judas' thirty pieces of silver we hunger for clinching of the deal as we acquire more and more material possessions and even as we destroy the very source of our existence.

And in case you forgot today is Earth Day! When last did you plant a tree?

So let's talk water. The native people UNDERSTOOD the relationship between themselves and Nature. They did not coin the buzz words 'sustainable development'. They lived it! Women understood the harmony more than men did. They understood the difference between the taking of natural resources and the giving it back or replacing what was used. It explains why they survived long enough to have begat this super race of scientists and know-it-alls – we civilized creatures who are now self-destructing.

I have wanted to share two little pieces of information that are relevant to this topic at a time when T&T's political fever is firing up the tribes. Thing is you can't talk survival without talking politics. One is never far from the other. In a little book by Robert J.C. Young titled *Postcolonialism - A Very Short Introduction* he reminds us that it was Gandhi's influence that rubbed off on women like Mira Behn and Vandana Shiva who initiated the Chipko movement in India. These were the 'tree-hugging' women.

Women sensitized to the flooding caused by tree removal that affected centuries of their own families' survival were taking action. They confronted the status quo and those who in the name of post-colonial development had begun the rape even earlier. It was they the colonizers who exploited their timber without any concern for its consequences. The movement resulted in confrontations between developers and their own village men who were in denial about the intimate relationship between water, the indigenous trees like the silk cotton and their own survival.

In Brasso Seco where the dead-end-ness of the road and the seemingly unending drive act as a deterrent to exploiters, the mountains exhale oxygen a bit more freely. The air is cleaner, the trees are a healthier green and Nature is at peace.

Well almost...for there are those who see endless money in the form of christophene vine-growing. There is one heartening piece of good news however. The ecology prevents the likes of coca and marijuana growing... or so I am told. You see, plants too have their 'druthers' and discriminate about where they thrive to their advantage!

Sometime over the years, we too admired the entrepreneurship of a gentleman who cleared some acres to experiment with first the growing of water melons. But christophene was a fast grower, loved the environment and after a few weeks into the rainy season promised daily harvests of fat plump jade green fruit right for stretching the chow miens popular in our Chinese food.

Now what is fascinating is how we who make the best Chinese food in the world (and this is no joke) were able to introduce christophene as a staple ingredient and spawn the growing of this previously little known fruit. And hear this - it is not common in Chinese culinary at all, let alone Cantonese food!

In today's Trinidad and Tobago with food as calorie-loaded as it is tasty, there is a demand for Chinese food that the newly-arrived Chinese is making *ole 'mas* with. The demand for christophene is phenomenal and, as with the 'Mack truck' syndrome when everybody wanted to make money with big trucks, christophene is seen as the current cash cow. Every Tom Dick and Harrylal wants to grow christophene on the road to Blanchisseuse and to Brasso Seco.

As we drive past the mountains wired with blankets of the christophene vine one wonders where the greed will stop. The thinking is that the more hi-jacking of the mountains for christophene, the deeper will the pockets become. Meanwhile this member of the cucumber or gourd family is a water drinker so visitors in search of a pristine interior are escorted by lengths of unsightly skeletal pipes that feed off the rivers from further up.

Now the second story begins with a question that I have asked in relationship to Haiti's denuded mountains. Where are the guardians of the people's patrimony to protect and provide the checks and balances so that we can continue to survive with Nature?

Before taking a look at ourselves in Trinidad and Tobago and WHO safeguards the lands from ongoing gang-rapes let us see WHY Haiti became as bald and barren and ravaged as it is today. I refer to my Thursday 21st January *JahajeeDesi* column about Haiti and the reference to the words of *Marguerite Laurent (Ezili Danto)* who reminds us that the people with a Vodun culture that reveres Nature (and here again like in India she refers to the oak-like silk cotton trees in particular) how on earth could they be expected to deforest their lands? But let me quote more of her verbatim:

In partnership with the US, the mulatto President Elie Lescot (1941-45) summarily expelled peasants from more than 100,000 hectares of land, razing their homes and destroying more than a million fruit trees in the vain effort to cultivate rubber on a large plantation scale. Also, under the pretext of the Rejete campaign, thousands of acres of peasant lands were cleared of sacred trees so that the US could take their lands for agribusiness.

When I hear Minister of Agriculture, Land and Marine Resources, Senator Arnold Piggott, talk about Agriculture and Agri-business as being separate entities as if the latter replaces the former, I tremble. Now these are the facts that our Caribbean children should be learning and discussing and questioning. THEY MUST UNDERSTAND THE PAST SO AS TO UNDERSTAND THE PRESENT.

There is so much more to relate about that visit to Brasso Seco but it will have to wait for another week.

The return trip takes us back to The Dial and presumably to God's presence in bustling Arima – (remember He is Trini) to the drive back into Port of Spain. As we go past Nestlé's I remember helping Michael J.Williams with his poui-planting many eons ago. How many people know that those delightful trees are the result of one citizen's vision and caring?

During the rest of the drive we are assailed by a radio station hosted by a chap who is called The Gladiator. It qualifies for raga raga boom box status. The programme is enlightening to his 'millions of listeners worldwide', for as he interacts with his audience it explains why Trinidad and Tobago has descended to the lowest common denominator of vulgarity. This despite the explosion of media houses in the country. For in the grossest and most bizarre of radio presentations I have ever heard he whips the listeners into frenzy with his mantra. "I vex wit Manning but ah votin' PNM."

Now it is left to the other side to respond with: "I vex wit de state of de country so ah voting Kamla".

And as a reminder that today is Earth Day - when last did you plant a tree?

46. POLITICS – THE ART OF THE ABSURD

PORT OF SPAIN: Thursday 29th April 2010

It's been seven weeks - yes – already - since my return to Trinidad and Tobago. There are times when I feel like I've just landed from Third Rock on some Star Trek episode as everything in attitude and appearance is so grossly alien that the words "Beam me up, Scotty" come to mind.

At other times it's like nothing has changed as we sit impatiently with fellow citizens in crowded waiting rooms of the Public Services for birth certificates and other ID pre-requisites that take weeks instead of the promised immediate delivery.

During this waiting season I've occupied myself with Barack Obama's *The Audacity of Hope.* So much of what he writes is familiar: the constant bickering of the warring parties; the petty grunging up of old mud-slinging; the chest-thumping and the mealy-mouthing of the hopefuls. It is driving me, yes, crazy! I have to remind myself this is democracy at work.

The new president of the United States of America has inherited the fall-out from the likes of investment bankers Goldman Sachs. There they sat a pitiful row of greedy young men yesterday pleading innocence at profiting from a national financial crisis. It called forth democratic Senator Carl Levin's wrath which he called "unbridled greed in the absence of the cop on the beat to control it".

I will come back to this greed as reading a *JahajeeDesi* posting that recalls the National Flour Mills' Rice Deal - NFM's $30m mystery - is enough to raise questions about what may lay in store for a new government. It was the first corruption scandal to rock the novel UNC administration back in 1998, and, definitely, one of the most remembered in the series of allegations of impropriety that still haunt the party.

The *Guardian* Special Report dated 8th May 2003 had ended a series on corruption as Sasha Mohammed took a look at the National Flour Mills Rice Scandal back then. We must not let this happen again!

When speaking with a number of on-the-fencers there is a definite reality here that must be addressed by the opposition platform should they work to win the trust of voters for these much needed ballots. It is not enough for the UNC PLUS coalition to employ the populist cry that Manning must go. Manning's departure will not solve T&T's

problems. It is the will of us all as patriots to improve our lot that will do so.

Steve Alvarez, Political leader of the Democratic Party of Trinidad and Tobago, has reminded us in his ominous posting, "There is a country to run" Tuesday, 27th April, 2010. He says: Consequently it is possible that on May 25th the new Alliance can awake to the realisation that they have in fact beaten the PNM and when all the victory celebrations are over they have a country to run.

It is a very good opportunity to read George Alleyne who also gives us a dire warning with his "End Silence on issues" (*Newsday* Wednesday 28th April). We need to debate the issues and foremost among them is crime that has overpowered the country. It has besieged the nation and we are not dealing with it. When we attempt to do so, even when discussing homosexuality at a prestige college with suggestions that the act may have been 'forced', the manner of presentation by *Gayelle* TV Channel reminds us that the country is truly sick.

The venerable Lloyd Best once remarked that the country is in need of serious psychiatric attention. It remains true and it seems that crime and the powerlessness of nations, their problems and the economy are endemic. In Greece, Standard and Poor's downgraded the country's debt to junk status. Elsewhere there was a strike against inflation in India called by the country's opposition parties and allies to protest rising food and fuel prices. And in between TV bytes of the British electoral candidates' walkabouts as to how they will fix the 'black hole', there were snippets of the Ukraine's legislature hiding under umbrellas as a brawl erupted and eggs rained down with smoke bombs in their parliament. This was because of a vote allowing the Russian navy continuity in using the port on the Black Sea despite retaining a cheaper home fuel.

In Trinidad and Tobago, we are constantly reminded of the absurdity that is politics. While we have had worse things than eggs rain down on our Parliament nevertheless at election time we continue to wallow in cesspits of trivia, pettiness and *comesse* while the main issues of the election campaign remain untouched. Sometimes while listening to the coarseness of the platform speakers it makes one want to puke. Okay - so I must understand that politics is war and the stakes are high for the combatants. But how does one get truth from untruths?

Well, the Trinidad and Tobago Chamber of Industry and Commerce has been planning for over a year a 'Presidential Debate' to have main contenders square off before each other on the level paying field that they are willing to provide. But Prime Minister Manning refuses to participate. He thinks it unnecessary. He has nothing to gain, he declares. He does not need it opting for walkabouts to convert the converted!

But this is like looking a gift horse in the mouth! There are so many questions that we want answered outside of the protective fronds of his balisier. Crime for starters is an issue that all of us want to know about. I WANT TO KNOW. How did we ever let it get SO out of hand?

MR MANNING, WE WANT TO KNOW!

Even as I write this the evening news speaks of the once pristine UWI campus being a terror zone where bandits not only rule but shoot to kill. This is not even about gang warfare here! Innocent people's lives are at stake and we are not debating this issue!

So this is why when Winston Dookeran, political leader of Congress of the People, appeared on Sunday evening's newscast, a gentle white-haired giant against a ghastly backdrop of surreal red figures, it took a little time to grasp the message. That morning he was making the point to reporters that crime was the biggest issue facing the nation and he had chosen to demonstrate this fact in front of the President's House on the northern end of the Savannah. Each cardboard figure represented a life that was lost to criminality – FIVE HUNDRED AND SIX of them over the past year!

And you guys are not debating this issue!

As if to underscore the carnage that continues, the weekend brought forth a slaughter house list - an increase of EIGHT more killings across the country. Again judging from the names and ages it remained black on black youths unleashing wave after wave of devastation upon each other. In the first twelve weeks of 2010 the murders in Trinidad and Tobago have climbed to 168 and April is not yet ended! Now if that isn't cause for alarm, I don't know what is.

But Crime is the number one issue that could cost Mr. Manning the elections and I daresay it is an issue that should Ms. Persad-Bissessar succeed it is one that she and her government will have to attend to with immediacy. In the very poignant column by Keith Smith (*Express* Tuesday 27th April) talking from inside the belly of PNM's Holy Ground in Laventille the atmosphere is heavy with the stench of death and the powerlessness of those still living there to have to overcome.

And yet if we are to listen to National Security Minister Martin Joseph in elevating the more than 400 police constables to the ranks of corporal last Friday, there is much to rejoice about, for an increase in their salaries is to come. Perhaps this incentive along with an increase in number of police vehicles will provide the magic wand to wish away the killing fields such as Trinidad and Tobago has now become infamously noted for with its daily register of victims in the nation's morgues.

So what we want to hear from both political platforms are answers to our country's anguish and at the top of the list is the crime situation. This is what we want to hear Messieurs Manning and Warner, Mrs. Persad-Bissessar and Ms. Marlene McDonald acting upon.

We do not want to hear any more bacchanal. We already know it all. We do not want to be bombarded with all those tired boring TV advertisements. Some enterprising hot shot agency should do a survey on how many consumers are turned off rather than on by those repetitious irritating sameness. So you LOSE customers rather than gain and money saved can be better put to more useful ways and even in a wiser distribution of the same ads.

In fact what has to be done in a new dispensation is to audit the number and cost of media advertisements with accountability for their sources. The taxpayers should not have to bear the brunt of clearly partisan ads such as are the Vision 20/20 ads currently in promotion of government. And as in the USA control measures must be established so that all electoral funds are transparent and equally based.

George Alleyne has written in his column in *Newsday* 28th April of the non-articulating of parties' policies on other issues like, say, minimum wage structure, or say legislation to protect against unscrupulous contractors. If anything an ad showing balance sheet of oil and gas revenues with attendant profit and loss statements including wastage and inconsistencies should be advertised. WE WANT TO KNOW all the details. Accountability is what the population should pledge itself to watch-manning (pardon the pun) regardless of whosoever gets in on May 25th. This is good opportunity to put our *macco-ing* to good use. It is what we are good at.

Where the People's National Movement's articulation of its industrialization programme and its Vision 20/20 is concerned, there are too many fuzzy areas where clarity and transparency are absent or simply unexplained.

So, yes, Mr. Manning, many of us want to know. Perhaps you should rethink your walkabouts and spend some more time outside the Balisier Curtain and in the harsh glare of an impartial representation of the nation's constituents.

Let's hear what you have to say in a fair and square debate with Mrs. Persad-Bissessar. Or, in this season of warring absurdity, is it that you're not man enough to really face the lady?

47. NO GOODWILL IN A SEASON OF RAGE

PORT OF SPAIN: Thursday 6th May 2010

It is an open season of waiting for things to happen in my life. I'm bored stiff in this gated community and want to jump onto a political platform where the real excitement is. I remember my time as an ONR candidate in 1981 and then later in 1986 with the NAR in support of Dr. Emanuel Hosein in Tunapuna. And as a reminder to those who do not understand how the former helped the latter it was with an unprecedented whopping victory of 33 to the 3 PNM seats back then. Remember! The time for change had come. The time for change has come again.

Dr. Hosein reminds me that his victory bagged over 10,000 votes to Dr. John Scott's 5,000. But he adds sadly that it is different now as the Tunapuna constituency has been gerrymandered making it a fairly safe constituency for PNM's Ms. Esther Le Gendre. Congress of the People's Dr. Winston Dookeran he sees as having to work harder for his UNC/COP Partnership seat.

My feelings after watching the news yesterday of 100 students attacking - meaning TERRORIZING - the villagers of lower Caura Road in El Dorado tell me otherwise. Mr. Dookeran has the seat made for him as no parent must continue to support the failure of Minister of Education Esther Le Gendre. The children are at risk and they must be saved. But more on this later.

Now in 2010 after a 12-year absence nothing seems to move - for example, as simple a thing as renewing one's driving permit unless – unless there is the arrival of a letter to collect my ID card from the Elections and Boundaries Commission's office in Port of Spain. A visit to the NIB and joining the lineup of senior citizens to collect the grant that used to be called a pension is still denied me. So that blinking ID card is the open-sesame to it all!

Now it makes one wonder what in the world of high tech and world-class-dom to which our Prime Minister Manning aspires could be keeping back for SIX weeks the production of a plastic card? All the information is already obtained and checked in an office designed for so important and urgent a public service. In fact it IS the season of urgency with the General Elections just 17 days away.

According to the young woman I've telephoned today at the EBC office and who is not allowed to identify herself, the normal waiting time is six to eight weeks! They've already checked out my living quarters four weeks ago so what IS the problem? I want to know if I can vote without an ID card. She says yes - just check the last place I've voted. Now that was Cipriani Labour College back in 1996. Thing is apparently I never did collect my ID card. Will that name be erased if my new voting station now carries my new ID? She cannot say as the onus is on me to follow through.

I'm lucky though as while my info was still posted my husband's was cancelled so he had to go through another procedure of restoration. Don't ask me why. As much like the best-selling *Bobbsey Twins* we have managed to do things fairly much together in the past. Now his task included finding someone older than himself by at least five years to vouch for a NEW affidavit of his birth! We advised the young woman at the desk that we would have to check out such a person at the Lapeyrouse Cemetery!

Another area of frustration is the incessant drilling of the next door apartment-in-renovation and the maddening traffic with that raga raga music on what turns out to be a main road in this residential area. I can identify with Mr. Ishmael Samad. In his *Memoirs of a Mad Man* in the *T&T Review* 3rd May he relates how his experiences of simply trying to be a good citizen can backfire. I want to rally the neighbours to visit whomsoever is the Parliamentary representative of the area but intolerant as I am to fence-sitters I prefer to do like Mr. Samad and trot up and down the road with a sandwich board sign marked "Residential Area − Observe the Speed Limit - Please no music." You see like Hazel Brown I'm an action person of the same mint.

Or else I could put up signs that warn speedsters and noisy muffler freaks of fines or warning that they are on CCTV. My theory on these noisemakers is that there is a latent anger that expresses itself in this blatant disrespect for others. It translates itself in other ways as in the gutter-type media and comedy shows that brand the society with the common denominator of "low class." Is this the persona we want to showcase as Mr. Manning's World Class? Are these supporters − advertisers, media and parents of this grunge and sludge − aware of these "role models" for our youths? Are we really serious about tourism?

Shame! Shame on us and our government for allowing our country to sink to such lows!

I have even played with the idea of mixing my own cement (at risk of dodging bullets in the middle of the night) and laying down 'sleeping policemen' or zebra crossings for those sons-of-guns. Forget the police as Mr. Samad was to learn in his 'good citizenship' encounters and pox on the hierarchy of decorated National Security officers who make promises they do not keep.

It is already two months since our return to Trinidad and Tobago. Having got past the novelty of gawking at the new façade of the country – familiar gingerbread houses with new layers of cosmetic surgery; empty towering high-rises; fluttering 2 million dollar flag in front of Movie Towne (I don't know how we ever lived without it!); good tasty Trini food; cheery embraces (long time no see, where have you been?) it is reason to get out Derek Walcott's crap detector.

Is there happiness in Paradise? Someone replies that we have our humour still intact. He is referring to the television ad that showcases Cro Cro and Sugar Aloes and their audience doubling up with laughter in anticipation of the likes of this Mother's Day Comedy Extravaganza. Am I losing my own sense of humour? Recently I have chided Rickey Singh for making reference to Trinidad's 'hilarious bacchanal politics'.

With two and a half weeks more to go before Judgement Day, there is a queasy feeling that the Prime Minister himself has enunciated. It is going to be an election like no other. THIS IS SERIOUS BUSINESS as so much is at stake. And no amount of reducing the election to the lowest common denominator of hilarity and smut is excusable. People are prickly sensitive and all it will take is a response to a provocation to trigger a fracas as courted recently in the UNC/COP St Joseph's meeting when Candidate Herbert Volney was speaking.

The latest is the news making TT$5 million hit on Kamla Persad-Bissessar! Never before has T&T elections been so deadly and the fight is not yet fully engaged! But we must remember that the stakes for the national treasury and people's hearts and minds are high.

CNC3 Tuesday evening's question put to viewers confirmed Mr. Manning's desperation when it recorded a 92% concern over violence in the coming elections. Just 8% thought that we are not that way inclined. We are not a violent people - never mind that by morning a chap was found in an Enterprise/Chaguanas back lane with not one nor two but MULTIPLE bullets pumped into his body. It has brought the murders in our little country to 179 (*Express* count) so far for the year! It shouts too of hatred, anger, and crime that is OUT OF HAND. There is never word nor visible follow up on each of these horrendous crimes. So they have now become a way of life making us a rogue country – a failing state -- and a reason for demanding answers from our next government hopefuls.

But you know what is scary about that murder? People heard the explosions about midnight but it took a gardener to discover the body in the early morning. Were there neither cell phones, land lines nor other ways to get help? Where and when were the police contacted? A resident interviewed on television was scared stiff as he spoke of the hellish fear that people now live in. WE ALL KNOW THAT! SO WHY ARE WE SO BLOODY COMPLACENT!

And yet this issue of crime which is the number one priority in the country is hardly an election issue. Here is the opportunity for the media in lieu of government action to highlight and provide a platform for crusade in its position as the Fourth Estate. Where are the blaring front-page editorials that should have condemned this morning's lead story, namely, that the police have reported a hit on someone's life! Where are the faces of the criminals?

The truth is I had difficulty locating that particular murder (referred to above) in the newspapers and when it was finally discovered in *Express* (Wednesday 5th May) it was sidelined without any detail. As for *Newsday's* four men missing since 23rd April and the missing labourer who was 'going down the road' last Wednesday, it seems their story is gone and it's business as usual with the hunt on for more and more *comesse* rather than what is the next government going to do to fix this sad rich little country of ours.

This is why I can identify with the 'mad people' of the country as perceived in the likes of Mr. Percy Villafana now a national icon, only because he was honest enough to tell the Prime Minister Manning "No More". So what's wrong with that? And there is Mr. Ishmael Samad who takes citizens' arrests very seriously. He acts, sometimes hastily but HE TAKES ACTION. So what's wrong with that? This is more than many of us can do.

One can understand fully the predicament of an intelligent and sensitive public servant seated in the highest echelons of the land but who in his conscience feels impotent to bringing about a solution to the criminal problems he faces daily. That is, unless he does the mad thing and jumps into the problems in the hope of bringing about change. This was what Justice Herbert Volney did by resigning from the Judiciary to offer himself as an election candidate for St. Joseph. A surprisingly mad action perhaps even for himself, but one with which he now feels comfortable.

He is as comfortable with himself as a UNC/COP candidate as is Ms. Marlene McDonald who defended her PNM stewardship as Minister of Community Development, Culture and Gender Affairs on a one-on-one interview with Shelley Dass-Clarke on *CNC3* Television. Both women were excellent and comfortable with their own self-confidence. What this interview did was to provide a peek into the moment of truth (for some of us the moment of rage that is a self-righteous anger – madness if you will). For Ms. McDonald it was that denial of an injustice that she perceived as a child at not being able to enter the front door of that family home in Cascade where her grandmother was considered a servant.

For former Justice Herbert Volney as with Messers Villafana and Samad, the moment of truth or madness may have come when they came face to face with themselves and the option that presented itself for changing their lot. I pray that care, good sense and righteousness will prevail in their fight for good citizenship.

The same goes for every citizen who votes for a safe, happy and wise Trinidad and Tobago on Monday, 24th May.

48. MR. MANNING, HAVE YOU EVER BEEN THROWN TO THE STREET AND ROBBED?

PORT OF SPAIN: Thursday 13th May 2010

It is 11 o'clock on Wednesday morning and up by the Elections and Boundaries Commission office a young man sits on the curb outside the Scott Building. He is working. He watches the two women who have come to check the office for long promised IDs. They are not yet ready as since your snap election date things have got pretty hectic with the processing of these plastic cards despite the fact that the crowds have dwindled since our application date early last month. What did they say? Six to eight weeks. And they mean it.

The women decide to make the best of the day out and excitedly they set off down Frederick Street planning to pay bills and lunch somewhere downtown. They are happy and free. I am with our daughter Deborah. Our men are busy elsewhere at work.

We have crossed Oxford Street and edging down the pavement on Frederick Street alongside a brick wall with coiled razor wire. The young man from by the EBC office stalks his prey and pounces. He pushes between us and brings me down onto the pavement. There is a split second to register what is happening to me. A heavy-set round-faced chap of about thirty, clean-shaven, short-haired and of cinnamon brown complexion is on top of me in the road and is wrenching my Grandmother's gold bracelets from my right hand even while clutching my handbag. I am screaming and do not even know that he has been successful in his quest for gold. "What are you doing to her?" Deborah is screaming too and pounds him.

He gets up and runs. I see he is wearing a thin white jersey with holes and bright stripes. Around the corner, he pulls it off and dashes bare-backed heading east toward Charlotte Street. He has shed the jersey along with an empty knapsack with names penned on it. It is the only evidence for the police to work with.

Mr. Manning, I don't know if you have ever been yourself the victim of an assault. The unprovoked attack on an innocent citizen by someone intent on causing harm is an act of terrorism. It traumatizes. It is a violation of one's basic human right to walk the streets unmolested and in peace.

People tell me later that day that this is something that happens many times every day in Trinidad.

I've since read that Sir Ellis Clarke was himself a victim in 2004 when the country's first President was attacked by four armed bandits, who stole $1,200 and also drove off with his Audi.

My gold bracelets are priceless; there is no price tag that can be placed on their sentimental value. Their pleasant jingle has comforted me during childbirth while they bring sober assurance during difficult times with promises that everything is going to be all right. Later, at a downtown jewellery store, we ask the price of a single gold bracelet. It is put at TT$4,300 for a single and thinner bracelet!

How much would the thief get for my thick pair? Various bystanders have their say. He may get a few hundreds for a drug fix, or, giving him the benefit of Makandal Daaga's doubt, enough to buy milk for his child. Or, maybe he just wants to give his woman a gift! Perhaps he will pass it on to a middle man who will then sell it to an unscrupulous jeweller who may well be the bigger culprit in encouraging and sustaining these criminal acts.

Another question: What is DOMA (Downtown Owners and Merchants Association) doing about such traders? What is its president Gregory Aboud doing?

I tell you, Mr. Manning, TRINIDAD AND TOBAGO IS UNDER SEIGE!

But all these thoughts come later. Humiliated and hurt, I struggled up after screaming bloody murder for my assailant to leave me. As he runs off, two older men tackle him with one jamming him against a passing car. But the predator is swift and escapes across Charlotte Street into the warren of buildings beyond. A young man in dark green shirt saunters past with cell phone attached to an ear. He shows little interest in me even as he doubles back across Oxford Street. Is he also busy at work?

I asked the police who arrive promptly on mobile patrol from St. Ann's.

Why? Mr. Manning. Isn't there enough legitimate work to go around even as you look outside for new labourers? As you yourself have reminded us in your 2010 PNM manifesto the unemployment rate has dropped to dramatic lows that must make the rest of the world envious of our enterprise!

Today, Thursday, as I nurse my bruised body, I tremble with fear as to where we are heading as a nation. The beleaguered Central Police Station (old Police Headquarters) on St. Vincent Street that we visited yesterday still reflects the grandeur of a colonial past when the country worked. The constables there are helpful but weary as they display mug shots of criminal offenders and assure us that with our help these offenders will be brought to justice.

When caught they are put on an identification parade and thereafter starts court proceedings that present new problems of legal efficiency because of case overload. Courage too is needed in placing the victims at further risk by exposing them in court. Even jurors become at risk as happened on Wednesday when the trial judge in a murder case aborted the trial after one of the jurors received a telephone threat in the jury room. How long this will last and with how many more acts of violence to go is what former High Court Justice Herbert Volney is publicly talking about on his own political platform because clearly there is need for change at the basic level of law enforcement and legal procedure.

Let me remind you of that reality for in the heat of the electioneering it is easy to forget the alarming figures of that ECLAC Report on Judicial Systems in the Americas 2006-2007. You should take a look at Table 3 Criminal Cases Resolved in High Court with reference to Total; numbers found Guilty; numbers found Not Guilty; and cases dismissed.

Figures recorded began in 1998, the year that I left Trinidad for China. By 2010 just before returning the Attorney General was to announce in a Ria Taitt article *Express* February 3rd that More judges coming: DPP gets big staff increase. Opposition Senator Wade Mark said while the Opposition welcomed the development, the question that had to be asked was: Why did it take Government so long (six and a half years)?

Senator Mark said the Government also needed to pay attention to the magistracy. We know that the backlog at the level of the magistracy is extremely huge, he said. The figure being bandied about was a backlog of 400,000 cases.

There are 400,000 cases, Mr. Manning, and yet this is not your central pillar of your PNM Manifesto!

I am copying this to Mrs. Persad-Bissessar as she too may have seen the *Newsday* front page today. It shows the open coffin of a murdered woman at her own funeral where her corpse and her family are being guarded by a plain-clothes policeman with a high-powered rifle. So this is what we have come to.

Come Tuesday May 25th Mr. Manning, you might well find yourself seated as Leader of the Opposition and Mrs. Persad-Bissessar will then have inherited your portfolio of governance as leader of a UNC Partnership.

But this does not free the rest of the nation of the task of caring for each other. Whichever way the population votes the future is in the hands of ALL OF US WHO CALL THIS HOME and WHO SAY THAT WE LOVE TRINIDAD AND TOBAGO.

The collective responsibility, whether as voters, as Leader of the Government, or as Leader of the Opposition in this democracy of ours, is to bring about peaceful and responsible change in our daily lives. Women, men and children must feel safe to walk our streets, roads and traces without fearing that they would be attacked, robbed and victimized.

49. A DATE WITH DESTINY

PORT OF SPAIN: Thursday 20th May 2010

These are the times that try men's souls.
– Thomas Paine

In four days' time, on Monday 24th May, the people of Trinidad and Tobago will vote in a new government. Their choice of Patrick Manning's People's National Movement government or Kamla Persad-Bissessar's

People's Partnership will definitively define us as a certain kind of nation. Are we going to keep the devil that we know or risk change for the she-devil instead? Exactly what calibre of people we are remains to be seen and to be judged by the regional and international community.

It is indeed scary to consider that we are afraid of change and will continue to place our hopes for a better life on the party that Eric Eustace Williams founded in 1956 even though it seems to have lost the claim to morality in public affairs. After all, it is just such fear that produced a second term for George W. Bush in 2004. It was his tenureship that saw an on-going entanglement in the unending wars in Iraq and Afghanistan. The global oil crisis and the collapse of the world economic order before his departure in 2008 have played a direct role in the predicament that we now find ourselves in the twin-island Republic of Trinidad and Tobago.

In fact were it not for President Bush's quest for oil, and the premium prices that caused oil to shoot up to over US$100 a barrel, our country would not have found itself in the euphoria of an unprecedented materialism and greed that provided the powerful opportunities for the creation of a dictator and the unpopularity that the post of Maximum Leader now attracts.

Last Sunday evening Mr. Manning commandeered prime time on all the media to dance rings around his three questioners in a staged airing of his interview. By Monday night he had seized the opportunity to present his *State of the Nation* report to another staged and captive audience subjected to the impressive details of his party's Vision 20/20. The glorified figures and projects past and future spoke of a quality of life befitting the windfalls that fell into the hands of a government with billions of dollars to spend.

This week is seeing a flurry of goodies for the nation. There is The Public Transport Service Corporation

(PTSC) yesterday that received 85 new buses from a Chinese supplier at a cost of $66 million. Twenty-five will replace old PTSC buses and the others will be used on rural routes, Works and Transport Minister Colm Imbert said yesterday. (*Express* 19th May).

There is T&T being given patent approval (finally!) for the G-pan and this is expected to reap benefits for the country as inventor. This was disclosed by Prime Minister Patrick Manning during the PNM's political meeting at the Diamond Vale Co-operative, Wendy Fitzwilliam Boulevard, Diego Martin, on Tuesday. (*Newsday* 20th May)

There is National Minister of Security Minister Martin Joseph turning the sod for the new St. Joseph Police Station and there is Health Minister Jerry Narace with $250 million fund for sick children; and Arima gets an $800,000 Social Services centre opened. It seems a good thing to call regular elections after all!

Meanwhile the People's Partnership under the leadership of Kamla Persad-Bissessar who, like a Joan of Arc continues to perform bravely, is engaged in battle to win the hearts and minds of the undecided voters. Scratch the fundamentalists who are genetically programmed to say, "my grandfather, father and now me is PNM to de bone"

It is not an easy week and the nation that is politicised as never before wishes that Monday 24th May would come and be done as quickly as possible. To quote Michael Harris who on Monday 17th May wrote in the *Express,* "as we go to the polls to select the next government of Trinidad and Tobago nothing is certain and it would be a brave man or an inveterate gambler who would want to make, at this point, any prediction as to the outcome."

Now remember that was said on Monday!

The result he says is that people find themselves in a 'tizzic' or a state of 'cognitive dissonance' to the point where one's normal behaviour, feelings and beliefs are in contradiction. Of course the only ones spared are the fundamentalists on both sides whose mindset is a blind belief in whichever party or candidate to which they pay homage.

Nevertheless for many of us there is a churning in our stomachs. You can't eat; you can't sleep; you just want your side to win. How much nastier can it get? I swear that the nervous excitement has brought on an angina.

As I continue to wait for a letter that announces my ID - what comes instead is the polling card so I can vote. Neither my husband's card - nor ID - has as yet arrived. Meanwhile it is easy to hum the popular jingles like "We movin' on wit Kamla" or switch easily to chip along while floor-sweeping with "Manning going back..." but when all is said and done the easiest one of all is Crazy's "Patrick Manning have to go."

To add to the cerebral dysfunction the people are jumping fences if not putting them up as happened on Tuesday evening when the UNC Partnership was bolted out of the George Earl Park in St. Joseph. One reason given by the Tunapuna/Piarco Regional PNM held Corporation was that the last time it was used by the UNC its playing equipment was damaged.

As if that wasn't enough there were the Yellow People (UNC) whose attire was so attractive that by this morning young PM Look-Alike Joel Primus, PNM contender for Fyzabad, appeared on TV6's morning programme resplendent in sunshine yellow with matching tie.

The Red People (PNM) were feverishly working up a 'tizzic' of their own with First Mate Rowley's pronouncements - the most blatant being that his worst fears were PNM losing and the other side winning. Marlene McDonald PNM Port of Spain South contender meanwhile was decrying the pasting of her face on *Facebook* over someone else's ample figure.

To make matters worse the Blue People (Baptist Council of Elders) yesterday threw in their support in favour of the People's Partnership. The Spiritual Head of the Church, Episcopal Archbishop Barbara Burke at a press conference held yesterday, called on all Baptists to either vote for the Partnership, or to "hold their vote," according to today's *Newsday*. The group shifted allegiance in a television appearance that they were neglected by The Reds and hence will not be voting for them.

As one listens each evening to the opposing platform speakers it is with nervous tension that you hope that your side will not make a *faux pas* and blow it for the party one leans toward. On Tuesday evening it must have been the case for some PNM stalwarts who learnt of the breaking news story as the UNC Partnership meeting was locked out of the George Earl Park in St Joseph.

By the same token for those who looked toward St Joseph's Partnership candidate Herbert Volney and UNC Chairman's Jack Warner's fiery contributions to the Partnership bandwagon, there is always the danger that one or the other could put their foot in their own mouth. So while Candidate Volney managed to escape any political incorrectness of the evening, it was guest speaker Candidate Warner who walked a thin line with revelations of the PNM opponent. His words made me scream "Don't go there, Jack! We're just five days away. The battle is almost won. Don't be tempted by the devil!"

Nevertheless Warner went in and continued there up to last evening's telecast in Palmiste exposing what seems to be another chink in the amour of Volney's political opponent St Joseph's Kennedy Swarathsingh.

But it is true that politics is war and in war anything goes. And this IS war! It is certainly not the time to question the ideals of what means justify what ends or vice versa. Forget love across the fence! It just gets nastier.

Besides, the stakes are high as Dr. Rowley reminded us on Tuesday evening when he shared his Diego Martin platform with his PM. And so in the coming days even while we consoled ourselves that "we are not a people like that" and "we respect our democracy" nevertheless the blatant acts of bold-faced criminality and vulgarity we have been experiencing over the past years make one cringe at the possibilities for disorder and mayhem by a recalcitrant rogue group.

But all is not lost in this Paradise of ours for beneath every racial colour and creed of the Good, the Bad and the Ugly of the land lies a True Trini whose love for Trinidad and Tobago is waiting to be tapped into. One has only to remember the Strike Squad of 1990 and the more recent Soca Warriors in the World Cup in Germany 2006 and even more recently the out-pouring of one love for our cricket team and for the earthquake victims in Haiti.

There is a national spirit of unity and a latent goodwill that is there. No matter where in the world we may roam, Trinidad and Tobago is home. Where else are we going? For example, just after my mugging on Frederick Street last week when I was deciding that I/we cyar live wid dat - something unexpectedly wonderful happened.

One morning at eight o'clock the white car backed out of its space in our compound, revved up with the usual madness and headed through the arthritic electronic gate. By the time I got through the multiple locks of the veranda, it was in time to see the driver staring back at me and risking on-coming traffic as he caught my solemn shaking of the head in condemnation.

But at 5:15 pm that day, there was a knock on the door and a young man asks politely: "Remember me?" He introduces himself and said that he was the chap who revved up his car engine each morning. He explained that his engine was in dire need of change and promised to go easier in future. He was real sorry for disturbing the peace.

And then there was the phone call from Mr. Gregory Aboud, President of DOMA (Downtown Owners' and Merchants' Association.) He was responding to my last week's questions about his thinking on the thuggery in broad daylight on Frederick Street and the trading in stolen gold by unscrupulous businessmen.

He was most understanding and was articulate about a range of factors that include a concern that the culprits responsible for the Frederick Street sidewalk bombings are still at large. But what was remarkable was his admission that people in business are guilty of not being involved and that "we have not spoken in a way that is responsible to people". It is the humble admission for a new beginning – a new vision as he says, of what is a good country.

As we count down the hours to exercise our franchise on Monday 24th May, it is time to pledge ourselves to honouring the legacy of our democratic freedoms to choose the way we want to live TOGETHER AS ONE PEOPLE. Whatever happens we must continue to make this country of ours a better place than it is, a place where fear and disrespect must be replaced by a genuine love and caring for each other. In the end we are one family in our beloved Trinidad and Tobago.

50. THIS IS A VICTORY OF THE PEOPLE!

PORT OF SPAIN: Thursday 27th May 2010

On Monday 24th May 2010 the people of Trinidad and Tobago went to the polls and voted overwhelmingly for Kamla Persad-Bissessar and her team in the People's

Partnership. By 9:15 that evening the digital map on line television screen changed colours from the 50/50 red of the PNM and yellow of the People's Partnership to an almost total yellow, representative of the imminent victory. Tobago's wipe-out, from red to yellow, was the beginning of the celebration of what was to come for Trinidad and Tobago.

Kamla's People's Partnership was leading and to some viewers it was a symbolic purge of the vitriolic blood-red that was responsible for the impasse that the country now found itself – a country plagued with crime and mired in corruption. Its leadership over the past eight years was tending toward megalomania-cy with Prime Minister Patrick Manning veering towards a frightening dictatorship.

By 9:30 that evening the results that change was inevitable with a landslide victory for the People's Partnership of 29 seats to the People's National Movement's 12 seats was cause for joy. Change was possible and the people recognised that they were the holders of the power to make it happen. By 9:40 p.m. that night Kamla's victory was making Trinidad and Tobago proud.

This day of deliverance stands as a historic date for our twin-island nation in ushering its first female Prime Minister. But not only was it that date with destiny – a day of redemption when the people clearly defined the road that they chose to take, it was also a re-endorsement for the democratic principles enshrined in the Trinidad and Tobago Republican Constitution of 1976.

The very first chapter of the constitution identifies the Recognition and Protection of fundamental human rights and freedoms of its citizens. It was cause for a personal reflection on the re-entry to my native land. Two weeks short of three months since my return from China I was roughed up and robbed of a pair of gold bracelets in broad daylight on Frederick Street. It was a violation of my right to walk the streets freely and safely.

As an addendum several women were to respond online of similar assaults on their persons over the years with KB speaking of an almost identical robbery of her bracelets as far back as ten years ago! My own mother-in-law never recovered from such an incident and that was on Piccadilly Street in the eighties!

On Election Day Monday, despite having been given an ID number on application receipt and frequent checking with the Electoral and Boundaries Commission Office, my husband who had applied at the same time as I did for an ID card on 13th April was unable to vote as his name was not on the voters' lists. Reason given by the EBC office on Election Monday: "pending". Why? He had fulfilled all the requirements that the EBC demanded, so this was an infringement on his constitutional right to vote. And thus another human right was violated.

Now the irony of these events is that having lived in a country run by a Socialist Government, we were never the victims of any violation of basic human rights. Everywhere bureaucracy takes its own time but even in cities with more than 12 million we were never threatened or denied the right to live free and unmolested.

I will go as far as to say that while teaching contracts stated the lines between proselytizing and teaching, we were never once questioned about our methodology or content of lectures. We, and British and American teachers, were never bothered.

The road that I have traveled between China and home is recorded over the past fifty weeks in a series of columns posted courtesy this *JahajeeDesi* group site. It was sparked by the murder of 10-year old Tecia Henry and was to bring me into daily monitoring of Trinidad and Tobago's on-line newspapers.

It is curious that our relationship thanks to Richard Seecharan as moderator celebrates not only a golden anniversary – this is the fiftieth of these postings - but the culmination of a joyous rise in celebration that this column supported and flagged. It happened when Kamla Persad-Bissessar was considering her daring leap into the leadership of the United National Congress back on January 24th and continued its support during the tumultuous pathway as Leader of the Opposition on February 24th to the present time.

The path less traveled by women in the deadly battle of politics that is seen as a male preserve proved a dangerous battleground and minefield for Kamla as over the past weeks we sat transfixed to the media waves as night after night the contenders engaged in battle. She was in the middle and holding steady.

Last week was the longest week for the nation as the battle was being waged. Each night as the TV screens changed from the hysteria of Mr. Manning's red platforms to the reflective mood of Ms. Persad-Bissessar's yellow and Mr. Winston Dookeran's white t-shirt clad followers there was a glaring difference in the modus operandi of both parties. To tell you the truth, even though I tried impartially to weigh the good, the bad and the ugly of both platforms, I often took relief in returning to the much more sober routine of the People's Partnership where the 'loose cannons' were kept in check by an organized ethic of presentation material.

Yesterday, 26th May, as Kamla Persad-Bissessar prepared to be sworn in as the next Prime Minister and first woman Prime Minister of Trinidad and Tobago we prayed for her health, safety and leadership. The road ahead is not an easy one as the very nature of democracy implies confrontation between two opposing factions and that demands resolution.

Democracy if we are to listen to US President Barack Obama's words in his book, *The Audacity of Hope*, is just that, but he also says that the pluses of a diverse group of constituents that make up the Democrats provide a platform for unity. There is much we can learn from the American model where accountability and award by merit are honoured.

So the new Prime Minister will be held responsible for her promises, one of the foremost being that her win is a victory of the people. The people, by the very nature of our history, are divided into two major ethnic camps the descendents of India and Africa. The majority of these remain loyal to roots that provide 'safety' or 'immunity' from the rest. It is a blueprint for the 'them' and 'us' the most divisive concept that exists in any society. This was evident in the responses to reporters coming out of both camps on election night.

For example, it did not take long before the absence of 'other' performers (meaning non-Indian) from the Rienzi Complex stage on Monday night was noted. Nor was the heart-rending grief of women (African) missed when they poured out their 'what we go do now?' that the PNM was no longer in charge.

Kamla's portfolio is heavy with both the physical duties of securing the daily wherewithal of her now-one-million-plus constituents AND the spiritual resuscitation of a nation that for a time was bereft of belief.

Her first test as Prime Minister has taken the form of fixing the perennial flooding that affects Central. She has hit the ground running with her team by visiting the sites and meeting with the Disaster Preparedness people. But PM Persad-Bissessar has the goodwill of the people with her.

Yesterday I listened to Hazel Brown on the television morning show with Jessie-May Ventour. It was further endorsement by Hazel who had welcomed me back three months before with the words "I going down Rienzi to help Kamla."

My fellow activist from the days of HATT (Housewives Association of T&T) when we worked on the Minimum Wages Bill for women with a focus on household helpers spoke about teaching a man how to fish rather than giving him a fish. She spoke against giving milk to mothers rather than teaching them the value of breast-feeding and about the use of white sugar and flour against food like pumpkin and bhagi.

These ideas and actions are basic practical building blocks that ALL women can provide in coming out to put out country back together. This transcends political hand-outs and political rhetoric.

Kamla must tap into the groundswell of support which lies out there. Afra Raymond said it when he spoke about her need to come out of the small pool to help move the country forward. She must widen the circle as there are good people out there not tapped into and who want to offer themselves.

Believe me there are. And I can assure our new Prime Minister that there are among the women out here, a vast pool of us 'shy' and 'retired' professional and non-professionals in every nook and cranny of our twin-islands who are bored to heck at home and who would really love the opportunity to come out and help build our communities.

I end by making a plea to all of us who are members of the 'silent majority'. There are going to be opportunists and saboteurs among us who will bring only embarrassment or grief to the new dispensation. To all of you out there I say be vigilant. Do not be afraid to speak out and act accordingly. We ARE the government and we must help those we have just elected to work for a communal good.

51. A TALE OF EPIC PROPORTIONS

PORT OF SPAIN: Thursday 3rd June 2010

Trinidad and Tobago continues to spin its own tale of epic proportions even as it enthralls viewers who nightly watch the stories unfold on the television evening news. So, much like the Indian epic poem *Ramayana* or the Chinese classic *Journey to the West* ours is equally chaptered into the most interesting of human experiences underscored by such human passions of love and hate, generosity and greed, peace and war, crime and punishment.

The past six weeks saw one such chapter of Trinidad and Tobago's epic story unfold as the then reigning monarch marshaled his troops to battle an increasingly disgruntled populace. Either through divine inspiration, prophetic oracle or perhaps absolute self-confidence he announced the date that once and for all would settle the dispute as to whether or not there was any doubt about his maximum leadership. After all, he knew about *The Art of War* having been a veteran in skirmishes since his indoctrination into the tribal party from 1971.

The mystical date of May 24th on which the masses were to re-affirm their allegiance was pulled from the pocket of his imperial robe. Never mind this date was by his own admission already settled upon by him one year into his new mandate with the mesmerizing 'other circles' marking 'other dates' just in case the calendar page should slip out his pocket. This was to 'confuddle' the finder so as never again to let a leakage to occur. He feared it would have been leaked to the enemy camp as had happened he said when he called a snap election in 1995. It cost him the throne even though it was only temporarily lost.

Ensuing weeks witnessed the spectacle of battle as each side - one brandishing the red of the Imperial troops and the other the yellow and white of the Proletariat's Partnership engaged in skirmishes and bloody warfare. The Emperor as he was commonly known would exit his palatial quarters each day and be driven past his towering edifices in a regal chariot that bore the license plate with the presidential coat-of-arms. This he had commissioned as talk had it that he was setting himself up as Executive President for life and the hotel opposite the Grand Savannah was to be the residential quarters for his Elite Guard.

It is interesting to note that mas' man extraordinaire Peter Minshall had already likened the gargantuan Hotel and National Academy of Performing Arts (NAPA) akin to slugs copulating on the site of the old Princes' Building. Peter's irreverent elegance on the subject we'll leave for another day. The Monarch, however, saw it as the 'Pearl of the Caribbean' and in favorable comparison with the iconic Sydney Opera House which incidentally is nowadays in serious trouble re-financing its upkeep.

There were times when the Emperor would even shed the red robes of his Balisier Cult devotees to don naval uniform as he tried to steady the rudder of the SS PNM. Aboard was his nemesis, a First Mate known for his vociferous questioning of the Captain whom he accused of shipwrecking the Ship of State and vaguely threatening a mutiny and trial.

It was this same spectacle at sea that would be used in the propaganda of the other side to show the unsteadiness of the vessel on turbulent waters as the First Mate shrilled, "I am a sailor..." each night on TV while threatening that there would be a court marshal once the ship had dry-docked.

By 9:30 on that eventful evening of Monday May 24th the Yellow Queen, so called by virtue of supportive battle garb, flags and bunting of the opposition crusade, was swept into power on the flood tide of love and gentility. Hers was a well-orchestrated campaign with four-star Generals and one Chairman of the Joint Chiefs of Staff – a colourful character – fondly dubbed Jack-in-the-box and soon to become Jack-of-all-trades who secured for her not one but TWO decapitations within a matter of months. A third head was still to fall.

The heads that were now placed at the feet of the Yellow Queen were that of the former Tribal Leader, a cantankerous old warrior in her own camp whom they called the Silver Fox; the other head was that of the Emperor who bore the impressive initials of PM. This could be conveniently switched from initials of his own given birth names to mean that of resident Prime Minister, or even to that of Project Manager.

This latter acronym of PM was to be the fatal weapon that found him wanting in explanation of a colossus place of worship in the high bush of Guanapo forests. Project Manager of that edifice - whosoever he (or she) might be - was indeed the director/owner/employer of the Shanghai Company with its own staff of workmen imported from China. Whose money, from whence it was coming and to whom it was going, remained challenges for the coming dispensation to seek. Answers must be forthcoming to a questioning electorate.

When the battle was over and the conceding of defeat was duly registered, it now remained the lot of the victors to examine the results of the people's will and to take stock of the damage and the spoils of war. Was there really TT$19.5 billion untouched and waiting in the treasury? It had been advertised before the Election date by the Emperor as being still there in the Heritage and Stabilization Fund.

So damaging were the results to the incumbents that all the supporters on beholding their Emperor as being truly naked began jumping up and down in *tootoolbay* denial/frenzy in front the Hall of the Balisier. The truth is that their Emperor had subjected them to a defeat at the stained fingertips of the People's Partnership Coalition with a total of 432,026 votes cast or 59.81% with 29 seats while the People's National Movement received 285,354 votes cast or 39.50% with 12 seats according to the Election and Boundaries Commission figures.

What's more with just 12 out of 41 seats garnered, the Emperor having wagered his previous 26 seats safely in hand for so ignominious a defeat, he now had to contend with the promised mutiny started on board the battered vessel that had barely made it to shore. First Mate's promise of a court-marshal was impending.

As in the Indian epic poem, composed in Sanskrit around 300 BCE when Rama of royal birth lost his throne and was banished to the forest with wife Sita and half-brother Laksmana, another kind of tale was happening here in the twin-island paradise where this epic is set. Would the Emperor now be banished to the forest with his wife and half-brothers to spend 14 years in exile?

The epic drama continues but would the Emperor be resurrected one day to deal with his rambunctious First Mate, the dejected other eleven of his Members of Parliament, an irate band of raging Balisier devotees who now admit that he had taken them overboard the SS PNM with him. But worst of all, there were these new yellow people with rainbow colour hybrids, a dazzling threat to his boring monochromous red Imperial estate. How dare this recalcitrant assortment of a coalition (that he foretold could not last) how dare they lay hands upon his treasures!

What lies in store for the newcomers? As the epic story unfolds it is interesting to take a look at what history records in the first week of their victory.

Truly from the hills of Laventille to the plains of Caroni and across the waters to Tobago as the Yellow Queen sang out, there is a wholesome wind of change blowing across the lands. People are smiling once more. The spoils of war however will present a challenge for the Queen and her Four Star Generals. The problems inherited are enormous and topping the list of fixings is the criminality – the main issue around which her crusade had rallied.

The path that her country must NOT follow is the stark reminder of a sister isle where to extradite or not to extradite to the USA a notorious drug lord remains a national as well as an international issue. The country of the Yellow Queen is leaning toward the entanglement of global drug-trafficking, gun-running, ghettoes with teenage delinquents and that coupled with its oil wealth is temptation enough for terrorism as well as white-collar crime to prosper.

And then there is the national culture of a country spoilt by its materialism and attitude to a Trini lifestyle that boasts as many as 20 public holidays each year. Some of them like today's Corpus Christi are becoming as redundant as the historical period in which they were set.

And then there is a work ethic or lack of thereof so that as the nation rises to the dawn of a new day, supervisors are finding it difficult to make it to work before ten o'clock; clerical staff lounge as was discovered on Tuesday in the Electoral and Boundaries Commission Office on Frederick Street as they await the President's official closing of the ballot count. Until then the machinery for dispensing ID cards on which citizens depend for processing Old Age pensions and National Insurance claims and driving permits is put on hold.

In one bank on the crowded St James Main Rd, where accommodation for clients have not kept pace with its multi-million dollar profits recently declared, one is left to wonder whatever did the past administrations do about a real vision and the development of the cities in a 21st century that blessed us with so much wealth. Port-of Spain and the East-West corridor towns of San Juan, Tunapuna and Arima remain embarrassing unplanned eye-sores.

Do these places have Mayors? What about POS Mayor Murchison Brown, can he really be proud of being the longest serving mayor to a capital city that stinks?

According to a *Guardian* report by Richard Lord on 30th June, "The PNM is ready" for the Local Government elections and even as he was about to off load his Mayoral chain to the eager-beaver Louis Lee Sing, his claim to fame was "the corporation was engaged in a reconstruction of sidewalks in the city, and was awaiting approval from the Local Government Ministry for a similar exercise to be done near residential areas.

For the sake of posterity couldn't he have checked with the Brazilian Portuguese or Chinese as to making those sidewalks decoratively tiled and interesting? Oh gosh man! Theirs is a delight to walk on.

He said the establishment of One Woodbrook Place (upscale housing project – still at time of writing unoccupied white elephants) was one of the most interesting private/public sector initiatives. He said the restoration of Memorial Park—which he described as a shrine—was a personal project of his, as mayor. Brown said a one-day seminar being held in conjunction with the UN Habitat Programme will be launched at City Hall on Friday."

Wait a minute, has Mr. Brown visited the characterless Woodford Square and Lord Harris'? Where have those monuments to our history gone?

One ventures out of the traffic grid to gingerly skirt filthy insane people and youths...always suspicious idling black youths... inside the bank is horribly crowded as customers mingle with security guards; the employees are unwilling, sour and dour. It lends credence to the black humour that Trinis really doh like to work.

But there is an excitement in the air that tells of a new order. People are willing to support the Yellow Queen and her court of ministers. Over the next one hundred and twenty days, the electorate will be supportive, perhaps forgiving even of the disappointments that are bound to occur with promises of this, that and the other.

However, the population now electrified, energized and hopeful thinks that better days are ahead; but they are aware too that they must be watchful. No more must apathy allow the freedom for some to laud it over others or to pilfer the national treasuries in exchange for votes and favours. No more must they sit unconcernedly as individuals get away with murder literally and figuratively. No more must friends in high places work to grant favours to their connections regardless of a perceived 'pay-back-time' to party funders nor to family and friends. NO MORE! And no more licentiousness, Mr. Ministers! NO MORE! We need role models for our youths.

Makandal Daaga is now reaping some of the good seed he has sown with his recent appointment as Caricom's Ambassador Extraordinaire. He has reminded us emotionally with his hand to heart as he exhorted from the People's Partnership campaign platform: "WE ARE THE GOVERNMENT."

It is a good enough thought to keep in mind.

We must never forget this chapter of our epic tale. It is one that the collective 'we' are writing.

52. LET THE GAMES BEGIN!

PORT OF SPAIN: Thursday 10th June 2010

Now that the sweetness of the honeymoon is ending, it is with alacrity that change is happening. On board the SS Partnership, under the captaincy of a woman the crew is energetically flexing its muscles. Meanwhile on dry dock, the First Mate now in line to full Captaincy of the SS PNM, is losing no time in matching up with a selection of robust women. They are to assist the impending court marshal he talked about while on the tossing boat. But first he must get busy with that pesky upstart Jack-in-the-box - or rather - Jack-of-all-trades on the victory ship next door.

It is open season for Politics in Trinidad and Tobago once more.

So let the games begin!

In 2010 the revolution we expected in Trinidad and Tobago DID come to pass. In fulfilling the 20-year cycle that established 1970 as the Year of the Black Power uprising and 1990 as the Year of Trinidad and Tobago Under Siege by a Muslimeen group, we expected that something extraordinary was bound to happen in 2010.

What happened was that a woman named Kamla Persad-Bissessar did the unbelievable in deposing her tenacious Party leader Basdeo Panday and in going on to remove the country's seemingly invincible Prime Minister Patrick Manning, now revealed as the self-same Project Manager he slyly alluded to in that infamous television interview prior to the May 24 elections.

Remarkable too was her charisma. It created the mystique of the election platform's charm enough to meld the warring male factions within the rank and file of opposition-splintered groups including her own United National Congress. The Congress of the People, the

Movement for Social Justice, the National Joint Action Committee and the Tobago Organization of the People were to unite into a formidable People's Partnership.

Trouble-makers within the ranks were put under heavy manners where some party-watchers suspect that true to their nature they are just biding their time to undermine her good works. Meanwhile the gentility continues to weave its magic as she goes about the people's business efficiently and charming everyone into her rapture of caring for the nation...and not...as she reiterates, for individual partisan-seeking interests.

As the days unfold however, the nation is watching the wish-lists of the various groups all of which are naturally tacked on to how much money there remains in the nation's coffers. It was no surprise to hear the supporters of the defeated People's National Movement bemoaning their lot as to "who would take care of we now."

It was always surprising though to hear some people in higher social brackets complain of crime and corruption in high places not to mention high prices while declaring that they 'voting Manning' because HE GAVE THEM "free education, free transport and free medicine." But neither crime nor corruption was an issue for them.

So what are Prime Minister Kamla Persad-Bissessar and her team discovering already? It does not take a degree in Economics to understand the revenues and expenses of a budget sheet. It does not take a degree in Political Science either to understand that electoral platform promises are sometimes just that. They are indeed promises that politicians hope will be fulfilled once they are in office. But this is where the best made plans of mice and men sometimes backfire.

Who knows if there is anything left in the treasury coffers to sustain those promises? Have we been living within our means and for how long can we do so? Or, are we really on the brink as new Minister of Finance Winston Dookeran feared?

Shaliza Hassanali reported in the *Guardian* on Sunday 6th June on the state of the country's debt and as to whether the Government would be able to deliver its campaign promises to citizens. Dookeran replied: "Yes; there is no question that the country is facing debt. We have commitments and we will honour them. We will have to order our priorities."

But the new government faces a daunting task of running the country as reality checks kick in and consternation is reflected in Minister Dookeran's face. It makes me think of what breadwinner Hubbard looked like when his Old Mother Hubbard went to the cupboard to fetch her poor dog a bone. The priorities are as numerous as lessons to be learnt!

Take Greece, for example, that proud country that gave us the blueprint for rational thought. Today there is bacchanal in the streets as the plebs try to understand their crippling debt crisis.

What caused the Greek financial crisis? "Did the 2004 Olympics spark Greek financial crisis?" asks Derek Gatopoulos, an *Associated Press* Writer on June 3rd. He writes: Prime Minister George Papandreou blames the debt crisis on decades of poor management, putting off unpopular reforms, and vast clientele networks set up by political parties, promising government jobs, social security perks and loss-making regional projects to win votes. Was it the same for Trinidad and Tobago under the PNM leadership? So much for déjà vu!

Okay, now let's take a look at Germany. "German president quits over military remarks" by Geir Molson. *Associated Press* reported on 1st June: President Horst Koehler stunned Germans by resigning Monday after being criticized for appearing to link military deployments abroad with the country's economic interests — creating a new headache for Chancellor Angela Merkel. Koehler, a member of Merkel's Christian Democrats, cited a week of criticism over a radio interview he gave following a visit to German troops in Afghanistan. In that broadcast, he said for a country with Germany's dependency on exports, military deployments could be "necessary . . . in order to defend our interests, for example, free trade routes."

Uh, Oh! It's necessary to watch what you say and what you DO! So Ministers do be careful! *Telegraph.co.uk* reported on Friday 4th June that the presidency is supposed to be above the political fray and carries little real power but traditionally it functions as the nation's moral voice.

Remember how much trouble our own President George Maxwell Richards had in putting together an Integrity Commission... again? And no sooner than Minister Keith Rowley put down the Bible as the sworn-in Leader of the Opposition, he was barking up the Integrity tree at Minister Jack Warner's perceived conflict of interests as Minister of Works and Transport and Vice-President of FIFA. And draw blood he did as last evening's news announced that the Integrity Commission promptly ruled against Minister Warner's dual roles as being of conflicting interests.

Then let's look at Japan's predicament with Prime Minister Yukio Hatoyama demitting office! He failed to make good on an election promise. The *Trinidad Guardian* editorial on Thursday 3rd June reminded us of the dangers for parties in opposition to make serious financial commitments without having a full grasp of the state of the treasury.

Mr. Hutoyama had come to office just eight months ago on the strength of his promise to the electorate that he would remove the unpopular Futenma American Military base on the island of Okinawa. Thing is it would overturn a 2006 deal between Japan and the USA! Sometimes there are cows that are most sacred.

What all this has to tell us is that there are many lessons for reference and those still to be learnt by our hard-working partnership of the people. The newly-appointed must walk a thin straight line especially since the country has been seen to have matured politically with its unprecedented voter turn out like never before in history.

The record shows a 70% turn out with a total of 722,322 votes cast. Added to that was the number of citizens registering once the election date was announced and the remarkable number of young people seen to participate in the process especially those en courant with the new Information Technology.

Two weeks into government the People's Partnership continues to perform in a remarkable revolution with Kamla Persad-Bissessar's daring to go where no one else has gone before. Pardon me for this sexist remark, but her womanly nature does seem to give her attitudes of generosity and humility where in the macho world of male superiority such virtues are seen as weaknesses. She makes work seem so easy!

At the moment there is enough goodwill to sustain her governance well past the first one hundred and twenty days. She must not let the Babel distract her however.

Beside the first salvo of Opposition Leader Dr. Keith Rowley delivered yesterday there was deposed minister of Works Colm Imbert who without giving Warner's Priority Bus route revamp a chance 'put goat mouth' on its feasibility while admitting that there were many, many studies going back 20 years! This is according to Joel Julien in the *Express* on 5th June.

The challenge always will have to be "doing the right thing" as the new opposition loses no time to oppose. Besides, with newly-appointed Opposition Chief Whip

Marlene McDonald, T&T's epic story promises to be interesting.

Now one of the virtues that the new administration will have to call forth is patience as many are the malpractices, bad attitudes and intrigue (*comesse*) that will have to be sorted out and explained to a public some of whom will prefer to hear what they want to hear. For example, there is the matter of the over one hundred taxi drivers who were promised $500 to transport the constituents of a PNM candidate on Election Day and who remained unpaid that evening. Gosh! That's $50,000 already! Oil money flowing like flood water! Now WHOSE money was being used to pay them?

How many other maxi-taxi pools were there to service all 41 constituencies? There is an update on this story in the *Guardian* on 9th June by Radhica Sooraj: "Maxi-taxi drivers await $$ from PNM". Dhanraj Soodeen, who owns a fleet of maxi-taxis, said more than 20 drivers were hired by the PNM to transport supporters to the various rallies. "I own seven maxis and six of them were used in the campaign," he said. He added that the maxis were contracted by the PNM Point Fortin office to transport supporters to various locations, including Macoya, Manzanilla, Cunupia and Balisier House. Soodeen said that in the last week before the election, payments were withheld. He claimed that the PNM owed him more than $15,000.

The math could be a challenge for the Integrity Committee should there be a breach of party and government integrity here as Soodeen continues: "I spoke to someone in the office and they said that in total, they owed more than $287,000 in outstanding fees for transportation and catering," he said. Soodeen said several of them went to Works Minister Jack Warner to get help. He said Warner was contacted in South Africa and he agreed to pay the PNM fees.

Something smells fishy here! Why would several of them feel that they had to go to Jack Warner for help? Has a precedent been set here with the Ministry of Works paying past PNM's electioneering fees? And why would Jack Warner AGREE to pay the PNM fees?

Another TV newscast showed disgruntled workers who were hired BEFORE elections on a month's contract but who now discovered that they were fired. The cameras showed them shouting abuses of 'tief'. WHO were they referring to? The people who signed them up OR the new administration that halted the projects so as to better understand and take stock?

But these are little teensy-weensy matters. Let us look at the bigger affairs that the new government must attend to with haste. Already there are the UDeCOTT improprieties on the plate along with Petrotrin's humongous headaches as reported by Donstan Bonn in the *Express* of 4th June: "Petrotrin is experiencing severe financial difficulties brought on by high cost overrun of its refinery upgrade and the $12 billion lawsuit filed by New York based fuel producer World GTL Inc. We are looking at allegations of malfeasance in Petrotrin's gas optimisation process and poor decision making in its procurement practices

We have not even looked at the WASA allegedly-signed contract with an Israeli firm whose address is a mail box number. How much of our money has already changed hands and how do we get it back? How to undo the *comesse* without our new leaders leading themselves into temptation?

The nation now more fully conscientized, is not going to sit back and let anyone get away with murder. Not again. I hear it in the wonderfully interactive media whether though newspaper and online blogs or though video and audio news waves. The people are engaged and in whichever social rung they are questioning and talking out.

As in China when foreigners gripe about the news censorship ofFacebook, YouTube and Twitter, one must be reminded that democracy is alive and well in the new Information Technology of a Global Village where citizens communicate freely with their cell phones and online AND BEIJING IS LISTENING. They've got to IF they are going to be relevant and avoid social unrest.

In Trinidad and Tobago there is an eager new participation in the government process with the invitation for newcomers to come aboard the People's Partnership.

It is enough to tempt me to throw in my own little piece of something for whatever it is worth. And by the by, we finally get to see a photo of The Prophetess, the Rev. Juliana Pena in yesterday's *Guardian* (June 9th) story by Michelle Loubon. The well-dressed mulatresse is the key to Mr. Manning's dilemma over the multi-million dollar Lighthouse of the Lord Jesus Christ Church in the Heights of Guanapo.

We could take pattern from the Chinese Yuan Ming Yuan Imperial Gardens in Beijing that were destroyed twice by European Allied Forces who plundered its treasures. It remains a sacred museum of the people – an untouched relic of arrogance, greed and a grim reminder of NEVER AGAIN must such an assault be inflicted on the people.

It will do well for Dr. Rupert Griffith as new Minister of Tourism to liaise with China through its Embassy for ideas on the 'HOW TO' proceed with a vibrant tourism industry that remains rewarding (financially and culturally) for all concerned. A nicely-packaged eco-trip to the Guanapo site will be a sober lesson in our history with an enjoyable commune with Nature reminding all visitors that a gentle revolution of 2010 was made possible by a woman named Kamla.

But then the Chinese workmen in the employ of the Shanghai Construction Company were back yesterday. The multi-million dollar structure is already being dismantled. Well, so much for history and evidence in the mysterious Lighthouse of the Lord Jesus Christ Church in the Heights of Guanapo.

53. KAMLA'S SANTIWAH

PORT OF SPAIN: Thursday 17th June 2010

Santiwah is the Trini dialect word for *santa aqua.* In Spanish it means Holy Water blessed in an ecclesiastical ceremony on Gloria Saturday following the Good Friday of Christian Lent. According to Roman Catholic tradition this water is sacred and will ward off evil spirits. By extension "bush bath" came into the vernacular as a means of washing the body with water and local herbs with the same effect.

I grew up in a household where my grandmother was a firm believer in these ablutions of body and soul and would sprinkle the holy water generously or *santiwah* with a sprig of sweet broom so as to cleanse and purify our living quarters as need arose.

Sylvia Moodie-Kublalsingh was to discover this as reported in the Journal of Ethnobiology and Ethnomedicine. Hispanic prayers are used in Latin America for healing and against mal yeux (maljo). These spanish-romanic prayers, like the 'oracion' prayer, are used during 'santowah' (santigual). The ceremony includes sweet broom (Scoparia dulcis) which is used to sprinkle holy water.... These prayers (magic rather than religion) are said to have come to the New World with the conquistadors.

Hmn-n-n-n... one wonders what happened after the Africans and Indians from both east and indigenous communities had added their own beliefs to the mix of cleansing rituals.

The rains and subsequent flooding that accompanied the installation of Kamla Persad-Bissessar as the first woman Prime Minister of Trinidad and Tobago during the last week of May might as well be interpreted as divine blessings by the spiritual among us. We may even go a step further to re-iterate that God is indeed a Trini.

Now it is three weeks later and the miracles continue as the changes Mrs. Persad-Bissessar promised at her swearing-in ceremony begin to kick in. Saturday's evening news showed the Prime Minister in working clothes cleaning up a water-way and promising action on plastic waste along with re-cycling opportunities and legislation that will assist in an ongoing C&B–T&T Clean and Beautify Trinidad and Tobago.

The Chinese initiated their nation's ban on plastic shopping bags before the Olympics in 2008 and have been diligently working at fixing their pollution by planting avenue trees like mangoes that remove traffic pollutants. Their recycling business that is as indigenous as it is lucrative often escapes the skeptical foreign experts who fail to include the ubiquitous street dealers-in-scrap among the Nation's employed. It is at this point that I like to remind those interested that among the world's richest is a woman in China, Zhang Yin, who started out by collecting scrap paper and who is now worth an estimated US$3.4 billion.

Knowing how impressive these figures are to most people one watcher named John Laumer writing in *Design & Architecture (Recycled)* June 11th 2010, put her beyond the worth of US talk show host Oprah Winfrey and J.K Rowling of Harry Potter fame.

As we move toward Sunday 27th June, the Prime Minister is calling for all hands on deck to clean up the country. It will be a time for community interaction and one that should bring old and young regardless of creed and race to make T&T as beautiful and as livable as can be. It would be the start of true oneness as each takes responsibility for the environment with promise of follow-up to maintain and support laws against offenders.

But can we really work together? Already where we live in Diego Martin which is the red North West promontory you see on that yellow election map is controlled by the winning PNM candidates who include Dr Amery Browne (DM Central) on one side of my street and Colm Imbert (DM N/E) on the other. Both are PNMites and one wonders whether or not those without a leaning toward the defeated candidates Nicole Dyer-Griffith (COP) and Garvin Nicholas (UNC) will want to join forces to tidy up our environs. In DM West there is the formidable Dr Keith Rowley (PNM) and the heavy-weight Rocky Garcia (COP).

As the days progress we will see, as I am yet to respond to the many who have become excited at the prospects of cleaning up our country and as one notes the wealth of goodwill that the May 24th People's Partnership victory has stirred up throughout the country.

In talking about cleaning up, it is with that genuine interest that the population is tasting its power and, as Michael Harris spoke about in his *Express* Monday June 14th column titled "In search of solid ground," who *is going to give little quarter and tolerate foolishness even less.* We WANT to know everything.... whether the Prime Minister and Minister Jack Warner will seek a political or an ethical answer - or both - on the question of a perceived 'conflict of interest' - to whether or not the evidence of the Guanapo Church site is being monitored on an on-going basis.

According to today's *Express* Akile Simon's "Guanapo church looted", the People's Partnership seems to have lost out already on its guardianship as Attorney General Anand Ramlogan passed the buck to the Integrity Commission. Apparently 'their wide-ranging sweep of power' seems to have become exhausted after the unusual spurt of energy expended on Rowley vs. Warner.

The People's Partnership risks another loss again unless they act NOW on those Cashew Gardens squatters.

In the uncharted waters Harris speaks about in which both political parties now find themselves, there is much cleaning up to be done. All eyes are naturally on what is there in the Government's piggy bank and so it continued during this past week as Minister of Finance Winston Dookeran confirmed his anxiety over the projected negative growth.

Now remember, according to the last government's Vision 20/20 Pathway to the New Trinidad and Tobago, 'T&T has emerged as the economic and financial leader of the Caribbean and is one of the fastest growing economies in the western hemisphere.' This looked undoubtedly good and expectedly so with an energy sector averaging 14.8% per year and an annual growth of 9.2% since the Iraqi invasion of US President George W. Bush in 2003. Other goodies in the booklet tell us about that Revenue Stabilization account balance of TT$11.6 billion in 2007 up from TT$400 million in 2002.

By the May 24th 2010 Election date government TV ads boasted of the TT$19.5 billion in 'untouched funds' but the new Minister of Finance by Friday 11th June was to announce his concerns over the fact that no funds were put in during 2009-2010. Yet former Finance Minister Karen Nunez-Tesheira said that on April 30th she had signed a warrant of deposit of over TT$650 million into the Heritage and Stabilization Fund (HSF) and that the fund was nearly TT$19 billion. We need Minister Dookeran to clarify this matter. It was a mistake for which he has since apologized.

Now we are talking lots of money here and while this HSF is a legal requirement to maintain the rainy day funds in the piggy-bank and even as the foreign reserves remain healthy at US$8 billion (TT$48 billion) so that the country is not likely to starve over the next three years, the fact is that we will experience a second year of negative growth in balancing our budget.

As I understand the book-keeping we are living beyond our means as we rush to the Central Bank and Treasury to see 'dramatic declines' that the Minister has put at an expected TT$788 million "therefore we are in fact borrowing to support current expenditure," he says. No wonder Minister Dookeran looks so worried!

Now as we spent the last three months pursuing our ID cards without which we could not proceed to pursue such entitlements as Old Age Pension aka Grant and National Insurance claims, nor Drivers' permits, it is with curiosity that one comes face to face with the people and how they are affected by the money windfall.

From the starting point of acquiring the newly-minted birth certificates and marriage certificate at the Ministry of Legal Affairs down on South Quay, up to Frederick Street to the Elections and Boundaries Commission Office and to the Ministry of Social Services on Duke and Richmond and finally to the NIB offices on upper Abercromby Street, there was a chance to really meet the voters.

Throw in a couple visits to the squalor of downtown where Affidavits now come for a princely sum of $160 each, one gets to meet the mother struggling with her baby and a red plastic bag of necessities while in a taxi. There is an old woman, both feet bandaged as she sits awaiting attention for her grant. The people here are definitely among the wretched of the earth. It shows in their faces and on the prostrate forms of vagrants on the sidewalks.

Thirteen weeks later, with experiences that include being roughed up on Frederick Street and robbed of a $10,000 pair of gold bracelets, we are finally at the NIB office. It is where one must go before even thinking pension/grant. Somehow the insurance affects the pension – negatively, but that bridge is still to be crossed.

The public here is better appointed with one retiree decked off in suit and tie while filling out his forms. Perhaps he thinks that his attire will help. The clerks are slow, bogged down in bureaucracy despite the myth of 'a paperless society'. There is definitely a better class here even if the lines are miserably long and the people fidgety.

Today as I look at the *Newsday* story by Nalinee Seelal 16th June 2010 and reflect on the salary scale now made possible by our new-found wealth, the mind boggles as it jumps to the little old lady with her bandaged feet and who must have been quite an eye-full in her younger days. She waits patiently to chase after her monthly grant of $2,000.

It is a time to question God when another woman in a nearby office could have had her income jump from $56,000 per month to $70,000. Just like that! Or was she a miracle worker? It was the farewell announcement by one Executive Chairman named Calder Hart bestowed upon his young acting CEO on the day he resigned from office.

Yup! There's a mighty lot to be done by the new People's Partnership in cleaning up our own Augean stables. Some things just ain't righteous.

54. OF TREES AND CRAP!

PORT OF SPAIN: Thursday 24th June 2010

I have abandoned my original scheme that was to choreograph *A Long Hot Summer in a Season of Illogic.* I had planned to focus on idle controversies like the call by Works and Transport Minister Jack Warner for Mr. Eric St. Cyr, leader of the Integrity Commission, to resign. The argument on whether it is unethical and/or unlawful for Mr. Warner to retain his Ministerial post with his FIFA Vice-Presidency is but one of the charming constitutional wrangles that distracts us from the real work at hand of managing and bringing order to our land.

It is politics I know but one must be vigilant against these calculated distractions! And the fact is they come from every corner of the population, from every nook and cranny that there is someone with a grievance or a vested interest. And the new Government that is wary about spending money must face what seems to be a legacy of profligacy.

Tomorrow, for example, the People's Partnership Government will be debating in Parliament the result of the country's search for a Commissioner of Police that seemed to have overlooked anyone in our Police Service. Or, to put it another way, it could be faced with the need to spend more money on an exercise that should have produced the right man years ago. But the disease as we know, the disease of spending large sums on salaries and consultancies, has been discovered in almost every state enterprise and every state board.

Now I would like all those who worked hard to bring about this change to pay particular attention to what I am about to share.

Like most newly-elected party leaders the National Alliance for Reconstruction occupied the vacated seats of their predecessors with new energies directed at serving the people. Their fall from a victorious high of 33 seats to the People's National Movement's 3 seats in 1986 to their annihilation in 1991 must not be forgotten. Or else, history will repeat itself.

One of the contributors to the devastation was due to a simple but very human error and that was a perceived bad attitude by everyone who was not of the NAR, especially by members of the public service. Thing is that the newly-elected guardians, excited and euphoric still with the headiness of victory, continue to make these same mistakes that they do not see but which could easily contribute to their downfall.

In their zealousness to convert and bring about change, it is easy to throw out the baby with the bathwater in winning or rather not winning friends and influencing or turning off people.

Prime Minister Kamla Persad-Bisessar seems to have succeeded in having a positive attitude and her humility has served her well both on the campaign trail and now on the highest platform of leadership. Rather than make her wishy-washy, her simplicity, her lack of arrogance and the directness that she brings to her openness, are admirable. Nevertheless she rules with discipline.

The same admiration goes for the open manner in which Minister of Finance Winston Dookeran interfaces as I can testify when meeting him last Saturday by chance on the Caura Royal Road cleaning the shoulders with his team. Prakash Ramadhar who visited Tobago yesterday to meet with Tobago House of Assembly Orville London seemed to exude that same out-goingness which is needed to charm adversaries and the electorate. Vasant Bharath is exemplary in his diction and well-grooming.

Unfortunately the same cannot be said for other newcomers whose faux pas must be corrected immediately

IF there is going to be a one-love in the desire for all to work to make this place a better one than we know it.

Let me begin with Mr. Warner whose revelations were most welcome on the People's Partnership platform. He balanced the soberness of the other speakers and brought a degree of who-dun-it mystery that the audience anticipated. Now that he is in Parliament he has to shed the pop-star halo and wear the hat as parliamentary representative of the people WITHOUT BEING DISTRACTED by the rowdies.

In a word, Mr. Warner has to set his priorities and not fall prey to the vicissitudes that come with office. His constant defense/attack, the most recent being the call to Mr. St. Cyr, is not necessary. It is not a priority. The Integrity Commission will stay in office or fall by its works. If necessary Mr. Warner could have pressed the case for action of the plundering of the Guanapo Church steel and scaffolding that is very possibly OUR MONEY. But this is what the Attorney General is already doing.

Or, is he?

As I have written before the People's Partnership CANNOT afford to make mistakes and I have already highlighted one of them as being that of Mr. Carlos John publicly front-lining himself with the party. One must ask how much support, that is, credibility in the partnership, is being lost each time he flaunts an appearance.

Similarly, whenever a member of the new leadership inadvertently makes a gaffe one must ask oneself how many more votes have been lost. It is with this in mind therefore that I now question the attitude of another minister of the new government.

I have no doubt that the new Minister of Health Therese Baptiste-Cornelis is well meaning. She is bringing her expertise, her youth and her energy to a difficult area of the public services. Her very first test was that visit to the Eric Williams Medical Complex when her team was greeted with a bomb scare. She wasted no time in her enthusiasm to declare that she would be taking no crap and she explained that CRAP was the acronym for Continuous Recurring Administrative Problems.

I liked her spirit and her words. She was cute and forgiving supporters were quick to say, "Well done! What we need is discipline!" But then she went on to Tobago and incurred the wrath of the Assembly.

We-l-l-l... that was not so good.

Supporters of the government are going to be less forgiving by calling on her in-experience in dealing with a bunch of public servants in whom laissez faire is a well-cultivated art if not a well-known congenital trait.

I will go on to cite some very current encounters with the public servants to prove that not only is the trait of apathy endemic in Trinidad and Tobago's work culture BUT because of its long existence, overcoming this disease will require deliberate bedside manners rather than radical surgery.

Yesterday I visited the Ministry of Agriculture in Curepe to seek legal advice that came out of a meeting with Food Production Minister Vasant Bharath. The office was sparsely peopled and after helping me to fill out forms the young female attendant abandoned me to hold what seemed to be a tete-a-tete with two young male clerks. I finally had to take up the forms and walk to find the legal gentleman after about half an hour. One wondered why the three senior-looking supervisors did not occupy them with work, and one also wondered whether or not the office was over-staffed.

That meeting resulted in directing me to the Arima Warden's office to pursue something called a RPO (Real Property Ordinance) "instrument". There, of the three young women, pretty but idle, one seemed unfamiliar with the word "instrument" repeated from my meeting in Curepe. She finally went to fetch a senior clerk who seemed to have taken offence at the use of "high language" as she called it. That visit ended with a useless attempt at tracking said RPO as the "book could not be found".

The final example of our present work culture that our new government has to deal with is exemplified by the Prime Minister's initiative of *Clean and Beautify T&T* that takes place on Sunday.

You may have noticed that there is no hot-line number to call. Blame it on the inherited bureaucracy that ties itself up in knots; blame it on the insecurity of new guardians to guard the rebellious guards; or you could blame it in the indelicacy of attitude that IF you only dare risk being threatening in the form of being "DE OTHER SIDE" or the new kids on the block like Mr. Warner and Ms. Baptiste-Cornelis, you run the risk of losing out. And the entire People's Partnership does so too.

This morning I was following up on behalf of the Diego Martin gung-ho group headed by Hazel Brown and Robert Torry a certain ministry responsible for Highways to get permission to plant trees and clean off the defacing election stickers. There was seemingly no problem with the latter and since the Diego Martin Regional Corporation seems to be doing a good job with cleaning our part of the drains and canals and also the highway borders, our contribution was to be the planting of trees.

Now therein lies the problem. If our tree-planting is going to be a model for the country, as I/we were touting it to be, then it will have to go through a process of bureaucracy so that there is a plan. Okay, understood. So what about the Prime Minister's C&B -T&T on Sunday?

Thing is that the cleaning part is no problem (although the political parties responsible for putting up those posters should be held responsible for taking them down with the understanding that what after next Sunday?

Will it be a return to those horror shots of garbage as we saw last night on CNC3TV in San Juan?

The Beautifying part IS the problem according to the Ministry and so I wonder if Prime Minister Persad-Bissessar in her own enthusiasm realises that we cannot go planting lovely little flowerbeds on the highway as there is a right way to proceed. Perhaps that is why as she must now be learning there is no hotline number on that pretty C&B - T&T commercial.

Between 7:00 am this morning Thursday to 9:30 at time of writing, my Ministry lady has gone through calls to La Pastora to be advised on WHAT kinds of trees to plant...to a request that should be made by letter...to the Permanent Secretary somewhere whose plate was as full as my lady's... to now. So while a couple of us are gung-ho planning to plant trees between KFC and the T-Junction on the Diego Martin Highway AFTER Sunday they are likely to be uprooted. Hazel Brown, veteran activist as she is says: "We'll plant anyway. Their plate is too full to come and uproot!"

As we await the paperwork and the different levels of approval, the People's Partnership must understand that there must be more ways to bell the cat than with showing "an attitude".

What Mr. Warner and Ms. Baptiste-Cornelis must understand is that we must use sometimes a carrot rather than a stick to encourage people and to work as always for the ONE BEAUTIFUL NATION that we are.

55. ZAI JIAN, OR, GOODBYE

PORT OF SPAIN: Thursday 1st July 2010

It is time to say goodbye. I have agonized as to when to end my weekly contributions to *JahajeeDesi* postings site. But one must know when to go and much as in my favourite words of Ecclesiastes in the Holy Book one must recognize that there is a time for everything under the sun. There is truly a season for every activity under the heaven.

Over the past fifty-five weeks many are the people from all corners of the globe to whom I have reached out and for whom the wonders of this instant technology have allowed to reach back and touch me. So, many thanks go out to Deosaran Bisnath the creator of this cyber site and to Richard Seecharan who accommodated my musings with graciousness along the way. You have put me happily in touch with classmates and political mates and all the other kinds of soul mates imaginable.

Anthony Milne former *Express* colleague once joked when we met online earlier on, did I have a book in mind? Well you know, Anthony, even though you seem to have dropped out of circulation, each week in churning out my thoughts I often questioned why I was doing this. It was the same question that former Prime Minister Basdeo Panday asked when he visited that dream of ours on Frederick Street called *Caribbean Information Systems & Services* and wondered why anyone with sanity would put their everything into an electronic publishing and educational exhibit that pioneered touch screen computer technology.

Even Secretary General Dr. Edwin Carrington exclaimed on his visit that the Caribbean Basin Exhibit should hold place of honour in the National Library (NALIS) then under construction.

Each week I took comfort in the words of Gertrude Stein who said "I write for myself and strangers." Mostly though, apart from the couple of responses from readers who identified with what I was saying, or those whose welcome comments arrived to enhance positively or were constructively critical, in the final analysis it was the therapeutic feeling that I was doing something that was satisfying. I was taking part in what was going on at home. I am part of the change.

So, yes, Anthony, I am compiling one year of Diasporean reflections in the life of Trinidad and Tobago as viewed from China. It began with the murder of that little Tecia Henry on June 13th last year and ended with the heroic rise of Kamla Persad-Bissessar on May 24th of this year. I am even tempted to call the collection *From Tecia to Kamla.*

After 12 years of self-exile in the People's Republic of China it was time to pay closer attention to what was happening back home and so began the monitoring of the three daily on-line newspapers. What triggered the anger and the need to DO something was the rapid deterioration of a beloved country as viewed through the eyes of a native so far away from home.

For several weeks after the strangled body of the ten-year old was discovered beneath a building not far away from her home I began the morbid task of recording the daily blood-bath of what was turning Trinidad and Tobago into a notorious Gangster's Paradise. Not only was there an average of two and half felonies a day but killers and their victims were predominantly young African males. It was blamed on drug and gun-trafficking from South America with the resultant breeding ground for turf and gang warfare.

Who feeds them these guns that are AK47s with telescopic lenses? Let's put names and faces on those who market those poisons with names like "magic mushrooms". There are real people who have contributed to this war of terror currently being waged on our nation. When are we going to end it?

Even as I write these final words to a period in our lives the news reveal an unchanging pattern in its reports of crime, wanton wastage of money and allegations of new corruption. Lawlessness still stalks the land as we witness the brazen plundering of the unfinished church at Guanapo and we understand the scene in the courts where yesterday according to Justice Anthony Carmona *even the courthouse has become an unsafe place with the brazen action of criminals.*

Have we really only ex-changed our government? How very, very sad!

The political structure such as existed was headed by a second term of the People's National Movement under Prime Minister Patrick Manning. The bizarre thing was that not only was the government side-lining the priority that was and still remains crime but, right before our eyes we were beholding the morphing of an ordinary citizen nicknamed 'Patos' into an idiotic creature now known as 'The Emperor' who deluded himself into thinking he was wearing the finest of robes. Surrounding him were sycophants who lived the fantasy with him even while holding on to his robes and feathering their million-dollar nests.

It was also a good time to do so as the country - with God himself being a Trini - was being showered with US dollars that paid for the people's birthright in the form of its mineral wealth of oil and gas. No wonder the brag was that our little country had escaped the ravages of the world recession and our unemployment rate was a commendable 5%.

There were lots of fine buildings going up, wonderful projects in train and while many were comforted with a health care that provided free medicine I was later to discover that while the cheaper ones could save a person TT$70 at a time the blows were administered in the other medicines that cost more than three times its equivalent in China. But still, many people were comfortable and therefore untouched so that a sister-in-law could advise me that on my return to Trinidad "do what other people do and live around it."

In such a situation one becomes immune from the tragedies and I was to discover another youth, shot in the back of his head, was soon to become just another statistic. A mirasmic hot pepper in the Super market for .59 cents was just inflation while absurd real estate and over-priced commodities was just someone doing 'good business' rather than skullduggery.

But some people were NOT sitting around and Kamla Persad-Bissessar, with help from those who understood how to play the game of politics, soon had her taking leadership of her United National Congress party. She went on to oust the un-oustable Basdeo Panday taking leadership of the Opposition in Parliament and by partnering her UNC with the rival parties that included Winston Dookeran's Congress of the People; Errol McLeod's Movement for Social Justice; Makandal Daaga's National Joint Action Committee; Ashford Jack's Tobago Organization of the People, she was able to humble Patrick Manning's PNM with a 29/12 defeat in the General Elections on May 24.

Now having said all this with the rest being history let's take a quick look at what we have at the end of the new People's Partnership victory. Now into its second month and with a honeymoon that has just about ended, rushed as it was with getting straight down to the business of battling floods and cleaning drains, and making promises of forensic public service investigations before putting things in place, what do we have?

Well, to be brutally honest, not a whole lot. And if the Prime Minister is going to prove herself a leader she has to make bold moves at risk of becoming that same type of leader whom Steve Alvarez, Political Leader of the Democratic Party of Trinidad & Tobago describes in his piece titled "Why Governments Fail." Here he talks of people looking for a saviour to whom they can bring their woes. This person or group eventually becomes maximum leader.

He says: Simply put governments and some corporations fail because they place greater emphasis on the ability of the humans instead of relying on appropriate structures.

His "structures that supersede the discretion of those elected to serve" are ones which are guidelines to be followed so that people check in to work and KNOW what they are supposed to do. A visit to any public services office will still expose idle workers who openly gab about whether it's going to be roti or jerk for lunch. It explains too the obesity that stalks the land and Minister Winston 'Gypsy' Peters Minister among others had better take heed and watch his health.

In talking about structures I think too of Joanne Blackman, Programme coordinator of the Ministry of Works Highway Division, whose Beautification Unit is designing a structure for the entire country. I understand. This means appropriate plants for appropriate landscaping and correct distancing from road in a planned and organized manner.

In other countries urban/rural beautification is professional business and does not depend on the whims of CEPEP workers sticking the fast-growing hybrid frangipani here and there. Clumps of this boring funereal white-flowering shrubby tree stick out all over the country as this botanical newcomer threatens to become invasive.

But to return quickly to what the Peoples' Partnership has demonstrated over the past five weeks in office. Certainly the new Government scored with its rapid response to the ensuing floods and clean-up campaign nationwide. The Prime Minister is to be commended. BUT SHE/THEY HAVE THEIR HANDS FULL AND ARE NOW STUMBLING IN THE DARK. IT SEEMS THAT IT IS DIFFICULT TO GET ANYTHING MORE DONE!

Crime which was (and still is) top priority saw the immediate installation of Brigadier John Sandy and a charmed Parliamentary opening that united both sides of the floor in excising the Canadian Neal Parker from the post of Police Commissioner.

As the days unfold however there are notable areas of failure that are beginning to surface. If Prime Minister Kamla Persad-Bissessar is to survive successfully in a leadership still to be tested, her scores are being based on the following tests:

•CRIME – Trinidad and Tobago continues to be under siege with unabated terror

•GUANAPO CHURCH – abandonment of responsibility to stop removal of materials; inability to find Rev. Juliana Pena despite Interpol; justice and answers to people of T&T; AG Anand Ramlogan, when he puts the onus of responsibility on the Integrity Commission, looks like Pontius Pilate

•CASHEW GARDENS SQUATTERS – closure needed

•EXTRADITION - Failure to bring to a close extradition proceedings against Steve Ferguson and Ish Galbraransingh

•MONEY - The handing out of large sums of money for medical attention. This begs the question on two counts: a) Why is the United States the choice? Surely Cuba or India could provide the medical assistance for a much more reasonable fee than TT$0.6 million in the United States for ONE needy child's attention! b) Isn't this a perception of buying support or fulfilling a promise at any cost? Will the Children's Fund stretch at this rate?

UDeCOTT – action, lots of this needed

These are just a few of the red flags that members of the electorate are watching and evaluating. And then there is Jack Warner, the Honourable Minister of Works and Transport, Chairman of the United National Congress and, generally speaking, a much beloved son of the soil. As Queen Maker he must be always on guard.

If no one in the People's Partnership has picked up on his promise to open the Priority Bus Route by June 16th but, since he was away at FIFA World Cup Opening in South Africa it was postponed to sometime in July, you'd better believe that Mr. Rowley as Leader of the Opposition already has. (It was opened today actually for the experimental 3-month trial run within specified hours.)

Now that the euphoria of change through accommodating a partnership and the charm of our own beloved lady Prime Minister continues to beguile, we must ALL wake up to the reality that nation-building is a together affair. We may have surfed some easy waves as we started out on this brand new five-year expedition, but the weather portends rough sailing.

On the boat alongside, it won't take much for the SS PNM to ride the rough waters over the SS Partnership. And perhaps the first storm, Local Government Elections, is going to be the decisive test! We should know that it was never going to be easy sailing, but in the end we remain one family.

MAY GOD BLESS OUR NATION!

POSTSCRIPT

An imaginary conversation with my husband about the state of Trinidad and Tobago

Monday morning.

Should I buy all three newspapers today?

You ask me that every morning and my answer is always yes.

I know but you fret over the reporting and the lack of taste. I think that I could reduce the amount of angst in your day.

Thanks but I don't want to miss out on anything.

How could you? No one is being trained on any of the newspapers. They are the same reporters on the job every day. And all of them it seems are running for political office. Only the commentaries make good reading even if everyone is writing on issues that often seem warmed-over noodles.

I don't think that could be avoided. The verities never change. Have you forgotten the moral storm that erupted when Herbert Volney announced his resignation from the Bench and his entry into politics? Even Ken Gordon was outraged.

Oh, Ken is the moral right! I liked Volney when I read some of his criticisms in China, and I was surprised that he was so outspoken. I agree with Ken however that his leap into politics lacked candour and discretion. It encouraged people's suspicions about the independence of judges. It could come back to haunt the People's Partnership.

Do you think a vigorous press helps us to see through men's actions? Do you get the feeling the news desks are being run by a bunch of sissies?

Sissies?

I am talking metaphorically. I am not talking gender. They seem to be people with little vision and no guts. I mean there is no planning, no crusade, and no tough investigative work. Was the fire that killed a family in their home at San Juan politically inspired? Was the home really fire-bombed as the press claimed at first? What is the truth about the alleged $5 million hit on Kamla Persaid-Bissessar? What is the truth about Jack Warner and the Soca Warriors? What is the truth about Suruj Rambachan and the Scott Drug Report? Will we go through another general election with the Opposition bringing back these zombies to confuse the electorate?

You are hoping that by the year 2015 all the unanswered questions about Udecott and the church at Guanapo Heights would be investigated and dealt with. Those who do the crime, as Kamla says, must do the time.

I want a more enlightened electorate. I want to see people who have done wrong meet the punishment they deserve. But the Government of the People's Partnership needs a strong, well-trained press to help it just as it needs a strong, hard-working Opposition and a strong, incorruptible police service. The People's Partnership and the Tobago Organisation of the People won't be able to bring about changes alone. Every man and woman alive today must be vigilant and must help in our development even if they did not vote. There's too much babble. No one is listening.

What you are saying is Trinidadians and Tobagonians must not allow the present government to slide back into the dictatorship that Mr. Manning made of the government of the People's National Movement. It must be honourable and not lose touch with the people.

That's right. Already there is a distracting - almost deliberate it seems - pitting of the tribes against each other. And we are doing this to ourselves! So much for unity and ONE T&T! We must not let Ms. Persad-Bissessar and her ministers forget that the government belongs to the people and must act with the interests of the people in mind. All the people - not just those who voted for it. Its actions must be transparent.

Isn't that concept always an ideal? Where in the world are there governments that place the interests of the people above their own survival and above the profit of groups that support them? Even in the great United States of America there are vested interests that control the government and manipulate even the President to act in their favour.

You are thinking of Halliburton and the National Rifle Association? Do you think Dick Cheney and Charleston Heston were able to do this? Do you think the pharmaceutical companies do this and it is the reason why governments seem powerless in controlling the costs of medical care today? Why vaccines and surgical work cost so much and are prohibitive to the people in small states like ours?

I am certainly concerned about the latter but the truth is I really don't care how much Dick Cheney influenced Mr. Bush into going to war with Saddam Hussein to gain control of Iraqi oil. There are issues that are too large for a single individual to deal with and that is the purpose of the United Nations and governments around the world. Wasn't that the feeling you got when you read Gore Vidal's *Dreaming War*? Wasn't it one of frustration? But on a national and regional basis I believe Trinidadians and Tobagonians must be aware, when they vote a party or an individual into government office, that the political party or candidate of their choice would serve the whole community and not just a section of it. Even in American-controlled Iraq we witnessed the irreconcilable violence between Shiites and Sunnis when the Americans kept favouring the former.

Tuesday afternoon.

Shah Hosein called. I was surprised. What was he doing in Trinidad I wondered? His parents had long since died and his siblings, all but Eman, had emigrated.

Well, why is he in Trinidad?

I have come for some tests, he told me. My heart.

His heart? I am sorry.

We had grown up across the Eastern Main Road in Tunapuna. I remembered that at one time our parents had felt we would marry. You know how parents like to match-make from cradle!

What happened?

Well, Shah went to the University of the West Indies in Jamaica and I went to Marygrove College in Detroit. Shah graduated and married a Jamaican whom his mother said looked like me.

And you?

That part you know.

And now Shah is back. His heart is troubling him, he said. Do we have better doctors in Trinidad? And has the People's National Movement put in place a better and more efficient medical service than they have in Jamaica?

Mr. Hubert Volney could answer that better than I can! Or, your niece, the new Minister of Health.

You still don't think that the Minister was given preferential treatment, do you?

I hate to think that some poor bloke who had been waiting for life-saving surgery succumbed because Mr. Volney jumped the queue, but I see your point that he is a Government Minister. I just want to believe that the system is equitable and doesn't play favourites.

It's equitable enough to allow Shah to piggy-back our health care.

Why are you picking on Shah?

I am not. I just want him to tell me that medicines and medical care are cheaper in Trinidad than in Jamaica. It hasn't been so for me. Debbie Goden paid twice what I used to pay in China for a pack of aspirins. Nearly forty dollars. And my high blood pressure tablets cost four times what I paid in Guangzhou. But why should he come to Trinidad for tests for his heart when he has spent two thirds of his life in Jamaica? Didn't he pay taxes there?

Why are you back in Trinidad after spending twelve years in China?

No, no. Don't do this. You are comparing lychees with ackees. I haven't come back home because the Ministry of Health, or the government, offers me a better health scheme. I am here because you figured that it was time to come back to Trinidad. I am sure that if it hadn't been for the snap election we would not have stayed a day longer than it was necessary to get our new ID cards. That took a lifetime! And in the end it was whom I knew. The little fuss I made with Leslie Fitzpatrick at the EBC office might have helped.

Little fuss? You hollered at the man! You mean coming back was so bad? You don't like what you see? You don't like Mr. Manning's tall buildings? You don't like Movie Towne? You don't like NAPA, the National Academy for the Performing Arts? You must admit that the city looks different.

Are you out of your mind! Port of Spain looks tackier than I left it. The entire Eastern Corridor is a pig pen, not just the Red House with its scaffolding that people say has been there for years. I haven't been to many places since we are back, but it is just as if there was no city planning anywhere and nothing is finished. It takes a really PNM bigot to say that the Party got the jewel in the crown when it retained hold of the Port of Spain Corporation and the mayoralty in the July Local Government election. You have seen the barbed wire and the burglar-proofing. It's a garrison city. Even your sister's and brother's homes in Tunapuna are tightly shut every day. The wind never shakes the curtains as we knew it did in Guangzhou.

So nothing has pleased you? Not even my friends? What a grump you've become! What about the new airport?

The new 1.2 billion dollars Piarco International Airport? God, if Jack Warner and the People's Partnership are thinking putting more teeth in anti-corruption laws, Ish Galbaransingh and Steve Ferguson would have a hard future ahead of them, judging from those bloggers you read to me. The airport is a bloody shame! I can't explain to you the shock I felt when we landed there in March. Every new airport we have seen in China is a hundred times more attractive. I knew instinctively that coming back to Trinidad was a mistake.

You are not going to make friends with that attitude.

Make friends? What are you talking about? I didn't go to Chaguaramas looking for any Farmers' Market and finding just a stall and arguing with everyone in sight that we could do better.

I scandalised Phyllis Davidson. She kept telling me to hush. And the other Trinidadians we met were just as embarrassed by my comments. They must have thought I had escaped from a mental home. But you have to blame Margaret Hunte. She had raved about the fruit and produce you could get there that she said were grown by Cubans. I went expecting a bazaar atmosphere with a coffee shop and fried bakes. What I met was a single stall.

Vasant Maharaj, the Minister of Agriculture, has his job cut out for him.

He seems to be able to handle it though. I like what I have seen of him so far.

He will have to. You could get more in the supermarkets than twelve years ago – coconut water and accra for example – but the prices for all of these foods are prohibitive. How much did you say you had to pay for a single hot pepper? Fifty-nine cents?

I didn't buy it. I am not that crazy!

The Central Bank has warned against inflation and the cause, as you know, is rising food prices. Just look at what I was asked to pay for a bottle of honey. One hundred and sixty dollars! In Beijing I used to pay forty-three yuan, which is about forty TT dollars. It's a worldwide worry but you keep comparing the cost of things in Trinidad with the prices you paid in Guangzhou and Beijing. That's why you hate to go shopping with Debbie and Victor. You think they don't look at prices and this attitude you say just sends up prices. Well, they don't have to. They don't have children, not even a pet.

I know but they have hearts of gold. They have overcome their generation's dependence and bitterness.

Wednesday night.

Do you think the world has changed and people are not so self-sufficient today?

You mean they expect the government to take care of every problem, from birth to the grave?

Well, yes. And the rest who are doing fine don't see that they are part of the problem when they do nothing to bring about change They hide behind closed doors and windows and they are not as charitable as in the past. It's every man for himself. Those who can't get by on CEPEP or some other ten-day programme seem prepared to kill or maim you for "a food."

For a food?

I know. Even the language today sounds barbaric. But a food is what they beg for at traffic lights when they are not offering to clean your windscreen or expecting you to buy water, soft drinks or nuts.

Do you think they ever approached Mr. Manning to give them a food?

With his outriders present?

You have forgotten. The PNM is the party that loves you.

Sorry. I thought that was only an election slogan.

You know I believe there is less of a family life than there was in our youth but this is a phenomenon that is mostly among Afro-Trinidadian families. Look at the successes of Indo-Trinidadians in education, from primary school to university. Prime Minister Kamla Persad-Bissessar has pointed to her own achievements in education. It's a fact that Indian children as doing better in schools than African children. And don't give me the excuses that Professor Selwyn Cudjoe makes about slavery.

You think what he says are excuses and not a serious warning about the disenchantment of black youth?

I do. I know that the Jews haven't given up speaking about the Holocaust and the Americans about 9/11 but I find the constant reminders of the past tiresome.

And yet, you know it is said that if you forget the past you will relive it?

I really do not think that people learn anything from history. You said you knew him as a boy?

Who? Cudjoe? Yes. My memory is that he grew up in the Tacarigua Orphanage during the years I went to the Tacarigua E.C. School. Maybe he lived there with his parents. I didn't know anything about his family. He seems proud of his past and has written a lot about Tacarigua.

And today he is a professor at Wellesley College! How was it that he survived his past? It doesn't seem that he was born with a gold spoon in his mouth. And if he has overcome a disadvantaged past, why haven't other Afro-Trinidadians who had possibly as tough a time as he had?

You don't think that slavery and colonialism that followed it have made an impact on Afro-Trinidadians and the two things are responsible for the feeling of discrimination and inferiority in our society?

Give me a break! We are celebrating Emancipation Day and making long speeches about our independence and achievements. Makandal Daaga is our Cultural Ambassador to governments in the Caricom region.

I am glad that he has a place in our government but frankly I don't understand what role Kamla expects him to play. It's not the same as when Dr. Williams made Kamaluddin Mohammed Minister of the Caribbean Free Trade Area. Or, is it?

No, I don't think so. I think Williams's intention was to cut Kamal's wings.

But it didn't work. Kamal proved his resilience.

You went to college with Daaga too, didn't you? And you were present when on February 26 1970 he stormed the Roman Catholic Cathedral with other members of the National Joint Action Committee. Archbishop Pantin you said didn't view their actions as a desecration of the church.

That's right. I spoke with him on that day.

And what about Professor Roy Preiswerk? Didn't he say that he had observed a new confidence among the people?

That's what he told me.

So the record shows that a lot of Afro-Trinidadians have overcome their squalid history.

Overcome?

Listen to me. More than a hundred and fifty years have passed since slaves brought to the West Indies from Africa have been freed. I know that freedom hasn't been the same for everyone and some are luckier in their choices than others. But too many Afro-Trinidadians still behave as if emancipation is a myth and they must still depend on handouts from the government.

Handouts? You think that the party of Dr. Eric Williams has encouraged this mentality and that it was evident during the PNM campaign?

I am sure it has. And the party has encouraged some other ugly features in our society. We saw two examples of this ugliness or meanness in the election campaign. The first was the decision to shut the park in St. Joseph where the People's Partnership was to hold one of their meetings and the second was to deny the People's Partnership permission to launch their Party's manifesto at the Library. I know you will say, it's politics, but it was mean and the meanness at the top of government usually filters down to the lowliest public servant until the entire society is mean and to cure it all we need to have a revolution as happened in France two centuries ago.

Is that what nearly happened in Trinidad and Tobago in 1990?

No, I don't think so. 1990 was a criminal activity by a group of power-hungry men. And I believe that the way we eventually dealt with that situation, the weakness and the stupidity of the law and the courts, is what has encouraged the crimes we are experiencing today.

Thursday morning.

I have been thinking of what we said last night about the circumstances that followed the failed coup of 27 July 1990. It's not just the law and the courts. The people must also take blame.

You mean all of us including your sisters and my friends who say we must live around the crime.

That's correct. Very few people are prepared to stand up and condemn the crimes taking place. They say that the police are inefficient and are incapable of solving murders and robberies that take place in broad daylight but they don't seem to realize that the majority of crimes have always been solved by eyewitnesses' reports and not by lawmen willing to lay down their lives or by forensic science the kind of which we see on CSI Miami. We must stand up and declare our support for law and order. We must risk our skin. We must become the eyes and the ears of our police service.

But it is difficult to stand up for men in government office who are weak and inarticulate and who give no sign that they are able to make a difference. The last Minister of National Security was as much a clown as the Minister of Sport was when he paid $2 million to put up a flag at the National Stadium. And what about the Commissioner of Police? Are people calling him Failbert?

James Philbert? I don't think that's fair. He's not responsible for the last government's failure to find a suitable replacement after spending $8 million on applicants from all over the world. And the twelve members of the party in the new House of Representatives, led by Dr. Keith Rowley, didn't even have the courage to vote for the Canadian Dwayne Gibbs. I too deplore the need to find an outsider to head our police service but this search for a Commissioner of Police was the work of Mr. Manning and his government. Now the remnant in Parliament is acting as if the problems of crime have nothing to do with them.

It could be a bonus however. Don't you think so?

What is? Getting a foreigner with foreign experience? That's what Jack Warner has said. But you know in all these things it is how you look at the specific example. Take Warner's own problem with the Opposition and the Integrity Commission over the business of being a Minister of Government and a Vice-President of FIFA. The Commission and Dr. Rowley say it was an ethical problem and that Warner could not serve two masters. The Attorney General viewed it as a legal matter and produced legal opinion, including that of former President, Sir Ellis Clarke, to say that there's no legal problem. I thought from the beginning that it was always a political problem if there was a problem. How the electorate, or rather the people of Trinidad and Tobago, would view Jack Warner's commitment to his Ministry of Works. And that to me is how Prime Minister Kamla Persad-Bissessar viewed it. Can he do both jobs successfully? This is where a maverick minister could become the Prime Minister's Achilles heel.

So it's always politics? Where is the morality in public affairs that Dr. Williams made the cornerstone of his party?

For that matter where is the slogan of Discipline, Production and Tolerance? And what about his promise that there would be no Mother Africa and no Mother India? And, finally, what about his pledge to the children of the nation that their future is in their schoolbags? If you look around you would wonder if he said all these things but that's the job of politicians, to get the populace thinking that there is always more hope than despair in their lives.

Friday morning.

We are going this morning to the National Insurance Board. It's the only government office that has shown us a spirit of care and concern. Many of the public servants at the Ministry of Legal Affairs and the Elections and Boundaries Commission didn't seem to care about serving the public. What is the name of the young woman who looked after our NIS claims?

Sharon Davis. And the others who called to tell us the status of our claims were as polite and helpful.

I remember. Ms. Williams and Ms. Roy.

This is what the Ministry of the People has to do. It has to remake the minds and hearts of public servants. These three young women show that public servants could perform in the best tradition of what we once called the Civil Service.

Do you remember the tale of Dame Partington in the Reverend Sydney Smith's story who was seen with mop and broom vigorously pushing away the Atlantic Ocean?

I haven't read the story. Tell me about it.

The Atlantic Ocean beat Mrs. Partington.

I am not surprised. What is your point?

Politics is like the Atlantic Ocean and we are like Mrs. Partington.

Will politics always beat us?

I think that like Mrs. Partington we should always put up a good fight.

And you think that with Kamla we can do this?

I am going to say, yes.

Even though you say it is with more hope than conviction?

I guess it is too early in the morning for me to be passionate about anything except breakfast. I don't know how those guys do it on early morning shows. Are they on prescribed drugs? I once tried valium when I did an editorial for Radio Trinidad. But I gave up both after a few weeks.

So, it's Kamla all the way with you.

Yes. Right now I don't feel I am wrong. And I don't want to look a gift horse in the mouth.

Me too. I guess she will stumble from time to time, or, seem to do so. But she has a lot of people, not just David Chin and Monica Gopaul, watching her and making sure she doesn't do so too often and that every time she falls she gets up and shakes her fist at the Opposition. We are none of us infallible, not even God who made man in his own likeness.

A fallible God? That doesn't sound like you and I am sure that the good Sisters of Cluny and Father Reginald Hezekiah will be furious with this idea and with me. There is a group of priests who always thought I was a heathen, or worse, a communist, even when I was editor of the *Catholic News*. This Father Hezekiah might even agree to hanging in my case if the government ever made apostasy a capital offence. I don't think the nuns would go that far.

I am lost. Nothing of religion I say today sounds like the good little Convent girl you wooed and won. You are remaking me in your image. I should appeal to Sr. Marie-Thérèse for help.

The deed's done. We have been married for 47 years, darling. See how well you wear the mask!

FEEDBACK

From: Satnarine Balkaransingh

Dear Friends, The pain being experienced by the loss of yet another child on the altar of barbarism and insensitivity is being felt by all of our far flung patriots and friends. Here is a letter from Rhona Baptiste from China. Her comments and questions are those on the lips of all of us. How can we honestly tell Rhona that something is being done to bring this society back to a state of normalcy? The disgrace, disrespect, arrogance, and violence - psychic and physical are everyday occurrences at every level of the society, especially at the leadership level. There is the need to exorcise the 'evil' that stalks the land/country starting with ourselves first, for after all we are inextricably interconnected, by this same energy field, to which we apply different names.

Sat

From: Cyber Mate

Young girls, some as early as 14, leave home to go with men, both young and older ones, to escape the brutality and poverty of home life and the boredom and lack of attention at school, not anticipating where this leads.Their parents do not want to find them.

We need small half way houses for teens. The churches can focus on this

On another note; many older folks are brutalized at home. We need to go back to a modern version of the 'poor houses' in every regional corporation. 'Poor' meaning - where they do not have to pay - for 2 reasons. (The country is riddled with the mentally disturbed.)

1. to escape brutality

2. to relieve the 'good' daughters and some sons of the pressure of seeing after geriatrics.They have to make a life of their own.

We need small, state-of-th-art free homes for

1. the demented from every walk of life.

There are more middle class demented people than we admit. I'm not talking about addicts.

How does this fit into violence?

It does. Many of these people are victims of violence, physical and psychological, that few families ACKNOWLEDGE. ACKNOWLEDGEMENT, the key to change.

Cheers

CM

From: Stephen Cadiz

Rhona, Your note on parenting and education says it all. I am reading a book entitled "The Bottom Billion" by Paul Collier which is about failed states and what can be done to correct the situation. T&T, not yet a failed state but on the way, may very well end up as one of them if we do not make an about turn.

Proper parenting is definitely one of the first things we must do.

Just a quick note, YESTT had a wonderful start to its education program on Referendum and Recall and we are now adding Proportional Representation to the list. We had a visiting Professor Mads Qvortrup, University College of London, lead the lecture series and based on the reaction by the general public we are on the right road, even though the road is a very long one.

We will be having another forum, possible in September, were we will have both local and international presenters discussing the 'nuts and bolts' of the various processes.

We hope to bring serious and permanent change to the politics of T&T where all voices will be heard so when parenting is becoming an issue we can deal with it without having to wait for an election and hope we have a change in the Administration.

POWER TO THE PEOPLE!

Stephen

From: Danielle Gladney

Dear Rhona, Had to congratulate you on your excellent article on In your-face vulgarity. I was born in Trinidad but have lived abroad most of my life. I loved going to Trinidad for carnival and taking visitors all through my years in Europe. I was always playing mas in Poison, then Skandal-Us.

I too am appalled by the vulgarity that has been exposed during the carnival time by men and women of the nation where foreigners and children are the audience among others. Nothing really surprises me anymore in Trinidad because I was there for a couple of years to see about my mom and my childhood house before leaving again for shores beyond.

I am really ashamed about the attitudes not only for carnival but for those during everyday life in Trinidad. I have never been exposed to so much disrespect and unconcern from the people who belong to the country where I was born as I was during the period I had to be there recently. People have lost the morals and dignity, the respect for themselves and others. There is no compassion.

Sincerely,

Danielle Gladney

From: Peggy Mohan

Rhona:(a propos 'jahaji bundle'): The word jahaji is Bhojpuri (not Hindi), and means (especially in places like Trinidad) someone who has travelled by ship to the diaspora lands: an original migrant. The Bhojpuri word for the ship itself is jahaaj. Bhojpuri is the language spoken directly east of the Hindi region. In Hindi the word for ship is jahaaz. Since the story of the migration to the diaspora lands isn't part of Hindi folklore, a jahaazi would simply mean a sailor.

From: Peggy Mohan

Hi, Rhona, The Bhojpuri word Bhowji actually means elder sister-in-law. It has kind of become extended in meaning, as young people no longer know what it means. (If you have Hindi-speaking friends, they would recognize the word as 'Bhabhi-ji').

I guess Bhowji would make roti :) But being traditional, she would call the stuffed rotis by their old Trini name: dalpuri. (People from India, unless from Bihar or Bengal, would call these 'stuffed parathas', or 'dal-parathas', as roti in India means any flatbread without oil made on a griddle or a tandoor, and any meat or vegetables served with them don't count as 'roti'. And they would make them from wholewheat flour).

A Bhojpuri word that does mean 'Tantie' is Mausi, (pronounced 'mousy'), and it means mother's sister. (The words for father's sister or father's sister-in-law also exist, but aren't as well known).

Peggy

From: Madeline Coopsammy

Dear Rhona: As usual you hit on the problem. Enjoyed your thoughts, tho' some of them are rather sad to contemplate.

I was teaching at an inner-city school in Winnipeg where there were lots of refugee and immigrant children from South East Asia. Most of them were well behaved except for a boy or two now and then. One of my colleagues, a born and bred white Canadian used to say that when she retired she would open a school for "little docile well behaved Asian girls" One thing I did notice, though as the Filipino population got more comfortable in the Canadian milieu, these brown-skinned boys would dye their jet-black hair in shades of red and brown or almost blonde.

But never the girls.

What did that say about equality between the sexes? We're talking about ten and eleven year olds.

I was at a West Indian picnic one day and the children were running races. This woman was cheering on her son, then turned to us and said, "Why we like our boy children more than the girls?" I could have hit her, but said nothing as I didn't know her.

Another thought. Did those smart people in China ever think about the consequences of the one child policy? Numerous people in North America have gone to China to adopt little babies and they are all girls. I know two at least.

I also read that the men in their twenties (or thirties?) can't find any women to marry. Ha!

Cheers.

Madeline

From: Ron Ramcharan

Rhona, This afternoon Pat came home from her Rotary gathering just after 2 o' clock. When she parked the car on the road she saw 2 fellas walking down and then back up the road. They just walked by. She came in, closed and wrapped the chain around the gate as usual, so the dogs won't push it open and come inside.

She asked Dolores, the maid, to show her what the pump repair man had done and they went to the back to see. She came in the kitchen and Dolores went upstairs. A few minutes after, she was standing on a chair, packing some of the things she had bought when she saw one of the fellas in the kitchen with his arm raised with a cutlass. She immediately started a number of alto screams, her lungs are in very good condition. The neighbour said he thought that someone was being beaten down the road.

The man threatened her telling her to shut up but he didn't know her well. The dogs were having their siesta at the back and the noise invited the tall one, roth/alsatian, to investigate. The other fella had just walked past the kitchen door and went towards the back. He met the other 2 dogs, very big pure roth and roth/pompek. The 2 persons vanished, seemingly into thin air. The Police were there in about 5 minutes.

It may be that they were not from the area and did not know we had dogs. After they saw her reach inside and they did not see any activity they jumped the gate. It would have been interesting to see what would have happened if the dogs were in front or on the porch.

Pat is OK with a sore throat.

Ron

From: Madeline Coopsammy

Dear Rhona, Just some reflections on the state of the nation of T&T.

When the young people see that there is so much wealth in the island and in the world via the satellite TV and they are still scrunting because our education system still only caters to the middle and upper classes and they see no way out except through drugs and crime, what can we expect?

A government that builds a luxury P.M residence with labour from China (let's not go there right now) gives make-work projects (CEPEP, etc.) to the unemployed instead of investing in training them for future jobs in the building and other industries, closes down the sugar industry when other countries are finding ways to utilize the product, (and what about our rum?) will not give the retrenched Caroni workers the lands they have been promised, continues to use the outmoded 11-plus exam now called SEA, which only children of wealthy and middle class parents can pass, as they use expensive tutoring after school and weekends, while the poor fail the exam and enter the second-class schools, shady dealings by Calder Hart and associates, a Justice system which does not seem to be the fair and square one we always knew, in which the Judges and lawyers were incorruptible. There are lots more, but I too, feel the despair you feel for our beloved island. I go there every winter, not by choice, but for family and in-law connections, and wonder what I'm doing there, except avoiding a harsh Prairie winter. (And then trying to keep cool)

Cheers.

Madeline

From: Diana Mahabir-Wyatt

Rhona, I just got back from a Commonwealth Human Rights Conference in London attended by Human Rights Defenders from all over the Commonwealth, and having listened to their stories of trials and tribulations which were appalling, I could only thank God that I live in T&T where we can say anything we want to ...and often do, criticizing the Government.. .never mind they ignore us...we are not arrested or tortured for what we say. We have put our Chief Justice on trial and no one died as a result...we have put the head of the opposition on trial and he's still there talking all kinds of what anywhere else would be regarded as traitorous nonsense....our Law Association comes out in public against the Attorney General and no one is arrested. The Commissioner of Police apologizes to the public for the transgressions of his Police Force. And changes do happen...mostly long after we protest. There are tire burnings and marches and placarding fests. We do it in song and in writing, and the radio talk shows would be closed down any where else for the seditious things callers-in say, and they would be found and arrested for the things they fearlessly and often stupidly come out with... even the Prime Minister just tries to go in person to protest, but no one ends up anonymously in jail. Too many macocious people to know what is happening and criticize. But then we go home alive to protest another day.

Have you forgotten what we really live like?

We are fallible, wrong-headed and often, simply stupid, but we have more exercise of human rights than most of the Commonwealth Countries that I listened to with tears in my eyes.

We need to improve and ensure that we do not end up like most of them, but for God's sake, Rhona, don't make us sound like we are what we are not. If you want to fight, come home and fight....don' t challenge from a distance on the basis of what we all know are the sensational press reports that focus on the very real negatives and forget the even more very real positives which don't sell papers.

Even the poorest people help others that they regard as even poorer than they are. We have no civil war. We don't incarcerate suspected terrorists with no proof like the USA. We try to protect even the rights of illegal immigrants, Our terrorists are still around and building Mosques whereas anywhere else they would be behind bars anonymously facing "rendition" in places we've never heard of. We have rogue cops that do things they shouldn't do and everyone gets to know about it and comment.

Our...mainly female...judges are not questioned except in the courts, by lawyers who take things to the Supreme Court. We all bitterly criticize the government for their building programs while poor people can't get a lot of the other drugs they need that are not on the list, but we have a free drug program for everybody that is better than that in the USA...we have free tertiary education. and.. such as it is ... free health care and free school lunches for children that need them. Come on...we are very imperfect. and small and stupid, but we are not vicious or cruel.

Diana

From: Diana Mahabir-Wyatt
Dear Rhona, I've always enjoyed your writing ......it is lively and readable and usually balanced, informative and fun. In fact I really started to read JahajeeDesi because of your wonderful articles on China.Your reply to me was, as was to be expected, also lively and fun to read. You may not agree with me, but you express your dis-agreement so well that I enjoyed reading it.

I wonder if I may be allowed to make two small corrections. I never said that Trinidad was a paradise (It isn't, just that I am glad I live here) .or referred to 'nasties' in the press.(as I worked peripherally in the press for about 15 years I would never have referred to my erstwhile colleagues using that term) that was perhaps an unnecessary embellishment on your part. As you know, I have been, for 35 years, the head of the Coalition Against Domestic Violence, and deal with the very dark underside of Trinidad every day. If anyone knows T&T is not a paradise, I do. My point was a comparative one where violence and corruption around the Commonwealth is growing. We are not exempt, but we are not nearly as bad as many of the other members of the Commonwealth. Portraying me as just a conservative buisness person is surprisingly one sided coming from you. I somehow expected something different, but the last thing I want to or will get into is a long debate with you on the issue. Your perception is your perception and I will let it rest there. Yes, I am in business...I have had to support a family for all these years. I don't get paid for my work with victims of domestic violence or for human rights advocacy, but like you, we have to eat!

Second correction. I know Karen and am very fond of her. We have worked together on many many projects involving womens' rights. And she is justifiably apprehensive, but no one has been arrested for sedition in T&T other than Abu Bakr since Colonial times. And even that case has never been heard and I don't think these articles or anyone's comments in these pages compare to Abu Bakr's acts in the sedition stakes. I agree with her that we have to be constantly vigilant though lest we end up like the other Commonwealth countries I referred to. I was one of the first people faced with the riot police in St James during the Drummin at the Summit incident a few months ago and it was truly frightening. Fortunately wiser heads prevailed, and they were called off. No one has been arrested and charged for these things for a very long time...half a century... and that is because women like Karen and me and hundreds of others fight and protest to keep it from happening. We don't do it because we are black or white, but because we are women... black, white, Chinese, Indian and various mixtures thereof, because we believe in a common cause which is trying to keep T&T from sliding further into the kinds of abuses we see happening elsewhere.

Perhaps what we both hope is that you will work with us in our efforts. Kindest regards.

Diana

From: Marlene Cuthbert

Rhona, Yes, RESPECT! That's the key word used by First Nations people in Canada. I had the opportunity while in Windsor to learn from a marvellous teacher who was Potowatami in the majority Ojibwe Native Indian reserve....

I can't imagine how you keep so closely in touch with T&T from China - great analysis!

Cheers,

Marlene

From: Diana Mahabir-Wyatt

That is the brilliant commentary that causes me to still read this Blog. So many other comments are too narrowly focused and partisan. Can we please have more of these?

Rhona has always been an objective and intelligent observer (never mind that I disagreed with her attack on me, which I answered and let go). China has become a daily presence in all the Caribbean countries in which I work. I wish she could come back for a month or two and see the daily presence of Chinese workers in our countries and our streets. This has been with the full agreement with all of our Caribbean Governments. Work permits are pre-agreed.

Government to Government contracts have brought in these industrious, efficient workers to take over where our own people would not agree to simple things like safety regs and building codes, according to Construction Project Managers that I have talked to. Where locally employed workers simply refused to attend safety induction training sessions on building sites, saying that "they didn't need them". The Chinese workers not only attended, but also complied. A disgruntled Trini construcction worker said to me, grudgingly "They work better than we do and faster, and don't complain." There is a real culture difference here. And this is true. I can't object to any of that. People are now trying to get Chinese companies to do their domestic walls and foundation work because our own people. Government workers included simply are inefficient. And they get good results. On time and within budget.

And there is a real socio-political change taking place. The Chinese government-to government agreements mean not only increased local infrastructure, but it has implications for foreign affairs. Who owes who and for what? And what does that mean for our future?

How many of our people can speak Mandarin or Cantonese? Some of us do. One of my friends, a Trini from a Chinese heritage family was born in T&T. She spesks fluent Cantonese, and Mandarin, which she learned at home as a child, and when we go into a Chinese restaurant she orders and we get the best service and food imaginable. Most of our really good Chinese restaurants are owned and run by Chinese people who don't speak English well, so they have to hire a few locals to take orders and deal with customer complaints. While their ethnic Chinese staff learn English. She was born here when her parents came from China after unimaginable abuses, with a justified resentment, which her family has passed down from generation to generation, and still feel. All her many brothers and sisters speak the languages and will be in a good position when the socio-political power shifts... which it will... given the debts the Caribbean Governments now owe to the Chinese Government.

Like typical Caribbean people, we go for the short term benefits, and we are getting them. Chinese Companies now build much of the new infrastructure of most of our islands from Bahamas to Guyana most of which I work in (and don't forget that we collectively still have 18 or 20 votes in the UN) and no one, as far as I have seen has done an analysis of what this means for our collective future. Selwyn Ryan where are you now that we need you? Question: Are there implications for a new kind of colonialism?

Rhona is right. We got rid (sort of) of the British colonialism. Are we about to replace this with a Chinese colonialism? They seem to be doing it much more cleverly than the Brits did.

I'd really like to have Rhona's observant brain doing an analysis on this. Few of us have had an opportunity to live and work in both countries as she has. Can she help us understand what is going on and ... more deeply... from a socio-political perspective... why?

Diana

From: Sheilah Solomon
You are both right and both among the most valuable resources that T&T has to face these very challenging times.

Rhona, last week I attended the UTT launching of project/book coordinated by Lawrence Scott which recorded the lives of Golconda Estate community, at which the various parties made their personal presentations, some even in music and poetry. And I looked at the audience - literally every creed, race and class honouring and enjoying - and beginning to understand each others' histories. And in the close-to-the ground NGO communities where Diana labours to protect women and girls, volunteers are still keeping their fingers in the dyke.

Diana, there is no doubt that the dyke is about burst and it threatens to flood us all. So we need some clear-headed strategy for getting to the root of the problem and fixing it once and for all.

The root of the problem is that while democratic institutions exist - now under stress - in our country, genuine democracy has never really taken root here. Citizens, individually and collectively, have no influence let alone control over their representatives. That is the issue I have addressed in the 2 attached papers.

Having absorbed the concept, both of you could make a tremendous contribution to urging groups to participate in the

Carnival Band strategy. The idea is to create a (hopefully) non-violent event choreographed for international and local media - and therefore for local political consumption.

Bless you both!

Sheilah

From: Winston Dookeran

Dear Rhona, I enjoy reading your articles but yours on 'the danger of race' prompted me to send to you my piece on fixing the politics, which is attached. I hope you have time to read it. Continue writing - good for the soul of so many of us

Winston Dookeran

From: Raffique Shah

Dear Rhona, Didn't get a chance before to welcome you and Owen back home. Reading your "POS1" article, I couldn't help laughing. Seriously, did you expect positive changes in this negative land?

Maybe two, three years ago, when the "high rise" madness began, I wrote a column titled "Look down, not up". I warned the government that things like battlefield-scarred pavements, stink drains, dilapidated buildings, etc., were in dire need of our oil-dollars attention. The skies asked us for nothing!

Better we had fixed the ground on which we walk or drive (and how I'd love to cycle!) than to improve our skyline. I note you have been to the electoral office (I haven't mustered the courage yet), the Legal Affairs mess and the barricaded Clico building. Wait till you go to licensing and see haggard-looking clerks pull up some old, dusty files that look like scraps from the 17th Century! And hope that the PM's new campus opens before you need to go to the BIR!

Still, for all the mess, welcome home. Call me. I work from home--hardly ever venture into POS weekdays.

Regards,

Raffique

From: Stan Algoo, Canada
Hi, Rhona, Loved the poetic piece Port-of-Spin. Very nuanced fair, observant and sympathetic to the civil servant trying to do a good job. Your comment proposing country before self is the only premise for genuine change.

Dr. Allan McKenzie captures this sentiment more perfectly than any I have read. Perhaps Dookeran is trying to do what Dr. McKenzie understands.

Looking forward to your future pieces.

Thks

From: Margaret D. Wilde
Rhona, Thanks for the pictures! And I really enjoyed "Port of Spin." Your earlier posting on Esther LeGendre sort of set the stage for this ambivalent homecoming; I'm not surprised, and I suspect you aren't either. Owen must be saying "I told you so," but I'm glad you're giving Paradise One a fair try. I have always been a strong advocate of reversing the brain- and talent-drain, and with you two I'm really rooting for Trinidad to get back what it almost lost.

It was a wonderful visit here, and I hope you'll stop in again on your way back (whenever that is, and to wherever, for however long). Meanwhile, please keep me on your email list. I look forward to following your reflections, and also your thinking on which Paradise is "home" now.

Greetings to Owen, and a special hug to you from us both.

Margaret

From: kid5rivers
Sister Rhona! Don't be despondent ---thinking, too, is a lonely business. Your writing stimulates the thought processes. Please don't stop! And, please, publish your work online if already you aren't?

God bless! And regards to Owen.

Richard Wm. Thomas

From: Margaret Hunte

Rhona, Well I remember when Dr. Williams died and I, together with the rest of the nation, was so unable to imagine T&T governed by anyone else. Who we go put? Couldn't see the way forward. Sheer habit had us all stultified. I don't want to be in the 'PNM for ever' box.' But I am hoping to find some positive reasons to vote for UNC-A... Kamla's personal style, restraint, decorum and positive talk need to be backed up by a solid manifesto to begin with.

M.

From: Ron Patterson

Dear Mrs. Baptiste, I have just finished reading you piece on the upsurge of Kamla Persad-Bissessar, our new Prime Minister. Your words were inspiring, thought-provoking, and cautionary.

As a resident of Florida for the past 15 years, I have assisted in hosting fund raisers for Ms. Kamla and have met her on a few occasions. On one of these occasions, she jokingly cautioned me about the repercussions of my support, given the fact that my niece is married to John Jeremie (ex-Attorney General)! Be that as it may, many of us in the U.S. long for the days when we could walk the streets of our country in relative peace and safety, without the imminent threat of being mugged or worse. We worry about the disparity between the "haves" and "have-nots." We worry about the lack of improvement in the basic infrastructure of the country. All of these are areas of discontentment in the population who have been at the mercy of the powers that be.

I am happy and hopeful at the events of the past few days. Our people need to give Ms. Kamla a little breathing space to carefully plan her options - going off half-cocked will do no good - neither to her team nor to the people of T & T. You cannot undo in one year what has been taking place over past decade.

This email was not meant as an opportunity to vent. Rather, it is a chance to reflect where we have been and what the future could hold for us. I welcome your insightful and thought-provoking column. Please continue to give us your input - it is most informative.

    With best regards,
    Dr. Ron Peterson

    From: Peter Minshall
my dear Rhona
welcome home darling
and Owen
it has been hard on you
I felt a deep knife wound
when they threw you to the ground in the street and snatched
    your grandmother's bangles right from off your wrist
it hurt me personally
yes
right from off your wrist is how to say it proper
right from off your wrist woman
right in the broad daylight road
right from off your wrist
that is too criminal
nobody did warn you?
woman do not wear jewelry in town no more
oh Lord
bangles is such a precious private thing to thief
it come close to spiritual rape
bangles is deep deep female family thing
Indians really don't know how much they influence spread
    through in these parts just with bangles alone
all those long years ago
bangles
long before independence
all my white girl cousins on the sugar estates in Guyana did get
    gold bangles at birth
and mothers did always hand down bangles to their daughters
white mothers, black mothers, brown mothers, bangles was the
    female family heirloom

I did real hurt to read your grief
been reading you since all those school and classroom anecdotes
     and quiet reflections from China
your brief sojourn in Los Angeles
your reflections
always illuminating
your return
and now the loud brash ugly noise of Trinidad
Home

     From: Peter Minshall
     Re: NAPA (National Academy of Performng Arts)
when at the beginning we first saw it rising we thought what the
     fuck
igloos on a tropical island?
then it gradually began to become harmful
monstrous
frightening
lunatic and utterly absurd and unbelonging to us
an eighteenth century opera house interior hermetically sealed
     in a capsule
and we looked at it again in utter horror as it grew and gradually
     took shape
a nest of copulating slugs at the Southern end of the Savannah
and horror of horrors
they compared it to the Sydney Opera House
which was site specific
a promontory by the bay overlooking the sea
and the citizens of Sydney hosted an international competition
     for their opera house
and a Danish architect won it
because his opera house rose like a set of billowing sails from
     the sea
or a majestic cluster of seashells
but we have slugs
growing out of the southern end of the savannah

humping each other
we do not even have the name of an architect
we were never consulted
nor were our needs or our site consulted by the faraway chinese
because it was simply a deal
a chinese backside fuck of a little black island that did not know
    its art from its elbow
the gold bangles from the grandmother get snatch from the
    woman wrist just so in the street
easy easy so
aunty Beryl want to bawl
all the ancestors in grief
we ass dark
why it is this napa afraid to look the savannah in its face?
why it is that every other proper house around the savannah
    does look at the savannah with eye wide open?
napa have six big mouth and six big eye
the eye and them just like a fly
multifaceted in every direction dull and evil
the biggest of all turn from the savannah looking greedy on a
    little black angel in memorial square
why?
napa is beelzebub
a monster mas out of hell to torment us till we dead
a useless monstrosity born out of the tragic abyss that lies
    between nignorance and enwhitenment

From: Mahendra Mathur
Rhona writes: "As in the Indian epic poem, composed in
Sanskrit around 300 BCE when Rama of royal birth lost his
throne and was banished to the forest with wife Sita and half-
brother Laksmana, so too it was happening here in the twin-
island paradise where this epic is set. Would the Emperor now
be banished to the forest with his wife and half-brothers to
spend 14 years in exile?

"Would a demon king carry off the Emperor's wife and would he then have to enter into an allegiance with Sugriva, king of the monkeys, and Hanuman, the monkey general, who would help him rescue her? Would the Emperor think his party was worth such an alliance?

"The epic drama continues as first the Emperor must be resurrected enough to deal with his rambunctious First Mate, the dejected other eleven of his Members of Parliament, an irate band of raging Balisier devotees who now admit that he had taken them overboard the SS PNM with him. But worst of all, there were these new yellow people with rainbow colour hybrids, a dazzling threat to his boring monochromous red Imperial estate. How dare this recalcitrant assortment of a coalition (that he foretold could not last) how dare they lay hands upon his treasures!"

It is a fantastic article and deserves a place in the literature of Trinidad and Tobago. But I am afraid it also has one error and one ambiguity.

To compare the Emperor with Rama is not only erroneous but sacrilegious too. Rama went to the forest not because he lost his throne but in compliance to the word given by his father to his step-mother. He gave up his throne also for the same reason. The Emperor had to leave because of an 'ignominious defeat'.

It is not clear who are monkeys with whom the Emperor can enter into an 'allegiance' and who is the monkey king and who is monkey general. No uncommitted 'monkeys' are visible in Trinidad and Tobago at present.

Mahendra

From: Cyber Mate
Rhona, Interesting introduction. I like it.
There are people who get meagre pensions from the gov't like me and other teachers who worked their 30+ years and who no longer work in other jobs. So the so-called 'poor' will be doing better than 'middle class' senior citizens as time goes by.

I'm off for my CDAP. Colm Imbert said recently that he introduced it. Thanks to him because the other medicines are well over $300 every month. I will probably join the list of paupers shortly unless I use my imagination and get cracking soon.

C.M.

From: Bharath Boochoon
Hi...I have always enjoyed your articles. I will miss them, but do keep me informed as where you might be posting your articles. Just maybe you may want to stay a bit longer as I feel your job is not done.

Thanks
Bharath Boochoon

From: KB
Dear Rhona, "It was the same question that former Prime Minister Basdeo Panday asked when he visited that dream of ours on Frederick Street called Caribbean Information Systems & Services and wondered why anyone with sanity would put their everything into an electronic publishing and educational exhibit that pioneered touch screen computer technology."

Thank you for bringing this memory back to me. This project has been one of the most, if not the most, interesting examples of visionary thinking and action that I have seen in this country. It was so futuristic that even now some twenty-something years later, this country has not yet fully embraced this technology. However, if the nation and the new government are ready to utilize the talent of local people, I think that one of the greatest contributions that you and Owen can make is to help to establish Visitor Information Centres all over Trinidad and Tobago using this technology.

I want to take this opportunity to thank you for reinforcing my view that here in Trinidad and Tobago we have many 'guided spirits' who are inspired to take the country forward. What the politicians need to do is find all these people and facilitate them to implement their ideas. Politicians must disrobe themselves of fear and insecurity and the feeling that "I must do it; it is my ideas that I must implement." Many politicians, as soon as they have ascended to public office, shut themselves out from the people with whom they have communicated, planned and organized all through the struggle. They stop answering their telephones, stop returning calls and stop participating in the blogs and returning emails. When you are an activist and you become a Minister, you simply get the opportunity to implement the things that you have agitated for. It is useful to remember the people with whom you agitated for those things because these are the people who can help to have them implemented. What do you think?

KB

Madeline Coopsammy (Mitchell)
Dear Rhona, You are no longer going to be writing for the website, but you haven't said what you will be doing. Writing the book, I expect. Or back to China?

I just finished reading Raoul Pantin's book, Days of Wrath, about the 1990 coup. I also read his Black Power Day, both of which are very enlightening as to the state of affairs in our country from 1970 to 1990. I was away for both of these, so found the details of value.

But only one month into a P.M's job, when everything had been falling apart for so long, so much corruption was rampant and only the rich and well connected were able to prosper, I don't envy the lady. Her job is a tough one.

Our country, by the way, since you and I were in school, has promoted a whole scale Carnival culture, encouraging a laxity and freeness for the month before Carnival, with all the schools' having calypso contests and Carnivals, and what not. I love Carnival, but it was for the adults, except the Kiddies' Carnival, not a total take–over of its culture, to the exclusion of other art forms.

Just an outsider's view and from one who still loves her roots and culture.

Best wishes.

Madeline

From: Peggy Mohan

Rhona, As in the Indian epic poem, composed in Sanskrit around 300 BCE (Actually, it's a much older story. The version written down by Valmiki was in Sanskrit, yes, but the story is older than that; Tulsidas wrote down a version in Braj, 'Old Hindi'; there are, however, tribal and Jain versions of the story, and versions outside India; one friend of mine, Murad Ali Baig, says he even knows of a Central Asian version, where even the place names were familiar. It may be safest to simply say: 'As in the Ramayana, the ancient Indian epic...')

...when Rama of royal birth lost his throne... (well, not exactly: his father had a number of wives, and while Rama was the oldest son, and was arguably the best candidate to succeed his father, primogeniture wasn't as inevitable as we now think it was, in India. One of his father's younger wives had 'pleased' him, and when he offered her anything she wanted, she asked for her son to be the heir to the throne, and Rama banished into the forest. So Rama was not yet king. Safest to say: 'when Rama of royal birth lost his chance of becoming king...')

...and was banished to the forest with wife Sita and half-brother Laksmana, so too it was happening here in the twin-island paradise where this epic is set. Would the Emperor now be banished to the forest with his wife and half-brothers to spend 14 years in exile? (Ah: here is the 'problem'! In the Ramayana, Rama's banishment is seen as an injustice: he has, over the years, even evolved into a sort of ideal human figure -- though if you read the Ramayana he comes across as weak, and not particularly interesting. Manning's banishment, however, is seen as much deserved. Kind of like comparing Jesus with a common criminal, just because he, too, ended up on a cross...)

(You could, perhaps, couch this in language that suggests that this is how Manning must be seeing himself).

Would a demon king carry off the Emperor's wife and would he then have to enter into an allegiance with Sugriva, king of the monkeys, and Hanuman, the monkey general, who would help him rescue her? Would the Emperor think his party was worth such an alliance?

The epic drama continues as first the Emperor must be resurrected enough to deal with his rambunctious First Mate, the dejected other eleven of his Members of Parliament, an irate band of raging Balisier devotees who now admit that he had taken them overboard the SS PNM with him. But worst of all, there were these new yellow people with rainbow colour hybrids, a dazzling threat to his boring monochromous red Imperial estate. How dare this recalcitrant assortment of a coalition (that he foretold could not last) how dare they lay hands upon his treasures! (Again: a lot of crossing of lines: it won't be easy to work this out. Rama, as I said, is a positive figure. It would almost be easier to have Manning as Ravana, the one who abducted Sita -- T&T? -- only to be beset by a motley group who, in the end, defeat him and get her back...) (Sita is often used as a metaphor of things like this: the misunderstood artist... the country...)

From: Peggy Mohan

Rhona, There are many-many Ramayanas, in India and outside, though the Valmiki Ramayana (in Sanskrit) and the Tulsidas Ramcharitmanas (in medieval Hindi, or Braj) have emerged as the two best known.

There are many folk versions, and even a version where Rama and Sita are brother and sister.

In one version, Sita is Ravana's daughter, buried in the ground by his wife, who had been told that this child would cause her husband's death (and she was found by Janak ploughing his field, and became known as the daughter of the

Earth). Ravana's sin, in this version, was to have fallen in love with his own daughter.

In a tribal Ramayan, Sita is encouraged by the women in her chamber to describe Ravana, and pushed to draw him on the wall. At this moment Rama comes into the room, and in his hurt he banishes her...

The Sanskrit playright Bhavabhuti, in Uttararamacharitam uses Sita as a metaphor of the artist, always being misunderstood and hounded by critics. There are also modern versions, some written by feminists. And there is a Chinese one, which ends very early, when the old king dies, and Rama consoles his brother who has come to give him the news. Rama's words to his brother become the important message.

In Indonesia Ramayana theatre is very popular, and often a vehicle for safely making political comments on the present order. And Rama and Sita are both Muslims, as are most Indonesians.

And, last but not least: think of our own jahaji journey to Trinidad! Many of us left Ayodhya itself, crossing not a forest but the kala pani, and staying not 14 years, but more like 140, several lifetimes...

An evergreen story!

Peggy

From: Margaret Hunte

Rhona, All true. But re politics, remember a no-vote amounts to a vote for whoever the rest of us choose, tho I agree the choice is not enticing at all. Take a trip down Tucker valley and buy some of the luscious veggies and pawpaw on sale at the farmers market on Saturday mornings very cheap and luscious, grown under the supervision of Cubans. But then go to Macqueripe and see how the PNM in its haste to "develop" have turned the natural into the unnatural! We just swim out to sea and close our eyes!

Love. M.

From laurel ince

Rhona, your essay makes fascinating reading, beginning as it does in Guanzhou in September, 2009, spanning several decades and winding up in Port of Spain in 2010, undertaking as it goes along some weighty issues. And your observation that 'nostalgia trifles with the fantasy of a diasporean,' is especially telling. Not because it triggers any meaningful recall, for perhaps I have very few, but from the truly 'trifling' and nonsensical chant one heard in my time, 'chinee, chinee never die, with their flat nose and chinky eye...' If Merle Hodge had not documented it in the local literature, I would have sworn that it was peculiar to a small and idiotic group of country children. But just think of the many ways an imaginative governmental structure could have mobilized and benefitted from a set of cultural traditions vastly different from our own.

As for kin bigotry and jealousy being driven by hate, I wonder!

Ignorance, in the case of bigotry and pettiness, certainly must feed jealousy.

How else does one explain the absurdity of the conclusions which we draw about the other tribes and, of course, those drawn about us! I think now, in maturity, that as island people we might have used those early opportunities to extract the best from one another; distilled a whole new set of tribal attitudes from which the rest of the world would have benefitted.

In a way, it happened in the kitchen. I think too that when the Chinese came to our shores how very sure they would have been about thriving in those parts with the kindly climate and the endless possibilities for those with a willingness to work hard. Yes, one sees them all over China, perched precariously on the hillside performing amazing agricultural feats. There was a time when our people also worked very hard, but our tenuous attachment to Christianity provided neither the zeal nor the fundamental knowledge necessary to nurture and sustain us, and overtime the political directorate, themselves lacking, could hardly lead or aid us.

The bigger burden of the piece, the link between religion/family and the work ethic, is undoubtedly very real and very valid, similar in some ways, to the Hindus' and their explanation of their desire for success and wealth.

And because you brought it all back to the successes of those who recently wrote the SEA examinations, I look on in amazement as our children fall further and further behind.But these are weighty topics and will await our next encounter, hopefully not in the yard of a consulate.

Until ...

Laurel

From: Kirk Francois

Your article "Black on Black" is very interesting and I apprciate the fact that you took on all sides. I personally believe that we Trinis are too quick to blame politicians for everything. We bear some responsiblility for our apathy and expectation that politicians must solve all our problems. Worse is the manner in which we defame and demoralise our own country.

Despite what happens in Jamaica and Haiti, I have never met anyone from these two countries who did not have pride in their country and wanted to see it better.

I think our problem is that Trinis have such a poor view of their country and themselves, that they do not celebrate our successes; we focus on the failures and do not have enough national pride to try to deal with our problems or try to help the situation.

We just count ourselves as lost and run away and live elsewhere and ridicule those Trinis still in T&T. We behave as though every other country in the world is better than ours and we gleefully tell other people that. If we say it and believe it, then it will happen because we will not have the motivation to fix out problems.

Kirk

From: Avonelle Hector-Joseph

Mrs Baptiste or Aunty Rhona, as I called you and would continue to call you, excellent, excellent piece. I think we who supported the Partnership would do both the Partnership and our country a great disservice if we fail to be brutally honest. We accused some of the PNM supporters of being blind loyalists and many of us seem to be heading in that direction.

I agree that some of our previous AGs left much to be desired but, but I feel that we need not to ignore the signs that our present AG just please note I said just might need to be a bit more tactful. I already see a trend developing where it seems to be outrageous to even remotely suggest that anything could be wrong from the PP side. PNM failed to deal with its shortcomings and the population dealt severely with those short comings on May 24th. I trust that the leadership of the PP has its ears to the ground. Keeping your ears to the ground helps leadership to really keep a buzz on the ground swell.

So again, I'm not saying he is wrong or right (AG) just saying a little tact wouldn't hurt. A POINT TO CONSIDER IF JERIMIE DID/SAID THE EXACT THING RAMLOGAN SAID - WHAT WOULD THE RESPONSE OF US PARTNERSHIP SUPPORTERS BE. I think we need to be brutally honest with ourselves.

Avonelle

From: Ian Lambie

Hello, Rhona, Nice to hear from you. You having been away for so long, you can better appreciate the changes to your Country. Without now talking about the Politics, I agree that we are a very undisciplined people. But we have taken a long time in getting there. We are also governed by some very arrogant persons.

It is so bad that they no longer care about what the people, the electorate, are saying.

"Massa Day Done" sounded nice at the time but Dr.Williams not only replaced that then "Massa" with himself. But Dr.Williams did a little more than that which is the cause of our present dilemma. (An undisciplined Country) He centralised everything under his thumb.Nothing could have being done in the Public Service without his approval.

School Principals, Heads of Departments, the Commissioner of Police, the Comptroller of Customs were all shorn of their authority, but yet being held responsible for the efficiency of their respective Departments. How could that work? The disciplinary machinery was centralised in the CPO, and the Service Commissions were also supposed to insulate the Public Servant from political interference.

The Manning PNM Government found a way around the Service Commissions by establishing Private Companies under the name of "Authorities" e.g. Regional Health Authorities (Health Department or Ministry of Health) Airports Authority (Civil Aviation Dept.), TT Post (Post Office Dept.), the Chairmen and CEO of all these:"Authorities" being political appointees.

And now this PNM Government is determined (and if and when returned to power) to do the same thing with the Inland Revenue and the Customs and Excise Division, amalgamate them into the Revenue Authority with the Chairman all Board Members and the CEO being political appointees , responsible to the Minister of Finance.

A major difference with the Revenue Authority is that every employee of the present Inland Revenue and Customs and Excise will be "sent home"with VSEP.They will then be required to either apply for a transfer to another Government Department or apply for their "old job" in the new Revenue Authority, with far inferior terms and conditions of employment.

They are to be employed on contract which means that the receipt of a pension on retirement does not arise.No Pension for dem. But Pension for Parliamentarians who serve two terms in office.

Will selection for employment in the Revenue Authority be based on "political affiliation"? Remember that there will be no Service Commission involvement.

There are many other questionable procedures in the Revenue Authority Bill. Get a copy.

But will the establishment of the Revenue Authority result in improved efficiency in service to the Business Community and the General Public? It is doubtful.

I admit that at for many years there has been need for improvement in the level of service provided by many Public Service Departments, but in my opinion, having been a Public Servant for 35 years, 75 percent of the complaints of poor and efficient service is due to a continuing shortage of personnel, shortage of appropriate equipment and yes, I admit, the other 25 percent is due to indisclipine.

Indiscipline has "crept-up gradually on us, getting worse over the past 50 years, resulting in what it is today almost in every sphere of our daily lives. This has been caused, again in my opinion, by the demise in the authority of the Heads of Departments who became "Toothless Tigers" as Jules Bernard, a former Commissioner of Police, described himself as almost powerless, when inefficiencies in the Police Service were being highlighted.

At the same time true and genuine "Supervisor" in the Public Service becoming a thing of the past.

When a Supervisor reports a "junior' for some indiscretion or misbehaviour, the Supervisor soon finds himself/herself on the defensive. It aint easy. I have had the experience on more than one occasion as a Supervisor of Customs and Excise.

As a result of the "veto powers" of the Prime Minister many persons consider him to be "a Dictator".He had rejected the nominee of the Public Service Commission for the post of DPP on numerous occasions and similarly the nominee by the Police Service Commission for the post of Commissioner. He correctly says that he is acting within the Law. The post of Solicitor General has been vacant for too many years and similarly for many top posts in the Public Service.

Even within the PNM, Manning as Political Leader continues to reject for reasons known only by him, those popular candidates nominated by the various Constituency Groups for example in the rejection of nominees for the up-coming General Election, Penelope Beckles (an MP with a very good track record), Roberts, etc.,

Manning says that he is acting within the "Constitution of the PNM". And do you know what, despite all the numerous failings, rumoured corruption (not proven), of some Members of Government, etc., it appears to me that the PNM Base remains intact. What hurts me a great deal is that the majority of qualified persons in the Country, the professionals at UWI, the Medical Doctors, the Engineers, the Economists, the Financial Experts, the Management Consultants, the Certified Accountants, the Quantity Surveyors, etc. are all silent and witnessing our Country being raped and destroyed.

Even the Public Servants who will soon "get their necks cut" by a PNM Government, i.e. Public Servants who have traditionally and for more than 100 years, enjoyed security of employment will no longer do so. They will be employed on Contract (rumoured to be on 2-year contracts) and importantly no longer receive a Pension during their "Golden Years" after Retirement, will still vote for the PNM, committing harakiri.

As small as my pension is, with no increase in 22 years, together with subsidies from our children, we have been able "to keep the wolf from the door". '

I did not intend to talk politics but it is so much a part of our daily lives it cannot be avoided.

Fondest regards to you and to Owen.

Ian Lambie

From Laurel Ince

Rhona, Thanks for sharing your final article, Zai Jian, or Goodbye from Port of Spain. Quite a ride you have had. Yes, it's self-explanatory and makes me wish that I had had the opportunity to see some of your other pieces. I was especially interested in Alvarez' identification of the missing structures in the society which give rise to our ad hoc way of doing things, and the resultant adjustments/accommodations which Trinis make. For sure, we are either a flexible people or we have become so immune to bad treatment that we fail to recognize it when it is meted out to us. So my question is, does distance only sharpen the vision or does it just give us opportunities to compare ourselves with others? And of course your answer could start a whole new set of feature articles.

It's July 4th, Independence Day, and I had a really great experience this morning, witnessing a Black American celebration of the day. I came away from a church service being extremely grateful for that experience and wondering if anyone can seriously doubt the allegiance which a people feel and have for a country, the singing, the ceremony, the sentiments....

Laurel

From: Sheila Maharaj
Seeta Ram, Rhona, bahin (sister).

It is great to see you posting at Jahajee again thus givng us Trinis an opportunity to read your well articulated opinions on a welter of subjects.

I am sorry though to see you have gone to China once more. I was hoping that you would stay in glorious TT and wade into the smarty pants we have as governance and keep them on their toes.

We still live in that small saving hope.

Do take care and we look forward to many more articles
Warmest blessings.
Sheila

APPENDICES

1. Victory Speech

Address by Ms. Kamla Persad-Bissessar at the Rienzi Complex in Couva on Monday May 24, after the People's Partnership won the 2010 general election.

Rienzi Complex, I am overwhelmed by your love!!!
I am humbled by your devotion!!!
I am honoured by your trust!!!
As Prime Minister-elect of the Republic of Trinidad and Tobago, may I say how grateful I am by your overwhelming response to the People's Partnership. And may I thank God for the guidance that has brought us here to this victory.
Over the past month I have asked for your hand, today you gave me your hand in trust; you gave me your love, support and confidence. I am so deeply humbled. The honour which you now accord me is without parallel. I accept it with deep gratitude and affection.
My brothers and sisters, your confidence today illuminates the theme of unity of all our peoples, to which we in the People's Partnership have devoted our lives. THIS is a Victory of the People. You, the people, have won.
The bells of freedom have rung resoundingly across our great nation. You have freely chosen the government you want to lead you. And the voice of the people is the voice of God.
The changing of the guard is an indicator that our democracy is still preserved and there can be nothing of greater importance for this nation.
And tonight you have good cause to celebrate albeit in moderation. You have earned the right to feel

good about what you have achieved. But let this not be a night we say Kamla or the People's Partnership won; let it be said that the Republic of Trinidad and Tobago was secured.

Let history record that each of you took part in a process that ensured the will of the people was carried out.

Congratulations to the people of Trinidad and Tobago! And I wish to make special mention of Tobago in our partnership. No longer will you have to feel like the ones left out. Tobagonians, welcome to your future equal participation in the affairs of our twin island state!

This victory only occurred because we listened to people from all walks of life.

Tonight I give you my solemn pledge. I pledge tonight that I will never stop paying attention to your needs. I will ensure that the leadership of the People's Partnership responds accordingly. No one will be left out.

Tonight I offer my hand to all those who did not feel assured to give us their confidence today. I want to assure you that we will work for all of Trinidad and Tobago. We will work twice as hard to gain your faith and trust!!! As a nation WE WILL ALL RISE!!!

The unbelievers said that they were mere words, a slogan and a flamboyant phase. Even when our opponents tried to downgrade our clarion call to unity, we built our collective strength and character around our belief that WE WILL RISE!! We were brave enough to face our challenges.

To each of you I offer a hand of genuine partnership in the important task of rebuilding our nation. Party loyalty to me after an election is of no more significance than the colour of your eyes or the texture of your hair or the colour of your skin.

To the supporters of the People's Partnership I cannot begin to express how much your words of encouragement have inspired me. This has been quite a journey for me and one which has brought so many people by my side along the way. So it would be difficult to individually thank them all but it would be remiss of me if I failed to mention the dedication and support of my husband Gregory and my children.

It is never easy on a family when your wife and mother juggles her roles with her political life and so tonight I pay tribute to them for the way they have endured these years with love and selflessness.

And to my niece, my special daughter, Lisa, thank you my love for being there for me. Lisa endured and sufficed so much during this difficult time, she bore the greatest trauma that can face us, that of a victim of criminals. Lisa, I thank you and love you.

To Usha, Roopchand, Arlene, Vishnu, Karen, Silvy, and Reesa, all the ladies and gentlemen at Siparia Constituency office and here at the Rienzi Complex, for the late nights and the long hours, for the dedication and the resolve, I thank you, and I love you all!

May I also say a special thanks to the members, supporters and well-wishers of my party the glorious United National Congress!!

January 24 seems so long ago. It was 120 days ago that you gave me your sacred trust to lead our great party. Now I am so humbled to have delivered to you the Government of the Republic of Trinidad and Tobago!!

May I also thank all our UNC soldiers who laboured in the vineyards for the past decade during our most difficult days in opposition, all our members and officers who worked tirelessly to keep our party alive and keep our flag flying high and proud.

I am so grateful for your work and sacrifice that has brought to this historic moment. I love you all and thank you from the bottom of my heart.

I express my gratitude as well, to the founder and former leader, the Hon. Basdeo Panday, for his years of service and dedication to the cause of justice, equality and national unity. As Mr. Panday celebrates his 77th birthday tomorrow/today, from Rienzi Complex, we wish you a most pleasant and joyful day in the glory of the rising sun!!!!

But there can be no greater gratitude tonight than that which I express to all those who believed in themselves and this great nation of ours. Because of you we now stand on the cusp of a great moment in our history, one in which we begin the task of bringing people together to rebuild Trinidad and Tobago to make it safer, cleaner, more truly progressive than it has ever been before.

It will not be easy but the process is going to be as rewarding as it is challenging. And I begin that process from this very moment.

In fact, I can admit to you now that I had started working on what needed to be done before Day One. Tonight, not tomorrow, tonight, I begin the task of selecting the most capable, competent, committed patriots to be a part of the leadership in the country's various Ministries. And I will do so without fear or favour.

There will be continuity in all sectors of governance with a greater emphasis on consultation, accountability and retention of all critical policies that will be needed to ensure administrative and economic stability in transition.

There will not be the old politics of dismantling programmes and projects and plastering of new names just to stake a political claim, rather, there will be responsible, collaborative and proactive governance to provide the equitable representation and administration that every citizen, regardless of affiliation or persuasion deserves.

Obviously, the process will require a level of consultation with the members of the People's Partnership and your representatives and I am confident that we will share the same perspectives on what is required to get the job done effectively and immediately. I look ahead to the next few years with enthusiasm and great expectation. And I can assure you that I will lead a government filled with compassion and concern.

The campaign promises must now become government policies. I can guarantee you a government that is accountable and transparent. You can hold me to the promise of the change which you so positively voted for tonight.

As I heard the results coming in and saw the trend I knew the time had come. A new page had been turned in our nation's history and the responsibility to each of you is now on my shoulders. I will not let you down.

I bring to my leadership not just political experience and government experience but I also carry into the office of the Prime Ministership the nurturing nature of a mother and grandmother and I will look after you all as my own.

And when someone asked me what was the first thing I would do as Prime Minister I instinctively replied, "To visit a few Children's Homes and Schools." And having said that, it is what I intend to do. And I guess I said that because this is where the change must all begin.

In closing, I wish at this juncture to pay special tribute to the Hon. Patrick Manning, Political Leader of the People's National Movement (PNM) who has been a most worthy and formidable opponent.

Whatever are our differences in ideology and policy, Mr. Manning has given over 30 years of his life to public service. While we may not agree on approaches and programs, we reserve and defend the right to disagree.

I thank him for his service to the people of Trinidad and Tobago and wish him all success in his future endeavours, I am almost certain that we have not heard the last of such an indefatigable political figure.

To the Candidates of the People's Partnership, those in the East West, North and South, those in Central and in Tobago, gird your loins, ban your bellies, the work is before us now.

And so as we celebrate tonight, let this be a call to duty, let this be a defining moment in our nation's life, a time of personal commitment as we all, you, you, you and you, and I, begin the work anew towards the change we all need, to build a better country for our children and their children .

Tonight, however, I quite understand that for all of you that it begins with a nationwide celebration. But, please, let us not lose a single one of you tonight through recklessness and carelessness. Be responsible. Don't drink and drive. Call the Arrive Alive team. Get home safely. I love you all and so do those who are waiting upon your return.

May God bless you all and may God bless our Nation.

2. Oath of Office

Remarks by His Excellency Professor George Maxwell Richards TC, CMT, Ph.D, President of the Republic of Trinidad and Tobago on the Occasion of the Taking and Subscribing the Oath of Office of the Prime Minister of the Republic of Trinidad and Tobago, the Honourable Kamla Persad-Bissessar, at Knowsley, Queen's Park East, in Port of Spain on Wednesday 26 May 2010.

The Honourable Kamla Persad-Bissessar, newly elected Member of Parliament for Siparia and Dr. Gregory Bissessar

The Honourable Mr. Justice Ivor Archie, Chief Justice and Mrs. Archie

Your Excellency Archbishop Thomas Gullickson, Dean of the Diplomatic Corps

Pundit Bramdeo Maharaj, President of the Inter Religious Organisation

Specially Invited Guests

Members of the Media

Other Distinguished Ladies and Gentlemen:

In the year 2007, it was felt that the Ceremony of Taking and Subscribing the Oath of Office of the Prime Minister, which normally took place at The President's House, in the presence of one or two witnesses, should be held at a venue where a wide audience could be accommodated. This was to signal the inclusion of the people of Trinidad and Tobago in such an important occasion in the life of our country.

Today, we have come to another milestone in our relatively short history. For the first time, Trinidad and Tobago will have, as its Head of Government, a woman, in the person of Mrs. Kamla Persad-Bissessar. This we must applaud.

By their action on May 24th 2010, the people of this country have shown their willingness to open avenues of possibility for all of our citizens. They have made a powerful statement of endorsement and of intent, certainly regarding the gender factor, which, in spite of our protestations to the contrary, has, from time to time and in significant ways, registered a deficit in our dealing with our women.

Lest I be misunderstood, let me say that there is no gainsaying that our women have made tremendous strides, in the public as in the private sector. Nevertheless, I would not be far off the mark, if I were to aver that there have existed and continues to exist a certain reservation, on the part of too many of us, men as well as women, in genuinely respecting the ability as well as the entitlement of women. As a consequence, many of us, at least subliminally, do not repose full confidence in our women to act independently or patronage of one kind or another. The evidence is there and healthy, honest debate on the matter should not be set aside. The statistics and common knowledge of female achievement and capability, in every sphere and at every level, warn us against that.

The current circumstance offers us opportunity to consider where we are as a people and to examine the pillars on which we stand. Not only the Prime Minister, but all who have put themselves forward for public service and have been accepted as representatives of the people, must be clear about their duty. They must be mindful of the people, must be clear about their duty. They must be mindful of the Constitution of our Republic which declares inter alia, that 'the people of Trinidad and Tobago...have asserted their belief in a democratic society in which persons may, to the extent of their capacity, play some part in the institutions of national life and thus develop and maintain due respect for lawfully constituted authority.'

It is for the leadership in our Parliament to use the avenues available to them to ensure that those words have life, as they guide the affairs of the country.

I thank the outgoing Prime Minister and his government for their contribution to the nation and wish them well.

I congratulate Mrs. Persad-Bissessar on her success and now invite her to come forward to take the Oath of Office.

3. Oath Taking Ceremony

Address by Prime Minister Kamla Persad-Bissessar at her Oath Taking ceremony at Knowsley on 26 May 2010.

My fellow citizens, it gives me great pleasure to address you for the very first time as Prime Minister of the Republic of Trinidad and Tobago.

This has been quite a journey for me. It is the summary of a life in public office that spans some 25 years but one which most people will long remember for its past five months.

As you all know, I was elected on February 24th of this year as Political Leader of the UNC, and on March 24th became Leader of the Opposition and now I humbly received the honour to have been elected Prime Minister on May 24th 2010.

But that is far as I will indulge myself in personalising the sequence of events, of far greater importance is enormous responsibility I now bear along with the leadership of the People's Partnership and our administration to address the urgent social issues at hand and move the nation forward.

Change has indeed come. The time has arrived to open a new chapter in our nation's history.

It's time for all of us to stand together side by side. Trinidad alongside Tobago. Members and supporters of all political persuasions, citizens all, arm in arm.

Today we start the work of transforming the hope and promise of change into the reality of change.

And while we leave the euphoria and the emotion of the election behind us, what we do not stray from is the unity the election has forged.

This morning we leave the labels behind and we move forward as one nation – all committed to the same goal – a safer, more prosperous and just Trinidad and Tobago where we all have opportunity and equality.

No more labels. No more prefixes of Afro and Indo nor North and South nor East, West corridors. The election is over. It was a means towards an end. Now as citizens of Trinidad and Tobago we are all beneficiaries of the mandate given by the people. This is a victory for all citizens.

Our love of country must now move to the forefront.

And we must recommit ourselves to our nation and to ourselves.

We are not checking party cards or keeping notes on supporters' lists.

The task of rebuilding Trinidad and Tobago will require the participation of everyone and you are all invited to sit at the nation's table.

Our country has had enough of top down government. We're going to reverse that order of things.

Throughout the campaign, we were clear about our plans. And so today we begin the process of making them government policy.

My fellow citizens, the task ahead of us is challenging and we need all our nation's talent, all our nation's wisdom, all our nation's people on board with us.

It's time to build a future which we can all share, hold pride in and pass on to our children with confidence.

We have been given an immense opportunity for developing Trinidad and Tobago in ways many might not have thought possible.

The abundant talent of our people in so many spheres is world renowned and we are blessed with rich natural resources. There is no reason why our nation cannot reach heights of development never seen before.

This development must not be measured in the grandeur of tall structures as an architectural manifestation of how far we have come but by the level of human development of our people, by the extent to which the needs of people have been satisfied, by the way things just work well, by the degree of safety and security that our people and the nation enjoy, by the enabling environment created for business to flourish and a renaissance of the arts and culture to emerge, by the mutual respect we hold for each other, by the level of education provided to our young ones and the quality of care given to our little children and by the success we achieve in addressing the very pressing social concerns, such as poverty alleviation, domestic violence and child abuse. These are just some of the ways in which our development must be measured.

What happens from this day forward is in our hands. It is up to us.

And so the challenge before us is to stay as one people.

We must never allow the seeds of separation to regain hold on our soil.

This afternoon, the new chapter we turn is a fresh start for all of us.

Over the next few days I will be making the appointments of members of my cabinet following consultations with the leadership of the People's Partnership. I promise you it will be comprised of the most competent, committed and qualified individuals.

On composition of the Cabinet my administration will bring Tobago into the core administration of government. And I formally announce this afternoon that there will be an establishment of a Ministry of Tobago Development as we look to bring our sister isle on as equal partners in the development of our twin-island state.

Our administration will be addressing social and economic restructuring in the medium term as we look to fast track the changes so urgently required. We will be targeting Ministries to give an account on specific deliverables within a timeframe, as an example, food production. This will be a performance driven formula that measures results and holds those in authority accountable to meeting their goals and objectives.

Under the Office of the Prime Minister, special emphasis will be placed on restoring the dignity and effectiveness of Parliament. In this context, the Red House will remain the Seat of the Parliament.

Parliamentary oversight on key issues has gone into abeyance and in an effort to ensure Parliament is not just a rubber stamp we will be making immediate steps to institute Parliamentary reform under the Office of the Prime Minister.

The People's Partnership government I lead will be moving towards the delivery of an early budget after candid assessments are conducted on the state of the nation's finances and economy. The budget provisions based will be developed to give effect to the priorities of the new direction of our new government.

At the conclusion of this afternoon's ceremony, one of my first acts as Prime Minister will be to meet with the Head of the Office of the Disaster Preparedness and Management along with the Permanent Secretary in the Office of the Prime Minister, Sandra Marchack, to discuss the current flooding in various parts of the island and the impending increased level of flooding. Arising out of those discussions, a release will be issued on the decisions arrived at and the course of action to be taken.

This situation underlines the need of our new administration to fast track all assessment and begin the process of implementing both short term and long term solutions in so many areas including those such as drainage and irrigation.

A tour of some of the affected areas has already been conducted by members of the incoming administration this morning and a report is being compiled on the needs of the affected areas.

In light of the urgency of this situation and my need to address it I will now crave your indulgence to leave hastily and do apologise for having to forego the usual formalities that accompany occasions such as this.

On behalf of the Government of the People's Partnership, may I thank you all for being here and to express once more my deepest gratitude to the people of Trinidad and Tobago for their overwhelming support.

May God Bless you all and May God Bless our Nation.

4. Swearing-in Ceremony

Address by Prime Minister Kamla Persad-Bissessar at the swearing-in ceremony of the Ministers of Government, at Knowsley on 28 May 2010.

Fellow citizens, as Prime Minister of the Republic of Trinidad and Tobago it gives me great pleasure to present to you the members of the Cabinet of the People's Partnership Government.

These twenty four men and women are the leaders who will represent the interests of the people.

I wish to make this address to all of us gathered here as members of the Cabinet and let the nation witness the following watchwords of our governance.

May I say to each of you that each day, you are expected to dedicate all of your energies towards ensuring that the people's needs are being addressed.

All of us are held accountable to the people. Ours is a monumental task but it is one which is equally rewarding because there can be no greater call than that of national service.

We must accept no mediocrity. Neither must we contribute to it in any way.

There must be no room for arrogance.

We must be faithful to a leadership style that is firm but humble, passionate and impatient for great achievements but ever conscious of the correct procedures.

We have to be ever mindful that the nation is looking at us expectantly. No one out there expects excuses, they want results. No one expects us to create miracles, but simply to work hard enough as though we know could produce them.

Lead by example. Follow by learning to listen.

All of this is as much my mantra as it is your own.

As of now, each of us is on trial. We begin to be tested as of this very moment. We carry a huge responsibility to get this nation back on track.

So we must discover how to turn obstacles into opportunities, discover new ways of solving old problems. Inspire others by our enthusiasm and positive outlook.

As members of the Cabinet of the People's Partnership we are stewards of the nation's future. What a legacy we can leave behind. What an incredible privilege and honour given to us to serve in this way. What a phenomenal opportunity to make such a contribution to country.

My caution is never to become aloof, never lose sight of the true purpose of the position you hold. Stay grounded. Keep connected to the people. Earn their respect by the way you serve them.

As Chief Servant Makandal Daaga would say, the people are the government. We are servants of the people. We work for the people. Diligently and entirely and always in their interest.

The talent and commitment of this group assembled here this afternoon cannot be denied. Sure, many of you are new to this but that means you bring fresh ideas and new perspectives. Government cannot be about doing the same things and expecting different results.

The days will be long and the nights sleepless but the rewards will come from knowing that we are improving the lives of others and creating the kind of nation of which we can all be proud.

One of the hallmarks of our government must be that we serve every citizen with the same dedication regardless of their political affiliation. And we must never display any kind of party symbol during the conduct of our work as the government of Trinidad and Tobago in or out of Parliament.

Transparency and accountability must be evident in all government matters. We must be exemplars of the society, returning sound, traditional values of ethics and morals back into government. Honesty must be one of the given qualifications of anyone who hopes to serve the people.

Harness the best of our nation's human resources to give reality to the change so many voted for. Disregard which party any qualified individual comes from or what ethnic group or religion or anything else that defines them in any way other than their competency and genuine commitment to serve the people.

"The people are the government." Please take these words and frame them on every desk of each of your Ministries and recommit to them every single day of each month you are privileged to be in service to the nation.

Thank you for coming forward in the way each of you has to contribute to the large task of rebuilding our great nation. I pledge to you all that I will be a leader who in turn listens and that my decisions will only be arrived at after collaboration and always in the interest of what best serves Trinidad and Tobago. There is no room for personal egos, no time for personal agendas, and no opportunity for self glorification. This is not about us, it is about the people. And they have the power to dismiss us anytime.

Congratulations to each of you. The entire nation now awaits your performance. And your job expectations actually began on Monday night so we have some catching up to do already so let me not delay you any further. God bless and guide us all as we embark upon this inspired journey of national service.

And may God bless our Nation.

5. List of Ministers and Parliamentary Secretaries Sworn In:

Mr. Austin Jack Warner — Minister of Works and Transport

Mr. Winston Dookeran — Minister of Finance

Brigadier John Sandy — Minister of National Security

Ms. Carolyn Seepersad-Bachan — Minister of Energy and Energy Affairs

Dr. Surujattan Rambachan — Minister of Foreign Affairs

Mr. Rudrawatee Nan Ramgoolam — Minister of Public Administration

Mr. Fazal Karim — Minister of Science, Technology and Tertiary Education

Ms. Therese Baptiste-Cornelis — Minister of Health

Mr. Emmanuel George — Ministry of Public Utilities

Mr. Vasant Bharath — Minister of Food Production

Ms. Mary King — Minister of Planning, Economics and Social Restructuring and Gender Affairs

Mr. Chandresh Sharma — Minister of Local Government

Dr. Roodal Moonilal — Minister of Housing and the Environment

Mr. Stephen Cadiz — Minister of Trade and Industry

Dr. Rupert Griffith — Minister of tourism

Mr. Herbet Volney — Minister of Justice

Dr. Glen Ramadharsingh — Minister of the People and Social Development

Dr. Tim Gopeesingh — Minister of Education

Mr. Nizam Baksh — Minister of Community Development

Mr. Prakash Ramadhar — Minister of Legal Affairs

Mr. Errol McLeod — Minister of Labour, Small and Micro Enterprise Development

Mr. Anil Roberts — Minister of Sport and Youth Affairs

Ms. Vernella Alleyne Toppin — Minister of Tobago Development

Mr. Winston Peters — Minister of the Arts and Culture

Ministers in the Ministries

Mr. Rudranath Indarsingh — Ministry of Works and Transport
Mr. Clifton de Coteau — Ministry of Education
Mr. Delmon Dexter Baker — Ministry of Tourism
Ministers of State
Mr. Colin Jefferson Partap — Office of the Prime Minister
Mr. Rodger Dominic Samuel — Office of the Prime Minister

Parliamentary Secretaries

Mr. Kevin Christian Ramnarine — Ministry of Energy and Energy Affairs
Ms. Stacy Alana Roopnarine — Ministry of Sport and Youth Affairs
Mr. Jairam Angad Seemungal — Ministry of Legal Affairs
Ms. Nela Khan — Ministry of the Arts and Culture
Ms. Ramona Ramdial — Ministry of Planning, Economic and Social Restructuring and Gender Affairs

6. President's Address

Address by His Excellency Professor George Maxwell Richards TC, CMT, Ph.D, President of the Republic of Trinidad and Tobago, on the Occasion of the Ceremonial Opening of the Tenth Parliament, on Friday 18 June, 2010 at 1.30 p.m.

The Speaker of the House of Representatives, the Honourable Prime Minister, the Honourable Leader of the Opposition, other Members of Parliament:

Having determined, by Proclamation dated 4th June, 2010, that the Tenth Parliament of the Republic of Trinidad and Tobago should begin with a Session to be held at the Red House in Port of Spain, on Friday 18th June, 2010, at 1.30 p.m., I am happy to be here, this afternoon, as we continue with the Ceremonial Opening of this, the First Session.

I acknowledge the presence of the Honourable Mr. Justice Ivor Archie, Chief Justice, Sir Ellis Clarke, former President, Members of the Diplomatic Corps, distinguished visitors from overseas, particularly our CARICOM family, and other Distinguished Ladies and Gentlemen.

I congratulate every person who has been elected or selected to serve the people of our country, following the general elections of 24th May, 2010. I recognize you as individuals, bringing your particular expertise and skills to bear on the tasks ahead, but also as a part of a collective, working together in the Parliament, and outside, regardless of political affiliation, to take the business of the Trinidad and Tobago forward.

It is the first time in the history of our nation that we have at the helm of government, a woman, and it is fitting that special acknowledgment be given to that fact, a fact which you have recognized merits applause for the many things that it connotes. Let us see this for what it is:

evidence of the process of maturing that has been taking place, the women of Trinidad and Tobago positioning themselves in order to secure a more visible profile in leadership roles, in every aspect of life in our country.

For those who have eyes to see, this is not happenstance or something that has occurred by chance. It strikes me that the rewards of embracing opportunities for education, in its broadest sense, as well as gaining relevant experience in the various avenues of national life are evident, and the women of this country ought to be keenly aware of the signals that are being sent. A more gentle caring society, yes, but there must be no room whatever
for patronage.

The country has come out of a rigorous, if not most bruising election campaign, and, as the then Prime Minister-elect stated, as the result of the polls became clear, "the elections are over". These are profound words which we would all, every single one of us, do well to remember and to embrace, with scrupulous exactitude. We are now witnessing a handing-over process which appears to be going well and it is my hope that all who are involved will be sensitive to the need to ensure a smooth transition, so that the country can settle down in this new dispensation. I extend best wishes to the new Prime Minister and her team, as I do to the new Leader of the Opposition and his team. Professional public servants, representing a continuum and dedicated to the welfare of our country, are there to help you.

Much work needs to be done to build upon the past; adjusting, as necessary, and forging ahead with appropriate thrust. In this context, in considering our several independent institutions established under our Constitution which guides the Executive, we must be careful to properly assess their value. The pace of delivery of some of them may not quite meet the demands with which consigning them to history. I advocate, rather, that the conditions under which they function be dispassionately examined, in order to ensure that they are properly equipped to fulfill their tasks and moreover, that these conditions are such as to consolidate their independence as guardians of our democracy.

As I have said, at another time in this House, while policy decisions are the business of the government and the Parliament, executing of policy relies heavily on agents of the state and others, throughout the national community, at every level of the society.

The matter of productivity is relevant, and in the context, also, of world competitiveness, where there has been considerable slippage in respect of Trinidad and Tobago. As I mentioned, not long ago, we have slipped from forty-second place on the Global Competitiveness Index in 2002/2003 to eighty-sixth in 2009/2010, out of one hundred and thirty-three countries. But productivity does not suddenly occur, in a vacuum. It is a culture and a way of life that must be nurtured. While leadership in the labour movement, understandably, negotiates to secure the best compensation for the country's organized labour, from which others may benefit, even so, much greater productivity than is now the case must be required of the work force. This is not applicable only in the formal sector, but across the board.

Moreover, the education system must be so structured and managed as to encourage a correct attitude to productivity and a better understanding of what this means for our country, in terms of poverty alleviation and eradication, becoming more self-sufficient, and being at the forefront of development.

Poverty alleviation and eradication will not become reality in a culture of low productivity. There is no question but that there are those in our society who must be assisted because of their financial circumstances, but rogrammes of such assistance, particularly at the lower age bracket, must be so organized as to enable recipients to work their way out of dependence on State benevolence. We ask ourselves: How far must State benevolence go? What are the entitlements of the people? How much of these entitlements must a government provide? These are matters that can be debated from different perspectives and it is certain that different and opposing views will persist, for a long time.

We all know that a government must take the lead in the provision of certain basic services, for example, health care, water, electricity, roads and transportation and we expect that the pace of development in these areas will be accelerated. Housing is another area in which an aggressive policy must be pursued. The private sector will continue to play its part, responsibly recognizing, it is hoped, that the market is way beyond the reach of the working and middle classes and collaborate in doing something about it, in order to pull back the working poor from homelessness. Make no mistake, Ladies and Gentlemen, the working poor are a reality, but they are not as recognizable as the indigent among us and so, their plight can easily be ignored, while others take centre stage. How much is expected of the government and how are the needs to be met? I leave this burning question before you in the hope that fairness and responsible action be the bedrock on which decisions will be taken.

Everyone, including the most vulnerable, has a part to play in the economy and it is a responsibility about which, as a people, on the whole, we must have greater awareness. This is a fact that must be inculcated in ourchildren. Artisans, providers in our indigenous and evolving food culture, home makers, technicians and professionals, exponents of the arts, for example, must all assume their places in moving the economy forward. I am of the view that not enough attention is paid to the informal sector. And so, our people have forgotten the sewing machines, the bakers' ovens, the homemade hot pepper sauce and confectionery, to name just a few items of cottage industry, which have sometimes provided the means necessary to produce the next generation of highly qualified and distinguished persons. Too many of us have forgotten, or do not know, about small beginnings and sacrifice.

By seeking a recognized and critical space for that category of potential contributor, I am by no means suggesting that we keep our manufacturing sector, for example, in the early twentieth century mode. We must have an advanced state-of-the-art manufacturing sector based on the use of new and established scientific and technological knowledge, embracing the potential role of existing technologies such as biotechnology, nanotechnology, new materials, as well as information and communications technology, which have broad applications and which impact the economy.

But in continually seeking to modernize that sector, so that we may be competitive in international trade, we must, at the same time, be mindful of the hard lessons of other countries. Ways and means must therefore be found to avoid further dislocation of the work force by recalling the skills to which I have referred, as examples, in order to restore the dignity and independence of those who are currently at the lower levels of the economic ladder, but who, through appropriate government policy, must be encouraged to see the possibility of upward mobility.

Full time employment is a highly desirable goal, but whatever the statistics say, in that regard, does not alter the fact that if we work little, at our full time or part time jobs, the country will not go forward. Flexi-time, which is already a feature in this country, in the public service at least, will not assist productivity, if beating the traffic results only in workers having breakfast on the job, instead of at home, thereby cutting down the eight hour work day to seven, if not less. While there are those who go beyond the call of duty, our current level of productivity, generally, is not at all acceptable.

This leads me to the matter of innovation, in the context of job creation which education in its proper sense must encourage. In this regard, there is ample room for innovation on the part of our people, not least our young people, at the post secondary stage of education. As for diversification, how can we rate ourselves? This is a much overworked word in our vocabulary of plans, and in this area we have come up short, very short. Our heavy dependence on the oil and gas sector, with its inherent vicissitudes, cannot continue. Other revenue generating industries must be developed to buffer the economy against possible shocks in the international environment.

There are undeniable possibilities, for example, in agriculture, which must be geared towards the goal of food sufficiency and the consequent reduction in our massive food import bill. This would also require policy decisions and development in areas allied to that sector. There are many other avenues for diversification and in which the government can no doubt take the lead. But ways must be found to so communicate the vision that thepeople, all over the country, regardless of traditional occupations, become a part of the process and are encouraged to make the choice of taking the opportunities offered.

The concern regarding diversification, which, so far, has remained largely in the realm of discussion, rests not only on the matter of income, which is very important, but there are environmental conditions or considerations as well. The time has long since come for us to harness and employ alternative sources of energy, some of which are already available to us and it is my hope that, with the new environmental legislation signaled by the Minister of

Energy and Energy Affairs, serious steps will be taken in that regard.

I have sought, Ladies and Gentlemen, over the past several minutes, simply to highlight a few areas in which government, in its broad sense, by deliberations brought to the Parliament by the people's representatives, might engage the national community in decisions that have as their objective greater success in our nation's future. But the government must be careful to leave room for people to define what success means to them androom for them to achieve that success.

Parliament provides a forum where the interests of the people can be vigorously pursued and secured by legislation that provides the greatest good for the greatest number. This responsibility towards the people of ournation must not be subordinated, in the cut and thrust of political engagement. On both sides of the political divide, constituents expect to be properly represented, issues being paramount.

Discipline, law and order must be watchwords that guide our living, in this country. At the level of leadership, we have a particular charge, in this context, to avoid mixed signals. Therefore, much as we may be temptedotherwise, we need to give deep consideration to reining in ourselves so that our collective voice may achieve maximum benefit for all our citizens.

Robert Louis Stevenson is reported to have said that "Politics is perhaps the only profession for which no preparation is thought necessary." I believe that there are those who have discovered otherwise and those of you who are new to the arena may want to consider an approach different from that which is suggested in the famous essayist, novelist and poet's remark.

In closing, may I exhort that you strive to make this forum attractive to the youth of our nation, to whom we must pass the baton of leadership. Let us maintain a proper tone, eschewing adversarial stances as a constant feature and respecting the separation of powers, according to our Constitution. Let us conduct our business, in this Parliament, in decency and in order, regarding one another as persons who have been blessed with the privilege of serving in the highest forum in the land and for which privilege history will hold us accountable.

May God grant you wisdom and may God bless our nation.

7. Members of the House of Representatives

1. Alleyne-Toppin, Vernella TOP Tobago East
2. Baker, Delmon TOP Tobago West
3. Baksh, Nizam UNC Naparima
4. Browne, Amery PNM Diego Martin Central
5. Cadiz, Stephen UNC Chaguanas East
6. Cox, Donna PNM Laventille East/Morvant
7. De Coteau, Clifton UNC Moruga/Tableland
8. Dookeran, Winston COP Tunapuna
9. Douglas, Lincoln COP Lopinot/Bon Air West
10. Gopee-Scoon, Paula PNM Point Fortin
11. Gopeesingh, Tim UNC Caroni East
12. Griffith, Rupert UNC Toco/Sangre Grande
13. Hospedales, Alicia PNM Arouca/Maloney
14. Hypolite, Nileung PNM Laventille West
15. Imbert, Colm PNM Diego Martin North/East
16. Indarsingh, Rudranath UNC Couva South
17. Jeffrey, Fitzgerald PNM La Brea
18. Khan, Fuad UNC Barataria/San Juan
19. Khan, Nela UNC Princes Town
20. Manning, Patrick PNM San Fernando East
21. Mark, Wade Speaker of the House
22. McLeod, Errol UNC Pointe-a-Pierre
23. McDonald, Marlene PNM Port-of-Spain South
24. McIntosh, Patricia PNM Port-of-Spain North/St. Ann's West
25. Moonilal, Roodal UNC Oropouche East
26. Partap, Collin UNC Cumuto/Manzanilla
27. Persad-Bissessar, Kamla UNC Siparia
28. Peters, Winston UNC Mayaro
29. Ramadhar, Prakash COP St. Augustine
30. Ramadharsingh, Glenn UNC Caroni Central
31. Rambachan, Surujrattan UNC Tabaquite
32. Ramdial, Ramona UNC Couva North
33. Roberts, Anil COP D'Abadie/O'Meara

34. Roopnarine, Stacy UNC Oropouche West
35. Rowley, Keith PNM Diego Martin West
36. Samuel, Rodger COP Arima
37. Seemungal, Jairam UNC La Horquetta/Talparo
38. Seepersad-Bachan, Carolyn COP San Fernando West
39. Sharma, Chandresh UNC Fyzabad
40. Thomas, Joanne PNM St. Ann's East
41. Volney, Herbert UNC St. Joseph
42. Warner, Jack UNC Chaguanas West

8. Members of the Senate

1. Abdulah, David UNC
2. Al-Rawi, Faris PNM
3. Ali, Basharat Independent
4. Armstrong, James Independent
5. Balgobin, Rolph Independent
6. Baptiste-Cornelis, Therese UNC
7. Baptiste-McKnight, Corinne Independent
8. Beckles-Robinson, Pennelope PNM
9. Bharath, Vasant UNC
10. Cudjoe, Shamfa PNM
11. Drayton, Helen Independent
12. George, Emmanuel UNC
13. Hamel-Smith, Timothy President of the Senate
14. Henry, Lester PNM
15. Hinds, Fitzgerald PNM
16. Karim, Fazal UNC
17. King, Mary COP
18. Maharaj, Danny UNC
19. Moheni, Embau UNC
20. Oudit, Lyndira UNC
21. Panday, Subhas UNC
22. Prescott, SC, Elton Independent
23. Ramgoolam, Rudrawatee Nan UNC
24. Ramkhelawan, Subhas Independent
25. Ramkissoon, Harold Independent
26. Ramlogan, Anand UNC
27. Ramnarine, Kevin UNC
28. Roopnarine, Ted PNM
29. Sandy, John UNC
30. Watson, Patrick COP
31. Wheeler, Victor Independent

9. Indian Arrival Day

Message by Prime Minister the Hon. Kamla Persad-Bissessar on 31 May 2010.

Fellow citizens of Trinidad and Tobago, it gives me great pleasure to extend greetings to the entire Nation on the 165th Anniversary of the Arrival of our East Indian forefathers to these shores. More than just a day of rememberance, it is a day when we must give thanks to God, and celebrate the human spirit's triumph over seemingly insurmountable odds, to build a legacy of strength, discipline and tolerance that has helped make us what we all are today as a nation.

Indeed my brothers and sisters, the journey of our East Indian forebears was long and arduous, and didn't come cheaply. It took patience, vision, belief and a spirit of sacrifice to begin a new life in a strange land, with the hope that one day, their offspring would reap the rewards of that sojourn.

And while the East Indian experience was unique in its own way, as would have been for those who made their life's journey to these shores from Africa, China, Europe and the farthest reaches of the globe, there were many things that were common to all... but most important among these was a desire to enjoy life's greatest freedoms without fear, and in an atmosphere of peace, prosperity and harmony.

And this more than anything else has been the legacy that has found its greatest expression in our people, from all walks of life - in our music, our food, our dance, the way we interact with each other...It's a journey that has taken us all centuries to arrive at, and still the journey continues as we steadily improve the means by which we travel to the destination of our Nationhood.

For this reason the Ministry of Arts and Culture will be redesigned to become the Ministry of the Arts and Multiculturalism in order to give greater voice to the diverse cultural expressions of our common desires for individual and national identity.

There will be a realignment of policies including resource allocation, to allow for a more equitable recognition and fulfilment of the needs of the diverse proponents of our culture.

Our celebration of days such as this must be more than just a formality, but an active reaffirmation of this Governement's commitment to ensure that every creed and race finds an equal place in this land of ours.

To you all I wish a very happy, peaceful and enjoyable Indian Arrival Day.

May God bless us all.

10. CARICOM Meeting

Statement by the Hon. Kamla Persad-Bissessar, Prime Minister of the Republic of Trinidad and Tobago, at the Thirty-First Regular Meeting of CARICOM Conference of Heads of Government, in Montego Bay, Jamaica, on 5 July 2010.

It is my pleasure to address you at the Opening Ceremony of the Thirty-First Regular Meeting of CARICOM Heads of Government and a further privilege to be doing so here in Montego Bay, the tourism capital of Jamaica.

I would like to begin by expressing appreciation to our hosts, Prime Minister Golding and the Government of Jamaica, for the warmth of the welcome extended to us and the superb arrangements that are so evident for this the Thirty-First Meeting of the Conference of Heads of Government of the Caribbean Community.

President Preval, since this is my first occasion to be in your presence since the tragedy which befell your nation on January 12 of this year please allow me to extend deep sympathy to the government and people of Haiti and to recommit the efforts of Trinidad and Tobago in assisting the recovery of your nation.

The fortitude, dignity and resilience demonstrated by the people of our sister isle state of Haiti in the wake of this terrible event have won profound respect.

As some of you may know Jamaica was once my home for some fourteen years. I studied here, fell in love here, taught here and attended my first political meeting right here in Jamaica.

So in a sense one can say that Jamaica helped prepare me in becoming Prime Minister of Trinidad and Tobago. I guess if my political opponents knew this would occur they would have done everything in their power to ensure I stayed right here.

May I add that I also spent a few years in Barbados as well, in fact, my son is Barbadian born.

And I believe such experiences help to sharpen an understanding of that unique Caribbean identity and perspective.

During those early periods of my life I never dreamt I would be one day addressing such an esteemed group of Caribbean leaders at all much less as Prime Minister of my nation.

But I guess one can never underestimate the education of a Caribbean experience, especially that of a woman who encounters it.

This Conference is being hosted by the Government of Jamaica against the backdrop of change in the Republic of Trinidad and Tobago as well as within and outside the Region.

Trinidad and Tobago now joins many other States which have experienced administrative changes in the very recent past, namely, the United States, the United Kingdom and Suriname in contributing new perspectives and approaches to the issue of governance.

Mr. Chairman, the change in Government which occurred in Trinidad and Tobago will lead to certain shifts in the policy direction of my country.

However, I wish to assure you that Trinidad and Tobago's posture in relation to the Caribbean Community remains unchanged.

My Government stands committed to the ideals of widening and deepening of the regional integration process within the Caribbean Community.

My Government, in its pursuit to strengthen and deepen the relationship within the Community, has appointed His Excellency Makandal Daaga as CARICOM's Cultural Ambassador Extraordinaire.

Thirty-Seven years ago today in Trinidad and Tobago, the Caribbean Community and Common Market

(CARICOM) came into existence with the signing of the Treaty of Chaguaramas by Trinidad and Tobago, Barbados, Guyana and Jamaica.

This bold step towards closer regional economic integration, functional cooperation and the coordination of foreign policy represented a catalyst for a viable economic Community symbolizing hope for an improved quality of life for all in the Region.

Since then the Caribbean Community, like any other institution, has been forced to confront enormous obstacles and weather prolonged periods of major crises.

Notwithstanding, the Community has managed to endure and sustain progress with the same spirit of resilience and resolution which was manifested in its infancy.

We have also progressed economically as a Community to a degree where it can be safely said that there has been some reduction in poverty, however, we need to do much more. Poverty threatens human development, our children and our future. We must work harder to reduce poverty throughout the Community so that all our people can enjoy a higher standard of living.

We have also done well in the pursuit of functional cooperation in several important sectors, such as education, health, security, our response to natural disasters, development financing and the environment and have built regional institutional infrastructure to facilitate these sectors. We must do better especially with respect to preparation for natural disasters and the health of our people.

Democracy prevails throughout our Region as many freedoms which our people enjoy are firmly entrenched in our individual constitutions, as well as in many regional and international instruments, and other nations see our Caribbean society as a model of peace and social stability.

In our relations with the rest of the world, we have been able to speak with one voice on matters of common interest and concern.

In the process, we have enhanced not only our collective influence in decision making but also our image as proud and independent members of the family of nations.

Many of our citizens have been acclaimed around the world in all spheres of activity from sports to literature.

And may I take this opportunity to congratulate one of our CARICOM Heads of State, the President of Guyana, His Excellency Bharrat Jagdeo for being honoured by the United Nations with one of its highest awards for his work in the area of the environment, specifically Guyana's unique low carbon emission programme.

The award, called the Champion of the Earth, is a demonstration of our ability to create breakthrough ideas which the world can embrace.

In this regard may I say we have launched our own CBT&T, Clean Up and Beautify Initiative in Trinidad and Tobago, which is perhaps the largest collaborative effort between government and the private sector ever introduced. It involves not only the massive deployment of machinery and manpower to clear and clean our waterways and landscape but the introduction of tough Anti-Littering legislation imposed by a cadre of litter wardens. This combined with an on-going education programme is intended to create a sustained transformation of the Trinidad and Tobago environment. I long for the day when I can learn of a pan-Caribbean approach within a specific initiative in dealing with environmental issues.

The Petroleum Fund

And this brings me to the point of the Petroleum Fund which my nation proudly contributes towards for the benefit of the region. May I say that the new Trinidad and Tobago Government is firmly commited to sustaining and strengthening its commitment but I must express my concerns.

I believe there needs to be greater accountability to how the funds are being used so that the resources spent are allocated in accordance with what are the most urgent areas of need in our region. And may I please be permitted to suggest some of these areas.

The first is the environment. It is ironic that for islands so dependent upon our natural environment that so little attention is paid to the development of a sustained regional initiative in this area.

The second area in which these funds can be allocated is one very dear to me. And that is Education. We are sadly and rapidly losing our competitiveness here. And when we lose our competitiveness in education, we lose our future. And so I wish to put on the table an initiative regarding Education for our region. This is the cornerstone for any kind of development which we hope to see take place over time. And I speak about education in the broadest sense here. We have to develop an education programme that addresses the critical issues involving what is happening to our young people today. Across the Caribbean we are losing a generation to drugs, violence and prostitution. Again, I urge that we explore ways and means of dealing with this issue from a regional perspective.

And what can be of greater importance than the plight of children. In Trinidad and Tobago one of my party's campaign pledges which is being put in place now that we have formed the Government is the establishment of a Children's Life Fund of TT100 million dollars. The Fund will be supported by government and the private sector and used to assist underprivileged children who are in need of urgent medical attention. Why can't the Petroleum Fund be used for a similar purpose? Why not have a Caribbean Children's Life Fund?

I am sure the citizens of every one of our Caribbean territories would welcome such an initiative so that children in urgent need of medical attention can access it. Imagine what it means to a parent to be told their child is going to die because the medical attention required cannot be accessed due to lack of funds. I can think of no better way to utilise the resources of the Petroleum Fund. And again I urge that we explore this initiative.

The plight of women in our region who remain exploited and disadvantaged, single parents, child advocacy causes, these are some of the other areas in which I believe CARICOM has been too silent for far too long or is it that we just speak about it but achieve too little by way of implementation of policies that make a difference? What is being done to promote parenting, one that is not mother centered but parent centered where the father plays a greater role. This is an issue across our region. It is time to come away from meetings such as this with result oriented programmes on critical issues that determine the future of our region such as these.

As the Caribbean Community approaches its thirty-seventh year of existence, it finds itself confronted by new critical challenges that call for urgent responses.

Most of these challenges arise from the impact of globalization on the world economy.

They include an expanding WTO regime devoid of provisions for development targeted by the Doha Round of negotiations; geo-political fragmentation in the investment and trade systems of the Americas; increasing threats to national and regional security owing largely to drug trafficking in the Region; escalating prices for imported energy products; growing threats to food security because of shortages and inflationary prices; impending regional loss of coastal territory owing to the global impact of climate change; irreparable degradation of the Caribbean eco-systems owing to the absence of a regional regime to regulate their use and exploitation; fierce competition among developing countries for the limited sources of investment capital; and the spread of communicable and non-communicable diseases in certain areas of the CARICOM sub-region.

The time has come for us to re-examine whether the dynamism and versatility of the external environment has impacted on our ability to chart a clear and consolidated pathway to regional development.

Today the Caribbean Community should guard against taking a backward step in addressing the issue of an adequate institutional structure to implement the idea of "CARICOM as A Community for All".

Mr. Chairman, in my capacity as the Lead CARICOM Prime Minister with responsibility for matters relating to Crime and Security in the Quasi Cabinet, I wish to state that it is imperative that all Member States participate fully in the efforts to strengthen the peace and security of the Region. In the Caribbean, guaranteeing public safety cannot be confined to military and police action.

The dimensions of criminal activity are increasingly associated with human trafficking, repatriation of deportees, money laundering, the trade of illicit drugs and firearms and other forms of organised crime and terrorism.

Trinidad and Tobago is committed to bolstering the security of the Region as it is one of the cornerstones which must be strengthened to ensure that the foundation for the collective prosperity of our Region remains solid.

To all in our region, it is patently clear that the security challenge continues to threaten our development initiatives. We are called upon to always refine our framework and strategy, to work out the details and focus more of our attention and resources on destroying this enemy of our progress.

We must do no less. If we collaborate closely enough in this effort, we may well be able to eradicate this scourge and free our future generations to proceed unhindered, along their charted course of development.

Mr Chairman, I have noted with interest the wide range of issues which constitute our Agenda for this Thirty-First Meeting of the Conference.

I look forward to our discussions over the next few days with my colleagues Heads of Government, all of whom is endowed with the vision, courage, sagacity, and political astuteness to bring to reality the vision the founding fathers had for our Region.

I feel confident that as we share our expertise we will move our fellow citizens on the path of economic sustainability and social mobility.

I wish to extend my heartfelt appreciation, and that of the rest of my delegation to the Government and people of Jamaica for the kind hospitality we have enjoyed since our arrival. It is as I always remember it to be, warmly, sincerely Jamaican.

Mr. Chairman, Ladies and Gentlemen, I thank you.

11. Emancipation Day

Message to the Nation from the Hon. Kamla Persad-Bissessar Prime Minister of the Republic of Trinidad and Tobago on the occasion of the celebration of Emancipation Day on 1 August, 2010

Fellow citizens.

Today our nation commemorates the 172nd Anniversary of Emancipation in Trinidad and Tobago. That historic act on August 1, 1838, destroyed the moral and legal basis of a system, which allowed human beings to be classified as chattel and denied the most basic human rights.

Perhaps more significantly however, Emancipation set new terms for other groups coming into the society. No longer could anyone be legally defined as property. No longer could there be a denial of human rights. Emancipation set in motion a chain of events which would eventually lead to self – determination, independence and the building of an egalitarian society.

While Emancipation holds special significance for the descendents of the enslaved Africans who were brought to our shores; as a nation there is much we can all learn from the observance of Emancipation Day. Emancipation presents an opportunity to celebrate triumph over oppression. It salutes the indomitable spirit to persevere in the face of tragedy. It encourages us to look into our past without fear and delve further into our history. It is a re-affirmation of identity.

Today in Trinidad and Tobago we are blessed with the diverse heritage of ancestors who made tremendous sacrifices in the name of freedom. Let us continue to use the observance of Emancipation to honour their memory. Let us remember to tell their stories to every generation, so that they do not forget the origins of their parents and their fellow countrymen. Let us celebrate our history and use it as a beacon into our future.

As we commemorate Emancipation Day 2010, I ask you, fellow citizens of Trinidad and Tobago, to continue to embrace the hard-won freedom bequeathed to us by our forefathers. In our diversity let us recognize our strength. There is no room for divisiveness. The prosperity and development of our beloved country depends on our capacity to look beyond our differences and build a common destiny as one united nation.

Together, let us continue to work together and to draw on each other's experiences to create a Trinidad and Tobago of which we can all be proud to call home. Happy Emancipation Day to you all, God bless you all and may God bless our nation.

12. Local Government Elections

City of Port of Spain: (PNM)

St James West—Wendell Stephen (PNM);
St James East—Balliram Ramsuchit (COP)
Woodbrook—Cleveland Phillip Garcia (COP)
Northern Port of Spain—Keron Valentine (PNM);
Belmont East—Darryl Rajpaul (PNM);
Belmont North and West—Deanne Boucaud (PNM);
Southern Port of Spain—Ryan Junior Dunbar (PNM);
East Dry River—Isha Wells (PNM);
St Ann's River South—Ashtine Thomason (PNM);
St Ann's River Central—Natasha Young (PNM);
St Ann's River North—Nedra Marisa McClean (PNM);
Belmont South—Jennel Young (PNM);

City of San Fernando: (Partnership)

Marabella West—Gloria Calliste (COP)
Marabella East—Jason Williams (UNC)
Marabella South/Vistabella—Gobin Persad Sinanan (COP)
Pleasantville—Robert Parris (PNM)
Cocoyea/Tarouba—Daren McLeod (UNC)
Mon Repos/Navet—Shaka Joseph (PNM)
Springvale/Paradise—John Mark Chankersingh (UNC)
Les Efforts West/La Romaine—Anthony A Ramkissoon (UNC)
Les Efforts East/Cipero—Navi Muradali (COP)

Borough of Arima: (Partnership)

Calvary—Wayne John Bertrand (COP)
Arima North East—Patricia T Cedeno-Metivier (COP)
Arima West/O'Meara—Flora Singh (COP)
Arima Central—Clinton Jennings (COP)

Malabar North—Vedya Mahabir (COP)
Malabar South—Anthony Garcia (PNM)
Tumpuna—Hugo Ambrose Lewis (COP)

Borough of Point Fortin: (PNM)

Techier/Guapo—Sherwin St Hillaire (PNM)
Newlands/Mahaica—Janelle St Hilaire (PNM)
Egypt—Abdon Mason (PNM)
Cap-de-Ville/Fanny Village—Marilyn Ramnarinesingh (COP)
Hollywood—Kennedy Kendel Richards (PNM)
New Village—Kriscia Simon (PNM)

Borough of Chaguanas: (Partnership)

Felicity/Endeavour—Orlando Nehru Nagessar (UNC)
Edinburgh/Longdenville—Dwarka Singh (UNC)
Montrose—Gopaul Boodhan (UNC)
Cunupia—Renuka N Kangal (UNC)
Enterprise North—Narsingh Rambarran (COP)
Enterprise South—Ronald Heera (PNM)
Charlieville—Falisha Isahak (UNC)
Munroe Road/Caroni Savannah—Joey Samuel (UNC)

Regional Corporation of Couva/Tabaquite/Talparo:
(Partnership)
Chickland/Mamoral—Merle Mungroo (UNC)
Freeport/Calcutta—Anil Baliram (UNC)
St Mary's/Edinburgh—Sandra Ramsingh-Abdool (UNC)
Felicity/Calcutta/McBean—Allan Seepersad (UNC)
Perseverance/Waterloo—Annmarie Boodram (UNC)
California/Pt Lisas—Christine Soobram (UNC)
Balmain/Esperanza/Forres Park—Gangaram Gopaul (UNC)
Claxton Bay/Pointe-a-Pierre—Camille Elie-Govind (UNC)
Caratal/Tortuga—Suresh Pooran Maharaj (UNC)
Gasparillo/Bonne Aventure—Feeraz Ali (UNC)

Las Lomas/San Raphael—Dhanraj Saroop (UNC)
Longdenville/Talparo—Rana Persad (UNC)
Piparo/San Pedro/Tabaquite—Henry Awong (UNC)

Regional Corporation of Diego Martin: (Partnership)

Chaguaramas/Point Cumana—Enroy Slater (PNM)
Glencoe/Goodwood/La Puerta—Ricardo Garcia (COP)
Covigne/Richplain—Katty Ann Christopher (PNM)
Diamond Vale—Gail Donna La Touche (PNM)
Bagatelle/Blue Basin—Lisa Maraj (UNC)
St Lucien/Cameron Hill—Anne Letren (UNC)
Moka/Boissiere No.2—Nadine Maria Romany (UNC)
Morne Coco/Alyce Glen—Phillip Joseph Murray (UNC)
Petit Valley/Cocorite—Wazim Daniel (UNC)
Belle Vue/Boissiere No.1—Susan Rodriguez (UNC)

Regional Corporation of Mayaro/Rio Claro: (Partnership)

Biche/Charuma—Glen Ram (UNC)
Rio Claro South/Cat's Hill—Cyrilla Zola Cooper (UNC)
Rio Claro North—Hazarie Ramdeen (UNC)
Cocal/Mafeking—Keshrie Kissoon (UNC)
Ecclesville—Shaffik Mohammed (UNC)
Mayaro/Guayaguayare—Raymond Cozier (UNC)

Regional Corporation of Penal/Debe: (Partnership)

Palmiste/Hermitage—Roland Hall (UNC)
La Fortune—Amir J Junior B Saiphoo (UNC)
Bronte—Brian N Julien (UNC)
Debe East/L'Esperance/Union Hall—
Marsha Jaimungal-Khan (UNC)
Debe West—Skafte Awardy (UNC)
Penal—Shanty Boodram (UNC)
Barrackpore West—Premchand Sookoo (UNC)

Rochard/Barrackpore East—Vishnu Ramlakhan (UNC)
Quinam/Morne Diablo—Hyacinth Rampersadsingh (UNC)

Regional Corporation of Princes Town: (Partnership)

Reform/Manahambre—Judy Barbara Hart (UNC)
Ben Lomond/Hardbargain/Williamsville—
Akash A Manickchand (UNC)
Corinth/Cedar Hill—Winston D Chindra (UNC)
Inverness/Princes Town—Deryck Mathura (UNC)
New Grant/Tableland—Gowrie N Roopnarine (UNC)
Hindustan/Indianwalk/St Mary's—
Jules Vernon Downing (UNC)
Lengua/St Julien—Alvin Lutchman (UNC)
Fifth Company—Rafi Mohammed (UNC)
Moruga—Phillip Gonzales (UNC)

Regional Corporation of San Juan/Laventille: (PNM)
Maracas Bay/Santa Cruz/La Fillette—Lyndon Lara (PNM)
    Febeau/Bourg Mulatresse—Roger Charles Celestine
    (COP)
Morvant—Franz Lambkin (PNM)
Caledonia/Upper Malick—Jeffrey Anthony Reyes (PNM)
St Ann's/Cascade/Mon Repos West—
Kenrick Preudhomme (COP)
St Barb's/Chinapoo—Jason C Alexander (PNM)
Beetham/Picton—Akil Audain (PNM)
Success/Trou Macaque—Joel Harding (PNM)
Aranguez/Warner Village—Santam Ramjit (UNC)
Barataria—Harrylal Persad (UNC)
Petit Bourg/Mount Lambert/Champs Fleurs—
Kion Williams (PNM)
San Juan East—Nazeemool Mohammed (UNC)
San Juan West—Kwesi Junior Antoine (PNM)

Regional Corporation of Sangre Grande: (Partnership)

Toco/Fishing Pond—Martin Rondon (PNM)
Valencia—Lawrence P Lalla (UNC)
Manzanilla—Annand Soodeen (UNC)
Sangre Grande South—Patricia Debbie A Harris (UNC)
Vega De Oropouche—Ravi Lakhan (UNC)
Sangre Grande North West—Dayne Evan Francois (UNC)
Sangre Grande North East—Quincy Damian Luces (COP)
Cumuto/Tamana—Nirmal Singh (UNC)

Regional Corporation of Siparia: (Partnership)

Avocat/San Francique North—Rajwantee Bullock (UNC)
Siparia East/San Francique South—
Leo Christiani Doodnath (UNC)
Siparia West/Fyzabad—Doodnath Mayrhoo (UNC)
Otaheite/Rousillac—Chanardaye Ramadharsingh (UNC)
Brighton/Vessigny—Gerald Debesette (PNM)
Mon Desir—Balkaran Frank Ramjit (UNC)
Cedros—Fitzroy Paul Beache (UNC)
Erin—Morena M. Martin Frederick (PNM)
Palo Seco—Christine Neptune (PNM)

Regional Corporation of Tunapuna/Piarco (Partnership)

Maracas/Santa Magarita—Winston C Ramsaroop (COP)
Auzonville/Tunapuna—Esmond Irving Forde (PNM)
Curepe/Pasea—Rosanna Sookdeo (COP)
Caura/Paradise/Tacarigua—Sookdeo P Barath (COP)
Macoya/Trincity—Ria Boodoo (COP)
Five Rivers/Lopinot—Dianne Bishop (UNC)
Bon Air/Arouca/Cane Farm—Colin Kerwin Rodney (PNM)
    Valsayn/St Joseph—Graham Butcher (UNC)
Kelly Village/Warrenville—Khublal Paltoo (UNC)
St Augustine South/Piarco/St Helena—

Khadijah Ameen (UNC)
Mausica/Maloney—Steven Sam (PNM)
La Florissante/Cleaver— Erwin Augustine Hope (COP)

D'Abadie/Carapo—J-Lynn Roopnarine (UNC)
Blanchisseuse/Santa Rosa—Andrew V Mooteram (COP)
Wallerfield/La Horquetta—Brian Hayden Joseph (PNM)

13. Emancipation Kambule Procession

Feature address by the Hon. Kamla Persad-Bissessar at the Emancipation Kambule Procession at Brian Lara Promenade on 1 August 2010.

Greetings.

Cabinet and Parliamentary Colleagues,

Mr. Kambon and Executive Members of the Emancipation Support Committee: congratulations and thanks to you for your work over the years. I salute you,

Members of the Diplomatic Corps, Distinguished Guests, Members of the local and foreign media,

Ladies and Gentlemen,

Good Morning.

I stand here this morning honoured and humbled to join you in celebrating the 172nd Anniversary of Emancipation in Trinidad and Tobago.

I must admit that as I stand here, waiting in anticipation to witness Ms. Eintou Springer's production, "Freedom Morning Come" and to participate in the Kambule procession, I am overwhelmed by an incredible lightness of being.

It is your energy that I feel, your strength, your unconquerable spirit – the legacy bequeathed to us by the ancestors who survived institutionalised inhumanity, humiliation and violence and to emerge with hope, courage and the ability to persevere in the midst of unthinkable suffering to help build our great nation.

Today my friends we commemorate the 172nd Anniversary of Emancipation in Trinidad and Tobago, that momentous chapter in our history, which precipitated the most profound social transformation in our country - and indeed the other English-speaking territories - since the conquest and colonization of the region changed the demographic landscape.

As a turning point for the development of the nation, the impact of Emancipation cannot be overemphasized.

That historic act on August 1, 1838, destroyed the moral, legal and institutional basis of a system which allowed human beings to be classified as chattel and denied the most basic human rights.

More significantly, however, by uprooting the most insidious aspects of the old order, Emancipation set new terms for other groups coming into the society.

Oppression did not end with Emancipation, but there were qualitative differences in the laws which governed the newcomers to post-emancipation society.

Though not as horrendous as chattel slavery, the East Indians who came to these shores following emancipation, also suffered cruelties, indignities and injustice under the system of indenture.

However post-emancipation law dictated that no one could legally be defined as property.

There were formal contracts, there were rights and there were those persons who would ensure that society did not regress into the abyss of slavery.

Emancipation set in train the arduous journey to self-determination, independence and the building of a free, just and egalitarian society.

Indeed it is later in this same month that we would be celebrating our Independence on August 31st.

Therefore today, ladies and gentlemen, in remembrance of our African ancestors who refused to break under the sting of the whip, I say, "Amandla!Power"!

In tribute to all who toiled and to those who continue to work to break down the barriers of discrimination, suspicion and mistrust, I say, "Amandla! Power"!

Power to the triumph of the human spirit and the determination to purge from our society the negative legacy of oppression, domination and racism!

This year our Emancipation celebrations seek to reawaken the Spirit of Liberty.

Haiti

The theme is dedicated to our Haitian brothers and sisters, who continue to struggle, at all levels, to recover from the devastating earthquake of January 12th; yet demonstrate an indomitable spirit in the face of hardship.

We recall that Haiti was the first colonial territory to break free from the tyranny of slavery and walk the road to liberty.

Their war of liberation greatly influenced a tidal wave of action in the Caribbean, which eventually led to freedom for the enslaved Africans.

I join you in honouring the courage of the people of Haiti and stand in solidarity with them as they overcome yet another challenge to their liberty.

My government remains committed to assisting in the reconstruction of Haiti.

Black Power Revolution

The theme of our celebrations also commemorates the 40th anniversary of the Black Power Revolution in Trinidad and Tobago.

A significant milestone in our history and testimony to the determined will of a people, the Black Power Movement sought to redress inequalities in a system, which many believed prevented them from realizing their full potential.

As you know, the Government has recently recognised the efforts of a central figure of the 1970s movement for his contribution to the people of Trinidad and Tobago.

I speak of none other than People's Partnership member, Chief Servant Makandaal Daaga, who is now our CARICOM Cultural Ambassador Extraordinaire.

I salute you Ambassador Daaga.

<u>Multicultural T&T</u>

Today in Trinidad and Tobago we can take pride in our multicultural society where each group may experience and share one another's diverse cultural traditions.

We are blessed with a vibrant democratic system. We enjoy freedom of expression and we can revel in the many achievements of our people in the fields of sport, culture and academia.

However, ladies and gentlemen, we must guard against complacency.

We must jealously protect the freedoms for which our forefathers have sacrificed so much.

For many of them liberty came at the price of their own lives.

And, as with power, liberty is closely linked with personal responsibility.

All who truly understands the concept of liberty understands that free people not only serve themselves but also their families, their communities and their country.

Those we remember on this Emancipation Day – Toussaint, Daaga, Nanny, Bussa and Makandaal Daaga – fought not only for themselves but for their people.

When we internalize the concept of freedom we understand that we must work diligently together, to do right, to protect common interests and ensure peace and prosperity for all.

Some among us may argue that Emancipation holds no meaning for them.

They willingly accept the chance for a 'day off' but ascribe no real significance to the Holiday.

I challenge those citizens to look with new eyes at Emancipation Day.

The commemoration of Emancipation is a celebration of struggle and triumph over oppression.

It is an opportunity to delve deeper into history.

It is a re-affirmation of identity.

It is the awakening of consciousness and the courage to look into the past without fear and trepidation.

It presents a mechanism for the release from pain and a return to wholeness.

It is an opportunity for all of us to pause and reflect.

Ladies and gentlemen, I am certain that you will agree that for any Nation – particularly plural societies such as ours – to truly develop and prosper, each segment of the society must be fully integrated into the collective whole.

I am not speaking about denial of heritage or the suppression of identity.

Rather, "I belong here", must echo with conviction from the lips of every citizen of Trinidad and Tobago.

"I have a valuable part to play in the development of Trinidad and Tobago", must be the sentiment and stance of every citizen.

There is no reason to create artificial bounders around the celebration of our diverse cultural heritage.

In Trinidad and Tobago mandir, mosque, church or revival tent already co-exist in the same community, at times on the same street.

The notes of the African drum and the steelpan blend easily with the sounds of the sitar, table, tassa and dholak.

The religious observances, festivals and commemorations of Christmas, Divali, Eid-ul-Fitr, Phagwa Hosay and Chinese Arrival are eagerly anticipated and enjoyed by members of the wider population.

There are not many countries in today's turbulent world which can boast of this level of cultural tolerance and acceptance.

To our credit, we have created in Trinidad and Tobago an enviable model of cultural and religious harmony.

Today as we commemorate Emancipation, as we awaken the spirit of liberty, let us with one voice, one heart and one mind determine to create in Trinidad and Tobago a Nation where everyone finds acceptance and security; where no-one faces the stigma of alienation and where every creed and race truly find an equal place and space.

Happy Emancipation Day.

Ladies and gentlemen, I thank you.

May God bless you and May God bless our Nation.

All appendices courtesy:

Government of the Republic of Trinidad and Tobago
Government Information Services, Ltd.
www.gisltd.tt

www.ingramcontent.com/pod-product-compliance
Lightning Source LLC
Chambersburg PA
CBHW050553270326
41926CB00012B/2040